BOB DYLAN

THE EARLY YEARS • A RETROSPECTIVE

THE FOLKLORE CENTER

Presents

BOB DYLAN

IN HIS FIRST NEW YORK CONCERT

SAT. NOV. 4, 1961 **8:40pm**

CARNEGIE CHAPTER HALL

154 WEST 57th STREET • NEW YORK CITY

All seats $2.00

Tickets available at:

The Folklore Center
110 MacDougal Street
New York City 12, New York

GR7 - 5987

or at door

BOB DYLAN

THE EARLY YEARS • A RETROSPECTIVE

EDITED BY

Craig McGregor

NEW PREFACE BY

Nat Hentoff

DA CAPO PRESS

Library of Congress Cataloging in Publication Data

Bob Dylan: the early years: a retrospective / edited by Craig McGregor.
p. cm. — (A Da Capo paperback)
Reprint. Originally published: New York: W. Morrow, 1972. With new preface.
Includes bibliographical references.
ISBN 0-306-80416-6
1. Dylan, Bob, 1941- . 2. Singers — United States — Biography. I. McGregor, Craig.
[ML420.D98B6 1990] 90-38857
782.42162'0092 — dc CIP
[B] MN

10 9 8 7 6 5 4

The editor and publisher wish to thank CBS Records for its courtesy in supplying and allowing the use of Bob Dylan's record jackets.

Acknowledgment is due The Macmillan Company and Jerrold Schatzberg for permission to reproduce the front of the jacket of *Tarantula* by Bob Dylan. Photograph by Jerrold Schatzberg.

This Da Capo Press paperback edition of *Bob Dylan, The Early Years: A Retrospective* is an unabridged republication of the edition published in New York in 1972, originally entitled *Bob Dylan : A Retrospective*, here supplemented with a new preface. It is reprinted by arrangement with William Morrow & Company.

Visit us on the World Wide Web at www.dacapopress.com

Published by Da Capo Press, Inc.

Perseus Books is a member of the Perseus Books Group.

Manufactured in the United States of America

Contents

Preface

by Nat Hentoff

Before he became world-renowned, Bob Dylan enjoyed the prospect of fame. In contrast to the later legend who became as resistant to interviews as Greta Garbo, Dylan, when he was on the edge of breaking through, was generous with his time. And he could hardly wait to see himself in print. For a while we both lived in the same neighborhood and he'd stop me on the street to ask about something I'd written on him, "When's it coming out? When's it coming out?"

He also had—in addition to his chronic mockery—an extraordinarily imaginatively sense of fun. In this collection, there is an interview I did with him for *Playboy* (pp. 124-145). Toward the end of my introductory remarks, there is a passage that is not true. It says the interview that follows took place at the CBS Building in mid-Manhattan. *An* interview did take place there. It was relatively straightforward, without many surprises. *That* interview was never printed.

Dylan got a set of galleys of that first interview. One of the editors at *Playboy* had decided he would "smooth out" some of Dylan's conversation. And in the process much of what Dylan had said had been so eviscerated as to make him sound like he might be ready to be profiled in the *Reader's Digest*.

I had not yet read the galleys when Dylan called me on a Saturday morning. He was furious at what had been done to him. "Kill the piece," I said. "Tell them that if they run it, you'll expose them for committing fraud on their readers. And I'll back you up."

There was silence. And then Dylan said, "I got a better idea. We'll make up an interview."

"Right now?"

"Right now."

It took several hours. I still remember how stiff and sore my hand became. It was also often hard to keep writing because some of Dylan's bizarre and baroque answers to my straight-man questions were so funny that I kept breaking up.

His imagery, metaphors, and wondrously wild imaginings were utterly spontaneous. I did not change a word or a sequence. He himself was right pleased with it at the end. I sent it off to *Playboy* with Dylan's instructions. Every word had to be published. And every word was. Some of the editors and some of the readers were, to say the least, puzzled at what was going on in those pages.

There's no point giving illustrations of Dylan-the-Wild-Colonial-Boy when you have the whole interview in this book—a book that provides more multiply-dimensional perspectives on Dylan than I have read in any volume.

Indeed, this collection is likely to be the most durably illuminating set of views of Dylan, because in the years after, he became less and less accessible. It seemed as if the more aggressively he was trying to find out who Bob Dylan—and, for that matter, Robert Zimmerman—was, the more he didn't want to be distracted by people who thought *they* knew who he was.

He figured, for a time, that he'd found himself in fundamentalist Christianity. But something was missing. Then Orthodox Judaism appeared to have the roots he was longing for, and, for all I know at this writing, he has gone on another spiritual road.

I believe him when he says that some of the more unexpected and difficult-to-fathom lyrics in his "cryptic" songs were not consciously crafted. They came, he has said, by themselves. For those who aren't sure why they're on earth, all signs give promise. I expect that Dylan will be searching for signs all his life.

He is one of those who have no intellectual or spiritual place to rest. Nothing is ever enough. Whether it's religion or drugs or companions, the recurring obbligato of his life has remained: "Is this all there is?"

This aloneness—no matter how large and deferential his retinue—is his most fundamental characteristic. I felt it the first time, and every time thereafter, that I talked to him.

And this persistent feeling of being lost, even as money and applause rained down, accounts in large part for his appeal to so many people through time—because many of us are also looking for ourselves.

There was more, of course. Dylan became the very voice of the anti-war and civil-rights generation—primarily for the whites among them, although there was enough knowledge of black blues in many of his songs to indicate he was more than a voyeur when it came to black blues traditions.

He said later—to me and others—that he hadn't really put himself into those anti-war and civil rights songs. It was just a way to get known at the time, he said, a way to make money. I didn't believe that story then, I don't believe it now. What went on in his mind, I think, was: God forbid I should be considered responsible for some whole goddamn movement! Then people would expect me to *represent* the movement and do more for it, and then I'd be stuck.

Dylan guards his independence every which way he can. He still likes the crowds. He still needs them. For the idea of continually searching for more of himself—without the reaffirmation by audiences of the one thing he knows is indisputably his—would be too desolate a road. But he doesn't want those audiences to expect any more from him than he chooses to give them—in performance.

Dylan needs to be in control, for how else can he be secure in his insecurity? In 1976, at the start of his Rolling Thunder Revue tour, I was asked by *Rolling Stone* to report on this landmark event in the history of American culture. I asked to interview Dylan. Request was denied. It turned out that Dylan was angry at my wife, who had been quoted in the *New York Times* as saying that he wasn't a kid anymore—a kid riding the *Zeitgeist*. He was history, past history.

There was nothing even Bob Dylan could do to punish the *New York Times*, but he could bar from his presence anyone he chose, including the husband of the woman who had doubted his immortality.

I went on to interview others on the tour—among them, Joan Baez, Allen Ginsberg, and Bobby Neuwirth. Dylan's intelligence unit let him know what was happening, and toward the end of the tour, word came from the castle that Mr. Dylan would, after all, see me. I sent word back that I had enough material, thank you. Word has never come again from the castle.

He is not always wholly self-involved. In a 1989 interview with Dylan in the British magazine *Q*, Adrian Deevoy notes that after meeting the little boy of someone he knew, a package arrived for the child the next morning. "Bob had gone out and bought him a little hand-carved wooden chair and it had a note. 'To Matthew. Here's a chair for you. Hope you like chairs. Love, Bob Dylan.'"

Deevoy, later on, said to Dylan that his last live tour had hardly finished before the current one began.

"Oh," Dylan briefly looked at her, "It's all the same tour. The Never-Ending Tour."

The ceaseless tour is internal as well. And I wonder what Dylan thought when his perennial journey brought him to Paris in January, 1990, where he was named a Commander in France's Order of Arts and Letters. The ceremony took place, the Associated Press reported, "in a gilded reception room at the Palais Royal."

In presenting the gold and emerald medal to Dylan, France's Culture Minister, Jack Lang, said to him: "For many of us in France and in Europe you bring together an ideal of music and an ideal of poetry." (Many Americans continue to agree.) Dylan took a crumpled envelope from his pocket and responded—in French—"It [the award] moves me enormously."

In his book, *Performing Artist: The Music of Bob Dylan*, Paul Williams quoted Liam Clancy of the Clancy Brothers:

"Do you know what Dylan was when he came to Greenwich Village? He was a teenager, and the only thing I can compare him with is blotting paper. He soaked everything up. He had this immense curiosity, he was totally blank, and he was ready to suck up everything that came his way."

He's still doing it, from the Palais Royal to other less resplendent stops of The Never-Ending Tour.

New York City
May, 1990

Introduction

by Craig McGregor

The first time I heard of Bob Dylan was when Pete Seeger was touring Australia. It was back in the early 'sixties, and I was writing on pop, jazz and folk music for the *Sydney Morning Herald,* which is a sort of antipodean version of the *New York Times.* At his opening concert in Sydney, Seeger sang mostly traditional songs; but toward the end he began singing some contemporary songs by Tom Paxton, Malvina Reynolds, and one by "a young New York songwriter called Bob Dillon" (I had to check with Seeger later even to get the name right). It was "Who Killed Davey Moore?", and Seeger sang it superbly. It knocked me out. I still think it is one of the best of Dylan's early songs, with a moral concreteness that in too many of his other "political" songs fades off into melodrama and rhetoric. (A couple of years later, when composer/musicologist Wilfrid Mellers was in Australia, he wound up a lecture on the development of Western pop music by playing Ray Charles, the Beatles, and Seeger's recording of "Who Killed Davey Moore?"—he liked it too. I got to know Mellers, who is the most perceptive of the academic commentators on pop music; his article on Dylan is the last in this book.) When I reviewed the concert for the following morning's paper I was lukewarm about Seeger's treatment of traditional songs but excited by Dylan's reworking of the old "Cock Robin" ballad. Who the hell, I asked, was Dylan?

Who indeed?

A little later Dylan's records began arriving in Australia. The first to be released was *The Times They Are A-Changin'.* By then I was writing a regular column on pop culture, and I spent a rhapsodic half-page on Dylan and his album. The song that impressed me most was "With God On Our Side," though it worried me too: there was that lapse in the fifth verse, "fried," which is simply the wrong word, and there was that rather swooning ambivalence of the last verse—Dylan wrestling with the traditional Problem of Evil, and not prepared to give God away. Most critics seem to regard that song as a statement of atheism, but I have never thought so: Dylan has too tangible a concept of God, and that last verse is too supplicatory. It sounds more like someone who still wants to believe in God, but doesn't like what he is finding out about Him. By the time of "Gates of Eden" Dylan is on the way to a solution: he has turned toward a transcendentalism which derides not God but those who posture in His shadow. Religious symbolism continues as a major motif in Dylan's later work, rising to a crescendo in *John Wesley Harding* and then leveling off into what seems to be a sort of calm acceptance of belief in *New Morning*—but more of that later.

After *The Times They Are A-Changin'* Dylan's two earlier albums were released in Australia. Except for a couple of critics, and the folk fraternity, the reception was hostile. Then the other albums started coming out. By now Dylan was a world figure, and had become as important to young people in Australia as he had in the United States and the rest of the world; but the disk jockeys and mass media still lampooned him as part of their general attack upon youth culture—and its subversive politics. When Dylan went pop some of the older Left intellectuals who had supported him as a radical "folk" poet turned against him too: for a similar regression, chart the course of Irwin Silber, then editor of *Sing Out!* and an early champion of Dylan's, throughout this book. (It is to their credit that Silber and his Australian counterparts later came around to recognizing the importance of Dylan's explosion of folk into pop music, but it took them a long time. Some songwriters who were contemporaries of Dylan, notably Tom Paxton, performed the same double somersault: one of the most savage attacks ever made upon Dylan was by Paxton in a column titled "Folk Rot," written at the height of the folk/rock controversy. Unfortunately Paxton refused permission to allow the article to be reprinted here; he was the only author to do so.) Anyhow, I found myself as a sort of lone overground defender of Dylan. Even Richard Neville, co-editor of *OZ* magazine (he and two friends founded it in Sydney) and later a pop proselytizer, had attacked rock as "an asylum for emotional imbeciles." But young Australians were buying Dylan's records, despite the media barrage against him, and in enough numbers for ole Albert Grossman to figure maybe Bob should do something about it. So in April, 1966, Dylan, the Band, and Grossman arrived to tour Australia.

Sydney airport. Early morning. Gulls, bitumen tarmac, hip kids in knee-high boots, camel-hair jeans, Zapata moustaches. Boeing 707, in from Honolulu. Pause. Doors open, the first passengers disgorged, blinking in the unfamiliar sunlight. Another pause. Then Dylan. I assumed it must be he, though he looked smaller and frailer than I'd imagined. Descending the gangplank he was talking to some of the Band, but walking across the tarmac he was by himself: a tiny, lonely figure. Customs. Then, at last, into the main hall, where fans besieged him. He gallantly accepted a fifty-foot pop-art fan letter glued together from magazine and newspaper clippings, signed himself "The Phantom." Black corduroy suit, black suede high-heeled calf-length zipper-sided boots, dark glasses, a halo of long ringleted hair: Dylan, 1966. He held up his hands (look, no stigmata!), turned away and made it across to the Press room, where the TV cameras and reporters were waiting. The Band, wearing dark glasses and sombreros, and the greying bulk of Albert Grossman followed. Dylan was smiling, being obliging. He settled himself down on a sofa for the Press conference. The arc lights switched on. I sat down beside him, to his left. Downcast eyes, hooked Jewish nose. The crucifixion was about to begin.

It was soon obvious that nearly everyone there had already made up his mind about Dylan. Or their editors had. He was either a Protest Singer, or a Phony, or preferably both; and they weren't going to be put off by any of that shit about him just being someone who wrote songs. Nobody welcomed him: the first questions were hostile, brutal, stupid. Dylan tried to answer seriously at first, but it was a lost cause. A few mumbles. Nobody listened. A young guy from the *Sun* kept interrupting with a line of questions drilled into him by his paper: get him to admit he's a phony, that all this protest stuff is bullshit. . . .

"Isn't all this protest music a fake?"

"Huh?"

"It's phony, isn't it?"

"Huh?"

"Are you a protest singer?"

"I haven't heard that word for a long time. Everybody knows there are no protest songs any longer—it's just songs."

"If you aren't a protest singer, why does everybody say you are?"

"Everybody? Who does?"

"*Time* magazine."

"Oh, yeah."

"Why have you started playing rock and roll?"

"Is that what they call it?"

"Why have you gone commercial?"

"I have not gone commercial. I deny it" (with Bible-swearing hand upraised). "Commercial—that's a word that describes old grandmothers that have no place to go."

"Who are all these people with you?"

"That's the band."

"Why don't you play by yourself? Why do you need so many? Is this all a stunt? Are you a professional beatnik?"

"Huh?"

"Are you a professional beatnik?"

"Well, I was in the brigade once—you know, we used to get paid money—but they didn't pay me enough, so I became a singer."

"Why do you wear those crazy clothes?"

"I look very normal where I live. I'm conservative by their standards."

"Does it take a lot of trouble to get your hair like that?"

"No, you just have to sleep on it for about twenty years."

"Why don't you see more of your parents?"

"Huh?"

"What would you be if you weren't a songwriter?"

"A ditchdigger called Joe."

Dylan kept his cool throughout, answering each question in a mumbled hip patois, and had a gracious word for everyone—including Pete Seeger ("rambustacious") and the Beatles' songs ("sidesplitting"). I asked a couple of questions, but they got swamped in the torrent of hostility. Dylan didn't need any help. In the end I got up and walked across to the side of the Press room, where Grossman and the Band were standing watching the circus. "They don't even realize he's putting them down," I said to Grossman. He grinned.

Dylan made one or two attempts to get across. He wrote songs, he said, for himself; it was just an accident that other people liked them. Why didn't he write songs about Negroes? *What?* Why didn't he . . . ? He didn't write songs about Negroes because all people were different and you have no respect for me, sir, if you think I would write about Negroes as Negroes instead of as people. And he had changed his name to Dylan not because of the Welsh poet ("I don't care for Dylan Thomas") but because his mother's name was Dillon. At that stage he was still peddling that line.

At last the reporters gave it away. (In print they all attacked him. A PHONY! A CHARLATAN! They might as well have stayed at home.) Then Dylan gave a separate interview to a bland, buttoned-down TV smoothie who worked for the Australian Broadcasting Commission, the local equivalent of the BBC. The interviewer began confidently enough, but he didn't know anything about Dylan or pop music. By now Bob had warmed up, and after the interviewer had received a couple of rapid-fire, surrealistic responses he forgot his questions, ran a sticky finger around his collar, stumbled to a dead halt, signaled frantically to the cameras to stop, stared down at his feet, tried to think of something to say (Dylan's eyes boring into him like gun barrels), had an inspiration, signaled the cameras to roll, and asked the ultimate Dylan question: "And how long, Mr. Dylan, will you be in Australia?" BEAUTY!

By this time Grossman and Robbie Robertson were rolling in the aisles. The Press disappeared. Dylan was left alone, stretched out on the settee like an Ottoman seductress. "Hey, Bob—why don't you interview yourself?" Grossman yelled at him. Immediately, moving swiftly between settee and interviewer's seat, Dylan improvised an instantaneous parody of everything that had just happened.

Dylan: "How long is it since you saw your mother?"
Dylan: "About three months."
Dylan: "Why don't you see her more often? Doesn't she approve of your music?"
Dylan: "Well, my mother doesn't approve of it but my grandmother does."
Dylan: "I see you've got about twelve people there with you: what's that, a band? Don't you play pure music any longer?"
Dylan: "No, man, that's not a band with me. They're all friends of my grandmother. . . ."

It went on and on, a hilarious spoof, but by this time I was laughing too much to take notes. And I had to get home; I'd decided to write something about it all. But it wasn't over yet. On the way out Dylan was mobbed again by the kids who had given him the fifty-foot fan letter, a-jostle in jerkins and Toulouse-Lautrec blazers. One of them, a guy in short-cropped hair and moustache, was called Skull. "Nothing means anything, does it?" said Skull to Dylan, "that's what you're saying, isn't it?" Dylan hesitated. I could see he didn't want to hurt Skull, but he didn't want to be forced into another false corner either —shit, he'd just fought his way out of one. "No, I didn't say that," said Dylan. "You must mean that! Why did you sign yourself The Phantom then?" demanded Skull. Dylan looked at him. "Because you asked me to," he said kindly.

Next day, in an extraordinary break with tradition, the staid *Sydney Morning Herald* ran on the front page the article I wrote about Dylan. The sub-editors cut it in half, but they kept the title ("Bob Dylan's Anti-Interview") and all the stuff about Dylan putting down the Press and parodying the whole performance. They even left the last paragraph intact: "Like I said to Albert, this boy's got talent. Why don't you put him on the stage sometime? He could be as big as—well, as big as Robert Zimmerman née Dylan, who happens to be, quite simply, the most creative and original songwriter in the world today."

I was still at home when the telephone rang. It was Dylan's road manager. Was I going to Bob's concert at the Stadium that night? Hell yes, I was going to review it. Well, Dylan wanted to meet me.

The Stadium. A giant, ramshackle hangover from the turn of the century, built of timber and rusty galvanized iron. It reeks of liniment, blood, sawdust. Along the dark, subterranean corridors, ghostly pictures of long-forgotten boxers, champions of their time: Les Darcy, Vic Patrick, Jack Hassan, Leo Hennessy, Jimmy Carruthers. The Stadium was built specially for the world title fight at which Jack Johnson, after years of pursuit, finally caught up with the reigning white champion, Tommy Burns, and chopped him to pieces in the ring; there's still a photo of it there, Johnson with his shaven skull and huge, black body, Burns backing off with both gloves held up in fright, and one of the biggest crowds in Australia's fight history watching from beneath grim felt hats. A half-century later, another massive crowd, drawn to a different ritual: that breathless, uptight tension as you hit the lines outside, people clotting together, glare on, nightblack down, something moving, has it started . . . ? As I walk inside the main arena with my wife, Dylan's road manager, who has been waiting at the entrance, catches me by the arm. Come backstage at interval, OK? OK. Lights down, spots on. The stage is where the ring usually is, surrounded on all sides by infinite rows of seats and bleachers which stretch away into the darkness. The crowd is unusually quiet, expectant. At last Dylan comes on, alone: a frail puppet with acoustic guitar held uncomfortably across his chest, a harmonica rack around his neck. Golliwog hair, pale surreal face, wobbly neck, brown check suit. Without a word he launches into one of his old songs, simple strums on the guitar but blowing the mouth harp like a virtuoso, holding and straining the melody lines till you fear they'll snap. As soon as one song is finished he starts the next. The stage revolves jerkily, facing a different quarter of the audience each turn. On the far side some people keep shouting for "With God On Our Side." Dylan brushes them aside with his hand, a cool put-down, but at last sings "The Times They Are A-Changin'." For his last number before the intermission he sings "Visions of Johanna." It seems to go on and on and on. The tension is electric.

Release. People spill into the cool outside. We go up to Dylan's dressing room. He is squatting down on his heels on the floor, electric guitar already around his neck. Grossman and the Band are there. Dylan mumbles hello. Yeah, he dug what I wrote. People don't understand what he's into. He got the Band because the songs needed it; he wanted something to fill in the spaces between the words. (Muddy Waters: "Before that it had just been a harmonica and me or the mandolin and me. But you've got a lot of empty spaces. But when you've got four, five or six pieces working you've always got a full bed of music there for you, waiting on you.") He is jumpy, nervous, unable to keep still. I have to bend down to talk to him, end up squatting alongside like a courtier. What's he doing now? He's into movies, man. But not normal movies, different. Improvised? No, man, that's just a fashion. Different, dig? Dylan is worried about his electric guitar, the sound, is everything right? Robbie Robertson tells him, for the fifth time, where to plug in. Dylan is by turns plaintive, querulous, accusing. I get the clear impression the rest of the band is taking care of him: they treat him like a baby—respectfully, but like a baby. It occurs to me, for the first time, that he is stoned, and not on grass: he isn't anything like the calm, self-possessed guy I saw at the airport. Dylan turns back to me. What am I doing on a newspaper? I try to explain I'm a writer, I write books, but Dylan isn't listening. Editors cut you to pieces, man. You wanna get out. But I dig what you're tryin' to say. How does he find Sydney, playing here? Makes me feel really at home, man; just like Texas. I start asking him about this religious theme in his work, how it isn't God but God's acolytes he's attacking, but he cuts me down. Everyone's got it wrong, man. I am finding it hard to talk to him. Grossman wants to know about the feedback—is there any feedback out there? Feedback? There's a popping, hissing sound in the mike when Bob's up close, I say. No, says Grossman, grimacing, he's talking about *feedback*. I feel foolish. Dylan gets up, strides around the dressing room, a tiny white box. He finishes a cigarette, picks up a copy of the program; it includes his long "autobiographical" poem, "My Life In A

Stolen Moment." "Don't take any notice of that, man," says Dylan. "It's stuff I had to put out at first, y'know, PR stuff. . . ." He's still edgy, twitchy, hyperactive. Hey, come up to his hotel room after tomorrow night's show, huh? He's got the acetates on his next album, he wants me to hear them. OK. It's time for the second half. Robbie Robertson grabs hold of Dylan, points him toward the door. Dylan whirls, disappears. The Band troops out after him. Shouts, a shock-wave of applause. We walk back to our seats. Dylan has plugged in, the Band has plugged in, the noise is tremendous. You can only just hear Bob's voice, sawing away above the organ: "How does it fe-ee-e-l? How does it fe-e-e-l? To be on your own . . . ?"

Next night I hear the show again, and go up to Dylan's hotel room afterwards. It is in the center of Kings Cross, Sydney's entertainment district. Bob appears at the door of his room. "Hi, Craig. Come in." He is friendly, relaxed—normal. I walk inside. His bed is unmade and a copy of a paperback Bob has been reading is lying opened on the sheets, cover upwards. Norman Mailer's *An American Dream*. There are other paperbacks scattered around, magazines, toilet gear, bits and pieces. It looks like the room of any college kid: untidy, unpretentious, strewn with the paraphernalia of learning. I have a sudden rush of understanding for Dylan, because it is so familiar. Déjà vu. I feel, for the first time, I am going to get through to him. Hell, I might even have something to give him. We talk quietly for a few seconds, and Bob mentions that he is waiting for Albert to get back. Like a fool, I say I thought he was coming in just as I caught the elevator. Bob asks me to hold on for a few minutes and disappears down the hallway to the suite which has been hired for him and the Band. I wait, and pick up an acoustic Gibson guitar in the corner. It is the one Bob had been playing. The guitar is out of tune, so I tune it and play some slow blues. Then fingerpick some. I am into my fifth number, and wondering what in the hell has happened, when not Bob but Robbie Robertson walks in. "Bob says come down, he wants you to hear those songs."

I walk into the main suite. It is a big room. Grossman is there. And most of the Band. They are lounging back on sofas, untalking. Bob is slumped in an easy chair, motionless.

He is wearing shades. Head propped against the back of the chair, staring up towards the ceiling. He doesn't notice me enter. Grossman motions to Robertson. "What're we gonna do?" says Robbie. The others are looking at me. "Bob wants to play 'em to him, so play 'em," says Grossman. Robertson shrugs, gets out an acetate, puts it on the portable record player. "Most Likely You Go Your Way And I'll Go Mine." They are the acetates of *Blonde on Blonde,* not yet released. I sit on the floor, propped against a bed. It is a bad scene. I concentrate on the music.

After the first side has finished, Bob stirs. "What do you think of that, Craig?" He is mumbling. I feel stupid. First time through, I haven't been able to catch many of the words; like usual, I just let it wash over me. "I like the piano; I like the whole sound." Robertson makes a gesture of disgust. Bob says, "No, that's all right, it means something." Second side. Third side. Nobody says anything. Robertson obviously doesn't want to go on with it. Albert insists. Fourth side. Bob hasn't moved; he seems to have passed out. I get to my feet, thank Grossman, mumble something about how much I liked the songs. With some reservations. What? demands Grossman. Well, say, "Just Like A Woman"—too sentimental. Grossman rounds on me, real anger showing through that pudgy bland facade. "Bob has never written anything sentimental in his whole life!"

I walk towards the door, stop, turn backwards towards Dylan. He is still slumped in the chair, head tilted towards the ceiling. Behind the shades, eyeless. I am filled with a strange, shifting mixture of pity and remorse. Ave atque vale, Bob.

It should end there, really. But everything has its sequel. Except death. And even that sometimes. . . .

Just before Dylan left Sydney for the rest of his tour the local folk fraternity—singers, songwriters, musicians—decided to give a party for him. I was asked to invite him. "Will you be there?" he asks me on the phone. "Yes." "Okay, I'll come." The party is held in a terrace house in Darlinghurst, a slum of whores, artists and auto-repair stores. By midnight Dylan still hasn't appeared, and everyone is uptight. I play a few blues, split for home. Dylan arrives shortly afterwards. No one calls me. Later they tell me it is another bad scene: a couple of the Band put on a big act, Dylan puts the hard word on a blond model, everyone stands around in awe, until finally Jeff St. John, a crippled singer with a rock band called The Id, accosts Dylan and bombards him with weird questions. Exit Dylan.

Melbourne. My brother goes to see the show. "Dylan was stoned out of his mind," he writes me. "Nearly fell off the stage. Spent most of the show making up to his lead guitar player. . . ."

Perth. The Far West. Last stop in Australia before the tour of England. Dylan sends a message to me, via another writer. Try and make it to the States, man.

The States? Oh sure. Like fucking hell.

Five years later, I find myself in New York. Hence this book.

When I began it, I was going to write a long critical introduction, a sort of careful analysis and explication of Dylan's work; but really, the book itself does that. And better. So I wrote this instead. However, there are three strands to Dylan's work I'd like to add something about.

One is its Jewishness. No one can come from a Jewish background without being profoundly influenced by it, whether the process is one of acceptance, compromise or rejection. Dylan is no exception, and one doesn't need to know much about his change of name or his contradictory, carefully disguised relationship with his parents to realize it. (If confirmation *were* needed, one need go no further than Toby Thompson's *Positively Main Street,* in which he quotes Dylan's former girlfriend Echo Helstrom: "I casually said to Bob, 'Gee, *Zimmerman,* that's a funny name. Is it Jewish?' Well, Bob didn't answer anything at *all,* he just looked straight ahead with his face sort of funny. Later in the week John took me aside at school and said, 'Listen Echo, don't ever ask Bob about being Jewish again. He doesn't like to talk about it.' ")

Recently Dylan seems to have been rediscovering his Jewishness all over again, coming to terms with it. But the important thing is what it means for his music. It explains, I think, a certain self-pity which slops over into sentimentality in some of his songs (*pace* Albert Grossman); except for his very early work, and one or two songs on *John Wesley Harding,* Dylan has always reserved most of his compassion for himself. Its most obvious effect, however, has been to make religion one of the major themes—perhaps *the* major theme—in Dylan's music. Not only does he make use of Biblical symbolism and allusions throughout his work; the central problem of what one is to believe, of Man's relationship to God, recurs in song after song. In early ballads like "With God On Our Side" Dylan's personal dilemma is clear enough: God is either omnipotent and Evil, or not omnipotent and therefore not God. In middle-period songs like "Gates of Eden" and "Tombstone Blues" he is still struggling for some sort of resolution, and the prolonged struggle of one man's soul for faith is the source of the apocalyptic note in much of his writing at this time. *John Wesley Harding* is the breakthrough: it is a penitent's album, ridden with shame, guilt and desire for atonement—Dylan's *Ash Wednesday* as surely as "Desolation Row" was his *Waste Land.* In many ways, in fact, Dylan's metaphysical progress (from rebellion to spiritual confusion to acceptance) has been very similar to that of a poet whom he has read and sometimes derided, T. S. Eliot. But the logical summation of Dylan's religious impulse had to wait two more albums, till *New Morning.* "Three Angels" is a quietly affirmative statement of belief, peace, contemplation; the spoken monologue, the calm low-key background, are almost perfect. "Father of Night" is nothing more nor less than a psalm, a hymn of praise to God—less successful, because Dylan only narrowly skirts cliché, and he has to bear comparison with his Biblical predecessors. Still, it's a fitting conclusion. And, somehow, almost predictable. A long day's journey into belief.

(Of course, this could be wrong. I am writing not long after the release of *New Morning,* and nobody else seems to think this way: Greil Marcus, in the *New York Times* review, calls "Three Angels" a joke; Ellen Willis, in the *New Yorker,* thinks it's a "spoof"; other critics have dismissed the last two songs as typical Dylan put-ons. They don't seem like that to me. We'll see.)

A second strand to Dylan's music which has been largely undiscussed is its "gay" component. It's almost as though the critics have maintained a conspiracy of silence about this, though Robert Shelton, Steven Goldberg and John Gordon refer to it briefly; most of the others have restricted themselves to veiled references to Dylan's strangely "androgynous" image, or to discussing whether or not the woman on the jacket of *Bringing It All Back Home* really is Dylan in drag. Who cares? What counts, again, is the music. There is a camp bitchiness, a penchant for the cheap put-down, which limits the effectiveness of too many of his songs, from "Positively Fourth Street" to some of the tracks on *Blonde on Blonde;* it's significant that one of the best love songs Dylan has ever written, "It Ain't Me, Babe," expresses a similar rejection without indulging in such a spiteful cutting edge. A few songs, such as "Ballad of a Thin Man," deal openly with homosexual experiences; when Dylan was in Australia I criticized it as an "in-group" song, and he quickly defended it as dealing with "something else altogether." In others the camp references are more covert, more deliberately camouflaged.

Dylan is a master of masks. If any proof were needed, his skillful manipulation of the mass media and his deliberate choosing among images to present to the public are sufficient. More importantly, Dylan uses masks in his songs as well. In many of them he seems to be writing about himself in the second or third person, as though distancing himself from and then addressing himself; so that the "you" in the song is really "I." It's a common enough device in literature and everyday speech, but Dylan has taken it further by seeming to create an alternative persona; and often the persona he chooses is a woman. He once told an interviewer that "Queen Jane Approximately," which he regarded as one of his best songs, was about a man; is the man Dylan himself? Certainly a song such as "Just Like A Woman" gains an extra dimension in meaning from such an interpretation, which also rescues that last line in the chorus ("breaks just like a little girl") from banality; it's interesting that, when he sings the chorus for the final time, Dylan switches from "she" to "you" ("You make love just like a woman. . . ."). It's only in *New Morning* that Dylan seems confident enough to write, straightforwardly, a song like "The Man in Me" ("Take a woman like you to bring out the man in me"). Of course, Dylan's songs characteristically work at different levels of meaning; like any great work of art, the best of them set up reverberations which defy reduction to a single, unalterable explanation. And often it is impossible to separate the man from the mask. Dylan's involvement in, or response to, the gay scene has probably enriched and deepened his music, though it may also have introduced an unnecessary obscurity. And it may also explain why, like Jagger's, some of its sexuality rings a little false.

Finally, it's worth emphasizing again the personal nature of Dylan's music. Those who try to force him into one ideological straightjacket or another don't realize that Dylan has never been a political thinker, that if anything he is both anti-political and anti-intellectual; he seems to work more by instinct than anything else, and what we value about him are his insights and his poetry, his artist's ability to distill and shape, not to order. Some critics accept this, but foist a substitute title upon him: that of Culture Hero, or Spokesman For His Generation. Fans search his latest songs for messages to the world, commentators with stethoscopes search for the heartbeat of the counter-culture. But Dylan has always insisted he writes only for himself. Throughout his career he has shrugged off old roles and adopted new ones like sport jackets; those who hunger after his old declamatory songs of dissent, or the apocalyptic visions of the mid-sixties, are demanding from him a consistency which he has never claimed.

Dylan's extraordinary capacity for change is one of his great strengths as an artist. (As A. J. Weberman discovered, computer concordance and all, even his symbology has changed over the years.) Yet this quality is one which critics and admirers alike have found hardest to accept. Thus the sourness of Richard Meltzer and others about Dylan's recent work; the kernel of their complaint is that it *ain't like it used to be.* Nor is it; but those who bemoan this, as such, are as guilty as the critics who attacked Dylan earlier for not sticking to folk music. They are asking him to stand still. Dylan never has. In the last few years his music has lost some of its earlier intensity and power; he has never equalled that extraordinarily creative period during which, in less than a year-and-a-half, he produced *Bringing It All Back Home, Highway 61 Revisited* and *Blonde on Blonde.* But his work has gained other virtues. "All Along the Watchtower" is one of the best songs Dylan's ever written, a brooding, philosophic reflection upon life which is the work of a mature artist; "Lay Lady Lay" is the distillation of a mood which has persisted in his work from "Corrina" onwards; and the *New Morning* album, though it contains more than its fair share of dross, includes two fine songs: "Sign in the Window" and "Three Angels." As well as being a great artist Dylan is also, simply, a man who has been through many of the changes we have been through ourselves, and is still going through them; the difference is that, unlike most of us, he has been able to write songs about what has been happening to him all the way along. Look to the songs. They are a precious record of one man's journey through darkness into light. Or vice versa. Ambivalence? Of course. We don't have to agree with Dylan: just listen.

Note

The material in this book is largely presented in chronological order. It follows Dylan's development from his first folk concerts through to the present day. Occasionally I've departed from strict chronology in order to explore certain themes, but this happens rarely. The articles have been reprinted unchanged, mistakes and all.

It's partly a source book, and partly a critical anthology. I'd liked to have included all of Dylan's album liner notes and poems, but I couldn't get his permission—and they are easily available on the album jackets anyhow. Don't forget his long poem/note on the sleeve of *Joan Baez in Concert/Part 2* (Vanguard VSD-2123). It should hardly be necessary to add that I disagree with much of what has been written in this book. What I've tried to do is represent the different points of view, and bring out the conflicts among them.

I've gained permission to reprint their work from virtually every writer and publisher in this book, but it proved impossible to trace one or two (Gil Turner, Jules Siegel, wherefore art thou?); I would be glad if they would contact me through the publisher. I'm grateful to all those who freely gave permission to include their work, and helped in so many other ways as well: especially Bob Christgau, Robert Shelton, Lillian Roxon, and Ralph Gleason. My thanks to Wilfrid Mellers, who wrote the concluding article on Dylan specifically for this book. *Sing Out!* let me go through every back issue and gave me permission to reprint anything I wished; I am deeply in their debt, and in particular to Happy Traum and John Cohen. The *New York Times,* and Seymour Peck, helped me with their files. My thanks also to Don and Sally Henderson, Ann McCarthy, and Bob Somma, editor of *Fusion* magazine, for help with research. Finally, my thanks to the following publications and publishers for allowing me to reprint material which first appeared in their pages: the *New York Times, Rolling Stone, Fusion, Sing Out!,* the *New Yorker, Playboy, Crawdaddy, Newsweek,* the *Chicago Daily News,* the *East Village Other, Ramparts, Long Island Press,* the New York *Daily News, Cheetah,* the *Washington Post,* and the *Village Voice.*

New York, 1971

Bob Dylan: A Distinctive Folk-Song Stylist

20-Year-Old Singer Is Bright New Face at Gerde's Club

by Robert Shelton

A bright new face in folk music is appearing at Gerde's Folk City. Although only 20 years old, Bob Dylan is one of the most distinctive stylists to play in a Manhattan cabaret in months.

Resembling a cross between a choir boy and a beatnik, Mr. Dylan has a cherubic look and a mop of tousled hair he partly covers with a Huck Finn black corduroy cap. His clothes may need a bit of tailoring, but when he works his guitar, harmonica or piano and composes new songs faster than he can remember them, there is no doubt that he is bursting at the seams with talent.

Mr. Dylan's voice is anything but pretty. He is consciously trying to recapture the rude beauty of a Southern field hand musing in the melody on his porch. All the "husk and bark" are left on his notes and a searing intensity pervades his songs.

Slow-Motion Mood

Mr. Dylan is both comedian and tragedian. Like a vaudeville actor on the rural circuit, he offers a variety of droll musical monologues: "Talking Bear Mountain" lampoons the overcrowding of an excursion boat, "Talking New York" satirizes his troubles in gaining recognition and "Talking Havah Nagilah" burlesques the folk-music craze and the singer himself.

In his serious vein, Mr. Dylan seems to be performing in a slow-motion film. Elasticized phrases are drawn out until you think they may snap. He rocks his head and body, closes his eyes in reverie and seems to be groping for a word or a mood, then resolves the tension benevolently by finding the word and the mood.

He may mumble the text of "House of the Rising Sun" in a scarcely understandable growl or sob, or clearly enunciate the poetic poignancy of a Blind Lemon Jefferson blues: "One kind favor I ask of you—See that my grave is kept clean."

Mr. Dylan's highly personalized approach toward folk song is still evolving. He has been sopping up influences like a sponge. At times, the drama he aims at is off-target melodrama and his stylization threatens to topple over as a mannered excess.

But if not for every taste, his music-making has the mark of originality and inspiration, all the more noteworthy for his youth. Mr. Dylan is vague about his antecedents and birthplace, but it matters less where he has been than where he is going, and that would seem to be straight up.

Stereo
COLUMBIA
Bob
Dylan

"Letter to Woody"—song by Bob Dylan

"It was written in the 1960th winter . . . in New York City in the drug store on 8th Street. It was on one of them freezing days that I came back from Sid and Bob Gleasen's in East Orange, New Jersey . . . Woody was there that day and it was a February Sunday night . . . And I just thought about Woody, I wondered about him, thought harder and wondered harder . . . I wrote this song in five minutes . . . it's all I got to say . . . If you know anything at all about Woody then you'll know what I'm trying to say . . . If you don't know anything about Woody, then find out."

—Bob Dylan

Reprinted with permission from *Sing Out!*, October–November, 1962.

Bob Dylan – A New Voice Singing New Songs

by Gil Turner

> Let me drink from the waters where the mountain
>   streams flood,
> Let the smell of wild flowers flow free through my
>   blood,
> Let me sleep in your meadows with your green grassy
>   leaves,
> Let me walk down the highway with my brothers in
>   peace.

These are the words of the most prolific young songwriter in America today. Bob Dylan has sung them, along with scores of songs he "put together," in coffee houses, nightclubs, taverns, "strip joints," living rooms and the stage of Carnegie Recital Hall. At the age of twenty-one he has won critical acclaim, a Columbia recording contract, and a clear place as a significant figure in American folk music.

In February 1961 Bob Dylan landed on the New York Island at the end of a zig-zaggy thumb ride across the country from South Dakota. He was wearing a pair of dusty dungarees, holey shoes, a corduroy Huck Finn cap and he had a beat-up Gibson guitar and two squeaky harmonicas. He wanted a try at singing his "folky" songs for the people in the big city and to meet the man whose life and music had had a great influence on his own—Woody Guthrie. He had first seen Woody in Burbank, California, a number of years before but had only the opportunity to watch and listen from a distance and say a brief hello after the program. The second meeting bridged the gap

Reprinted with permission from *Sing Out!*, October–November, 1962.

of several generations and began a friendship based on the love of good songs and a common view toward life.

Born in Duluth, Minnesota, in 1941, Bob Dylan began his "rambling" at the age of a few months. For the next nineteen years he made his home in Gallup, New Mexico; Cheyenne, South Dakota; Sioux Falls, South Dakota; Phillipsburg, Kansas; Hibbing, Minnesota; Fargo, North Dakota; and Minneapolis. He dates his interest in music and his own singing "as far back as I can remember." Everywhere he went his ears were wide open for music around him. He listened to blues singers, cowboy singers, pop singers and others soaking up music and styles with an uncanny memory and facility for assimilation. Gradually, his own preferences developed and became more clear, the strongest areas being Negro blues and country music. Among the musicians and singers who influenced him were Hank Williams, Muddy Waters, Jelly Roll Morton, Leadbelly, Mance Lipscomb and Big Joe Williams.

Dylan's first appearances in New York were at hootenannies held in the afternoon hours in Greenwich Village coffee houses. It was at one of these that I first heard him, blowing blues harmonica with singer guitarist, Mark Spoelstra. There was apparent in his singing, playing and lyric improvisation an expressive freedom seldom encountered among white blues singers. Bob Dylan in performance, however, is more than a blues singer. His flare for the comic gesture and the spontaneous quip, the ability to relate his thoughts on practically any subject from hitch-hiking to the phoniness of Tin Pan Alley, and make it entertaining, make Bob's stage personality. It is not a contrived, play-acted personality. One gets the impression that his talk and story-telling on stage are things that just came into his head that he thought you might be interested in.

Part of Dylan's magnetism lies in the fact that he is not the slightest bit afraid of falling flat on his face. If he gets an idea for a song or a story, he does it on the spot without worrying about whether it will come out exactly polished and right. There's a sense of "what's he going to do next?" Whatever comes it is often as much a surprise to the performer as to the audience. Harry Jackson, cowboy singer, painter and sculptor, summed up a Dylan performance rather graphically one night: "He's so goddamned real, it's unbelievable!"

Reality and truth are words that Bob Dylan will use often if you get him into a serious discussion about anything. They are his criteria for evaluating the world around him, the people in it (especially other folksingers), songs to sing and songs to write. If the reality is harsh, tragic, funny or meaningless, it should be thought about, looked at and described. Says Dylan, "I don't have to be anybody like those guys up on Broadway that're always writin' about 'I'm hot for you and you're hot for me—ooka dooka dicka dee.' There's other things in the world besides love and sex that're important too. People shouldn't turn their backs on 'em just because they ain't pretty to look at. How is the world ever gonna get any better if we're afraid to look at these things?" Some of "these things" are lynching, fallout shelters and peace. ("The best fallout shelter I ever saw is the Grand Canyon. They oughta put a roof on it and let all the generals and bigshot politicians go and live in it. They seem to like these fallout things pretty much so let 'em live in 'em.")

Although he can execute some intricate blues runs, do fancy three-finger picking and play in a variety of open tunings, Dylan sticks mostly to simple three-chord patterns and a rhythmic, driving flat-picking style. For him, the words are the important thing and don't need a lot of show-offy instrumental ballast to help them out. "I could sing 'Porgy and Bess' with two chords, G and D, and still get the story across."

His vocal style is rough and unpolished, reflecting a conscious effort to recapture the earthy realism of the rural country blues. It is a distinctive, highly personalized style combining many musical influences and innovations.

His first Columbia album, titled simply *Bob Dylan*, while capturing some really superb performances, does not show the breadth of his talent. It contains only one humorous selection —a talking blues about some of his own composition, "Song to Woody." With this relatively minor reservation, the record can be wholeheartedly endorsed as an excellent first album and also, incidentally, as a reflection of the growing maturity of the Columbia A & R department. According to advance reports, the second Bob Dylan album will contain a good deal more of his original songs which usually reveal him at his interpretive best.

Dylan's reception from the critics has been mixed and promises to stir up controversy as his audience grows. Robert Shelton of *The New York Times* finds him to be "bursting at the seams with talent" and is appreciative of his "originality and inspiration," while *McCall's* magazine regards him as "a young man with the style and voice of an outraged bear." Dylan's reaction to the latter: "Hah, they don't even know what a bear sounds like. Probably never saw one. Anyway, I don't even know if it's so bad to sound like a bear. When a bear growls, he's really sayin' somethin'." *Newsweek* says he "looks and acts like the square's version of a folksinger" (whatever that might be). A prominent critic privately dubs him the "Elvis Presley of folk music." The latter designation is not meant to be derogatory, but merely reflects his wide appeal to young audiences.

His night club appearances at Gerde's Folk City in New York have attracted predominantly youthful and enthusiastic audiences while the elders in the crowd seemed puzzled at his style of singing. Several teenage imitations of Dylan, harmonica, Huck Finn cap and repertoire, have already made their appearance in the Greenwich Village folksong scene. Although he maintains his performance is not consciously tailored for the young, the largest portion of his growing following is made up of persons near his own age.

While Bob is a noteworthy folk performer with a bright future, I believe his most significant and lasting contribution will be in the songs he writes, three examples of which appear in these pages. Dylan avoids the terms "write" or "compose" in connection with his songs. "The songs are there. They exist all by themselves just waiting for someone to write them down. I just put them down on paper. If I didn't do it, somebody else would." His method of writing places the emphasis on the words, the tune almost always being borrowed or adapted from one he has heard somewhere, usually a traditional one. I remember the first night he heard the tune he used for the "Ballad of Donald White." It was in Bonnie Dobson's version of the "Ballad of Peter Amberly." He heard the tune, liked it, made a mental record of it and a few days later "Donald White" was complete. About this song Dylan says: "I'd seen Donald White's name in a Seattle paper in about 1959. It said he was a killer. The next time I saw him was on a television set. My gal Sue said I'd be interested in him so we went and watched . . . Donald White was sent home from prisons and institutions cause they had no room. He asked to be sent back cause he couldn't find no room in life. He murdered someone 'cause he couldn't find no room in life. Now they killed him 'cause he couldn't find no room in life. They killed him and when they did I lost some of my room in life. When are some people gonna wake up and see that sometimes people aren't really their enemies but their victims?"

One night, two months ago, Bob came flying into Folk City where I was singing. "Gil, I got a new song I just finished. Wanna hear it?" The song was "Blowin' in the Wind," one of his best efforts to date in my opinion. I didn't recognize the tune at the time and neither did Bob, but Pete Seeger heard it and pegged the first part of it as an imaginative reworking of "No More Auction Block."

In one of his songs rejecting atomic war as a possible solution for differences among nations he says:

> If I had riches and rubies and crowns
> I'd buy the whole world and I'd change things around,
> I'd throw all the guns and the tanks in the sea,
> For they all are the mistakes of our past history.

His concluding lines for a "Ballad of Emmett Till":

> If you can't speak out against this kind of thing
> A crime that's so unjust.
> Your eyes are filled with dead man's dirt
> Your mind is filled with dust.
> Your arms and legs must be shackled and chained
> Your blood must cease to flow,
> For you would let this human race
> Fall down so godawful low.

From a lively song celebrating the bold actions of students on the civil rights front:

Red and white and brown and black,
We're ridin' this train on a one-way track
We got this far and we ain't turnin' back
We ain't gonna grieve no more.
There's a time to plant and a time to plow
A time to stand and a time to bow,
There's a time to grieve but that ain't now
We ain't gonna grieve no more.

Dylan's flare for the comic is usually put to use in the talking blues form. His "Talking Bear Mountain" is based on newspaper stories of counterfeit tickets sold for an excursion and the resultant overcrowding of the boat. "Talkin' New York" satirizes some of his early troubles in the big city. "Talkin' Havah Nagilah" was made up especially for members of the audience that shout out requests for songs way out of his line.

Dylan is adamant in his insistence that his songs remain as he has written them without being watered down. There is at least one major record company A & R man bemoaning Dylan's stubbornness in refusing to alter one of his songs. He wanted to use "Gamblin' Willie" for one of his popular recording stars, but wanted a verse changed so that the cause of Willie's gambling became an unfortunate love affair. Dylan refused on the ground that Willie was a real person whom he knew and the change would not conform to the truth as he knew it.

Dylan's plans are simply to keep on singing wherever people want to hear him (but preferably not in night clubs) and putting down songs as fast as they come into his head. The present record is five songs in one night. The latest is a song about blacklisting, inspired by the case of John Henry Faulk. The chorus of it goes:

Go down, go down you gates of hate,
You gates that keep men in chains.
Go down and die the lowest death,
And never rise again

Bob Dylan Sings His Compositions

Folk Musician, 21, Displays Originality at Town Hall

by Robert Shelton

Bob Dylan, a folk musician who breaks all the rules of song writing except those of having something to say and of saying it stunningly, gave a program of his compositions at Town Hall last night.

Mr. Dylan is 21 years old, hails from Hibbing, Minn., wears blue jeans, presumably has little to do with barbers, and resembles a Holden Caulfield who got lost in the Dust Bowl.

He plays excellent guitar and one of the most inventive harmonicas to be heard these days. His voice is small and homely, rough but ready to serve the purpose of displaying his songs. The songs are among the best written in this country's folk vein since Woody Guthrie stopped composing.

Mr. Dylan's compositions don't fit into any pigeonhole; the minute you have one characterized, it flies away. His lyrics mix a silo sermon out of Guthrie's conversational folksay with a dash of Rimbaud's demonic imagery or even a bit of Yevtushenko's social criticism. Whether his verse is free or rhymed, whether the mood is somber, crusading, satiric, subjective or fanciful, Mr. Dylan's words and melodies sparkle with the light of an inspired poet.

Despite the singer's age, he is very deeply concerned with the world around him. He cares about war, poverty, injustice and discrimination. He wants to know "Who Killed Davey Moore?" Yet there was not a cliché in any of these topics, which lesser folk composers tend to turn into hollow slogans.

Mr. Dylan's mastery of mood built up an almost physically discomforting intensity in "Hollis Brown," a song about death on a South Dakota farm. "Hard Rain's Going to Fall," about the pollution of the atmosphere with fallout, generated similar tension through repetition and an inexorable guitar beat. There was comic relief throughout, in mockbumbling stage business or "a 1930 ragtime tune I wrote last week." The reading of a poem to Guthrie won an ovation at the concert's close.

It was a memorable evening of new songs by an incredibly gifted song writer. Our thanks to Harold Leventhal, the producer, for straying from the sure box-office attraction to present a young giant.

STEREO
THE FREEWHEELIN'
BOB DYLAN

"Don't Think Twice, It's All Right"—song by Bob Dylan

". . . it isn't a love song. It's a statement that maybe you can say to make yourself feel better. It's as if you were talking to yourself. It's a hard song to sing . . . I can sing it sometimes, but I ain't that good yet."

—Bob Dylan

Reprinted with permission from *Sing Out!*, December–January, 1964.

Only Human

Driftin' and Learnin'

by Sidney Fields

All the things that once churned inside Bob Dylan when he was knocking about America are pouring from him now.

These past six years he's written over a hundred songs, with rare perception, covering everything from nuclear fallout and integration to a lover's lament or his own loneliness.

Some like "Hard Rains Are Going to Fall" are in his current best-selling album, "The Free Wheelin' Bob Dylan." Others, like "Blowin' in the Wind," and "Don't Think Twice, It's All Right," are hits by Peter, Paul, and Mary, and Bobby Darin.

Dylan is twenty-one, wears faded dungarees, uncut hair, an assumed hillbilly accent, and has been an on and off resident in Greenwich Village (where else?) for over two years. Before that he was trying to cover every highroad and by way of the country.

"The itch to move, to see, and hear, was always there," he says. "But I didn't want to see the atomic bathrooms and electronic bedrooms and souped up can-openers; I wanted to watch and feel the people and the dust and ditches and the fields and fences."

His parents and a younger brother are still in Hibbing, Minnesota, which he first tried to leave when he was ten, with his guitar and harmonica. He got 900 miles away before police picked him up and sent him home by train.

"I got walloped, but not hard enough to make me stay," Dylan says. "I took off again at 12, and five times after that,

Reprinted from *New York Mirror*, September 12, 1963.

getting caught and walloped each time. But when I was 18 I made it."

He touched about every state, trying to earn his keep by telling stories of what he saw, but eating more regularly when he trimmed hedges, mowed lawns, or any work he could get. His first New York job earned him $2 for a one-night stand in a village coffee joint. When another folk singer made a record for Columbia he was asked to accompany her on the harmonica. Columbia signed him. He made his first album, and was given a Town Hall debut.

The program notes about himself came from "My Life in A Stolen Minute," a long autobiographical poem. Part of it goes: "With my thumb out, my eyes asleep, my hat turned up an' my head turned on, I'se driftin' an' learnin' new lessons."

His voice is small, but telling, and what he sings in his own penetrating way has all the bright rhythm of a poet aware of the world.

Since his Town Hall appearance he has appeared at colleges and folk festivals, coast-to-coast, and in London and Rome. He has been on the Ed Sullivan show; on stage at Carnegie Hall. He gives a second Carnegie Hall concert next October 27. Of late he has shown up on the same stage with Joan Baez in "impromptu-on-purpose."

After his first album, titled simply *Bob Dylan*, he concluded, "That's not me. There was only a couple of my stories on it." He was happier with his second. "I wrote all the stories except for one or two songs."

His songs always start as stories. When he was on the road he became a fine teller of other people's stories. But he quit that.

"Because Dickens and Dostoievski and Woody Guthrie were telling their stories much better than I ever could," Bob Dylan says, "I decided to stick to my own mind."

Satire on Birch Society Barred From Ed Sullivan's TV Show

by Val Adams

A song satirizing the John Birch Society was barred from Ed Sullivan's television show on Sunday night by the Columbia Broadcasting System, which said it was controversial.

The network's stand was opposed by Mr. Sullivan and by Bob Precht, producer of the program, who had approved the lampoon of the right-wing organization.

It was to be sung by Bob Dylan, 21-year-old folk singer. Mr. Dylan was told by a network representative after dress rehearsal on Sunday afternoon that the song could not be presented. He did not appear on the show as scheduled.

The song, written by Mr. Dylan, is entitled "The Talking John Birch Society Blues." It is one of several John Birch songs of recent months. One version was performed on Saturday evening by the Chad Mitchell Trio on "Hootenanny" over the American Broadcasting Company television network.

Al Grossman, Mr. Dylan's manager, said Mr. Precht approved the song at an audition last week. At a rehearsal of the television show on Saturday, Mr. Grossman said, the song met the approval of Mr. Sullivan.

The manager said that after dress rehearsal Sunday afternoon, he and the singer were told by Stowe Phelps, editor of program practices for C.B.S. television, that the song could not be used.

Yesterday a spokesman for C.B.S. said "we have no comment" on the matter.

Mr. Precht said the Sullivan show hoped to present Mr. Dylan at some future time. The singer has a recording contract with Columbia Records, a subsidiary of C.B.S., Inc.

Northern Folk Singers Help Out at Negro Festival in Mississippi

Special to *The New York Times*

Greenwood, Miss., July 6

Three Northern folk singers led by Pete Seeger brought a folk-song festival to the Deep South this evening.

They sang in the yard of a Negro farm home on the edge of a cotton patch three miles south of here. The song festival, or hootenanny, was sponsored by the Student Nonviolent Coordinating Committee, which has been conducting a voter registration drive among Negroes in Mississippi delta towns for more than a year.

The festival was attended by 250 to 300 persons. Most of them were Negroes. There were a score or more of young white people, plus several white newsmen and a television camera crew of four white men from New York.

Three cars with white men in them were parked in a lane across the highway from the scene of the sing. There was also a highway patrol car with two policemen sitting along the road. There were no incidents.

Joining Mr. Seeger in leading the songfest, in which most of the audience joined at one time or another, were Theodore Bikel and Bobby Dillon, who like Mr. Seeger, are white. There was also a Negro trio, the Freedom Singers, from Albany, Ga.

All paid their own expenses for the trip and sang without a fee.

One of the more popular songs presented by a local singer was one dedicated to Medgar W. Evers, the Mississippi field secretary of the National Association for the Advancement of Colored People, who was slain last month in Jackson, Miss. A Greenwood man, Byron de La Beckwith, has been indicted in the shooting.

The refrain of the song was that the man who shot Mr. Evers didn't know what he was doing and should be forgiven, "he's only a pawn in their game."

The sing was to have begun at 10 A.M., but it was a blistering hot day, with a high of 97 degrees. So it was postponed until the sun had almost gone down, and it proceeded into the night.

STEREO
THE TIMES THEY ARE A-CHANGIN'
BOB DYLAN

"My past is so complicated you wouldn't believe it, man . . ."

Bob Dylan, to William Bender,
in the *New York Herald Tribune,*
December 12, 1965

The Crackin', Shakin', Breakin' Sounds

by Nat Hentoff

The word "folk" in the term "folk music" used to connote a rural, homogeneous community that carried on a tradition of anonymously created music. No one person composed a piece; it evolved through generations of communal care. In recent years, however, folk music has increasingly become the quite personal—and copyrighted—product of specific creators. More and more of them, in fact, are neither rural nor representative of centuries-old family and regional traditions. They are often city-bred converts to the folk style; and, after an apprenticeship during which they try to imitate rural models from the older approach to folk music, they write and perform their own songs out of their own concerns and preoccupations. The restless young, who have been the primary support of the rise of this kind of folk music over the past five years, regard two performers as their preeminent spokesmen. One is the twenty-three-year-old Joan Baez. She does not write her own material and she includes a considerable proportion of traditional, communally created songs in her programs. But Miss Baez does speak out explicitly against racial prejudice and militarism, and she does sing some of the best of the new topical songs. Moreover, her pure, penetrating voice and her open, honest manner symbolize for her admirers a cool island of integrity in a society that the folk-song writer Malvina Reynolds has characterized in one of her songs as consisting of "little boxes." ("And the boys go into business/ And marry and raise a family/ In boxes made of ticky tacky/ And they all look the same.") The second—and more influential—demiurge of the folk-music microcosm is Bob Dylan, who is also twenty-three. Dylan's impact has been the greater because he *is* a writer of songs as well as a performer. Such compositions of his as "Blowin' in the Wind," "Masters of War," "Don't Think Twice, It's All Right," and "Only a Pawn in Their Game" have become part of the repertoire of many other performers, including Miss Baez, who has explained, "Bobby is expressing what I—and many other young people—feel, what we want to say. Most of the 'protest' songs about the bomb and race prejudice and conformity are stupid. They have no beauty. But Bobby's songs are powerful as poetry and powerful as music. And, oh, my God, how that boy can sing!" Another reason for Dylan's impact is the singular force of his personality. Wiry, tense, and boyish, Dylan looks and acts like a fusion of Huck Finn and a young Woody Guthrie. Both onstage and off, he appears to be just barely able to contain his prodigious energy. Pete Seeger, who, at forty-five, is one of the elders of American folk music, recently observed, "Dylan may well become the country's most creative troubadour—if he doesn't explode."

Dylan is always dressed informally—the possibility that he will ever be seen in a tie is as remote as the possibility that Miss Baez will perform in an evening gown—and his possessions are few, the weightiest of them being a motorcycle. A wanderer, Dylan is often on the road in search of more experience. "You can find out a lot about a small town by hanging around its poolroom," he says. Like Miss Baez, he prefers to keep most of his time for himself. He works only occasionally, and during the rest of the year he travels or briefly stays in a house owned by his manager, Albert Grossman, in Bearsville, New York—a small town adjacent to Woodstock and about a hundred miles north of New York City. There Dylan writes songs, works on poetry, plays, and novels, rides his motorcycle, and talks with his friends. From time to time, he comes to New York to record for Columbia Records.

A few weeks ago, Dylan invited me to a recording session that was to begin at seven in the evening in a Columbia studio on Seventh Avenue near Fifty-second Street. Before he arrived, a tall, lean, relaxed man in his early thirties came in and introduced himself to me as Tom Wilson, Dylan's recording producer. He was joined by two engineers, and we all went into the control room. Wilson took up a post at a long, broad table, between the engineers, from which he looked out into a spacious studio with a tall thicket of microphones to the left and, directly in front, an enclave containing a music stand, two microphones, and an upright piano, and set off by a large screen, which would partly shield Dylan as he sang, for the purpose of improving the quality of the sound. "I have no idea what he's going to record tonight," Wilson told me. "It's all to be stuff he's written in the last couple of months."

I asked if Dylan presented any particular problems to a recording director.

"My main difficulty has been pounding mike technique into him," Wilson said. "He used to get excited and move around a lot and then lean in too far, so that the mike popped. Aside from that, my basic problem with him has been to create the kind of setting in which he's relaxed. For instance, if that screen should bother him, I'd take it away, even if we have to lose a little quality in the sound." Wilson looked toward the door. "I'm somewhat concerned about tonight. We're going to do a whole album in one session. Usually, we're not in such a rush, but this album has to be ready for Columbia's fall sales convention. Except for special occasions like this, Bob has no set schedule of recording dates. We think he's important enough to record whenever he wants to come to the studio."

Five minutes after seven, Dylan walked into the studio, carrying a battered guitar case. He had on dark glasses, and his hair, dark-blond and curly, had obviously not been cut for some weeks; he was dressed in blue jeans, a black jersey, and desert boots. With him were half a dozen friends, among them Jack Elliott, a folk singer in the Woody Guthrie tradition, who was also dressed in blue jeans and desert boots, plus a brown corduroy shirt and a jaunty cowboy hat. Elliott had been carrying two bottles of Beaujolais, which he now handed to Dylan, who carefully put them on a table near the screen. Dylan opened the guitar case, took out a looped-wire harmonica holder, hung it around his neck, and then walked over to the piano and began to play in a rolling, honky-tonk style.

"He's got a wider range of talents than he shows," Wilson told me. "He kind of hoards them. You go back to his three albums. Each time there's a big leap from one to the next—in material, in performance, in everything."

Dylan came into the control room, smiling. Although he is fiercely accusatory toward society at large while he is performing, his most marked offstage characteristic is gentleness. He speaks swiftly but softly, and appears persistently anxious to make himself clear. "We're going to make a good one tonight," he said to Wilson, "I promise." He turned to me and continued, "There aren't any finger-pointing songs in here, either. Those records I've made, I'll stand behind them, but some of that was jumping into the scene to be heard and a lot of it was because I didn't see anybody else doing that kind of thing. Now a lot of people are doing finger-pointing songs. You know—pointing to all the things that are wrong. Me, I don't want to write *for* people anymore. You know—be a spokesman. Like I once wrote about Emmett Till in the first person, pretending I was him. From now on, I want to write from inside me, and to do that I'm going to have to get back to writing like I used to when I was ten—having everything come out naturally. The way I like to write is for it to come out the way I walk or talk." Dylan frowned. "Not that I even walk or talk yet like I'd like to. I don't carry myself yet the way Woody, Big Joe Williams, and Lightnin' Hopkins have carried themselves. I hope to someday, but they're older. They got to where music was a tool for them, a way to live more, a way to make themselves feel better. Sometimes I can make myself feel better with music, but other times it's still hard to go to sleep at night."

A friend strolled in, and Dylan began to grumble about an interview that had been arranged for him later in the week. "I hate to say no, because, after all, these guys have a job to do," he said, shaking his head impatiently. "But it bugs me that the first question usually turns out to be 'Are you going down South to take part in any of the civil-rights projects?' They try to fit you into things. Now, I've been down there, but I'm not going down just to hold a picket sign so they can shoot a picture of me. I know a lot of the kids in S.N.C.C.—you know, the Student Nonviolent Coordinating Committee. That's the only organization I feel a part of spiritually. The N.A.A.C.P. is a bunch of old guys. I found that out by coming directly in contact with some of the people in it. They didn't understand me. They were looking to use me for something. Man, everybody's hung up. You sometimes don't know if somebody wants you to do something because he's hung up or because he really digs who you are. It's awful complicated, and the best thing you can do is admit it."

Returning to the studio, Dylan stood in front of the piano and pounded out an accompaniment as he sang from one of his own new songs:

> "Are you for real, baby, or are you just on the shelf?
> I'm looking deep into your eyes, but all I can see is
> myself.
> If you're trying to throw me, I've already been tossed.
> If you're trying to lose me, I've already been lost. . . ."

Another friend of Dylan's arrived, with three children, ranging in age from four to ten. The children raced around the studio until Wilson insisted that they be relatively confined to the control room. By ten minutes to eight, Wilson had checked out the sound balance to his satisfaction, Dylan's friends had found seats along the studio walls, and Dylan had expressed his readiness—in fact, eagerness—to begin. Wilson, in the control room, leaned forward, a stopwatch in his hand. Dylan took a deep breath, threw his head back, and plunged into a song in which he accompanied himself on guitar and harmonica. The first take was ragged; the second was both more relaxed and more vivid. At that point, Dylan, smiling, clearly appeared to be confident of his ability to do an entire album in one night. As he moved into succeeding numbers, he relied principally on the guitar for support, except for exclamatory punctuations on the harmonica.

Having glanced through a copy of Dylan's new lyrics that he had handed to Wilson, I observed to Wilson that there were indeed hardly any songs of social protest in the collection.

"Those early albums gave people the wrong idea," Wilson said. "Basically, he's in the tradition of all lasting folk music. I mean, he's not a singer of protest so much as he is a singer of *concern* about people. He doesn't have to be talking about Medgar Evers all the time to be effective. He can just tell a simple little story of a guy who ran off from a woman."

After three takes of one number, one of the engineers said to Wilson, "If you want to try another, we can get a better take."

"No." Wilson shook his head. "With Dylan, you have to take what you can get."

Out in the studio, Dylan, his slight form bent forward, was standing just outside the screen and listening to a playback through earphones. He began to take the earphones off during an instrumental passage, but then his voice came on, and he grinned and replaced them.

The engineer muttered again that he might get a better take if Dylan ran through the number once more.

"Forget it," Wilson said. "You don't think in terms of orthodox recording techniques when you're dealing with Dylan. You have to learn to be as free on this side of the glass as he is out there."

Dylan went on to record a song about a man leaving a girl because he was not prepared to be the kind of invincible hero and all-encompassing provider she wanted. "It ain't me you're looking for, babe," he sang, with finality.

During the playback, I joined Dylan in the studio. "The songs so far sound as if there were real people in them," I said.

Dylan seemed surprised that I had considered it necessary to make the comment. "There are. That's what makes them so scary. If I haven't been through what I write about, the songs aren't worth anything." He went on, via one of his songs, to offer a complicated account of a turbulent love affair in Spanish Harlem, and at the end asked a friend, "Did you understand it?" The friend nodded enthusiastically. "Well, I didn't," Dylan said, with a laugh, and then became somber. "It's hard being free in a song—getting it all in. Songs are so confining. Woody Guthrie told me once that songs don't have to do anything like that. But it's not true. A song has to have some kind of form to fit into the music. You can bend the words and the metre, but it still has to fit somehow. I've been getting freer in the songs I write, but I still feel confined. That's why I write a lot of poetry—if that's the word. Poetry can make its own form."

As Wilson signalled for the start of the next number, Dylan put up his hand. "I just want to light a cigarette, so I can see it there while I'm singing," he said, and grinned. "I'm very neurotic. I need to be secure."

By ten-thirty, seven songs had been recorded.

"This is the fastest Dylan date yet," Wilson said. "He used to be all hung up with the microphones. Now he's a pro."

Several more friends of Dylan's had arrived during the recording of the seven songs, and at this point four of them were seated in the control room behind Wilson and the engineers. The others were scattered around the studio, using the table that held the bottles of Beaujolais as their base. They opened the bottles, and every once in a while poured out a drink in a paper cup. The three children were still irrepressibly present, and once the smallest burst suddenly into the studio, ruining a take. Dylan turned on the youngster in mock anger. "I'm gonna rub you out," he said. "I'll track you down and turn you to dust." The boy giggled and ran back into the control room.

As the evening went on, Dylan's voice became more acrid. The dynamics of his singing grew more pronounced, soft, intimate passages being abruptly followed by fierce surges in volume. The relentless, driving beat of his guitar was more often supplemented by the whooping thrusts of the harmonica.

"Intensity, that's what he's got," Wilson said, apparently to himself. "By now, this kid is outselling Thelonious Monk and Miles Davis," he went on, to me. "He's speaking to a whole new generation. And not only here. He's just been in England. He had standing room only in Royal Festival Hall."

Dylan had begun a song called "Chimes of Freedom." One of his four friends in the control room—a lean, bearded man—proclaimed, "Bobby's talking for every hung-up person in the whole wide universe." His three companions nodded gravely.

The next composition, "Motorpsycho Nitemare," was a mordantly satirical version of the vintage tale of the farmer, his daughter, and the travelling salesman. There were several false starts, apparently because Dylan was having trouble reading the lyrics.

"Man, dim the lights," the bearded friend counselled Wilson. "He'll get more relaxed."

"Atmosphere is not what we need," Wilson answered, without turning around. "Legibility is what we need."

During the playback, Dylan listened intently, his lips moving, and a cigarette cocked in his right hand. A short break followed, during which Dylan shouted, "Hey, we're gonna need some more wine!" Two of his friends in the studio nodded and left.

After the recording session resumed, Dylan continued to work hard and conscientiously. When he was preparing for a take or listening to a playback, he seemed able to cut himself off completely from the eddies of conversation and humorous byplay stirred up by his friends in the studio. Occasionally, when a line particularly pleased him, he burst into laughter, but he swiftly got back to business.

Dylan started a talking blues—a wry narrative in a sardonic recitative style, which had been developed by Woody Guthrie. "Now I'm liberal, but to a degree," Dylan was drawling halfway through the song. "I want everybody to be free. But if you think I'll let Barry Goldwater move in next door and marry my daughter, you must think I'm crazy. I wouldn't let him do it for all the farms in Cuba." He was smiling broadly, and Wilson and the engineers were laughing. It was a long song, and toward the end Dylan faltered. He tried it twice more, and each time he stumbled before the close.

"Let me do another song," he said to Wilson. "I'll come back to this."

"No," Wilson said. "Finish up this one. You'll hang us up on the order, and if I'm not here to edit, the other cat will get mixed up. Just do an insert of the last part."

"Let him start from the beginning, man," said one of the four friends sitting behind Wilson.

Wilson turned around, looking annoyed. "Why, man?"

"You don't start telling a story with Chapter Eight, man," the friend said.

"Oh, man," said Wilson, "what kind of philosophy is that? We're recording, not writing a biography."

As an obbligato of protest continued behind Wilson, Dylan, accepting Wilson's advice, sang the insert. His bearded friend rose silently and drew a square in the air behind Wilson's head.

Other songs, mostly of love lost or misunderstood, followed. Dylan was now tired, but he retained his good humor. "This last one is called 'My Back Pages,'" he announced to Wilson. It appeared to express his current desire to get away from "finger-pointing" and write more acutely personal material. "Oh, but I was so much older then," he sang as a refrain, "I'm younger than that now."

By one-thirty, the session was over. Dylan had recorded fourteen new songs. He agreed to meet me again in a week or so and fill me in on his background. "My background's not all that important, though," he said as we left the studio. "It's what I am now that counts."

Dylan was born in Duluth, on May 24, 1941, and grew up in Hibbing, Minnesota, a mining town near the Canadian border. He does not discuss his parents, preferring to let his songs tell whatever he wants to say about his personal history. "You can stand at one end of Hibbing on the main drag an' see clear past the city limits on the other end," Dylan once noted in a poem, "My Life in a Stolen Moment," printed in the program of a 1963 Town Hall concert he gave. Like Dylan's parents, it appears, the town was neither rich nor poor, but it was, Dylan has said, "a dyin' town." He ran away from home seven times—at ten, at twelve, at thirteen, at fifteen, at fifteen and a half, at seventeen, and at eighteen. His travels included South Dakota, New Mexico, Kansas, and California. In between flights, he taught himself the guitar, which he had begun playing at the age of ten. At fifteen, he was also playing the harmonica and the autoharp, and, in addition, had written his first song, a ballad dedicated to Brigitte Bardot. In the spring of 1960, Dylan entered the University of Minnesota, in Minneapolis, which he attended for something under six months. In "My Life in a Stolen Moment," Dylan has summarized his college career dourly: "I sat in science class an' flunked out for refusin' to watch a rabbit die. I got expelled from English class for using four-letter words in a paper describing the English teacher. I also failed out of communication class for callin' up every day and sayin' I couldn't come. . . . I was kept around for kicks at a fraternity house. They let me live there, an' I did until they wanted me to join." Paul Nelson and Jon Pankake, who edit the *Little Sandy Review*, a quarterly magazine, published in Minneapolis, that is devoted to critical articles on folk music and performers, remember meeting Dylan at the University of Minnesota in the summer of 1960, while he was part of a group of singers who performed at The Scholar, a coffeehouse near the university. The editors, who were students at the university then, have since noted in their publication: "We recall Bob as a soft-spoken, rather unprepossessing youngster . . . well-groomed and neat in the standard campus costume of slacks, sweater, white oxford sneakers, poplin raincoat, and dark glasses."

Before Dylan arrived at the university, his singing had been strongly influenced by such Negro folk interpreters as Leadbelly and Big Joe Williams. He had met Williams in Evanston, Illinois, during his break from home at the age of twelve. Dylan had also been attracted to several urban-style rhythm-and-blues performers, notably Bo Diddley and Chuck Berry. Other shaping forces were white country music figures—particularly Hank Williams, Hank Snow, and Jimmie Rodgers. During his brief stay at the university, Dylan became especially absorbed in the recordings of Woody Guthrie, the Oklahoma-born traveller who had created the most distinctive body of American topical folk material to come to light in this century. Since 1954, Guthrie, ill with Huntington's chorea, a progressive disease of the nervous system, had not been able to perform, but he was allowed to receive visitors. In the autumn of 1960, Dylan quit the University of Minnesota and decided to visit Guthrie at Greystone Hospital, in New Jersey. Dylan returned briefly to Minnesota the following May, to sing at a university hootenanny, and Nelson and Pankake saw him again on that occasion. "In a mere half year," they have recalled in the *Little Sandy Review*, "he had learned to churn up exciting, bluesy, hard-driving harmonica-and-guitar music, and had absorbed during his visits with Guthrie not only the great Okie musician's unpredictable syntax but his very vocal color, diction, and inflection. Dylan's performance that spring evening of a selection of Guthrie . . . songs was hectic and shaky, but it contained all the elements of the now-perfected performing style that has made him the most original newcomer to folk music."

The winter Dylan visited Guthrie was otherwise bleak. He spent most of it in New York, where he found it difficult to get steady work singing. In "Talkin' New York," a caustic song describing his first months in the city, Dylan tells of having been turned away by a coffeehouse owner, who told him scornfully, "You sound like a hillbilly. We want folk singers here." There were nights when he slept in the subway, but eventually he found friends and a place to stay on the lower East Side, and after he had returned from the spring hootenanny, he began getting more frequent engagements in New York. John Hammond, Director of Talent Acquisition at Columbia Records, who has discovered a sizable number of important jazz and folk performers during the past thirty years, heard Dylan that summer while attending a rehearsal of another folk singer, whom Hammond was about to record for Columbia Records. Impressed by the young man's raw force and by the vivid lyrics of his songs, Hammond auditioned him and immediately signed him to a recording contract. Then, in September, 1961, while Dylan was appearing at Gerde's Folk City, a casual refuge for "citybillies" (as the young city singers and musicians are now called in the trade), on West Fourth Street, in Greenwich Village, he was heard by Robert Shelton, the folk-music critic for the *Times*, who wrote of him enthusiastically.

Dylan began to prosper. He enlarged his following by appearing at the Newport and Monterey Folk Festivals and giving concerts throughout the country. There have been a few snags, as when he walked off the Ed Sullivan television show in the spring of 1963 because the Columbia Broadcasting System would not permit him to sing a tart appraisal of the John Birch Society, but on the whole he has experienced accelerating success. His first three Columbia albums—*Bob Dylan, The Freewheelin' Bob Dylan,* and *The Times They Are A-Changin'*—have by now reached a cumulative sales figure of nearly four hundred thousand. In addition, he has received large royalties as a composer of songs that have become hits through recordings by Peter, Paul, and Mary, the Kingston Trio, and other performers. At present, Dylan's fees for a concert appearance range from two thousand to three thousand dollars a night. He has sometimes agreed to sing at a nominal fee for new, non-profit folk societies, however, and he has often performed without charge at civil-rights rallies.

Musically, Dylan has transcended most of his early influences and developed an incisively personal style. His vocal sound is most often characterized by flaying harshness. Mitch Jayne, a member of the Dillards, a folk group from Missouri, has described Dylan's sound as "very much like a dog with his leg caught in barbed wire." Yet Dylan's admirers come to accept and even delight in the harshness, because of the vitality and wit at its core. And they point out that in intimate ballads he is capable of a fragile lyricism that does not slip into bathos. It is Dylan's work as a composer, however, that has won him a wider audience than his singing alone might have. Whether concerned with cosmic spectres or personal conundrums, Dylan's lyrics are pungently idiomatic. He has a superb ear for speech rhythms, a generally astute sense of selective detail, and a natural storyteller's command of narrative pacing. His songs sound as if they were being created out of oral street history rather than carefully written in tranquillity. On a stage, Dylan performs his songs as if he had an urgent story to tell. In his work there is little of the polished grace of such carefully trained contemporary minstrels as Richard Dyer-Bennet. Nor, on the other hand, do Dylan's performances reflect the calculated showmanship of a Harry Belafonte or of Peter, Paul, and Mary. Dylan off the stage is very much the same as Dylan the performer—restless, insatiably hungry for experience, idealistic, but skeptical of neatly defined causes.

In the past year, as his renown has increased, Dylan has become more elusive. He felt so strongly threatened by his initial fame that he welcomed the chance to use the Bearsville home of his manager as a refuge between concerts, and he still spends most of his time there when he's not travelling. A week after the recording session, he telephoned me from Bearsville, and we agreed to meet the next evening at the Keneret, a restaurant on lower Seventh Avenue, in the Village. It specializes in Middle Eastern food, which is one of Dylan's preferences, but it does not have a liquor license. Upon keeping our rendezvous, therefore, we went next door for a few bottles of Beaujolais and then returned to the Keneret. Dylan was as restless as usual, and as he talked, his hands moved constantly and his voice sounded as if he were never quite able to catch his breath.

I asked him what he had meant, exactly, when he spoke at the recording session of abandoning "finger-pointing" songs, and he took a sip of wine, leaned forward, and said, "I looked around and saw all these people pointing fingers at the bomb. But the bomb is getting boring, because what's wrong goes much deeper than the bomb. What's wrong is how few people are free. Most people walking around are tied down to something that doesn't let them really *speak*, so they just add their confusion to the mess. I mean, they have some kind of vested interest in the way things are now. Me, I'm cool." He smiled. "You know, Joanie—Joanie Baez—worries about me. She worries about whether people will get control over me and exploit me. But I'm cool. I'm in control, because I don't care about money, and all that. And I'm cool in myself, because I've gone through enough changes so that I know what's real to me and what isn't. Like this fame. It's done something to me. It's O.K. in the Village here. People don't pay attention to me. But in other towns it's funny knowing that people you don't know figure they know *you*. I mean, they think they know everything about you. One thing is groovy, though. I got birthday cards this year from people I'd never heard of. It's weird, isn't it? There are people I've really touched whom I'll never know." He lit a cigarette. "But in other ways being noticed can be a weight. So I disappear a lot. I go to places where I'm not going to be noticed. And I *can*." He laughed. "I have no work to do. I have no job. I'm not committed to anything except making a few records and playing a few concerts. I'm weird that way. Most people, when they get up in the morning, have to do what they *have* to do. I could pretend there were all kinds of things I *had* to do every day. But why? So I do whatever I feel like. I might make movies of my friends around Woodstock one day. I write a lot. I get involved in scenes with people. A lot of scenes are going on with me all the time—

here in the Village, in Paris during my trips to Europe, in lots of places."

I asked Dylan how far ahead he planned.

"I don't look past right now," he said. "Now there's this fame business. I know it's going to go away. It has to. This so-called mass fame comes from people who get caught up in a thing for a while and buy the records. Then they stop. And when they stop, I won't be famous anymore."

We became aware that a young waitress was standing by diffidently. Dylan turned to her, and she asked him for his autograph. He signed his name with gusto, and signed again when she asked if he would give her an autograph for a friend. "I'm sorry to have interrupted your dinner," she said, smiling. "But I'm really not."

"I get letters from people—young people—all the time," Dylan continued when she had left us. "I wonder if they write letters like those to other people they don't know. They just want to tell me things, and sometimes they go into their personal hangups. Some send poetry. I like getting them—read them all and answer some. But I don't mean I give any of the people who write to me any *answers* to their problems." He leaned forward and talked more rapidly. "It's like when somebody wants to tell me what the 'moral' thing is to do, I want them to *show* me. If they have anything to say about morals, I want to know what it is they *do*. Same with me. All I can do is show people who ask me questions how I live. All I can do is be me. I can't tell them how to change things, because there's only one way to change things, and that's to cut yourself off from all the chains. That's hard for most people to do."

I had Dylan's *The Times They Are A-Changin'* album with me, and I pointed out to him a section of his notes on the cover in which he spoke of how he had always been running when he was a boy—running away from Hibbing and from his parents.

Dylan took a sip of wine. "I kept running because I wasn't free," he said. "I was constantly on guard. Somehow, way back then, I already knew that parents do what they do because they're up tight. They're concerned with their kids in relation to *themselves*. I mean, they want their kids to please them, not to embarrass them—so they can be proud of them. They want you to be what *they* want you to be. So I started running when I was ten. But always I'd get picked up and sent home. When I was thirteen, I was travelling with a carnival through upper Minnesota and North and South Dakota, and I got picked up again. I tried again and again, and when I was eighteen, I cut out for good. I was still running when I came to New York. Just because you're free to move doesn't mean you're free. Finally, I got so far out I was cut off from everybody and everything. It was then I decided there was no sense in running so far and so fast when there was no longer anybody there. It was fake. It was running for the sake of running. So I stopped. I've got no place to run from. I don't have to be anyplace I don't want to be. But I am by no means an example for any kid wanting to strike out. I mean, I wouldn't want a young kid to leave home because I did it, and then have to go through a lot of the things I went through. Everybody has to find his own way to be free. There isn't anybody who can help you in that sense. Nobody was able to help me. Like seeing Woody Guthrie was one of the main reasons I came East. He was an idol to me. A couple of years ago, after I'd gotten to know him, I was going through some very bad changes, and I went to see Woody, like I'd go to somebody to confess to. But I couldn't confess to him. It was silly. I did go and talk with him—as much as he could talk—and the talking helped. But basically he wasn't able to help me at all. I finally realized that. So Woody was my last idol."

There was a pause.

"I've learned a lot in these past few years," Dylan said softly. "Like about beauty."

I reminded him of what he had said about his changing criteria of beauty in some notes he did for a Joan Baez album. There he had written that when he first heard her voice, before he knew her, his reaction had been:

> "I hate that kind a sound," said I
> "The only beauty's ugly, man
> The crackin', shakin', breakin' sounds're
> The only beauty I understand."

Dylan laughed. "Yeah," he said. "I was wrong. My hangup was that I used to try to *define* beauty. Now I take it as it is, however it is. That's why I like Hemingway. I don't read much. Usually I read what people put in my hands. But I do read Hemingway. He didn't have to use adjectives. He didn't really have to define what he was saying. He just said it. I can't do that yet, but that's what I want to be able to do."

A young actor from Julian Beck's and Judith Malina's Living Theatre troupe stopped by the table, and Dylan shook hands with him enthusiastically. "We're leaving for Europe soon," the actor said. "But when we come back, we're going out on the street. We're going to put on plays right on the street, for anyone who wants to watch."

"Hey!" said Dylan, bouncing in his seat. "Tell Julian and Judith that I want to be in on that."

The actor said he would, and took Dylan's telephone number. Then he said, "Bob, are you doing only your own songs now—none of the old folk songs at all?"

"Have to," Dylan answered. "When I'm up tight and it's raining outside and nobody's around and somebody I want is a long way from me—and with someone else besides—I can't sing 'Ain't Got No Use for Your Red Apple Juice.' I don't care how great an old song it is or what its tradition is. I have to make a new song out of what *I* know and out of what *I'm* feeling."

The conversation turned to civil rights, and the actor used the term "the Movement" to signify the work of the civil-rights activists. Dylan looked at him quizzically. "I agree with everything that's happening," he said, "but I'm not part of no Movement. If I was, I wouldn't be able to do anything else but be in 'the Movement.' I just can't have people sit around and make rules for me. I do a lot of things no Movement would allow." He took a long drink of Beaujolais. "It's like politics," he went on. "I just can't make it with *any* organization. I fell into a trap once—last December—when I agreed to accept the Tom Paine Award from the Emergency Civil Liberties Committee. At the Americana Hotel! In the Grand Ballroom! As soon as I got there, I felt up tight. First of all, the people with me couldn't get in. They looked even funkier than I did, I guess. They weren't dressed right, or something. Inside the ballroom, I really got up tight. I began to drink. I looked down from the platform and saw a bunch of people who had nothing to do with my kind of politics. I looked down and I got scared. They were supposed to be on my side, but I didn't feel any connection with them. Here were these people who'd been all involved with the left in the thirties, and now they were supporting civil-rights drives. That's groovy, but they also had minks and jewels, and it was like they were giving the money out of guilt. I got up to leave, and they followed me and caught me. They told me I had to accept the award. When I got up to make my speech, I couldn't say anything by that time but what was passing through my mind. They'd been talking about Kennedy being killed, and Bill Moore and Medgar Evers and the Buddhist monks in Vietnam being killed. I had to say something about Lee Oswald. I told them I'd read a lot of his feelings in the papers and I knew he was up tight. Said I'd been up tight, too, so I'd got a lot of his feelings. I saw a lot of myself in Oswald, I said, and I saw in him a lot of the times we're all living in. And, you know. they started booing. They looked at me like I was an animal. They actually thought I was saying it was a good thing Kennedy had been killed. That's how far out they are. I was talking about Oswald. And then I started talking about some friends of mine in Harlem—some of them junkies, all of them poor. And I said they need freedom as much as anybody else, and what's anybody doing for *them?* The chairman was kicking my leg under the table, and I told him, 'Get out of here.' Now, what I was supposed to be was a nice cat. I was supposed to say, 'I appreciate your award and I'm a great singer and I'm a great believer in liberals, and you buy my records and I'll support your cause.' But I didn't, and so I wasn't accepted that night. That's the cause of a lot of those chains I was talking about—people wanting to be accepted, people not wanting to be alone. But, after all, what is it to be alone? I've been alone sometimes in front of three thousand people. I was alone that night."

The actor nodded sympathetically.

Dylan snapped his fingers. "I almost forgot," he said. "You know, they were talking about Freedom Fighters that night.

I've been in Mississippi, man. I know those people on another level besides civil-rights campaigns. I know them as friends. Like Jim Forman, one of the heads of S.N.C.C. I'll stand on his side any time. But those people that night were actually getting me to look at colored people as colored people. I tell you, I'm never going to have anything to do with any political organization again in my life. Oh, I might help a friend if he was campaigning for office. But I'm not going to be part of any organization. Those people at that dinner were the same as everybody else. They're doing their time. They're chained to what they're doing. The only thing is, they're trying to put morals and great deeds on their chains, but basically they don't want to jeopardize their positions. They got their jobs to keep. There's nothing there for me, and there's nothing there for the kind of people I hang around with. The only thing I'm sorry about is that I guess I hurt the collection at the dinner. I didn't know they were going to try to collect money after my speech. I guess I lost them a lot of money. Well, I offered to pay them whatever it was they figured they'd lost because of the way I talked. I told them I didn't care how much it was. I hate debt, especially moral debts. They're worse than money debts."

Exhausted by his monologue, Dylan sank back and poured more Beaujolais. "People talk about trying to change society," he said. "All I know is that so long as people stay so concerned about protecting their status and protecting what they have, ain't nothing going to be done. Oh, there may be some change of levels inside the circle, but nobody's going to learn anything."

The actor left, and it was time for Dylan to head back upstate. "Come up and visit next week," he said to me, "and I'll give you a ride on my motorcycle." He hunched his shoulders and walked off quickly.

STEREO
Another
side
of
Bob
Dylan

"Bobby Dylan says what a lot of people my age feel, but cannot say."

—Joan Baez

"I like his whole attitude. The way he dresses, the way he doesn't give a damn, the way he sings discords and plays discords. The way he sends up everything."

—George Harrison

"I just have thoughts in my head and I write them. I'm not trying to lead any causes for anyone else."

—Bob Dylan

An Open Letter to Bob Dylan

Dear Bob:

It seems as though lots of people are thinking and talking about you these days. I read about you in *Life* and *Newsweek* and *Time* and *The Saturday Evening Post* and *Mademoiselle* and *Cavalier* and all such, and I realize that, all of a sudden, you have become a pheenom, a VIP, a celebrity. A lot has happened to you in these past two years, Bob—a lot more than most of us thought possible.

I'm writing this letter now because some of what has happened is troubling me. And not me alone. Many other good friends of yours as well.

I don't have to tell you how we at SING OUT! feel about you—about your work as a writer and an artist—or how we feel about you as a person. SING OUT! was among the first to respond to the new ideas, new images, and new sounds that you were creating. By last count, thirteen of your songs had appeared in these pages. Maybe more of Woody's songs were printed here over the years, but, if so, he's the only one. Not that we were doing you any favors, Bob. Far from it. We believed—and still believe—that these have been among some of the best new songs to appear in America in more than a decade. "Blowin' in the Wind," "Don't Think Twice," "Hattie Carroll," "Restless Farewell," "Masters of War"—these have been inspired contributions which have already had a significant impact on American consciousness and style.

As with anyone who ventures down uncharted paths, you've aroused a growing number of petty critics. Some don't like the way you wear your hair or your clothes. Some don't like the

Reprinted with permission from *Sing Out!*, November, 1964.

way you sing. Some don't like the fact that you've chosen your name and recast your past. But all of that, in the long run, is trivial. We both know that many of these criticisms are simply coverups for embarrassment at hearing songs that speak directly, personally, and urgently about where it's all really at.

But—and this is the reason for this letter, Bob—I think that the times they are a-changing. You seem to be in a different kind of bag now, Bob—and I'm worried about it. I saw at Newport how you had somehow lost contact with people. It seemed to me that some of the paraphernalia of fame were getting in your way. You travel with an entourage now—with good buddies who are going to laugh when you need laughing and drink wine with you and insure your privacy—and never challenge you to face everyone else's reality again.

I thought (and so did you) of Jimmy Dean when I saw you last—and I cried a little inside me for that awful potential for self-destruction which lies hidden in all of us and which can emerge so easily and so uninvited.

I think it begins to show up in your songs, now, Bob. You said you weren't a writer of "protest" songs—or any other category, for that matter—but you just wrote songs. Well, okay, call it anything you want. But any songwriter who tries to deal honestly with reality in this world is bound to write "protest" songs. How can he help himself?

Your new songs seem to be all inner-directed now, inner-probing, self-conscious—maybe even a little maudlin or a little cruel on occasion. And it's happening on stage, too. You seem to be relating to a handful of cronies behind the scenes now—rather than to the rest of us out front.

Now, that's all okay—if that's the way you want it, Bob. But then you're a different Bob Dylan from the one we knew. The old one never wasted our precious time.

Perhaps this letter has been long overdue. I think, in a sense, that we are all responsible for what's been happening to you—and to many other fine young artists. The American Success Machinery chews up geniuses at a rate of one a day and still hungers for more. Unable to produce real art on its own, the Establishment breeds creativity in protest against and nonconformity to the System. And then, through notoriety, fast money, and status, it makes it almost impossible for the artist to function and grow.

It is a process that must be constantly guarded against and fought.

Give it some thought, Bob. Believe me when I say that this letter is written out of love and deep concern. I wouldn't be sticking my neck out like this otherwise.

Irwin Silber

STEREO
Bob Dylan
Bringing It All Back Home

Newport Folk Festival, 1965

by Irwin Silber

The Festival's most controversial scene was played out on the dramatically-lit giant stage halfway through the final night's concert when Bob Dylan emerged from his cult-imposed aura of mystery to demonstrate the new "folk rock," and expression that has already begun to find its way into the "Top Forty" charts by which musical success is measured. To many, it seemed that it was not very good "rock," while other disappointed legions did not think it was very good Dylan. Most of these erupted into silence at the conclusion of Dylan's songs, while a few booed their once-and-former idol. Others cheered and demanded encores, finding in the "new" Dylan an expression of themselves, just as teenaged social activists of 1963 had found themselves summed up in the angry young poet's vision.

Shocked and somewhat disoriented by the mixed reaction of the crowd, a tearful Dylan returned to the stage unelectrified and strained to communicate his sense of unexpected displacement through the words and music of a song he made fearfully appropriate, "It's All Over Now, Baby Blue."

But if the audience thought that the Dylan scene represented a premature climax to the evening, more was yet to come. A double finale (presumably a Newport tradition by now) saw hordes of singers, musicians, self-appointed participants and temporary freaks take over the stage in a tasteless exhibition of frenzied incest that seemed to have been taken from a Hollywood set. One singer called it a "nightmare of pop art," which was one of the more apt and gentle of the comments heard in the audience. The stage invasion took place during the singing

Reprinted with permission from *Sing Out!*, November, 1965.

of Mrs. Fannie Lou Hamer, one of that incredible band of Mississippi heroines who are in the process of reshaping America for us all. It seemed as though everyone wanted to make sure they were in on the big "civil rights act," and a moment that might have become the highpoint of the entire weekend was suddenly turned into a scene of opportunistic chaos—duplicated once again after the inevitable Peter, Paul and Mary finale and reducing the meaning of Newport to the sense of a carnival gone mad.

At the height of the frenzy, it was easy to forget the music and the conviction that had come before. There were many who thought they sensed a feeling of revulsion even among some of the Newport directors who were themselves participating in the debacle. And when the end finally came, the crowd filed out to the sound of a mournful and lonesome harmonica playing "Rock of Ages." It was the most optimistic note of the evening.

Newport Folk Festival, 1965

by Paul Nelson

For all its emphasis on tradition and its quiet highpoints (Roscoe Holcomb and Jean Ritchie singing "Wandering Boy" was my favorite among many), Newport is still a place for the Big Moment, the Great Whan, that minuscule second of High Drama that freezes the blood and sparks the brain into the kind of excitement that stays forever in one's memory. Nothing approaching such a moment happened at Newport in 1964 (it was a dull circus), but Bob Dylan provided it on Sunday night this year: the most dramatic scene I've ever witnessed in folk music.

Here are two accounts of it, the first sketched quickly in my notebook at the time:

"Dylan doing his new R&R, R&B, R&? stuff knocked me out . . . I think his new stuff is as exciting as anything I've heard lately in any field. The Newport crowd actually booed the electric guitar numbers he did, and there followed the most dramatic thing I've seen: Dylan walking off the stage, the audience booing and yelling 'Get rid of that electric guitar,' Peter Yarrow trying to talk the audience into clapping and trying to talk Dylan into coming back, Yarrow announcing that Dylan was coming back, George Wein asking Yarrow in disbelief '*Is* he coming back?', Dylan coming back with tears in his eyes and singing 'It's All Over Now, Baby Blue,' a song that I took to be his farewell to Newport, an incredible sadness over Dylan and the audience finally clapping now because the electric guitar was gone, etc." (Dylan did only his first three numbers with electric guitar and band.)

Reprinted with permission from *Sing Out!*, November, 1965.

The second account is from a long report on Newport by Jim Rooney of Cambridge, Massachusetts:

"Nothing else in the festival caused such controversy. His (Dylan's) was the only appearance that was genuinely disturbing. It was disturbing to the Old Guard, I think, for several reasons. Bob is no longer a neo-Woody Guthrie, with whom they could identify. He has thrown away his dungarees and shaggy jacket. He has stopped singing talking blues and songs about 'causes'—peace or civil rights. The highway he travels now is unfamiliar to those who bummed around in the thirties during the Depression. He travels by plane. He wears high-heel shoes and high-style clothes from Europe. The mountains and valleys he knows are those of the mind—a mind extremely aware of the violence of the inner and outer world. 'The people' so loved by Pete Seeger are 'the mob' so hated by Dylan. In the face of violence, he has chosen to preserve himself alone. No one else. And he defies everyone else to have the courage to be as alone, as unconnected . . . as he. He screams through organ and drums and electric guitar, 'How does it feel to be on your own?' And there is no mistaking the hostility, the defiance, the contempt for all those thousands sitting before him who aren't on their own. Who can't make it. And they seemed to understand that night for the first time what Dylan has been trying to say for over a year—that he is not theirs or anyone else's—and they didn't like what they heard and booed. They wanted to throw him out. He had fooled them before when they thought he was theirs . . . Pete (Seeger) had begun the night with the sound of a newborn baby crying, and asked that everyone sing to that baby and tell it what kind of a world it would be growing up into. But Pete already knew what he wanted others to sing. They were going to sing that it was a world of pollution, bombs, hunger, and injustice, but that PEOPLE would OVERCOME . . . (But) can there be no songs as violent as the age? Must a folk song be of mountains, valleys, and love between my brother and my sister all over this land? Do we allow for despair only in the blues? . . . (That's all) very comfortable and safe. But is that what we should be saying to that baby? Maybe, maybe not. But we should ask the question. And the only one in the entire festival who questioned our position was Bob Dylan. Maybe he didn't put it in the best way. Maybe he was rude. But he shook us. And that is why we have poets and artists."

Indeed, that's why we have poets and artists. Newport 1965, interestingly enough, split apart forever the two biggest names in folk music: Pete Seeger, who saw in Sunday night a chance to project his vision of the world and sought to have all others convey his impression (thereby restricting their performances), and Bob Dylan, like some fierce young Spanish outlaw in dress leather jacket, a man who could no longer accept the older singer's vague humanistic generalities, a man who, like Nathanael West, had his own angry vision to project in such driving electric songs as "Like a Rolling Stone" and "Maggie's Farm."

And, like it or not, the audience had to choose. Whether, on the one hand, to take the word of a dignified and great humanitarian whose personal sincerity is beyond question but whose public career more and more seems to be sliding like that other old radical Max Eastman's toward a *Reader's Digest*-Norman Rockwell version of how things are (Pete's idea of singing peace songs to a newborn baby makes even the most middlebrow *Digest* ideas seem as far-out as anything William Burroughs ever did!); or whether to accept as truth the Donleavy-Westian-Brechtian world of Bob Dylan, where things aren't often pretty, where there isn't often hope, where man isn't always noble, but where, most importantly, there exists a reality that coincides with that of this planet. Was it to be marshmallows and cottoncandy or meat and potatoes? Rose-colored glasses or a magnifying glass? A nice guy who has subjugated and weakened his art through his constant insistence on a world that never was and never can be, or an angry, passionate poet who demands his art to be all, who demands not to be owned, not to be restricted or predicted, but only, like Picasso, to be left alone from petty criticisms to do his business, wherever that may take him?

Make no mistake, the audience had to make a clear-cut choice and they made it: Pete Seeger. They chose to boo Dylan off the stage for something as superficially silly as an electric guitar or something as stagnatingly sickening as their idea of owning an artist. They chose the safety of wishful thinking rather than the painful, always difficult stab of art. They might have believed they were choosing humanity over a reckless me-for-me attitude, but they weren't. They were choosing suffocation over invention and adventure, backwards over forwards, a dead hand instead of a live one. They were afraid, as was Pete Seeger (who was profoundly disturbed by Dylan's performance), to make a leap, to admit, to consider, to think. Instead, they took refuge in the Seeger vision as translated by the other less-pure-at-heart singers on the program, indeed, by all other than Seeger: the ghastly second half of Sunday night's program, where practically all forms of Social Significance ran completely out of control in a sickening display of egomania and a desperate grasping for publicity and fame (see Irwin Silber's account elsewhere in this section). The second half of Sunday night (from all reports) was more ugly and hysterical than anything in a Dylan song; and, remember, the impetus for it was not Dylan at all, but Pete Seeger. (Ironically, although the audience chose the Seeger vision, it was a hollow victory for Pete, who felt he'd failed badly.)

It was a sad parting of the ways for many, myself included. I choose Dylan, I choose art. I will stand behind Dylan and his "new" songs, and I'll bet my critical reputation (such as it may be) that I'm right.

Pop Singers and Song Writers Racing Down Dylan's Road

Musician's "Sound" Inspires a Variety of Entertainers in "Folk Rock" Idiom

by *Robert Shelton*

If imitation is the sincerest form of flattery, then Bob Dylan must be one of the most flattered performers in American popular music today.

The singer and song-writer, who will appear tomorrow night at the Forest Hills Music Festival in Queens, has fostered a trend that music circles call "the Dylan sound."

At least three groups and one individual who consciously style their singing after Mr. Dylan are listed high on popularity charts of recordings. Sonny and Cher, the Byrds, the Turtles and Donovan all have a strong Dylanesque quality in their recordings.

Many others, from the Beatles to Johnny Cash to the song-writing team of Barry Mann and Cynthia Weil, have publicly acknowledged their debt to Mr. Dylan. And John Lennon has even recorded a song in the Dylan mode.

In a telephone interview, Mr. Dylan, the often enigmatic folk performer, parried questions about his new imitators and the controversy over his fusion of folk music with rock 'n' roll, called "folk rock."

"Missing Something"

"It's all music; no more, no less," the twenty-four-year-old musician from Hibbing, Minnesota, said. "I know in my own mind what I'm doing. If anyone has imagination, he'll know what I'm doing. If they can't understand my songs they're missing something. If they can't understand green clocks, wet chairs, purple lamps or hostile statues, they're missing something, too."

Many pop-music insiders regard Mr. Dylan as the most influential American performer to emerge since the rise of Elvis Presley ten years ago. Some think he is on the brink of superstardom.

Mr. Dylan is a wiry, sharp-featured, sunken-eyed youth who affects a somewhat bizarre image. His hair has grown so long since he became interested in "folk rock" that the Beatles look clean-cut by comparison. After leaving Hibbing, he studied briefly at the University of Minnesota but flunked out of the science class, he says, "for refusing to watch a rabbit die."

He went on the road, playing at a carnival and elsewhere, until he got off the subway in Greenwich Village in the spring of 1961.

Since Mr. Dylan was discovered at Gerde's Folk City in September of that year, he has evolved through several composing and performing approaches. Each time he has changed he has brought an increasingly larger segment of the pop and folk music world with him.

The tousle-haired musician, who has written more than 100 songs, expressed a driving need to create and perform new material. "I get very bored with my old songs," he said. "I can't sing 'With God on My Side' for 15 years. What I write is much more concise now than before. It's not deceiving."

When Mr. Dylan first appeared in New York he was strongly under the influence of Woody Guthrie, the Oklahoma balladmaker. By the spring of 1963, with the popularity of his antidiscrimination protest, "Blowin' in the Wind," he became nationally known. His "Times They Are a' Changin'" was considered a credo for the discontented protesting collegians, for whom he became a spokesman.

Personal Expression

About a year ago he veered toward more personal expression with "Mr. Tambourine Man," a current hit. Last spring he introduced "folk rock" with "Subterranean Homesick Blues" and the currently popular "Like a Rolling Stone."

Some of Mr. Dylan's lyrics are obviously "camp" fantasies, while others are poetically profound. Many are sufficiently elliptical to spur squadrons of interpreters.

Mr. Dylan refused to express this avant-garde direction. "I have no idea what I'll be doing at Forest Hills Saturday," he said. "I'll have some electricity [electrically amplified instruments] and a new song or a couple or three or four new songs. Time goes by very fast up there onstage. I think of what not to do rather than what to do."

Show Sold Out; but Did Dylan?

by Joseph Gelmis

Forest Hills—There was anger in the grandstands and anguish on the stage as hipsters who felt betrayed roared disapproval of the new Bob Dylan sound Saturday night at Forest Hills Stadium.

Dylan, the composer of 100 folk songs of social interest; Dylan, the spokesman for the hippies and a whole younger generation of the disenchanted; Dylan, the non-conformist 24-year-old poet-singer-guitarist from Hibbing, Minn., whose lyrics have become more cynical and his hair longer and more unkempt as his popularity and bankroll grew; Dylan, all these things and more, was going rock'n'roll—complete with four-man combo behind him and electric guitars ablaze with neon lights.

"Traitor," some shouted as Dylan and his quartet finished a song. "Where's Ringo?" a young voice in the stands taunted. Then, from the seats where 15,000 faithful had defied temperatures in the low 50s and winds that boomed like doomsday through the microphone, a chant started: "Where's Dylan? We want Dylan. We want Dylan."

Dylan's only reply to the catcalls and gibes was a sad shake of the head and a plaintive: "Ah, ah, come on." He tried to ignore the hostility. Eventually, most of the crowd did become more polite, but less enthusiastic than it had been earlier. By concert's end, Dylan and his musicians slipped away ignominiously to the candy-striped tent behind the stage without a goodbye or a wave.

That it was the sound and not the singer who was booed was

Reprinted with permission from *Newsday,* August 30, 1965.

obvious. Dylan's concert, the last of the season at the stadium, was a sellout—sharing that distinction only with those by Frank Sinatra and Barbra Streisand. During the first half of the show, when Dylan sang his best-known protest songs, there was thunderous applause.

But after the intermission, Dylan introduced for the first time in the New York area his four accompanists: a pianist with a rinky-tink portable instrument, a drummer and two electric guitarists. Together they launched into ear-splitting renditions of Dylan songs. Dylan's sing-song voice was often inaudible against the electric cacophony.

The purists, the socially-conscious, the thousands of young boys who grew their hair long and wore rag-tag clothes—as tribute to their spokesman—were shaken. They had come to listen to the lone voice of youthful dissent against the evils of an adult world. And they got the Beatles, instead.

That his most fervent fans should resent Dylan's unpredictability and experimentation is ironic. Since he burst on the folk music scene four years ago, Dylan has changed styles several times—influencing the direction of musical tastes each time. But now, Dylan the innovator had disappointed the admirers of Dylan the social critic.

Bob Dylan Interview

by Nora Ephron & Susan Edmiston

This interview took place in late summer of 1965 in the office of Dylan's manager Albert Grossman. Dylan had just been booed in the historic Forest Hills concert where he abandoned folk purity to the use of electric accompaniment. He was wearing a red-and-navy op-art shirt, a navy blazer and pointy high-heeled boots. His fact, so sharp and harsh when translated through the media, was then infinitely soft and delicate. His hair was not bushy or electric or Afro; it was fine-spun soft froth like the foam of a wave. He looked like an underfed angel with a nose from the land of the Chosen People.

Some American folk singers—Carolyn Hester, for example—say that what you're now doing, the new sound, "folk rock," is liberating them.
Did Carolyn say that? You tell her she can come around and see me any time now that she's liberated.

Does labeling, using the term "folk rock," tend to obscure what's happening?
Yes.

It's like "pop gospel." What does the term mean to you?
Yeah, classical gospel could be the next trend. There's country rock, rockabilly. What does it mean to me? Folk rock. I've never even said that word. It has a hard gutter sound. Circussy atmos-

phere. It's nose-thumbing. Sound like you're looking down on what is . . . fantastic, great music.

The definition most often given of folk rock is the combination of the electronic sound of rock and roll with the meaningful lyrics of folk music. Does that sum up what you're doing?
Yes. It's very complicated to play with electricity. You play with other people. You're dealing with other people. Most people don't like to work with other people, it's more difficult. It takes a lot. Most people who don't like rock and roll can't relate to other people.

You mention the Apollo Theatre in Harlem on one of your album covers. Do you go there often?
Oh, I couldn't go up there. I used to go up there a lot about four years ago. I even wanted to play in one of the amateur nights, but I got scared. Bad things can happen to you. I saw what the audience did to a couple of guys they didn't like. And I would have had a couple of things against me right away when I stepped out on the stage.

Who is Mr. Jones in "Ballad of a Thin Man"?
He's a real person. You know him, but not by that name.

Like Mr. Charlie?
No. He's more than Mr. Charlie. He's actually a person. Like I saw him come into the room one night and he looked like a camel. He proceeded to put his eyes in his pocket. I asked this guy who he was and he said, "That's Mr. Jones." Then I asked this cat, "Doesn't he do anything but put his eyes in his pocket?" And he told me, "He puts his nose on the ground." It's all there, it's a true story.

Where did you get that shirt?
California. Do you like it? You should see my others. You can't get clothes like that here. There are a lot of things out there we haven't got here.

Isn't California on the way here?
It's uptight here compared to there. Hollywood I mean. It's not really breathable here. It's like there's air out there. The Sunset

Strip can't be compared to anything here, like 42nd Street. The people there look different, they look more like . . . you want to kiss them out there.

Do you spend a lot of time out there?
I don't have much time to spend anywhere: The same thing in England. In England everybody looks very hip East Side. They wear things . . . they don't wear things that bore you. They've got other hangups in other directions.

Do you consider yourself primarily a poet?
No. We have our ideas about poets. The word doesn't mean any more than the word "house." There are people who write *po*ems and people who write po*ems*. Other people write *poems.* Everybody who writes poems do you call them a poet? There's a certain kind of rhythm in some kind of way that's visible. You don't necessarily have to write to be a poet. Some people work in gas stations and they're poets. I don't call myself a poet because I don't like the word. I'm a trapeze artist.

What I meant was, do you think your words stand without the music?
They would stand but I don't read them. I'd rather sing them. I write things that aren't songs—I have a book coming out.

What is it?
It's a book of words.

Is it like the back of your albums? It seemed to me that the album copy you write is a lot like the writing of William Burroughs. Some of the accidental sentences—
Cut-ups.

Yes, and some of the imagery and anecdotes. I wondered if you had read anything by him.
I haven't read *Naked Lunch* but I read some of his shorter things in little magazines, foreign magazines. I read one in Rome. I know him. I don't really know him—I just met him once. I think he's a great man.

Burroughs keeps an album, a collection of photographs that illustrate his writing. Do you have anything similar to that?
I do that too. I have photographs of "Gates of Eden" and "It's All Over Now, Baby Blue." I saw them after I wrote the songs. People send me a lot of things and a lot of the things are pictures, so other people must have that idea too. I gotta admit, maybe I wouldn't have chosen them, but I can see what it is about the pictures.

I heard you used to play the piano for Buddy Holly.
No. I used to play the rock and roll piano, but I don't want to say who it was for because the cat will try to get hold of me. I don't want to see the cat. He'll try to reclaim the friendship. I did it a long time ago, when I was seventeen years old. I used to play a country piano too.

This was before you became interested in folk music?
Yes. I became interested in folk music because I had to make it somehow. Obviously I'm not a hard-working cat. I played the guitar, that was all I did. I thought it was great music. Certainly I haven't turned my back on it or anything like that. There is—and I'm sure nobody realizes this, all the authorities who write about what it is and what it should be, when they say keep things simple, they should be easily understood—folk music is the only music where it isn't simple. It's never been simple. It's weird, man, full of legend, myth, Bible and ghosts. I've never written anything hard to understand, not in my head anyway, and nothing as far out as some of the old songs. They were out of sight.

Like what songs?
"Little Brown Dog." "I bought a little brown dog, its face is all gray. Now I'm going to Turkey flying on my bottle." And "Nottemun Town," that's like a herd of ghosts passing through on the way to Tangiers. "Lord Edward," "Barbara Allen," they're full of myth.

And contradictions?
Yeah, contradictions.

And chaos?
Chaos, watermelon, clocks, everything.

You wrote on the back on one album, "I accept chaos but does chaos accept me."
Chaos is a friend of mine. It's like I accept him, does he accept me.

Do you see the world as chaos?
Truth is chaos. Maybe beauty is chaos.

Poets like Eliot and Yeats—
I haven't read Yeats.

They saw the world as chaos, accepted it as chaos and attempted to bring order from it. Are you trying to do that?
No. It exists and that's all there is to it. It's been here longer than I have. What can I do about it? I don't know what the songs I write are. That's all I do is write songs, right? Write. I collect things too.

Monkey wrenches?
Where did you read about that? Has that been in print? I told this guy out on the coast that I collected monkey wrenches, all sizes and shapes of monkey wrenches, and he didn't believe me. I don't think you believe me either. And I collect the pictures too. Have you talked to Sonny and Cher?

No.
They're a drag. A cat gets kicked out of a restaurant and he went home and wrote a song about it.

They say your fan mail has radically increased since you switched sounds.
Yeah. I don't have time to read all of it, but I want you to put that I answer half of it. I don't really. A girl does that for me.

Does she save any for you—any particularly interesting letters?
She knows my head. Not the ones that just ask for pictures, there's a file for them. Not the ones that say, I want to make it with you, they go in another file. She saves two kinds. The violently put-down—

The ones that call you a sellout?
Yeah. Sellout, fink, Fascist, Red, everything in the book. I really dig those. And ones from old friends.

Like, "You don't remember me but I was in the fourth grade with you"?
No, I never had any friends then. These are letters from people who knew me in New York five, six years ago. My first fans. Not the people who call themselves my first fans. They came in three years ago, two years ago. They aren't really my first fans.

How do you feel about being booed at your concert at Forest Hills?
I thought it was great, I really did. If I said anything else I'd be a liar.

And at the Newport Folk Festival?
That was different. They twisted the sound. They didn't like what I was going to play and they twisted the sound on me before I began.

I hear you were wearing a sellout jacket.
What kind of jacket is a sellout jacket?

Black leather.
I've had black leather jackets since I was five years old. I've been wearing black leather all my life.

I wonder if we could talk about electronic music and what made you decide to use it.
I was doing fine, you know, singing and playing my guitar. It was a sure thing, don't you understand, it was a sure thing. I was getting very bored with that. I couldn't go out and play like that. I was thinking of quitting. Out front it was a sure thing. I knew what the audience was gonna do, how they would react. It was very automatic. Your mind just drifts unless you can find some way to get in there and remain totally there. It's so much of a fight remaining totally there all by yourself. It takes too much. I'm not ready to cut that much out of my life. You can't have nobody around. You can't be bothered with anybody else's world. And I like people. What I'm doing now—

it's a whole other thing. We're not playing rock music. It's not a hard sound. These people call it folk rock—if they want to call it that, something that simple, it's good for selling records. As far as it being what it is, I don't know what it is. I can't call it folk rock. It's a whole way of doing things. It has been picked up on, I've heard songs on the radio that have picked it up. I'm not talking about words. It's a certain feeling, and it's been on every single record I've ever made. That has not changed. I know it hasn't changed. As far as what I was totally, before, maybe I was pushing it a little then. I'm not pushing things now. I know it. I know very well how to do it. The problem of how I want to play something—I know it in front. I know what I'm going to say, what I'm going to do. I don't have to work it out. The band I work with—they wouldn't be playing with me if they didn't play like I want them to. I have this song, "Queen Jane Approximately"—

Who is Queen Jane?
Queen Jane is a man.

Was there something that made you decide to change sounds? Your trip to England?
I like the sound. I like what I'm doing now. I would have done it before. It wasn't practical to do it before. I spent most of my time writing. I wouldn't have had the time. I had to get where I was going all alone. I don't know what I'm going to do next. I probably will record with strings some time, but it doesn't necessarily change. It's just a different color. And I know that it's real. No matter what anybody says. They can boo till the end of time. I know that the music is real, more real than the boos.

How do you work?
Most of the time I work at night. I don't really like to think of it as work. I don't know how important it is. It's not important to the average cat who works eight hours a day. What does he care? The world can get along very well without it. I'm hip to that.

Sure, but the world can get along without any number of things.
I'll give you a comparison. Rudy Vallee. Now that was a lie, that was a downright lie. Rudy Vallee being popular. What kind of people could have dug him? You know, your grandmothers and mothers. But what kind of people were they? He was so sexless. If you want to find out about those times and you listen to his music you're not going to find out anything about the times. His music was a pipedream. All escapes. There are no more escapes. If you want to find out anything that's happening now, you have to listen to the music. I don't mean the words, although "Eve of Destruction" will tell you something about it. The words are not really gonna tell it, not really. You gotta listen to the Stapes Singers, Smokey and the Miracles, Martha and the Vandellas. That's scary to a lot of people. It's sex that's involved. It's not hidden. It's real. You can overdo it. It's not only sex, it's a whole beautiful feeling.

But Negro rhythm and blues has been around underground for at least twelve years. What brought it out now?
The English did that. They brought it out. They hipped everybody. You read an interview asking who the Beatles' favorite singer was and they say Chuck Berry. You never used to hear Chuck Berry records on the radio, hard blues. The English did that. England is great and beautiful, though in other ways kinda messy. Though not outside London.

In what way messy?
There's a snobbishness. What you see people doing to other people. It's not only class. It's not that simple. It's a kind of Queen kind of thing. Some people are royalty and some are not. Here, man, somebody don't like you he tells you. There it's very tight, tight kinds of expressions, their whole tone of speaking changes. It's an everyday kind of thing. But the kids are a whole other thing. Great. They're just more free. I hope you don't think I take this too seriously—I just have a headache.

I think you started out to say that music was more in tune with what's happening than other art forms.
Great paintings shouldn't be in museums. Have you ever been

in a museum? Museums are cemeteries. Paintings should be on the walls of restaurants, in dime stores, in gas stations, in men's rooms. Great paintings should be where people hang out. The only thing where it's happening is on the radio and records, that's where people hang out. You can't see great paintings. You pay half a million and hang one in your house and one guest sees it. That's not art. That's a shame, a crime. Music is the only thing that's in tune with what's happening. It's not in book form, it's not on the stage. All this art they've been talking about is nonexistent. It just remains on the shelf. It doesn't make anyone happier. Just think how many people would really feel great if they could see a Picasso in their daily diner. It's not the bomb that has to go, man, it's the museums.

Contemporary Song

by Ewan MacColl

Politics are just as valid a subject for songs as any other kind of human activity; this does not mean that a song dealing with a political subject is automatically a good song; conversely, it is not automatically a bad song. In addition to the special criteria applied to traditional song, we have to ask ourselves whether a song also extends our awareness of reality, both in the terms of form AND content. Furthermore, does it—through its special form—increase our knowledge and understanding of the culture to which it belongs? Does it produce a simultaneous response of our emotions and intelligence? These are only some of the questions pertinent to our understanding of an art form—any art form. As I write these words, I am conscious of the fact that many readers of SING OUT! will be outraged by the idea that folk songs are subject to such highfalutin' criteria. It is obvious that you, in America, and we, in Britain, live in societies where our traditional music is more than a little broken down; we tend to think that this is the normal condition of all traditional music. It is not! At their best, our traditional songs and ballads are the creations of extraordinarily talented artists, working inside disciplines formulated over an extended period of time. It seems to me that the present crop of contemporary American songs has been made by writers who are either (a) unaware of these disciplines, (b) incapable of working inside the disciplines, or (c) are at pains to destroy them.

"But what of Bobby Dylan?" scream the outraged teenagers

Reprinted, in excerpt form, with permission from *Sing Out!*, September, 1965.

of all ages. Well, I have watched with fascination the meteoric rise of this American idol and I am still unable to see in him anything other than a youth of mediocre talent. Only a completely non-critical audience, nourished on the watery pap of pop music, could have fallen for such tenth-rate drivel. "But the poetry?" What poetry? The cultivated illiteracy of his topical songs or the embarrassing fourth-grade schoolboy attempts at free verse? The latter reminds me of elderly female schoolteachers clad in Greek tunics rolling hoops across lawns at weekend theater schools. "But think of his outspoken attacks against war!" It has been safe and fashionable to speak out against war ever since 1918; President Johnson consistently speaks out against war, even while he is sending bombers against the Vietnamese. It is perfectly safe to attack—providing the attack is in general terms; that way nobody gets hurt.

I have dealt with Dylan at some length since, for me, he exemplifies contemporary American song writing, a movement where journalism is more important than art, where flabby sentimentality and shrill self-pity take the place of passion.

Finally, it is, I believe, time for American folk revival writers to examine their intentions and to decide whether their objective is to "improve" pop music or to extend the tradition—it is a mistake to imagine that both objectives are identical.

Frets and Frails

by Israel G. Young

Bob Dylan has become a pawn in his own game. He has ceased his Quest for a Universal Sound and has settled for a liaison with the music trade's Top Forty Hit Parade. He has worked his way through dozens of singers and poets on both sides of the Atlantic, and he has left them all behind. Because he is a Genius, he need not, and does not, give credit to anyone—all the way from Jack Elliott to Allen Ginsberg. He has given up his companions for the companionship of the Charts. Currently, the Charts require him to write rock-and-roll; and he does. And he is no mere imitator. Where there is life, vivacity, statement, and protest in the original, Dylan has added a bitterness and loneliness that can't be helped. He adds a sense of violence that is cloaked by a brilliant obscurity. It leaves you depressed and alone instead of wanting to join with others in life and song.

As Dylan gets further and further away from his original leanings, there is no question that his singing voice has improved. But he doesn't always use his "better" voice. It depends on the market he is singing for. So as not to miss out on any markets, he sings with two voices, clear and unclear, and, I might add, with two sets of costumes. If necessary, he'll sing songs he repudiated. For example, he sang many songs in England he no longer sings here because the English audience is two years behind his American image. Next year, he'll be writing rhythm-and-blues songs when they get high on the charts. The following year, the Polish polka will make it, and then he'll

Reprinted with permission from *Sing Out!*, November, 1965.

write them, too. By then, he'll be so mired in the popularity charts that he'll be safe enough for the State Department to have them send him to entertain troops at whatever battlefront we're on at the time. As much as he's popular, the American Public would love to see him fall, just like Andy Griffith in *A Face in the Crowd* or Marilyn Monroe in real life. I don't think it's worth it, Bob. If you don't watch out, you'll become commercial.

Dylan Disowns His Protest Songs

Pop Singer Likes Success

by Frances Taylor

Now that he's on the charts where the best-sellers of the pop music world are listed, Bob Dylan disowns all the folk songs he wrote and the protest songs that made him famous.

He won't sing them any more (hasn't for several months now) and he doesn't plan to write any in the future.

Dylan, the adored king of folk music until recently, no longer wears the dungarees and boots that became the uniform of the hip kids who imitated him. His halo of red-brown hair is about the only outward sign of the old Dylan.

Inwardly he's calm and quite sure of his direction.

"I'm not a voice of their generation," he said in an interview in his manager's Manhattan office. "How can I be? I'm not their generation."

He's doing now, says Bobby, exactly what he's always wanted to do: blues, rhythm songs and song-stories in poetry that are startlingly beautiful . . . and mostly unintelligible.

He thinks of his best-loved songs such as "Blowin' in the Wind" and "With God on Our Side" as dead. "They're ghosts," he says.

When thousands of Long Island young people called for them at his recent, jammed concert in Forest Hills Stadium, Dylan "didn't hear that." He seems surprised on being told they called for those songs until they realized he had no intention of singing them.

Dylan does realize he was booed when he appeared for the second half of the concert with an electric guitar in his hands

Reprinted with permission from the *Long Island Press,* October 17, 1965.

and a noisy jazz combo behind him. He remembers that thousands of youngsters chanted "We want Dylan" and "We want the real Dylan" when he launched into rock and roll.

For those young people, we have some sad news. Today's twenty-four-year-old rock and roll expert is the real Dylan. Bobby himself says so.

"I never wanted to write topical songs," he explains. "Have you heard my last two records, *Bringing It All Back Home* and *Highway 61*? It's all there. That's the real Dylan."

Why, then, did he ever write anti-war songs and songs inspired by and inspiring to the civil rights movement?

"That was my chance," he says frankly. "In the Village there was a little publication called *Broadside* and with a topical song you could get in there. I wasn't getting far with the things I was doing, songs like I'm writing now, but *Broadside* gave me a start."

It also brought him the attention and friendship of Joan Baez, undisputed queen of folk music, and Pete Seeger, for many years a folksinger and composer known in many nations.

Joan Baez brought an almost unknown Dylan onstage two years ago at her own concert in the Forest Hills Music Festival. He wasn't an instant hit, his voice was almost harsh where now it's rich and stirring. But his songs were loved by tens of thousands of young people who began to buy any record he made. Soon he was their idol; he created one song after another on themes from the movement that swept every campus in the U.S.

What most young people don't realize is that "Blowin' in the Wind" made money . . . but not for Bobby. The trio who made the record got the lion's share. His income, right up to October of this year, was low enough to qualify him for an award from the American Society of Composers, Authors and Publishers. The ASCAP fund is for "young artists of merit" whose work brings them insufficient income.

Where he was once proud to be the angry young man of the music world, Bobby now takes comfort in his popularity. He can fill concert halls three or four times a week. His albums sell enormously. His blues and rollicking tunes are high up on every chart. He's also on top in England where "With God on Our Side" is bringing in ghostly money that banks accept.

"I'm writing now for the people who share my feelings," he says earnestly. "The point is not understanding what I write but feeling it."

Of course, thinking, feeling or just plain listening, Dylan's blues are superb and his new singing style is ingratiating. His wayout poetry is full of brilliant images and marvelous color as well as sharp wit.

Dylan thinks his newest work, "Desolation Row," is a more important piece of music than "Blowin' in the Wind." If you haven't heard the Desolation opus, it's a long, plaintively poetic piece about . . . chaos. In it Bobby writes of "Einstein disguised as Robin Hood" and of Ophelia whose "sin is her lifelessness" as well as of "heart-attack machine . . . then the kerosene." Fire and brimstone? Purgatory? Life itself is hell?

Where he's heading now is clear to Dylan and to his newest fans who are content with "Like a Rolling Stone" and "It Ain't Me, Babe." His older fans still play his older albums. Some of his followers still love "Blowin' in the Wind" and were happy to hear it played, only last week, as the finale in a Dylan salute by the Hullabaloo TV show.

His most devoted followers still hope Dylan will some day sing to them of reality, as he once did in clear, sharp tones and lyrics they can remember.

BOB DYLAN HIGHWAY 61 REVISITED

Recently at a concert his fans booed in protest—"We want Dylan." His reaction: "It doesn't bother me. These people who claim to be old fans picked up on me a year and a half ago. My old fans, the ones in the Village five years ago, they'll understand. I can't keep painting the same picture. These so-called fans expect the same picture. I could please them—it's very simple. What would it be worth—it would be putting them on. I'm not experimenting—been playing for fourteen years. I know what I'm doing. I played rock and roll when I was thirteen. I have no idea where this thing is going. I'll quit and take up something else if it becomes a drag. In fact, I'd like to write a Broadway play." His latest release: *Highway 61 Revisited,* which includes his hit "Like a Rolling Stone," and a new smasher, "Desolation Row."

Reprinted from *Vogue,* 1965.

Topical Song: Polarization Sets In

by Irwin Silber

Right now, we are hearing from Bob Dylan. His newest album, *Highway 61 Revisited* (Columbia CL 2389), is the logical extension of his last three LPs. Somehow, I feel that most critics (and admirers) of the "new" Dylan have missed the main point. They have made Dylan's electrification the point of demarcation between the old and the new. The fact is that "Desolation Row" is not less (or more) "folk music" than "The Death of Hattie Carroll." Whether what Dylan does should or shouldn't be called "folk" is about the most unimportant question one can ask.

Let us leave motivation aside for the moment. No one can climb into Bob Dylan's head and say, "Ah! This is why you're doing this or that or the other thing." We can only listen and evaluate what we hear. There are many artists who can be judged by technique alone: but it's a pretty poor level of appreciation, it seems to me, to say "So-and-so has a beautiful voice," as if a combination of produced tones can, by itself, create an emotional response. No, it is not by amplification or vocal technique that audiences have ever responded to (or rejected) Bob Dylan. It has always been by the substance of what he had to say—sometimes clearly articulated, sometimes couched in incredibly involved and frequently challenging symbolism.

Like it or not, by choice or necessity, Bob Dylan's thing is his message. Listening to *Highway 61 Revisited,* one realizes more clearly than ever before the essentially existentialist philosophy that Dylan represents, filtered, of course, through his own set of eye and brain images. Song after song adds up to

Reprinted with permission from *Sing Out!*, February–March, 1966.

the same basic statement: Life is an absurd conglomeration of meaningless events capsuled into the unnatural vacuum created by birth and completed by death; we are all living under a perpetual sentence of death and to seek meaning or purpose in life is as unrewarding as it is pointless; all your modern civilization does is further alienate man from his fellow man and from nature.

The existentialist philosophy is, in this form, uniquely a product of the 20th century mind. Since World War II it has become a significant force in western civilization. With a candid and non-hypocritical eye it has shown us much of the absurdity and pretentiousness of modern-day idealism. Unfortunately, it has not been able to replace its destroyed idols with anything but a void. As a result, it has frequently become social protest without a point of view. In essence, it says to us, there is no honesty in this world beyond what you yourself can perceive and choose to make honest.

If I have spent more time on philosophy than on music in this review of Bob Dylan's new record, it is because I believe that the music will not really be intellectually understood without it.

Let there be no mistake about it. Bob Dylan is a terrifyingly gifted artist—as both writer and singer. But, as with any important artist, we must ultimately come to grips with the substance of what he is saying. And underneath it all, this is what the fuss is really about. In the final analysis, I do not believe that Dylan's vision of the world is really where it's at. What he sees is there. But to stop and go no further is the path to either destruction or compromise. I'm not prepared to buy either.

Bob Dylan: Another View

by Paul Nelson

BOB DYLAN/ HIGHWAY 61 REVISITED
(Columbia CL 2389 and CS 9189)

Time, if nothing else, will vindicate Bob Dylan's "New Music" from the sad and even pathetic charges of Social Irresponsibility and Artistic Decadence leveled by the current representatives of the Thirties and Forties. Formal excellence and brilliant wit are seldom as appreciated at first glance as are the topical sensations of the hour. Yet, "The Hammer Song" and "Banks of Marble" are already dead, while "Mr. Tambourine Man," "Lay Down Your Weary Tune," and "Chimes of Freedom" become more impressive with each passing year. Bob Dylan requires no extreme rationalization, and his latest and best album no elaborate defense: the evidence of his style and vision is found in his songs.

It is a highly personal style-vision: Dylan's unyielding and poetic point of view represents a total commitment to the subjective over the objective, the microcosm over the macrocosm, man rather than Man, problems not Problems. To put it as simply as possible, the tradition that Dylan represents is that of all great artists: that of projecting, with the highest possible degree of honesty and craftsmanship, a unique personal vision of the world we live in, knowing full well that unless the personal is achieved, the universal cannot follow. Dylan's historical-political adversaries aren't interested in what one person may see; their myopia recognizes only the sweep of Masses and they daydream hopefully of thousands singing union songs in Central Park.

Reprinted with permission from *Sing Out!*, February–March, 1966.

From their Disneylandic yearnings, they demand their songs short, snappy, imbecilicly simple, and straight to the proletarian point. Thus, *Highway 61 Revisited* is considered corrupt and self-indulgent, and Dylan's gloriously ambiguous new works too rich for the People's blood. This is a time for bread, not cake, they rationalize, blissfully unaware that time invariably vindicates form over topicality; and poetry always outlives journalism.

Dylan has been heavily criticized for abandoning the protest movement. Irwin Silber, from his quaint but oddly charming vantage point, mobilizes the heavy artillery of the famed Silber Canon of Criticism and seeks to rout Dylan with such misguided ammunition as: 1) he used to be a Good Guy, now he's a Bad Guy; and, even worse, 2) He's an existentialist! The only answer to his first charge is a long sigh: oh-no-not-again. His second shot is as harmless as it is pointless, a confused missile that, upon exploding, had it any vital argument to it, would presumably wipe out, with Silber's blessings, among others, Sartre, Kierkegaard, Nietzsche, Heidegger, and Camus, along with Dylan. Silber plays with the word "freedom" as if it were his own personal toy. Indeed, it seems Dylan might be criticized with equal justice for having grown older, more thoughtful, and much smarter. He and Shirley Temple.

With the advent of *Highway 61 Revisited* (in my opinion, one of the two or three greatest folk music albums ever made), Bob Dylan has exploded, as Leslie Fiedler claims William Burroughs to have "exploded" the novel, the entire city folk music scene into the incredibly rich fields of modern poetry, literature, and philosophy; that he did it with his own personal blend of a popular music style, rock-and-roll, is all the more joyful and remarkable. He has, in effect, dragged folk music, perhaps by the nape of the neck, into areas it never dreamed existed, and enriched both it and himself a thousandfold by the journey. Now, for the first time, I think, with this album, we have finally progressed out of Then and into Now. With a Minnesota gypsy leading us, we have truly become contemporary.

Not that it's painless. For Dylan's main concern in *Highway 61 Revisited* is the classic American Dream, Innocence and Experience, a theme that has always haunted and tormented American artists, particularly in the twentieth century. The music of Bob Dylan is the music of illusion and delusion, of men deluded by women, of men and women deluded by surface appearance, a music of the tramp as explorer and the clown as happy victim, where the greatest crimes are lifelessness and the inability to see oneself as circus performer in the show of life. Thus, in "Ballad of a Thin Man," Dylan will choose the life of emotion rather than the life of reason: "You have many contacts among the lumberjacks to get you facts when someone attacks your imagination." And again, in "Tombstone Blues," the outcry against "useless and pointless knowledge." In the tender lovely "Queen Jane Approximately," Dylan offers some good advice to a popular woman folksinger (but one who "commissions clowns"). The last verse, to anyone familiar with the New York City folk scene, is brilliant: "Now when all of the bandits you turn your other cheek to/ All lay down their bandannas and complain/ And you want somebody you don't have to Speak To [my capitals]/ Won't you come see me, Queen Jane."

The charge that Dylan's new songs are vicious, morbid, humorless, and explorations into the death-wish can be easily refuted by anyone with a mind to think and an ear to listen. "Highway 61 Revisited" is a corrosively funny satire on the standard businessman-promoter's reply to anything, no matter what, as long as it makes money: "Why, yes, I think it can be very easily done!" "From a Buick 6" is pure joyous rock, and a hilarious song. The beautiful "Just Like Tom Thumb's Blues," with its unforgettable opening lines ("When you're lost in the rain in Juarez when it's Eastertime, too/ And your gravity fails and negativity don't pull you through"), is among other things, a retelling of the old joke of women loving men to death: "And you're so kind and careful not to go to her too soon/ And she takes your voice and leaves you howling at the moon." And the exquisite "It Takes a Lot to Laugh, It Takes a Train to Cry" is one of the most lyric and bluesy love songs in any tradition or any language.

"Desolation Row," a song over eleven minutes long (who else but Dylan could hold attention to a single performance for so long a timespan?), is clearly a major statement. Once again, we are in a dark, Felliniesque world of clowns and grotesques, but Dylan makes it clear that the tragic man is not the clown per se, but the clown who thinks he is something better. Accept the universal truth, Dylan says, accept chaos, and advance from there. We are all childfools and "Don't send me no more letters, no, not unless you mail them from Desolation Row."

The finest song on the album, and Dylan's greatest so far, I think, is "Like a Rolling Stone," the definitive statement that both personal and artistic fulfillment must come, in the main, by being truly on one's own. Dylan's social adversaries have twisted this to mean something very devious and selfish, but that is not the case at all. Dylan is simply kicking away the props to get to the real core of the matter: Know yourself; it may hurt at first, but you'll never get anywhere if you don't. The final "You're invisible now, you got no secrets to conceal/ How does it feel?/ How does it feel?/ To be on your own" is clearly optimistic and triumphant, a soaring of the spirit into a new and more productive present.

Much should be said here about the brilliance of Dylan's music itself, of his melding together so many diffuse fragments from so many folk and popular music traditions, of the great musicians who played with him on the album; but there is no space.

Let me close with two things. First, Dylan's own eloquent answer to the social critics: "I know there're some people terrified of the bomb, but there are other people terrified to be seen carrying a modern screen magazine." And, finally, from novelist John Clellon Holmes: "[Dylan] has the authentic mark of the bard on him, and I think it's safe to say that no one, years hence, will be able to understand just what it was like to live in this time without attending to what this astonishingly gifted young man has already achieved."

Bob Dylan Talking

by Joseph Haas

Bob Dylan, one of the most talented and controversial figures in American entertainment, will perform tonight in the second of two concerts in Arie Crown Theater of McCormick Place. When the 24-year-old performer sings his original compositions, in his highly distinctive way, millions of young people listen—at concerts and on his best-selling long-playing albums and single recordings. Wise parents, who want to understand what the younger generation is thinking, would do well to listen to him, too. Dylan is a difficult performer to classify—is he a protest singer, leader of the folk-rock cult, a rock'n'roller, or a natural progression in American folk music? He has been called all of these things, and perhaps the wisest course is not to try to classify him at all, but to let him speak for himself, about himself, at length and informally. This is what Panorama has done, and this is Dylan talking:

Will you sing any of the so-called folk-rock music in your concerts here?

No, it's not folk-rock, it's just instruments . . . it's not folk-rock. I call it the mathematical sound, sort of Indian music. I can't really explain it.

Do you dislike folk-rock groups?

No, no, I like what everybody else does, what a lot of people do. I don't necessarily like the writing of too many songwriters, but I like the idea of, look, like they're trying to make it, you know, to say something about the death thing.

Reprinted with permission from *Panorama, Chicago Daily News,* November 27, 1965.

Actually I don't know many of them. I'm 24 now, and most of them playing and listening are teen-agers.

I was playing rock'n'roll when I was 13 and 14 and 15, but I had to quit when I was 16 or 17 because I couldn't make it that way, the image of the day was Frankie Avalon or Fabian, or this whole athletic supercleanness bit, you know, which if you didn't have that, you couldn't make any friends.

I played rock'n'roll when I was in my teens, yeah, I played semi-professionally, piano with rock'n'roll groups. About 1958 or 1959, I discovered Odetta, Harry Belafonte, that stuff, and I became a folk singer.

Did you make this change so you could "make it"?

You couldn't make it livable back then with rock'n'roll, you couldn't carry around an amplifier and electric guitar and expect to survive, it was just too much of a hangup. It cost bread to make enough money to buy an electric guitar, and then you had to make more money to have enough people to play the music, you need two or three to create some conglomeration of sound. So it wasn't an alone kind of thing, you know. When you got other things dragging you down, you're sort of beginning to lose, crash, you know? When somebody's 16 or 25, who's got the right to lose, to wind up as a pinboy at 65?

By "making it," do you mean making commercial success?

No, no, that's not it, making money. It's being able to be nice and not hurt anybody.

How does your sound differ today?

It differs because it doesn't. I don't know, you see. I don't know exactly what to say rock'n'roll is. I do know that . . . think of it in terms of a whole thing. It's not just pretty words to a tune or putting tunes to words, there's nothing that's exploited. The words and the music, I can hear the sound of what I want to say.

Did you go into the folk field, then, because you had a better chance of "making it"?

No, that was an accidental thing. I didn't go into folk music to make any money, but because it was easy, you could be by yourself, you didn't need anybody. All you needed was a guitar, you didn't need anybody else at all. I don't know what's happened to it now. I don't think it's as good as it used to be. Most of the folk music singers have gone on, they're doing other things. Although they're still a lot of good ones around.

Why did you give up the folk sound?

I've been on too many other streets to just do that. I couldn't go back and just do that. The real folk never seen 42nd Street, they're never ridden an airplane. They've got their little world, and that's fine.

Why have you begun using the electric guitar?

I don't use it that much, really.

Some people are hurt because you've used one at all.

That's their fault, it would be silly of me to say I'm sorry because I haven't really done anything. It's not really all that serious. I have a hunch the people who feel I betrayed them picked up on me a few years ago and weren't really back there with me at the beginning. Because I still see the people who were with me from the beginning once in a while, and they know what I'm doing.

Can you explain why you were booed at the Newport Folk Festival last summer when you came on stage with an electric guitar and began singing your new material?

Like I don't even know who those people were, anyway I think there's always a little boo in all of us. I wasn't shattered by it. I didn't cry. I don't even understand it. I mean, what are they going to shatter, my ego? And it doesn't even exist, they can't hurt me with a boo.

What will you do when the success of your present kind of music fades?

I'm going to say when I stop, it just doesn't matter to me. I've never followed any trend, I just haven't the time to follow a trend. It's useless to even try.

In songs like "The Times They Are A-Changin'," you made a distinction between young and old thinking, you talked about the older generation failing to understand the younger?

That's not what I was saying. It happened maybe that those

were the only words I could find to separate aliveness from deadness. It has nothing to do with age.

What can you say about when your first book is coming out?

Macmillan is the publisher, and the title now is *Tarantula,* right now it's called that but I might change it. It's just a lot of writings, I can't really say what it's about. It's not a narrative or anything like that.

Some stories have said that you plan to give up music, perhaps soon, and devote your time to writing?

When I really get wasted, I'm gonna have to do something, you know. Like I might never write again, I might start painting soon.

Have you earned enough money so you have freedom to do exactly what you want?

I wouldn't say that. You got to get up and you got to sleep, and the time in between there you got to do something. That's what I'm dealing with now. I do a lot of funny things. I really have no idea, I can't afford to think about tonight, tomorrow, any time. It's really meaningless to me.

Do you live from day to day?

I try to. I try not to make any plans, every time I go and make plans, nothing really seems to work. I've given up on most of that stuff. I have a concert schedule I keep, but other people get me there. I don't have to do anything.

Do you ever hope to settle down to a normal life, get married, have kids?

I don't hope to be like anybody. Getting married, having a bunch of kids, I have no hopes for it. If it happens, it happens. Whatever my hopes, it never turns out. I don't think anybody's a prophet.

You sound quite pessimistic about everything.

No, not pessimistic. I don't think things can turn out, that's all, and I've accepted it. It doesn't matter to me. It's not pessimism, just a sort of sadness, sort of like not having no hopes.

What about religion or philosophy?

I just don't have any religion or philosophy, I can't say much about any of them. A lot of people do, and fine if they really do follow a certain code. I'm not about to go around changing anything.

I don't like anybody to tell me what I have to do or believe, how I have to live. I just don't care, you know. Philosophy can't give me anything that I don't already have.

The biggest thing of all, that encompasses it all, is kept back in this country. It's an old Chinese philosophy and religion, it really was one . . . there is a book called the *I-Ching*, I'm not trying to push it, I don't want to talk about it, but it's the only thing that is amazingly true, period, not just for me. Anybody would know it. Anybody that ever walks would know it, it's a whole system of finding out things, based on all sorts of things. You don't have to believe in anything to read it, because besides being a great book to believe in, it's also very fantastic poetry.

How do you spend your time when you're not on a concert tour?

I keep a regular bunch of hours. I just do what I have to do, not doing nothing really. I can be satisfied anywhere, I never read too much. Once in a while I write up a bunch of things, and then I record them. I do the normal things.

What about romantic reports about you and Joan Baez?

Oh, man, no, that was a long time ago.

On her latest album, about half of her songs are Dylan songs.

Heaven help her.

What about the story that you changed your name from Bob Zimmerman to Bob Dylan because you admired the poetry of Dylan Thomas?

No, God no. I took the Dylan because I have an uncle named Dillon. I changed the spelling but only because it looked better. I've read some of Dylan Thomas' stuff, and it's not the same as mine. We're different.

What about your family?

Well, I just don't have any family, I'm all alone.

What about a story that you invited your parents to one of your early concerts, paid their way there, and then when they were seated, you said on the stage that you were an "orphan," and then didn't visit them when they were in New York City?

That's not true. They came to a concert, they drove there on their own, and I gave them some money. I don't dislike them or anything, I just don't have any contact with them. They live in Minnesota, and there's nothing for me in Minnesota. Probably sometime I'd like to go back for awhile, everybody goes back to where they came from, I guess.

You talk as if you are terribly separated from people.

I'm not disconnected from anything because of a force, just habit, it's just the way I am. I don't know, I have an idea, that it's easier to be disconnected than to be connected. I've got a huge hallelujah for all the people who're connected, that's great, but I can't do that. I've been connected so many times. Things haven't worked out right, so rather than break myself up, I just don't get connected.

Are you just trying to avoid being hurt again?

I haven't been hurt at the time, the realization is afterwards. Just looking back on it, thinking about it, it's just like a cold winter.

Do you avoid close relationships with people?

I have relationships with people. People like me, also disconnected, there are a lot of disconnected people. I don't feel alienated, or disconnected, or afraid. I don't feel there's any kind of organization of disconnected people. I just can't go along with any kind of organization.

Some day I might find myself all alone in a subway car, stranded when the lights go out, with 40 people, and I'll have to get to know them. Then I'll just do what has to be.

Bob Dylan's words are his own. The questions were asked by Joseph Haas of the Panorama staff.

Bob Dylan

by Israel Young

There is no sparer story than the Bob Dylan story. It is simple and familiar. He came to New York five years ago to trade the West for wild and wooly Greenwich Village. He started his New York career as a disciple of Woody Guthrie via the technique of Jack Elliott. With the help of many friends he immersed himself in the entire range of American balladry. He soon became the first singer-writer to incorporate contemporary psychological ideas into the form of the traditional ballad stanza. He made contemporary words and ideas seem as if they were always there—and that is the work of the important artist.

He never said he was a writer of protest songs. He merely reflected accurately the healthiest feelings of the time. For four years Bob Dylan allowed himself to be considered in the "protest bag." The period of gestation from "protest" to "introspection" has since been improved upon. Phil Ochs is trying to get out after two years as a protest song writer but doesn't know how to get out. Donovan is almost out of it in less than six months. P. J. Sloane has identified himself with, and gotten out of, the protest movement with a single song "Era of Destruction." Businesswise this means that you need only write one "protest" song to be identified by the folkniks as a good guy. Forever after these schmucks will buy anything you will ever produce because they have infinite hope. In the case of Bob Dylan everyone conveniently forgot that he allowed Columbia Records to delete the "John Birch Society Talking Blues" from his second album. This was soon after he swore that Columbia

Reprinted from *East Village Other*, October, 1965.

would have its way "over his dead body." (I was hoodwinked at the time into arranging an abortive protest march against the entire matter which I cancelled by dumping signs and literature into the trash basket when Dylan and management pulled a noshow on our line of six brave marchers.) We forgot and never chided, for there was so much to come—books, novels, plays, movies, poetry. Our whole world was to be illuminated.

He made the poetry scene and reflected accurately the works of poets from Patchen to Ginsberg. He added the imprimatur of copyright and no one complained. He went to England and picked up marvelous morsels of tunes and songs to be presented to the American public "as only Dylan can." He became "bigger than Big Ben" and no one complained. And he left the poets and England behind. He really made no promises to them either. Just another little guy trying to make a living.

There seemed no heights to which Dylan could not attain. He had only to meet the right person. If he could only meet Malraux he could write treatises on civilization. If he could only meet DeGaulle he could resolve the world crisis. If he could only meet God he would write a new bible. And we would all be brought to Grace through his work.

These events did not take place. He returned to the great hope of American music—Rock and Roll. He electrified his guitar. He was now coming into his own. He took the raw force of Rock and Roll. He took out the protest and vivacity and statement and hope. He added his personal bitterness and loneliness. He beat his breast publicly for all of us. He brought us to ultimate loneliness, which is our fate, and left us there. It is not fair. It is sissy-stuff to go down to the bottom and not try to come up. The artist, in any society, must lift us while depicting our fate. This is not to say that Bob Dylan does not affect you. Your feet don't tap—your bodies don't move—but your stomach churns. If you have a weak spot he encompasses you, and you think "that's where it's at."

A man's private life is his own, but for the artist it is the matter of his art. The artist, finally, bares himself to us and we are moved. The artist exalts in his life and so we share it. The honest artist cannot be hurt. Jack Elliott can not be hurt as an interpreter. Allen Ginsberg can not be hurt as a creator. They are what they are. We share in their lives. We are moved. We are cleansed. We are made richer. Bob Dylan cannot exalt in his life now because it would upset the "image" he has cultivated among the record-buying public. He can be hurt. He is forced to a brilliant obscurity in his writing so that people will continue to buy his records. The same people he wants nothing to do with.

Why can't he just continue to sing and they just continue to send him invisible nickels and dollars? Don't Frank Sinatra and Ella Fitzgerald do the same thing? Yes and no. Yes, in that you pays your money and you takes your choice. No, in that they do not claim the holy title of a poet. Where he has obscured his words he has intensified his voice. His voice now tells the true story of Bob Dylan. He screams from the bottomless pit and it is truly heart-rending. But it is like sharing something dirty. It is no longer in the open arena of life's possibilities and we mourn for it.

Letters to SING OUT!

Dear Editor:

Folk fans the world over are mourning the death of Bob Dylan, who died at Carnegie Hall on Oct. 1, 1965. In a short but brilliant career, Mr. Dylan amassed fans and fame with his electrifying performances. He leaves a legacy of only four albums which contain some of the finest folk music ever written.

His last illness, which may be termed an acute case of avarice, severely affected Mr. Dylan's sense of values, ultimately causing his untimely death.

Probably the best indication of folk lovers, feeling at his death are given in Dylan's own words: "I'm not the one you want, babe, I'll only let you down."

I guess Mr. Dylan knew himself better than we did.

Kathleen Ivans
Whitestone, N.Y.

Dear Editor:

In the last few years, the gap between folk music and popular music has narrowed. If this trend continues the gap will disappear entirely . . .

The lyrics of popular music are not as inane as you claim them to be. Many of the blues songs you praise are of the same lyrical content; the depressed feeling, the blues, and the repetition of lines . . .

Bob Dylan's music is being brought to more attention than ever due to his single releases and songs done by Sonny and

Reprinted with permission from *Sing Out!*, January, 1966.

Cher, the Turtles, Barry McGuire, and the Byrds. These songs are done in good taste with respect for the lyric.

Please do not believe that popular music will lower the musical standards and eventually cloy the taste of the public. The standards are not that unstable and will welcome the new presentation of feelings.

Yours truly,
D. N. Stancoff
Chicago, Ill.

Dear Editor:

Congratulations to Paul Nelson! I could not agree with him more on his views on Bob Dylan. If people want "pure, unstained" folk music they can go into the hills and listen to some ignorant cowboy sing about dad's old whiskey still. Dylan is a poet above all, criticizing the world and its people; and if he wants to experiment with ways of expressing his genius he certainly should. Both Dylan and Nelson have my utmost admiration.

Polly Demuth
White Plains, N.Y.

Dear Editor:

What happened at Newport this year will not make or break folk music—or any part of it . . . I think Paul Nelson missed the whole point, (saying) Sunday night's audience was choosing Pete Seeger's humanism over Bob Dylan's art. The choice made had nothing to do with art or humanism—and even less to do with folk music. It was a choice of fanaticism over quiet conviction, of showing off over simply living what you believe . . .

Abbie Place
Ballston Lake, N.Y.

Dear Editor:

I don't like the new Bob Dylan. In the face of violence he has chosen to preserve himself alone . . . Art is not alienation although that seems to be what Mr. Dylan is practicing. The idea Mr. Dylan is to give, but people who think only of themselves don't know how. And an artist who thinks only of me, myself, and I cannot create art.

Irene Meltzer
New York

Dear Sirs:

I'm for Bob Dylan. You want Bob Dylan to be what he ain't. His is the "sound" of the sixties.

Like it or not—look for it or not—listen or not, it's Bob Dylan. The "hit parade" comes to him, cause he is the voice of young America, and says what they're a saying 'bout life, love, and people.

Maybe you've outlived your time, and it's new—the Limey Rock'n'Roll, but it's a message and it's coming across.

Moe Armstrong

Dear Sir:

Now that the commercial enterprise known as Bob Dylan has been wired for sound and gone electric SING OUT! will surely ceased to publish drivel about the Folk-Art of this product.

Frank Carlo
Los Angeles, Calif.

Dear Editor:

Yesterday's Hero

McCartney sings, backed up by celli,
And no one gets a pain in the belly.
Why do folkies, then, get cramps
On hearing Dylan play with amps?

Kristin White
Westport, Conn.

Dear Editor:

The oral tradition you so cherish is now in the hands of Top 40 radio. It is its logical heir. The medium is quite democratic and nothing becomes a genuine hit that doesn't deserve its place on the chart—no matter what you think!

The greater majority of Top 40 records are produced by small independents (not major labels—they lease masters as a rule) who have usually barely scraped together the bread for the studio time.

Dylan is bringing his personal distillation of hundreds of years of liberal and enlightened thought to the youth of America and the world in the greatest number possible, and is, in turn, spawning a generation of new writers and performers who share his courage in being blatantly honest and/or obscure even if it doesn't rhyme consistently.

Do you expect him to retain his limited-audience appeal when the same effort can reach millions? His drive, I'm sure, is not to "create art," but to communicate at all costs and to as many as will listen.

The fact is, he has caught the general ear while you have yet to be heard above a whisper.

Loren D Schwartz
Los Angeles 46, California

The Gap

by Studs Terkel

Let me tell you about Rose. She's sixteen and has a black heart tattooed on her pale arm. When I asked her why she dug protest songs, she said: "It just get t'rough to ya. 'At's all I can say." That's plenty. She's terribly excited about attending Dylan's concert in Chicago. (I'm not interested at all in the controversy, real or manufactured, raging about him. I don't give a damn whether his guitar is electric or acoustic. I'm a little hard of hearing on one ear, anyway. I found the *Sing Out!* debate between Paul Nelson and Irwin Silber fascinating but I find myself too old to mount either hobby horse.) What's important is that he gets through to Rose. The tattooed girl has been trying to get through to her mother, a lost soul, by sending her love poems. (It's beautiful poetry by an untutored bard, who has been to hell, purgatory and back.) To no avail. She did not get through.

Short-hand thoughts, neither merry nor mournful, on attending Dylan performance. 11/26/65

First half. Boy Alone. All business. Serious of mien. I, here; Thou, there. Edwardian uniform, expensive cut. Where have you been, my blue-eyed boy? Pucci your tailor? Small matter. Half dozen fairly strong searching songs. "Desolation Blues" awfully good. Suddenly, intermission. Rose overwhelmed: "I'm going back to recover my mind. He stole it."

Conclusion: Dylan controversy missed point by a Minnesota

Reprinted with permission from *Sing Out!*, February, 1966.

mile. Question of best of broadside balladeers becoming probing introspective poet wholly irrelevant. Excellent subject for high school debate, but irrelevant. Wry truth: Original become Show Biz wind-up doll. It sings, plays (doesn't talk), walks on, walks off. Have seen toy before. Called Sinatra at one time; Ella, at another. (Unlike, say, Billie Holiday or Woody Guthrie, for that matter. They were nobody's toys. Always, they revealed themselves in all their human vulnerability. This is the hallmark of an artist, Paul Nelson's dreary nonsense to the contrary. This was the Boy in the beginning—the one I had met two, three years ago; he had moved me profoundly. It was before the alchemy of commerce transmuted him into a Golden Boy Toy. The rich juices are still in him; witness "Desolation Row." Perhaps, there's still a chance, the Boy Poet will disenthrall himself from the grossness that has encircled him.) Goes over big, can't miss. Secret is in packaging.

Second half. Metamorphosis out of Kafka. Boy no longer alone. Four colleagues (La Dolce Vita paparazzi?), plugged into wall sockets. Organ glows fluorescently, all orange and green. A good night for Commonwealth Edison. Verse comes to mind, Woody—whom Boy is said to have visited about 553 years ago:

> I'm going to tell papa, I am, mama
> I'm going to tell papa, I am, haha
> He might not like it but I don't care
> 'Cause we'll have electricity and all.

Boy heads toward piano, ala Bix of another time. "Mr. Jones," a fine piece. Good bite. Lyrics audible. Returns to wall socket. Word or two occasionally heard way out there in wilds of third row. What's happening here, Mr. Jones? Whom is putting on whom? Not only is the executioner's face always well hidden. Perhaps Rimbaud is on stage or the other Dylan, he of South Wales. One never knows, do one? as Fats did say. And one never will. 'Cause we have electricity and all. Content is overwhelmed. Suddenly it's over. Boy nods ever so slightly. Minces off. No encores. House lights. Andy Frain ushers en garde. Look past you, as did Boy: cool; no nonsense.

Rose, highly impressed: "Man, he's home. He zooms right at

ya." I stare at mirror, across bar. The Gap is twin-level. Rose and I vs. the Establishment and one, equally as deep, between the tattooed girl and me. The flaw, Medea to the contrary, may be not in the stars but in me. Still, I ask: Where have you been, my blue-eyed boy? Comes the answer, blowing in the wind: Who said I was ever yours?

The Playboy Interview: Bob Dylan

A Candid Conversation with the Iconoclastic Idol of the Folk-Rock Set

by Nat Hentoff

As a versatile musicologist and trenchant social commentator, Nat Hentoff brings uniquely pertinent credentials to his task as interviewer of this month's controversial subject, about whom he writes:

"Less than five years ago, Bob Dylan was scuffling in New York—sleeping in friends' apartments on the Lower East Side and getting very occasional singing work at Gerde's Folk City, an unprepossessing bar for citybillies in the Village. With his leather cap, blue jeans and battered desert boots—his unvarying costume in those days—Dylan looked like an updated, undernourished Huck Finn. And like Huck, he had come out of the Midwest; he would have said 'escaped.' The son of Abraham Zimmerman, an appliance dealer, he was raised in Hibbing, Minnesota, a bleak mining town near the Canadian border. Though he ran away from home regularly between the ages of 10 and 18, young Zimmerman did manage to finish high school, and went on to spend about six months at the University of Minnesota in 1960. By then, he called himself Bob Dylan—in tribute to Dylan Thomas, according to legend; but actually after a gambling uncle whose last name was similar to Dylan.

"In the fall of that year, he came East to visit his idol, Woody Guthrie, in the New Jersey hospital where the Okie folk-singing bard was wasting away with a progressive disease of the nervous system. Dylan stayed and tried to scrape together a singing career. According to those who knew him then, he

was shy and stubborn but basically friendly and, beneath the hipster stance, uncommonly gentle. But they argued about his voice. Some found its flat Midwestern tones gratingly mesmeric; others agreed with a Missouri folk singer who had likened the Dylan sound to that of 'a dog with his leg caught in barbed wire.' All agreed, however, that his songs were strangely personal and often disturbing, a pungent mixture of loneliness and defiance laced with traces of Guthrie, echoes of the Negro blues singers and more than a suggestion of country-and-western; but essentially Dylan was developing his own penetratingly distinctive style. Yet the voice was so harsh and the songs so bitterly scornful of conformity, race prejudice and the mythology of the Cold War that most of his friends couldn't conceive of Dylan making it big even though folk music was already on the rise.

"They were wrong. In September of 1961, a music critic for The New York Times *caught his act at Gerde's and hailed the scruffy 19-year-old Minnesotan as a significant new voice on the folk horizon. Around the same time, he was signed by Columbia Records, and his first album was released early the next year. Though it was far from a smash hit, concerts and club engagements gradually multiplied; and then Dylan scored his storied triumph at the Newport Folk Festival in 1962. His next LP began to move, and in the spring of 1963 came his first big single: 'Blowin' in the Wind.' That same spring he turned down a lucrative guest shot on 'The Ed Sullivan Show' because CBS wouldn't permit him to sing a mordant parody he'd written about the John Birch Society. For the nation's young, the Dylan image began to form: kind of a singing James Dean with overtones of Holden Caulfield; he was making it, but he wasn't selling out. His concerts began to attract overflow crowds, and his songs—in performances by him and other folk singers—were rushing onto the hit charts. One of them, 'The Times They Are A-Changin',' became an anthem for the rebellious young, who savored its message that adults don't know where it's at and can't tell their children what to do.*

"By 1965 he had become a major phenomenon on the music scene. More and more folk performers, from Joan Baez to the Byrds, considered it mandatory to have an ample supply of Dylan songs in their repertoires; in one frantically appreciative

month—last August—48 different recordings of Dylan ballads were pressed by singers other than the composer himself. More and more aspiring folk singers—and folk-song writers—have begun to sound like Dylan. The current surge of 'protest' songs by such long-haired, post-beat rock-'n'-rollers as Barry McGuire and Sonny and Cher is credited to Dylan. And the newest commercial boom, 'folk-rock,' a fusion of folk-like lyrics with an r'-n'-r beat and background, is an outgrowth, in large part, of Dylan's recent decision—decried as a 'sellout' by folknik purists—to perform with a rock-'n'-roll combo rather than continue to accompany himself alone on the guitar. Backed by the big beat of the new group, Dylan tours England with as much tumultuous success as he does America, and the air play for his single records in both countries is rivaled only by that of the Beatles, Herman's Hermits and the Rolling Stones on the Top 40 deejay shows. In the next 18 months, his income—from personal appearances, records and composer's royalties—is expected to exceed $1,000,000.

"Withal, Dylan seems outwardly much the same as he did during the lean years in Greenwich Village. His dress is still casual to the point of exoticism; his hair is still long and frizzy, and he is still no more likely to be seen wearing a necktie than a cutaway. But there have been changes. No longer protesting polemically against the bomb, race prejudice and conformity, his songs have become increasingly personal—a surrealistic amalgam of Kafkaesque menace, corrosive satire and opaque sensuality. His lyrics are more crowded than ever with tumbling words and restless images, and they read more like free-verse poems than conventional lines. Adults still have difficulty digging his offbeat language—and its message of alienation—but the young continue to tune in and turn on.

"But there are other changes. Dylan has become elusive. He is no longer seen in his old haunts in the Village and on the Lower East Side. With few exceptions, he avoids interviewers, and in public, he is usually seen from afar at the epicenter of a protective coterie of tousle-topped young men dressed like him, and lissome, straight-haired young ladies who also seem to be dressed like him. His home base, if it can be called that, is a house his manager owns near Woodstock, a fashionable artists'

colony in New York State, and he also enjoys the run of his manager's apartment on dignified Gramercy Park in New York City. There are tales told of Dylan the motorcyclist, the novelist, the maker of high-camp home movies; but except among his small circle of intimates, the 24-year-old folk hero is inscrutably aloof.

"It was only after a long period of evasion and hesitation that Dylan finally agreed to grant this 'Playboy Interview'—the longest he's ever given. We met him on the 10th floor of the new CBS and Columbia Records building in mid-Manhattan. The room was antiseptic: white walls with black trim, contemporary furniture with severe lines, avant-garde art chosen by committee, everything in order, neat desks, neat personnel. In this sterile setting, slouched in a chair across from us, Dylan struck a refreshingly discordant note—with his untamed brownish-blond mane brushing the collar of his tieless blue plaid shirt, in his black jacket, gray vaudevillian-striped pipestem pants and well-worn blue-suede shoes. Sitting nearby also long-haired, tieless and black-jacketed, but wearing faded jeans—was a stringy young man whom the singer identified only as Taco Pronto. As Dylan spoke—in a soft drawl, smiling only rarely and fleetingly, sipping tea and chain-smoking cigarettes—his unspeaking friend chuckled and nodded appreciatively from the sidelines. Tense and guarded at first, Dylan gradually began to loosen up, then to open up, as he tried to tell us—albeit a bit surrealistically —just where he's been and where he's going. Under the circumstance, we chose to play straight man in our questions, believing that to have done otherwise would have stemmed the free-wheeling flow of Dylan's responses."

PLAYBOY: "Popular songs," you told a reporter last year, "are the only art form that describes the temper of the times. The only place where it's happening is on the radio and records. That's where the people hang out. It's not in books; it's not on the stage; it's not in the galleries. All this art they've been talking about, it just remains on the shelf. It doesn't make anyone happier." In view of the fact that more people than ever before are reading books and going to plays and art galleries, do you think that statement is borne out by the facts?

DYLAN: Statistics measure quantity, not quality. The people in the statistics are people who are very bored. Art, if there is such a thing, is in the bathrooms; everybody knows that. To go to an art gallery thing where you get free milk and doughnuts and where there is a rock'n'roll band playing: that's just a status affair. I'm not putting it down, mind you: but I spend a lot of time in the bathroom. I think museums are vulgar. They're all against sex. Anyhow, I didn't say that people "hang out" on the radio, I said they get "hung *up*" on the radio.

PLAYBOY: Why do you think rock'n'roll has become such an international phenomenon?

DYLAN: I can't really think that there is any rock'n'roll. Actually, when you think about it, anything that has no real existence is bound to become an international phenomenon. Anyway, what does it mean, rock'n'roll? Does it mean Beatles, does it mean John Lee Hooker, Bobby Vinton, Jerry Lewis' kid? What about Lawrence Welk? He must play a few rock'n'roll songs. Are all these people the same? Is Ricky Nelson like Otis Redding? Is Mick Jagger really Ma Rainey? I can tell by the way people hold their cigarettes if they like Ricky Nelson. I think it's fine to like Ricky Nelson; I couldn't care *less* if somebody likes Ricky Nelson. But I think we're getting off the track here. There *isn't* any Ricky Nelson. There isn't any Beatles; oh, I take that back; there are a lot of beetles. But there isn't any Bobby Vinton. Anyway, the word is not "international phenomenon"; the word is "parental nightmare."

PLAYBOY: In recent years, according to some critics, jazz has lost much of its appeal to the younger generation. Do you agree?

DYLAN: I don't think jazz has *ever* appealed to the younger generation. Anyway, I don't really know who this younger generation is. I don't think they could get into a jazz club anyway. But jazz is hard to follow; I mean you actually have to *like* jazz to follow it; and my motto is, never follow *anything*. I don't know what the motto of the younger generation is, but I would think they'd have to follow their parents. I mean, what would some parent say to his kid if the kid came home with a glass eye, a Charlie Mingus record and a pocketful of feathers? He'd say, "Who are you following?" And the poor kid would have to stand there with water in his shoes, a bow tie on his ear and soot pouring out of his belly button and say, "Jazz, Father, I've been following jazz." And his father would probably say, "Get a broom and clean up all that soot before you go to sleep." Then the kid's mother would tell her friends, "Oh yes, our little Donald, he's part of the younger generation, you know."

PLAYBOY: You used to say that you wanted to perform as little as possible, that you wanted to keep most of your time to yourself. Yet you're doing more concerts and cutting more records every year. Why? Is it the money?

DYLAN: Everything is changed now from before. Last spring, I guess I was going to quit singing. I was very drained, and the way things were going, it was a very draggy situation—I mean, when you do "Everybody Loves You for Your Black Eye," and meanwhile the back of your head is caving in. Anyway, I was playing a lot of songs I didn't want to play. I was singing words I didn't really want to sing. I don't mean words like "God" and "mother" and "President" and "suicide" and "meat cleaver." I mean simple little words like "if" and "hope" and "you." But "Like a Rolling Stone" changed it all; I didn't care anymore after that about writing books or poems or whatever. I mean it was something that I myself could dig. It's very tiring having other people tell you how much they dig you if you yourself don't dig you. It's also very deadly entertainment-wise. Contrary to what some scary people think, I don't play with a band now for any kind of propaganda-type or commercial-type reasons. It's just that my songs are pictures and the band makes the sound of the pictures.

PLAYBOY: Do you feel that acquiring a combo and switching from folk to folk-rock has improved you as a performer?

DYLAN: I'm not interested in myself as a performer. Performers are people who perform for other people. Unlike actors, I know what I'm saying. It's very simple in my mind. It doesn't matter what kind of audience reaction this whole thing gets. What happens on the stage is straight. It doesn't expect any rewards or fines from any kind of outside agitators. It's ultra-simple, and would exist whether anybody was looking or not.

As far as folk and folk-rock are concerned, it doesn't matter what kind of nasty names people invent for the music. It could be called arsenic music, or perhaps Phaedra music. I don't think that such a word as folk-rock has anything to do with it. And folk music is a word I can't use. Folk music is a bunch of fat people. I have to think of all this as traditional music. Traditional music is based on hexagrams. It comes about from legends, Bibles, plagues, and it revolves around vegetables and death. There's nobody that's going to kill traditional music. All these songs about roses growing out of people's brains and lovers who are really geese and swans that turn into angels—they're not going to die. It's all those paranoid people who think that someone's going to come and take away their toilet paper—*they're* going to die. Songs like "Which Side Are You On?" and "I Love You, Porgy"—they're not folk-music songs; they're political songs. They're *already* dead. Obviously, death is not very universally accepted. I mean, you'd think that the traditional-music people could gather from their songs that mystery is a fact, a traditional fact. I listen to the old ballads; but I wouldn't go to a *party* and listen to the old ballads. I could give you descriptive detail of what they do to me, but some people would probably think my imagination had gone mad. It strikes me funny that people actually have the gall to think that I have some kind of fantastic imagination. It gets very lonesome. But anyway, traditional music is too unreal to die. It doesn't need to be protected. Nobody's going to hurt it. In that music is the only true, valid death you can feel today off a record player. But like anything else in great demand, people try to own it. It has to do with a purity thing. I think its meaninglessness is holy. Everybody knows that I'm not a folk singer.

PLAYBOY: Some of your old fans would agree with you—and not in a complimentary vein—since your debut with the rock-'n'roll combo at last year's Newport Folk Festival, where many of them booed you loudly for "selling out" to commercial pop tastes. The early Bob Dylan, they felt, was the "pure" Bob Dylan. How do you feel about it?

DYLAN: I was kind of stunned. But I can't put anybody down for coming and booing; after all, they paid to get in. They could have been maybe a little quieter and not so persistent, though. There were a lot of old people there, too; lots of whole families had driven down from Vermont, lots of nurses and their parents, and well, like they just came to hear some relaxing hoedowns, you know, maybe an Indian polka or two. And just when everything's going all right, here I come on, and the whole place turns into a beer factory. There were a lot of people there who were very pleased that I got booed. I saw them afterward. I do resent somewhat, though, that everybody that booed said they did it because they were old fans.

PLAYBOY: What about their charge that you vulgarized your natural gifts?

DYLAN: What can I say? I'd like to *see* one of these so-called fans. I'd like to have him blindfolded and brought to me. It's like going out to the desert and screaming, and then having little kids throw their sandbox at you. I'm only 24. These people that said this—were they Americans?

PLAYBOY: Americans or not, there were a lot of people who didn't like your new sound. In view of this widespread negative reaction, do you think you may have made a mistake in changing your style?

DYLAN: A mistake is to commit a misunderstanding. There could be no such thing, anyway, as this action. Either people understand or they *pretend* to understand—or else they really *don't* understand. What you're speaking of here is doing wrong things for selfish reasons. I don't know the word for that, unless it's suicide. In any case, it has nothing to do with my music.

PLAYBOY: Mistake or not, what made you decide to go the rock'n'roll route?

DYLAN: Carelessness. I lost my one true love. I started drinking. The first thing I know, I'm in a card game. Then I'm in a crap game. I wake up in a pool hall. Then this big Mexican lady drags me off the table, takes me to Philadelphia. She leaves me alone in her house, and it burns down. I wind up in Phoenix. I get a job as a Chinaman. I start working in a dime store, and move in with a 13-year-old girl. Then this big Mexican lady from Philadelphia comes in and burns the house down. I go down to Dallas. I get a job as a "before" in a Charles Atlas "before and after" ad. I move in with a delivery boy who can cook fantastic chili and hot dogs. Then this 13-year-old girl from Phoenix comes and burns the house down. The delivery boy—he ain't so mild: He gives her the knife, and the next thing I know I'm in Omaha. It's so cold there, by this time

I'm robbing my own bicycles and frying my own fish. I stumble onto some luck and get a job as a carburetor out at the hot-rod races every Thursday night. I move in with a high school teacher who also does a little plumbing on the side, who ain't much to look at, but who's built a special kind of refrigerator that can turn newspaper into lettuce. Everything's going good until that delivery boy shows up and tries to knife me. Needless to say, he burned the house down, and I hit the road. The first guy that picked me up asked me if I wanted to be a star. What could I say?

PLAYBOY: And that's how you became a rock'n'roll singer?

DYLAN: No, that's how I got tuberculosis.

PLAYBOY: Let's turn the question around: Why have you stopped composing and singing protest songs?

DYLAN: I've stopped composing and singing anything that has either a reason to be written or a motive to be sung. Don't get me wrong, now. "Protest" is not my word. I've never thought of myself as such. The word "protest," I think, was made up for people undergoing surgery. It's an amusement-park word. A normal person in his righteous mind would have to have the hiccups to pronounce it honestly. The word "message" strikes me as having a hernia-like sound. It's just like the word "delicious." Also the word "marvelous." You know, the English can say "marvelous" pretty good. They can't say "raunchy" so good, though. Well, we each have our thing. Anyway, message songs, as everybody knows, are a drag. It's only college newspaper editors and single girls under 14 that could possibly have time for them.

PLAYBOY: You've said you think message songs are vulgar. Why?

DYLAN: Well, first of all, anybody that's got a message is going to learn from experience that they can't put it into a song. I mean it's just not going to come out the same message. After one or two of these unsuccessful attempts, one realizes that his resultant message, which is not even the same message he thought up and began with, he's now got to stick to it; because, after all, a song leaves your mouth just as soon as it leaves your hands. Are you following me?

PLAYBOY: Oh, perfectly.

DYLAN: Well, anyway, second of all, you've got to respect other people's right to also have a message themselves. Myself, what I'm going to do is rent Town Hall and put about 30 Western Union boys on the bill. I mean, then there'll *really* be some messages. People will be able to come and hear more messages than they've ever heard before in their life.

PLAYBOY: But your early ballads have been called "songs of passionate protest." Wouldn't that make them "message" music?

DYLAN: This is unimportant. Don't you understand? I've been writing since I was eight years old. I've been playing the guitar since I was ten. I was raised playing and writing whatever it was I had to play and write.

PLAYBOY: Would it be unfair to say, then, as some have, that you were motivated commercially rather than creatively in writing the kind of songs that made you popular?

DYLAN: All right, now, look. It's not all that deep. It's not a complicated thing. My motives, or whatever they are, were never commercial in the money sense of the word. It was more in the don't-die-by-the-hacksaw sense of the word. I never did it for money. It happened, and I let it happen to me. There was no reason *not* to let it happen to me. I couldn't have written before what I write now, anyway. The songs used to be about what I felt and saw. Nothing of my own rhythmic vomit ever entered into it. Vomit is not romantic. I used to think songs are supposed to be romantic. And I didn't want to sing anything that was unspecific. Unspecific things have no sense of time. All of us people have no sense of time; it's a dimensional hang-up. Anybody can be specific and obvious. That's always been the easy way. The leaders of the world take the easy way. It's not that it's so difficult to be unspecific and less obvious; it's just that there's nothing, absolutely nothing, to be specific and obvious *about.* My older songs, to say the least, were about nothing. The newer ones are about the same nothing—only as seen inside a bigger thing, perhaps called the nowhere. But this is all very constipated. I *do* know what my songs are about.

PLAYBOY: And what's that?

DYLAN: Oh, some are about four minutes; some are about five, and some believe it or not, are about eleven or twelve.

•

PLAYBOY: Can't you be a bit more informative?

DYLAN: Nope.

PLAYBOY: All right. Let's change the subject. As you know, it's the age group from about 16 to 25 that listens to your songs. Why, in your opinion?

DYLAN: I don't see what's so strange about an age group like that listening to my songs. I'm hip enough to know that it ain't going to be the 85-to-90-year-olds. If the 85-to-90-year-olds *were* listening to me, they'd know that I can't tell them anything. The 16-to-25-year-olds, they probably know that I can't tell *them* anything either—and they know that *I* know it. It's a funny business. Obviously, I'm not an IBM computer any more than I'm an ashtray. I mean it's obvious to anyone who's ever slept in the back seat of a car that I'm just not a schoolteacher.

PLAYBOY: Even though you're not a schoolteacher, wouldn't you like to help the young people who dig you from turning into what some of their parents have become?

DYLAN: Well, I must say that I really don't know their parents. I really don't know if *anybody's* parents are so bad. Now, I hate to come on like a weakling or a coward, and I realize it might seem kind of irreligious, but I'm really not the right person to tramp around the country saving souls. I wouldn't run over anybody that was laying in the street, and I certainly wouldn't become a hangman. I wouldn't think twice about giving a starving man a cigarette. But I'm not a shepherd. And I'm not about to save anybody from fate, which I know nothing about. "Parents" is not the key word here. The key word is "destiny." I can't save them from that.

PLAYBOY: Still, thousands of young people look up to you as a kind of folk hero. Do you feel some sense of responsibility toward them?

DYLAN: I don't feel I have any responsibility, no. Whoever it is that listens to my songs owes *me* nothing. How could I possibly have any responsibility to any kind of thousands? What could possibly make me think that I owe anybody anything who just happens to be there? I've never written any song that begins with the words "I've gathered you here tonight . . ." I'm not about to tell anybody to be a good boy or a good girl and they'll go to heaven. I really don't know what the people who are on the receiving end of these songs think of me, anyway. It's horrible. I'll bet Tony Bennett doesn't have to go through this kind of thing. I wonder what Billy the Kid would have answered to such a question.

PLAYBOY: In their admiration for you, many young people have begun to imitate the way you dress—which one adult commentator has called "self-consciously oddball and defiantly sloppy." What's your reaction to that kind of put-down?

DYLAN: Bullshit. Oh, such bullshit. I know the fellow that said that. He used to come around here and get beat up all the time. He better watch it; some people are after him. They're going to strip him naked and stick him in Times Square. They're going to tie him up, and also put a thermometer in his mouth. Those kind of morbid ideas and remarks are so petty—I mean there's a *war* going on. People got rickets; everybody wants to start a riot; forty-year-old women are eating spinach by the carload; the doctors haven't got a cure for cancer—and here's some hillbilly talking about how he doesn't like somebody's clothes. Worse than that, it gets printed and innocent people have to read it. This is a terrible thing. And he's a terrible man. Obviously, he's just living off the fat of himself, and he's expecting his kids to take care of him. His kids probably listen to my records. Just because my clothes are too long, does that mean I'm unqualified for what I do?

PLAYBOY: No, but there are those who think it does—and many of them seem to feel the same way about your long hair. But compared with the shoulder-length coiffures worn by some of the male singing groups these days, your tonsorial tastes are on the conservative side. How do you feel about these far-out hair styles?

DYLAN: The thing that most people don't realize is that it's *warmer* to have long hair. Everybody wants to be warm. People with short hair freeze easily. Then they try to hide their coldness, and they get jealous of everybody that's warm. Then they become either barbers or Congressmen. A lot of prison wardens have short hair. Have you ever noticed that Abraham Lincoln's hair was much longer than John Wilkes Booth's?

PLAYBOY: Do you think Lincoln wore his hair long to keep his head warm?

DYLAN: Actually, I think it was for medical reasons, which are none of my business. But I guess if you figure it out, you realize that all of one's hair surrounds and lays on the brain inside your head. Mathematically speaking, the more of it you can get out of your head, the better. People who want free minds sometimes overlook the fact that you have to have an uncluttered brain. Obviously, if you get your hair on the outside of your head, your brain will be a little more freer. But all this talk about long hair is just a trick. It's been thought up by men and women who look like cigars—the anti-happiness committee. They're all freeloaders and cops. You can tell who they are: They're always carrying calendars, guns or scissors. They're all trying to get into your quicksand. They think you've got something. I don't know why Abe Lincoln had long hair.

PLAYBOY: Until your abandonment of "message" songs, you were considered not only a major voice in the student protest movement but a militant champion of the civil rights struggle. According to friends, you seemed to feel a special bond of kinship with the Student Nonviolent Coordinating Committee, which you actively supported both as a performer and a worker. Why have you withdrawn from participation in all these causes? Have you lost interest in protest as well as in protest songs?

DYLAN: As far as SNCC is concerned, I knew some of the people in it, but I only knew them as people, not as any part of something that was bigger or better than themselves. I didn't even know what civil rights *was* before I met some of them. I mean, I knew there were Negroes, and I knew there were a lot of people who don't *like* Negroes. But I got to admit that if I didn't know some of the SNCC people, I would have gone on thinking that Martin Luther King was really nothing more than some underprivileged war hero. I haven't lost any interest in protest since then. I just didn't have any interest in protest to begin with—any more than I did in war heroes. You can't lose what you've never had. Anyway, when you don't like your situation, you either leave it or else you overthrow it. You can't just stand around and whine about it. People just get aware of your noise; they really don't get aware of *you*. Even if they give you what you want, it's only because you're making too much noise. First thing you know, you want something else, and then you want something else, and then you want something else, until finally it isn't a joke anymore, and whoever you're protesting against finally gets all fed up and stomps on everybody. Sure, you can go around trying to bring up people who are lesser than you, but then don't forget, you're messing around with gravity. I don't fight gravity. I do believe in equality, but I also believe in distance.

PLAYBOY: Do you mean people keeping their racial distance?

DYLAN: I believe in people keeping everything they've got.

PLAYBOY: Some people might feel that you're trying to cop out of fighting for the things you believe in.

DYLAN: Those would be people who think I have some sort of responsibility toward *them*. They probably want me to help them make friends. I don't know. They probably either want to set me in their house and have me come out every hour and tell them what time it is, or else they just want to stick me in between the mattress. How could they possibly understand what I believe in?

PLAYBOY: Well, what *do* you believe in?

DYLAN: I already told you.

PLAYBOY: All right. Many of your folk-singing colleagues remain actively involved in the fight for civil rights, free speech and withdrawal from Vietnam. Do you think they're wrong?

DYLAN: I don't think they're wrong, if that's what they see themselves doing. But don't think that what you've got out there is a bunch of little Buddhas all parading up and down. People that use God as a weapon should be amputated upon. You see it around here all the time: "Be good or God won't like you, and you'll go to hell." Things like that. People that march with slogans and things tend to take themselves a little too holy. It would be a drag if they, too, started using God as a weapon.

PLAYBOY: Do you think it's pointless to dedicate yourself to the cause of peace and racial equality?

DYLAN: Not pointless to dedicate yourself to peace and racial equality, but rather, it's pointless to dedicate yourself to the *cause;* that's *really* pointless. That's very unknowing. To say "cause of peace" is just like saying "hunk of butter." I mean, how can you listen to anybody who wants you to believe he's dedicated to the hunk and not to the butter? People who can't conceive of how others hurt, they're trying to change the world. They're all afraid to admit that they don't really know each other. They'll all probably be here long after we've gone, and we'll give birth to new ones. But they themselves—I don't think *they'll* give birth to *anything*.

PLAYBOY: You sound a bit fatalistic.

DYLAN: I'm not fatalistic. Bank tellers are fatalistic; clerks are fatalistic. I'm a farmer. Who ever heard of a fatalistic farmer? I'm not fatalistic. I smoke a lot of cigarettes, but that doesn't make me fatalistic.

PLAYBOY: You were quoted recently as saying that "songs can't save the world. I've gone through all that." We take it you don't share Pete Seeger's belief that songs can change people, that they can help build international understanding.

DYLAN: On the international understanding part, that's OK. But you have a translation problem there. Anybody with this kind of a level of thinking has to also think about this translation thing. But I don't believe songs can change people anyway. I'm not Pinocchio. I consider that an insult. I'm not part of that. I don't blame anybody for thinking that way. But I just don't donate any money to them. I don't consider them anything like unhip; they're more in the rubber-band category.

PLAYBOY: How do you feel about those who have risked imprisonment by burning their draft cards to signify their opposition to U.S. involvement in Vietnam, and by refusing—as your friend Joan Baez has done—to pay their income taxes as a protest against the Government's expenditures on war and weaponry? Do you think they're wasting their time?

DYLAN: Burning draft cards isn't going to end any war. It's not even going to save any lives. If someone can feel more honest with himself by burning his draft card, then that's great; but if he's just going to feel more important because he does it, then that's a drag. I really don't know too much about Joan Baez and her income tax problems. The only thing I can tell you about Joan Baez is that she's not Belle Starr.

PLAYBOY: Writing about "beard-wearing draft-card burners and pacifist income-tax evaders," one columnist called such protesters "no less outside society than the junkie, the homosexual or the mass murderer." What's your reaction?

DYLAN: I don't believe in those terms. They're too hysterical. They don't describe anything. Most people think that homosexual, gay, queer, queen, faggot are all the same words. Everybody thinks that a junkie is a dope freak. As far as I'm concerned, I don't consider myself outside of anything. I just consider myself *not around.*

PLAYBOY: Joan Baez recently opened a school in northern California for training civil rights workers in the philosophy and techniques of nonviolence. Are you in sympathy with that concept?

DYLAN: If you mean do I agree with it or not, I really don't see anything to be in agreement *with.* If you mean has it got my approval, I guess it does, but my approval really isn't going to do it any good. I don't know about other people's sympathy, but my sympathy runs to the lame and crippled and beautiful things. I have a feeling of loss of power—something like a reincarnation feeling; I don't feel that for mechanical things like cars or schools. I'm sure it's a *nice* school, but if you're asking me would I go to it, I would have to say no.

PLAYBOY: As a college dropout in your freshman year, you seem to take a dim view of schooling in general, whatever the subject.

DYLAN: I really don't think about it.

PLAYBOY: Well, have you ever had any regrets about not completing college?

DYLAN: That would be ridiculous. Colleges are like old-age homes; except for the fact that more people die in college than in old-age homes, there's really no difference. People have one great blessing—obscurity—and not really too many people are thankful for it. Everybody is always taught to be thankful for their food and clothes and things like that, but not to be thankful for their obscurity. Schools don't teach that; they teach people to be rebels and lawyers. I'm not going to put down the teaching system; that would be too silly. It's just that it really doesn't have too much to teach. Colleges are part of the American institution; everybody respects them. They're very rich and influential, but they have nothing to do with survival. Everybody knows that.

PLAYBOY: Would you advise young people to skip college, then?

DYLAN: I wouldn't advise anybody to do anything. I certainly wouldn't advise somebody not to go to college; I just wouldn't pay his *way* through college.

PLAYBOY: Don't you think the things one learns in college can help enrich one's life?

DYLAN: I don't think anything like that is going to enrich my life, no—not *my* life, anyway. Things are going to happen whether I know why they happen or not. It just gets more complicated when you stick *yourself* into it. You don't find out why things move. You *let* them move; you *watch* them move; you *stop* them from moving; you *start* them moving. But you don't sit around and try to figure out *why* there's movement—unless, of course, you're just an innocent moron, or some wise old Japanese man. Out of all the people who just lay around and ask "Why?", how many do you figure really want to know?

PLAYBOY: Can you suggest a better use for the four years that would otherwise be spent in college?

DYLAN: Well, you could hang around in Italy; you could go to Mexico; you could become a dishwasher; you could even go to Arkansas. I don't know; there are thousands of things to do and places to go. Everybody thinks that you have to bang your head against the wall, but it's silly when you really think about it. I mean, here you have fantastic scientists working on ways to prolong human living, and then you have other people who take it for granted that you have to beat your head against the wall in order to be happy. You can't take everything you don't like as a personal insult. I guess you should go where your wants are bare, where you're invisible and not needed.

PLAYBOY: Would you classify sex among your wants, wherever you go?

DYLAN: Sex is a temporary thing; sex isn't love. You can get sex anywhere. If you're looking for someone to *love* you, now that's different. I guess you have to stay in college for that.

PLAYBOY: Since you didn't stay in college, does that mean you haven't found someone to love you?

DYLAN: Let's go on to the next question.

PLAYBOY: Do you have any difficulty relating to people—or vice versa?

DYLAN: Well, sometimes I have the feeling that other people want my *soul*. If I say to them, "I don't *have* a soul," they say, "I know that. You don't have to tell me that. Not me. How dumb do you think I am? I'm your *friend*." What can I say except maybe feeling bad and paranoia are the same thing.

PLAYBOY: Paranoia is said to be one of the mental states sometimes induced by such hallucinogenic drugs as peyote and LSD. Considering the risks involved, do you think that experimentation with such drugs should be part of the growing-up experience for a young person?

DYLAN: I wouldn't advise anybody to use drugs—certainly not the hard drugs; drugs are medicine. But opium and hash and pot—now, those things aren't drugs; they just bend your mind a little. I think *everybody's* mind should be bent once in a while. Not by LSD, though. LSD is medicine—a different kind of medicine. It makes you aware of the universe so to speak; you realize how foolish *objects* are. But LSD is not for groovy people; it's for mad, hateful people who want revenge. It's for people who usually have heart attacks. They ought to use it at the Geneva Convention.

PLAYBOY: Are you concerned, as you approach thirty, that you may begin to "go square," lose some of your openness to experience, become leery of change and new experiment?

DYLAN: No. But if it happens, then it happens. What can I say? There doesn't seem to *be* any tomorrow. Every time I wake up, no matter in what position, it's always been today. To look ahead and start worrying about trivial little things I can't really say has any more importance than looking back and *remembering* trivial little things. I'm not going to become any poetry instructor at any girls' school; I know *that* for sure. But that's about *all* I know for sure. I'll just keep doing these different things, I guess.

PLAYBOY: Such as?

DYLAN: Waking up in different positions.

PLAYBOY: What else?

DYLAN: I'm just like anybody else; I'll try anything once.

PLAYBOY: Including theft and murder?

DYLAN: I can't really say I *wouldn't* commit theft or murder and expect anybody to really believe me. I wouldn't believe anybody if they told *me* that.

PLAYBOY: By their mid-twenties, most people have begun to settle into their niche, to find a place in society. But you've managed to remain inner-directed and uncommitted. What was it that spurred you to run away from home six times between the ages of ten and eighteen and finally to leave for good?

DYLAN: It was nothing; it was just an accident of geography. Like if I was born and raised in New York or Kansas City, I'm sure everything would have turned out different. But Hibbing, Minnesota, was just not the right place for me to stay and live. There really was nothing there. The only thing you could do there was be a miner, and even that kind of thing was getting less and less. The people that lived there—they're nice people; I've been all over the world since I left there, and they still stand out as being the least hung-up. The mines were just dying, that's all; but that's not their fault. *Everybody* about my age left there. It was no great romantic thing. It didn't take any great amount of thinking or individual genius, and there certainly wasn't any pride in it. I didn't run away from it; I just turned my back on it. It couldn't give me anything. It was very void-like. So leaving wasn't hard at all; it would have been much harder to stay. I didn't want to die there. As I think about it now, though, it wouldn't be such a bad place to go back to and die in. There's no place I feel closer to now, or get the feeling that I'm part of, except maybe New York; but I'm *not* a New Yorker. I'm North Dakota-Minnesota-Midwestern. I'm that color. I speak that way. I'm from someplace called Iron Range. My brains and feelings have come from there. I wouldn't amputate on a drowning man; *nobody* from out there would.

PLAYBOY: Today, you're on your way to becoming a millionaire. Do you feel in any danger of being trapped by all this affluence—by the things it can buy?

DYLAN: No, my world is very small. Money can't really improve it any; money can just keep it from being smothered.

PLAYBOY: Most big stars find it difficult to avoid getting involved, and sometimes entangled, in managing the business end of their careers. As a man with three thriving careers—as a concert performer, recording star and songwriter—do you ever feel boxed in by such noncreative responsibilities?

DYLAN: No, I've got other people to do that for me. They watch my money; they guard it. They keep their eyes on it at all times; they're supposed to be very smart when it comes to money. They know just what to do with my money. I pay them a lot of it. I don't really speak to them much, and they don't really speak to me at all, so I guess everything is all right.

PLAYBOY: If fortune hasn't trapped you, how about fame? Do you find that your celebrity makes it difficult to keep your private life intact?

DYLAN: My private life has been dangerous from the beginning. All this does is add a little atmosphere.

PLAYBOY: You used to enjoy wandering across the country—taking off on open-end trips, roughing it from town to town, with no particular destination in mind. But you seem to be doing much less of that these days. Why? Is it because you're too well known?

DYLAN: It's mainly because I have to be in Cincinnati Friday night, and the next night I got to be in Atlanta, and then the next night after that, I have to be in Buffalo. Then I have to write some more songs for a record album.

PLAYBOY: Do you get the chance to ride your motorcycle much anymore?

DYLAN: I'm still very patriotic to the highway, but I don't ride my motorcycle too much anymore, no.

PLAYBOY: How do you get your kicks these days, then?

DYLAN: I hire people to look into my eyes, and then I have them kick me.

PLAYBOY: And that's the way you get your kicks?

DYLAN: No. Then I *forgive* them; that's where my kicks come in.

PLAYBOY: You told an interviewer last year, "I've done everything I ever wanted to." If that's true, what do you have to look forward to?

DYLAN: Salvation. Just plain salvation.

PLAYBOY: Anything else?

DYLAN: Praying. I'd also like to start a cookbook magazine. And I've always wanted to be a boxing referee. I want to referee a heavyweight championship fight. Can you imagine that? Can you imagine any fighter in his right mind recognizing *me?*

PLAYBOY: If your popularity were to wane, would you welcome being anonymous again?

DYLAN: You mean welcome it, like I'd welcome some poor pilgrim coming in from the rain? No, I wouldn't welcome it; I'd accept it, though. Someday, obviously, I'm going to *have* to accept it.

PLAYBOY: Do you ever think about marrying, settling down, having a home, maybe living abroad? Are there any luxuries you'd like to have, say, a yacht or a Rolls-Royce?

DYLAN: No, I don't think about those things. If I felt like buying anything, I'd buy it. What you're asking me about is the future, *my* future. I'm the last person in the world to ask about my future.

PLAYBOY: Are you saying you're going to be passive and just let things happen to you?

DYLAN: Well, that's being very philosophical about it, but I guess it's true.

PLAYBOY: You once planned to write a novel. Do you still?

DYLAN: I don't think so. All my writing goes into the songs now. Other forms don't interest me anymore.

PLAYBOY: Do you have any unfulfilled ambitions?

DYLAN: Well, I guess I've always wanted to be Anthony Quinn in *La Strada*. Not always—only for about six years now; it's not one of those childhood-dream things. Oh, and come to think of it, I guess I've always wanted to be Brigitte Bardot, too; but I don't really want to think about *that* too much.

PLAYBOY: Did you ever have the standard boyhood dream of growing up to be President?

DYLAN: No. When I was a boy, Harry Truman was President; who'd want to be Harry Truman?

PLAYBOY: Well, let's suppose that you *were* the President. What would you accomplish during your first thousand days?

DYLAN: Well, just for laughs, so long as you insist, the first thing I'd do is probably move the White House. Instead of being in Texas, it'd be on the East Side in New York. McGeorge

Bundy would definitely have to change his name, and General McNamara would be forced to wear a coonskin cap and shades. I would immediately rewrite "The Star-Spangled Banner," and little school children, instead of memorizing "America the Beautiful," would have to memorize "Desolation Row" (one of Dylan's latest songs). And I would immediately call for a show-down with Mao Tse-tung; I would fight him *personally*—and I'd get somebody to film it.

PLAYBOY: One final question. Even though you've more or less retired from political and social protest, can you conceive of any circumstance that might persuade you to reinvolve yourself?

DYLAN: No, not unless all the people in the world disappeared.

"Well, What Have We Here?"

We have Bob Dylan, singer, songwriter, poet, who at 25 admits he's a millionaire but denies being a genius.

by *Jules Siegel*

Quick and little, Bob Dylan scrambled from the safety of a rented gray sedan and ran for his dressing room through a wildness of teen-age girls who howled and grabbed for his flesh. A cordon of guards held for a moment against the overwhelming attack. Then it broke and Dylan disappeared beneath yards of bell-bottoms and long hair. After a brief struggle he was rescued by one of his assistants, who methodically tore small and large girls off him, but it was too late. With a pair of enormous shears, a giant blond girl had snipped a lock of the precious Dylan hair and now was weeping for joy.

"Did you see that?" said Dylan in his dressing room, his pale face somewhat paler than usual. "I mean did you *see* that?" repeated Dylan, who tends to talk in italics. "I don't care about the hair, but she could have killed me. I mean she could have taken my eyes out with those scissors."

This is Bob Dylan's year to be mobbed. Next year it will probably be somebody else. But this year Bob Dylan is the king of rock'n'roll, and he is the least likely king popular music has ever seen. With a bony, nervous face covered with skin the color of sour milk, a fright-wig of curly brown hair teased into a bramble of stand-up tangles, and dark-circled hazel eyes usually hidden by large prescription sunglasses, Dylan is less like Elvis or Frankie than like some crippled saint or resurrected Beethoven.

The songs he writes and sings, unlike the usual young-love

Reprinted from *Saturday Evening Post*, July 30, 1966.

pap of the airwaves, are full of dark and, many insist, important meaning; they are peopled with freaks, clowns, tramps, artists and mad scientists, dancing and tumbling in progressions of visionary images mobilized to the massive beat of rock'n'roll. They often make very little logical sense, but almost always they make very good poetic sense. According to a recent poll, college students call him the most important contemporary poet in America.

He is certainly the only poet who gets his hair snipped off by shrieking teen-age girls, but Dylan has always been a defier of categories. His first fame was as a folk singer and folk-song writer. Last year he modified his style to what has been labeled "folk-rock," a blend of serious, poetic lyrics and rock'n'roll music, which has brought him his greatest commercial success but has alienated some purists who were his early fans. He is a singer whose voice has been compared to the howl of "a dog caught in barbed wire"; a performer whose stage presence includes no hip wiggling or even, until recently, any acknowledgment of his audience; a public figure whose press conferences are exercises in a new kind of surrealism in which reporters ask, "Are you planning to do a movie?" and Dylan answers, deadpan, "Yes, I'm going to play my mother."

Yet, Bob Dylan, at the age of 25, has a million dollars in the bank and earns an estimated several hundred thousand dollars a year from concerts, recordings and publishing royalties. He is even more popular in England and Europe than in America. Four hours after tickets went on sale for his recent London concerts at Albert Hall, the SOLD-OUT sign was put up, and at one time five of his LP albums were selling in the top 20 in London. One paperback book on him has already been published; a hard-cover book about him by Robert Shelton, folk critic of *The New York Times*, will be published this winter; a third book of photographs and text by Daniel Kramer is scheduled for winter publication. A two-hour documentary of his English tours will soon be released for theater showing; he is about to begin production of his own movie; ABC-TV has signed him for a television special. A book of his writings, *Tarantula*, is to be published by Macmillan late this summer, with a prepublication excerpt to appear in the *Atlantic Monthly*.

And although he is not nearly so popular as the Beatles, who have sold nearly 200 million records in four years, his artistic reputation is so great that in the recording business Dylan is ranked as the No. 1 innovator, the most important trend-setter, one of the few people around who can change radically the course of teen music.

"Dylan," says a folk-singer friend of his, "is the king. He's the one we all look to for approval, the one we're all eating our hearts out about, the one who proved you could make it with the kids without any compromises. If I didn't admire him so much, I would have to hate him. In fact, maybe I do hate him anyway."

Born Robert Zimmerman, May 24, 1941, in Duluth, Minn., Dylan is a product of Hibbing, Minn., an iron-ore mining town of 18,000 inhabitants about 70 miles from the Canadian border. The southwestern accent in his singing voice is apparently acquired; he speaks without it. His father is a prosperous, witty, small (five-foot-six), cigar-smoking appliance dealer. His mother, a deeply tanned, attractive woman, is described by acquaintances as extremely intelligent, well informed and very talkative.

Dylan has a brother, David, 20, who attends St. Olaf College on a musical scholarship, and in the family it was always David who was thought of as "the musical one." Abe Zimmerman remembers buying a piano ("Not an expensive one," he says) when Bob was 10. Bob took one lesson and gave up in disgust because he couldn't play anything right away. David, then five, began taking lessons and has been playing ever since.

Despite his initial impatience, Bob Zimmerman soon taught himself how to play the piano, harmonica, guitar and autoharp. Once he began to play the piano, says Mrs. Zimmerman, he beat the keys out of tune pounding out rock'n'roll. He also wrote—not only music but also poetry. "My mother has hundreds of poems I wrote when I was twelve years old," says Dylan.

As an adolescent, Dylan helped his father in the store, delivering appliances and sometimes attempting to make collections. "He was strong," Abe Zimmerman recently told an acquaintance. "I mean he could hold up his end of a refrigerator as well as kids twice his size, football players.

"I used to make him go out to the poor sections," Mr. Zimmerman said, "knowing he couldn't collect any money from those people. I just wanted to show him another side of life. He'd come back and say, 'Dad, those people haven't got any money.' And I'd say, 'Some of those people out there make as much money as I do, Bobby. They just don't know how to manage it.' "

In more than one way the lesson was well taken. Dylan today, while professing not to know anything about his wealth, appears to be a very good manager of money, careful sometimes to what might be considered stinginess.

A photographer friend of his recalls having to meet him at a hotel. "I called him," he says, "and asked if he wanted me to bring anything up for him. 'A container of tea,' Bobby said. I said, 'Bobby, they have room service in the hotel; you can have it sent up.' He thought about that for a couple of seconds and then said no, room service was too expensive." This was in 1965, the year that Dylan became a millionaire.

But Dylan learned more than frugality in the depressed areas of Hibbing. He learned, as Abe Zimmerman hoped he would, that there were people who knew nothing about middle-class life and middle-class values, people whose American dream had become a nightmare of installment debt. He seems to have felt a blood tie with them, based on a terrifying sense of his own peculiarity.

"I see things that other people don't see," he says. "I feel things other people don't feel. It's terrible. They laugh. I felt like that my whole life.

"My friends have been the same as me, people who couldn't make it as the high-school football halfback, Junior Chamber of Commerce leader, fraternity leader, truck driver working their way through college. I just had to be with them. I just don't care what anyone looks like, just as long as they didn't think I was strange. I couldn't do any of those things either. All I did was write and sing, paint little pictures on paper, dissolve myself into situations where I was invisible."

In pursuit of invisibility, Bob Zimmerman took to running away from home. "I made my own depression," he says. "Rode freight trains for kicks, got beat up for laughs, cut grass for quarters, met a waitress who picked me up and dropped me off in Washington." He tells of living with carnivals, of some trouble with police in Hibbing, of entertaining in a strip joint.

Be that as it may, he managed to finish high school at the appropriate time and even earned a scholarship to the University of Minnesota. Then the middle-class college boy from Hibbing began to remake his life and his image radically. He moved from his fraternity house to a downtown apartment. He began singing and playing the guitar and harmonica at Minneapolis' Ten o'Clock Scholar for two dollars a night; it is said that when he asked for a raise to five dollars, he was fired. He became Bob Dylan, and has since changed his name legally. This was not in tribute to Dylan Thomas, as the widely circulated legend maintains, but for some reason which he doesn't feel compelled to explain seriously.

"Get that straight," he says. "I didn't change my name in honor of Dylan Thomas. That's just a story. I've done more for Dylan Thomas than he's ever done for me. Look how many kids are probably reading his poetry now because they heard that story."

Dylan also gave up his very conventional college-boy dress—for his first professional appearance in Minneapolis he had worn white buck shoes—and began to develop his own personal style. At first, he was influenced by the uniform of folk singers everywhere—jeans, work shirt, boots, collar-length hair. Now that he's a rock'n'roll star, the uniform has changed. The boots are still part of it, but the jeans are now tight slacks that make his legs look skinnier than they are. The work shirt has been replaced by floppy polka-dot Carnaby Street English shirts with oversized collars and long, puffed sleeves. Sometimes he wears racetrack-plaid suits in combinations of colors like green and black. His hair seems to get longer and wilder by the month.

In December, 1960, Dylan gave up on Minnesota and took off for New York to try rock'n'roll, then in an uncertain state and dominated by clean-cut singers like Fabian and Frankie Avalon. It was not an auspicious time for someone who looked and sounded like Bob Dylan.

"I tried to make it in rock'n'roll when rock'n'roll was a piece of cream," he says. "Elvis had struck; Buddy Holly was dead; Little Richard was becoming a preacher, and Gene Vincent was leaving the country. I wrote the kind of stuff you write when you have no place to live and you're wrapped up in the fire pump. I nearly killed myself with pity and agony. I saw the way doors close; the way doors that do not like you close. A door that does not like you needs no one to close it. I had to retreat."

Retreat for Dylan was folk music and Greenwich Village. He was strong medicine for both—nervous, cocky, different from anyone else around.

Arthur Kretchmer, a young magazine editor, remembers meeting Dylan at a party: "There was this crazy, restless little kid sitting on the floor and coming on very strong about how he was going to play Holden Caulfield in a movie of *Catcher in the Rye,* and I thought, 'This kid is really terrible'; but the people whose party it was said, 'Don't let him put you off. He comes on a little strong, but he's very sensitive—writes poetry, goes to visit Woody Guthrie in the hospital,' and I figured right, another one. I forgot all about him until a couple of years later he was famous and I wasn't. You can't always be right about these things, I suppose." Both Kretchmer and his wife are now Dylan fans.

Says Robert Shelton, whose book about Dylan is to be published this winter, "He was so astonishing-looking, so Chaplinesque and cherubic, sitting up on a stool playing the guitar and the harmonica and playing with the audience, making all kinds of wry faces, wearing this Huck Finn hat, that I laughed out loud with pleasure. I called over Pat Clancy [an Irish folk singer, one of the Clancy Brothers] and he looked at this cherub and broke into a broad smile and said, 'Well, what have we here?' "

Not too long after that, Shelton wrote a laudatory review in the *Times* of a Dylan performance. About the same time, Columbia Records executive John Hammond met Dylan at the home of folk singer Carolyn Hester, whom Dylan was going to accompany on a new record Hammond was producing. Without hearing him perform, Hammond offered Dylan a two-year contract with Columbia, and immediately hit a snag.

Dylan, a minor of 20, refused to admit to having any living relatives who could sign for him. "I don't know where my folks are," he told Hammond. "I think I've got an uncle who's a gambler in Nevada, but I wouldn't know how to track him down." Taking another chance, Hammond finally let the boy execute the contract himself.

The young folk singer's first LP was called *Bob Dylan*. It cost $403 to produce and sold, initially, 4,200 copies. By way of comparison, Dylan's most recent record as of this writing, *Highway 61 Revisited*, has sold 360,000 in the United States. All together, it is estimated that 10 million Dylan records have been sold throughout the world. His songs have been recorded in more than 150 other versions by performers ranging from Stan Getz to Lawrence Welk, and the royalties, Dylan admits, have made him a millionaire.

In achieving this success, Dylan has had powerful allies. Not the least of these was Billy James, a young Columbia public-relations man who is now the record company's West Coast artist-relations director. It was through James's efforts that Dylan got his first taste of national publicity, but the singer's past was to come between them. In 1963, when Dylan was entering his first flush of fame with "Blowin' in the Wind," a song which became an unofficial anthem of the civil-rights movement and a major popular hit, *Newsweek* revealed that Bob Dylan was Robert Zimmerman and went on to suggest that not only was Dylan's name a fake but it was rumored another writer had created "Blowin' in the Wind." One part of the story was false—Dylan was the author of the song—but the other part, of course, was true: Bob Dylan was Robert Zimmerman.

Dylan was infuriated by the article and blamed Billy James for it. For two years the two did not speak. James won't talk about the incident at all, but people who know both of them say that Dylan attempted to get the public-relations man fired. Two years later, they met at a party and Dylan was all friendship again. When James mentioned the *Newsweek* affair, Dylan put an arm around him and said, "Thousands of people are dying in Vietnam and right at this minute a man is jumping off the Empire State Building and you got *that* running around in your head? Forget it!"

One of the great factors in Dylan's early success was his profound ability to articulate the emotions of the civil-rights revolution, which was developing its peak of power in the early '60's. Recognition of this talent came in dramatic form at the Newport Folk Festival of 1963.

Although he had already appeared once on the program, which is a sort of Hall of Fame of folk singing in action, he was called back to the stage at the end of the final concert. Accompanied by a stageful of folk stars, from Pete Seeger, the gentle "king" of folk music, to Joan Baez, the undisputed queen, Bob Dylan sang "Blowin' in the Wind" to an audience of 36,000 of the most important folk-singing fans, writers, recording executives and critics.

"How many roads must a man walk down before you call him a man?" they sang. "Yes, 'n' How many seas must a white dove sail before she sleeps in the sand? Yes, 'n' How many times must the cannon balls fly before they're forever banned? The answer, my friend, is blowin' in the wind, The answer is blowin' in the wind."

Recorded by Peter, Paul and Mary, "Blowin' in the Wind" was Dylan's first major hit, and very quickly there were 58 different versions of the song, by everyone from The Staple Singers (a screaming gospel version) to Marlene Dietrich. Almost overnight Dylan was established at the top of the folk-music field. Here at last, sighed the folk critics and the civil-rights people, was a songwriter with the true "proletarian" touch, one who could really reach the masses. For two years, Dylan was the musical spokesman for civil-rights, turning up in Mississippi, in the march on Washington, at the demonstrations and rallies.

"I feel it," said Joan Baez, whom Dylan had met before Newport, "but Dylan can say it. He's phenomenal."

For a while, Joan and Bobby were to be inseparable, the queen and crown prince of folk music. When Dylan went to England for a concert tour, Joan Baez went with him. As much as anyone's, it was her voice and authority which helped to create the charismatic reputation of Bob Dylan the folk singer.

These days Dylan and Baez are not as close as they used to be. When the rough cut of the film of his English tour was screened in Hollywood this spring, Baez was everywhere on the film, in the limousine, at the airport, singing in the hotel room. After the screening, Dylan said to the film editor, "We'll have to take all that stuff of Joan out." He hesitated and then added, "Well, it looks as if she was the whole thing. She was only there a few days. We'll have to cut it down."

Far more important to Dylan, however, was Albert Grossman, who took over Dylan's career and, to a great extent, his life. He is not only Dylan's manager, but also his confidant, healer and friend. Until recently, in fact, Dylan had no home of his own. He lived in Grossman's New York City apartment or the manager's antique-filled country home in Woodstock, N. Y.

He appears to be only vaguely aware of the extent or nature of his wealth, leaving the details to Grossman. "When I want money," Dylan says, "I ask for it. After I spend it, I ask for more."

Dylan has had his effect on Grossman, too, however. "I used to remember Albert as a nice-looking businessman, the kind of middle-aged man you would meet in a decent restaurant in the garment center," says one acquaintance. "Then, a while after he signed Dylan, I met him again. I couldn't believe it. I just couldn't believe what had happened to him. He had long gray hair like Benjamin Franklin and wire-rimmed spectacles, and he was wearing an old sweatshirt or something and Army pants. 'Albert,' I screamed, when I finally recognized him. 'Albert, what has Bobby done to you?' "

A measure of Dylan's relationship with his manager is found in the tone and style he uses in talking to Grossman. Even in the most ordinary conversation, Dylan can be almost impossible to understand. He is often vague, poetic, repetitive, confusing. But his flow of imagery can be startlingly precise and original, and the line of his thought brilliantly adventurous, funny and penetrating. So, in describing his music he will say, "It's all math, simple math, involved in mathematics. There's a definite number of Colt .45's that make up Marlene Dietrich, and you can find that out if you want to."

This kind of talk is not useful for more than a few situations. Nonetheless, it is the way Dylan speaks to fans, disk jockeys, reporters, acquaintances and, frequently, friends. It is not the way he speaks to Grossman. Then his voice often goes into a kind of piping whine, the voice of a little boy complaining to his father.

Thus, after a concert on the West Coast, at three o'clock in the morning, Dylan was told by a visitor that his voice was not heard over the blast of the electronically amplified rock'n'roll instruments. Grossman lay dozing on the hotel bed, his tinted glasses still on, a slight smile of repose on his heavy face.

"Al-*bert*," Dylan cried, "Albert, did you hear that? They couldn't hear me. Al-*bert*, I mean they couldn't *hear* me. What good is it if they can't hear me? We've got to get that sound man out here to fix it. What do you think, Albert?"

Grossman stirred on the bed and answered soothingly, "I told you in the car that the volume was too high. Just cut the volume by about a third and it'll be all right." Grossman went back to sleep, very much like an occidental Buddha, snoring lightly. Dylan was satisfied.

Grossman's formidable managerial talent is displayed most clearly when Dylan is on concert tour. From Grossman's New York office, the logistics of moving the singer and his crew from concert to concert halfway around the world are worked out with an efficiency that makes the whole operation seem effortless.

On the road the Dylan entourage usually consists of Dylan, his road manager, a pilot and co-pilot for the 13-seat two-engine Lodestar in which the group travels over the shorter distances (tourist-class commercial jets are used for overseas and transcontinental travel), two truck drivers who deliver the sound equipment and musicians' instruments from stop to stop, a sound man and five musicians—two guitarists, a drummer, pianist and organist. Grossman flies out from time to time to hear a concert or two and then returns to New York. On foreign tours he usually stays with the group throughout the trip.

Dylan's people are protective and highly attentive to his wants, and Dylan himself, given his status as a star, is neither especially demanding nor temperamental, even when things don't quite go according to schedule.

Last spring, for example, a concert in Vancouver was an acoustical disaster. The arena still smelled strongly of its last guests—a stock exhibition. It was perfectly round, with a flat dome that produced seven echoes from a sharp handclap in the center, and large open gates which let sound leak out of the hall as easily as if the concert were held in the open air. Although Dylan's $30,000 custom-designed sound system filled eight large crates with equipment, it could never fill this gigantic echo chamber with clear sound. To add to the problem, one of the small monitor speakers, placed on stage to enable the musicians to hear themselves play, was not working.

Dylan's concerts are divided into two halves. During the first, in which he played his acoustic guitar into a stage microphone, the sound was patchy; in some spots it was perfect, in others it was very bad. In the second half, however, in which rock'n'roll songs were played on the amplified instruments and electric guitars, the music was a garble of reverberation, and Dylan's voice was totally scrambled by the echo. The sound man sweated and twirled his knobs, but it was no use. At one point Grossman ran up to the stage to tell Dylan to stop "eating the mike," getting too close to the microphone and contributing to the electric jumble. The musicians, deprived of the monitor, watched each other tensely as they tried to keep their beat by observation rather than sound.

"Man, that was just terrible," Dylan said when he came offstage and hurried into the waiting car. "That was just awful. I mean that was worse than Ottawa, and Ottawa was the worst hole in the universe." He turned to each person in the car and asked them separately, "Wasn't that worse than Ottawa, and wasn't Ottawa the worst hole in the universe?" Everyone agreed that it was worse than Ottawa.

"That was really worse than Ottawa, and Ottawa was the worst, terrible, miserable hole in the entire universe," Dylan repeated, with a certain satisfaction. "Worse than Ottawa," he mused, and then laughing, turned around and said, "and anyone who doesn't think it was worse than Ottawa can get out of the car right now."

Later he and Grossman discussed the problem again, and it

was agreed that the fault lay in the arena, not in the equipment. In a better hall or a theater there would have been no trouble. Dylan's concern now was with the halls in which he was booked in Australia.

"Albert, it's no good in those arenas," he said. "I just would rather forget arenas and play theaters. To hell with the money, I mean I would much rather have a good show. Are we going to play any arenas in Australia?"

"We have to," Grossman answered, after quickly going through the Australia situation with Dylan. "We haven't enough big concert halls or theaters there. It's not America. The country is still undeveloped."

"Well, all right," said Dylan. "I mean if we have to, but I wish we could just play theaters and halls. I mean that place was worse than Ottawa and—" "Ottawa was the worst hole in the universe," someone chimed in.

"Yeah. The worst in the universe. And this was worse."

At no time, perhaps, was Dylan's closeness with Grossman more important than in 1965, the year Dylan turned from folk music to rock'n'roll. He had by this time cut three more albums, two of them, *The Times They Are A-Changin'* and *The Freewheelin' Bob Dylan,* outstandingly successful, not only in sales but in acclaim from the critics and the civil-rights activists. But he came back from a stunningly successful English tour with a feeling of *malaise* and a desire for change.

"After I finished the English tour," he says, "I quit because it was too easy. There was nothing happening for me. Every concert was the same: first half, second half, two encores and run out, then having to take care of myself all night.

"I didn't understand; I'd get standing ovations, and it didn't mean anything. The first time I felt no shame. But then I was just following myself after that. It was down to a pattern."

In his next album, *Bringing It All Back Home,* Dylan broke the pattern. Instead of playing either conventional "protest" as it was understood then, or using the traditional folk-music modes, he electrically amplified his guitar and set surrealistic verses to the rock'n'roll beat.

Ironically, it was one of the album's few nonrock songs that brought Dylan his first great success in the pop market. "Mr. Tambourine Man," recorded by The Byrds in a hard-rock version complete with falsetto, was a massive hit.

"When 'Mr. Tambourine Man' broke, we didn't know anything about Bob Dylan," says "Cousin Brucie" Morrow, a disk jockey on WABC Radio, New York. "Oh, I remember a few years ago we'd listened to a single of his. It didn't seem to fit the sound then, so we didn't play it. That was all I knew about Bob Dylan until The Byrds hit with "Mr. Tambourine Man." Then everyone was asking, 'Who's this Bob Dylan?' It's the only time I can remember when a composer got more attention for a hit than the performers did."

Then when Dylan released his new single, "Like a Rolling Stone," and his new album, *Highway 61 Revisited,* the folk fans knew Bobby was going to be a teen-age idol, and if he was a teen-age idol he wasn't theirs anymore. For people who had thought they owned Bob Dylan it was a bitter disappointment, and Dylan lost a great many people he thought were his friends. "A freak and a parody," shrieked Irwin Silber in the folk music magazine *Sing Out!* At the Newport Folk Festival of 1965, Dylan was booed off the stage. At his Forest Hills concert in September, the audience listened attentively through the first, folk, half of the program and then began to boo when the musicians came out for the rock'n'roll portion. This time Dylan did not walk off the stage as he did at Newport, but fought his way through the performance, supported by 80 percent of the crowd.

"Like a Rolling Stone" finally put Dylan across as a rock'n'-roll star. He wrote it in its first form when he came back from England. "It was ten pages long," he says. "It wasn't called anything, just a rhythm thing on paper all about my steady hatred directed at some point that was honest. In the end it wasn't hatred, it was telling someone something they didn't know, telling them they were lucky. Revenge, that's a better word.

"I had never thought of it as a song, until one day I was at the piano, and on the paper it was singing, 'How does it feel?' in a slow motion pace, in the utmost of slow motion following something.

"It was like swimming in lava. In your eyesight, you see your victim swimming in lava. Hanging by their arms from a birch tree. Skipping, kicking the tree, hitting a nail with your foot. Seeing someone in the pain they were bound to meet up with.

"I wrote it. I didn't fail. It was straight." "Like a Rolling Stone" climbed rapidly to the top of the charts. It was followed by "Positively 4th Street" and then by "Ballad of a Thin Man," and Dylan's lead was soon followed by other songwriters released from the inane bondage of the "I Love You, Teen Queen" straitjacket. Soon the airwaves were full of songs about the war in Vietnam, or civil-rights, or the general disorder of the world and society in America. It was quickly labeled "folk-rock," and the kids wolfed it down and are listening to it.

Along with the teen-agers, Dylan got a surprising bonus audience—the adult hip intellectuals who had just found out about rock'n'roll. National magazines began writing favorably about Dylan and rock'n'roll, and rock concerts became the social events of the intellectuals' seasons. Allen Ginsberg said, "He writes better poetry than I did at his age . . . I'd say he's a space-age genius minstrel more than an old library poet . . ." One Sunday, the magazine sections of *The New York Times* and *The New York Herald Tribune* simultaneusly published long articles on the poetry of Bob Dylan, complete with learned analyses and exegeses off the most fashionable academic-journalistic-sociological kind.

Dylan's reaction is predictably thorny. "The songs are not meant to be great," he said. "I'm not meant to be great. I don't think anything I touch is destined for greatness. Genius is a terrible word, a word they think will make me like them. A genius is a very insulting thing to say. Even Einstein wasn't a genius. He was a foreign mathematician who would have stolen cars."

Some of his recent songs have brought him new criticism: it has been claimed that the lyrics of "Mr. Tambourine Man" and his latest hit, "Rainy Day Women #12 and 35" ("Everybody *must* get stoned!"), are all about drugs and drug experiences. Grossman denies it. Dylan won't talk about his songs. "Don't interrupt me," he says. Talking about drugs, he is typically elusive.

"People just don't need drugs," he says. "Keep things out of your body. We all take medicine, as long as you know why you're taking it. If you want to crack down on the drug situation, the criminal drug situation takes place in suburban housewives' kitchens, the ones who get wiped out on alcohol every afternoon and then make supper. You can't blame them and you can't blame their husbands. They've been working in the mines all day. It's understandable."

During the past year Dylan has got married, fathered a son, Jesse Byron Dylan, and bought a townhouse in Manhattan's fashionable East 30's. Typically, he has attempted to keep all of this a secret. When his wife, a beautiful, black-haired girl named Sara Lownds, visited him in Vancouver and attended his concert, Dylan was faced with a problem: two disk jockeys were coming up to the dressing room to interview him; how was he to hide his wife from them? "Sara," said Dylan, opening a large closet, "when they arrive I want you to get in here." His wife looked at him quizzically but stepped reluctantly toward the open door. Dylan began to laugh, but it is a mark of the seriousness of his desire for privacy that his wife was ready to get into the closet.

The only thing anyone now will predict for certain is that Dylan will change. "I'll never decay," he says. "Decay is when something has stopped living but hasn't died yet, looking at your leg and seeing it all covered with creeping brown cancer. Decay turns me off. I'll die first before I decay."

The Austin Interview

REPORTER: What do you consider yourself? How would you classify yourself?

BOB DYLAN: Well, I like to think of myself in terms of a trapeze artist.

REPORTER: Speaking of trapeze artists, I've noticed in some of your recent albums a carnival-type sound. Could you tell me a little about that?

BOB DYLAN: That isn't a carnival sound, that's religious. That's very real, you can see that anywhere.

REPORTER: What about this "Ballad of the Thin Man"? This sounds as though it might have been dedicated to a newspaper reporter or something.

BOB DYLAN: No, it's just about a fella that came into a truck-stop once.

REPORTER: Have the Beatles had any influence on your work?

BOB DYLAN: Well, they haven't influenced the songs or sound. I don't know what other kind of influence they might have. They haven't influenced the songs or the sound.

REPORTER: In an article in *The New Yorker*, written by Nat Hentoff, I believe, you said you sang what you felt and you sang to make yourself feel good, more or less. And it was implied that in your first two albums you sang "finger-pointing songs," I believe.

BOB DYLAN: Well, what he was saying was, I mean, I wasn't playing then and it was still sort of a small nucleus at that time and by the definition of why do you sing, I sing for the people.

Interview in Austin, Texas, 1965.

He was saying, "Why do you sing?" and I couldn't think of an answer except that I felt like singing, that's about all.

REPORTER: Why is it different?

BOB DYLAN: Come on, come on.

REPORTER: What is your attitude toward your "finger-pointing" songs? He implied that you thought they were just superficial.

BOB DYLAN: No, it's not superficial, it's just motivated. Motivated. Uncontrollable motivation. Which anyone can do, once they get uncontrollably motivated.

REPORTER: You said before that you sang because you had to. Why do you sing now?

BOB DYLAN: Because I have to.

REPORTER: Your voice in here is soft and gentle. Yet in some of your records, there's a harsh twang.

BOB DYLAN: I just got up.

REPORTER: Could you give me some sort of evaluation as far as your own taste is concerned, comparing some of the things you did, like old music, say, "Girl from the North Country," which I consider a very beautiful-type ballad? Perhaps some of the things that have come out in the last couple of albums—do you get the same satisfaction out of doing this?

BOB DYLAN: Yeah, I do. I wish I could write like "Girl from the North Country." You know, I can't write like that any more.

REPORTER: Why is that?

BOB DYLAN: I don't know.

REPORTER: Are you trying to accomplish anything?

BOB DYLAN: Am I trying to accomplish anything?

REPORTER: Are you trying to change the world or anything?

BOB DYLAN: Am I trying to change the world? Is that your question?

REPORTER: Well, do you have any idealism or anything?

BOB DYLAN: Am I trying to change the idealism of the world? Is that it?

REPORTER: Well, are you trying to push over idealism to the people?

BOB DYLAN: Well, what do you think my ideas are?

REPORTER: Well, I don't exactly know. But are you singing just to be singing?

BOB DYLAN: No, I'm not just singing to be singing. There's a much deeper reason for it than that.

REPORTER: In a lot of the songs you sing you seem to express a pessimistic attitude toward life. It seems that "Hollis Brown" gives me that feeling. Is this your true feeling or are you just trying to shock people?

BOB DYLAN: That's not pessimistic form, that's just statement. You know. It's not pessimistic.

REPORTER: Who are your favorite performers? I don't mean folk, I mean general.

BOB DYLAN: Rasputin . . . Hmmm . . . Charles de Gaulle . . . the Staple Singers. I sort of have a general attitude about that. I like just about everybody everybody else likes.

REPORTER: You said just a minute ago you were preparing to go to classical music. Could you tell me a little about that?

BOB DYLAN: Well, I was going to be in the classical music field and I imagine it's going right along. I'll get there one of these records.

REPORTER: Are you using the word classical perhaps a little differently than we?

BOB DYLAN: A little bit, maybe. Just a hair.

REPORTER: Could you explain that?

BOB DYLAN: Well, I'm using it in the general sense of the word, thumbing a hair out.

REPORTER: Any attention to form?

BOB DYLAN: Form and matter. Mathematics.

REPORTER: What is your belief in a God? Are you a Christian?

BOB DYLAN: Well, first of all, God is a woman, we all know that. Well, you take it from there.

Dylan: A Few Years Older Than Israel

by John Gordon

In our time, defensive freakery, as exemplified by the put-on, has been developed most fully in the double-edged mordancies of homosexual humor. The archetypal homosexual joke (and by the *way,* dear, doesn't that *woman* on the cover of *Bringing It All Back Home* look *aw*fully like *you* know *who?*) is the drag queen—the man dressed as a woman who goes waltzing through the straights, provoking stony shock or nervous giggles—classically the two responses, both unsatisfactory, open to the victim of a successful put-on. Shakespeare plays around with this joke a lot in his comedies, not because he was necessarily gay, but because he knew a right dramatic image when he saw one. A drag queen, by turning himself into a mask of self-mockery, has in effect pre-empted our defensive ridicule, and thus undermined our comfortable superiority; he is saying: any name you want to call me I acknowledge, I'm living it out much more fully than you, my dear, with your crude insults, can understand; so what? Secondly, he is imitating a woman, and the straight's identity depends on a fairly idealized conception of woman. So he is saying: If I'm weird and disgusting when I *imitate* them, what are you, you asshole, when you spend your life *chasing after* them? Finally, most subversively of all, he is implying by his presence a world of shifting mirrors and masks where even something as primal as sexuality is not necessarily all that primal—not one of those bed-talk myths about fecundating the race or discovering your lost other half or plugging into the pith of the universe (read Norman Mailer for the other

Reprinted in excerpt with permission from *Fusion,* June 25, 1971.

metaphors) but maybe just kick-wicked fun, dressing up like dolls, diddling one another's thingy-wingies, a sport long ago unmoored from the rolling rounds of the Big Picture. Ribbons, and games, and masks and masks, and nothing behind them but more masks. And that, my dear, can't be; things fall apart, the center cannot hold—why the very fiber of *Amurr*icanism is weakened by such in-*sinn*-ua-*a*-shuns. Parlous, parlous. So the straight world is always at work re-etching the demarcations of its reality, just as the freak world, drawing on the lessons of its fancy-pants uncle, the gay world, is at work erasing them. Ridicule is a powerful weapon for both sides, but especially for the straights, if only in underscoring the reality of their standards for them; for the last ten years the all-time-popular straight witticism has been some variation on "Jeez. You can't tell if it's a boy or a girl anymore." But the artful high-power put-on, like the drag queen, effectively deadens that ridicule, and the superiority it gives, and all the latitudes and longitudes of convention it reaffirms. Which is why your mother probably stopped liking Bob Dylan round about *Bringing It All Back Home,* when he ceased being a recognizable variation on her own conventionally rebellious spawn ("Oh yes, our little Donald, he's part of the younger generation, you know."). (I couldn't care less about it incidentally, but none of the above should be taken as in any way speculative about Dylan's sex-life—saying he's a fag or anything like that, which would really be dumb, just as dumb as saying that anyone into rock or that kind of thing was a fag—Dylan for playing it, or me for writing about him, or you for reading about him.) (Though frankly I have my doubts about *you.*)

All this has the double-edged advantage of permitting privacy —and hence the possibility of personal development—within the constrictions of a public identity. It is the particular favorite, ironically, not of much mysterioso types with dark-stained pasts (who invariably opt for respectability), but rather of people like Dylan and the lumpen-bourgeois children he appeals to, coming from dull, blandly TV dinner childhoods and hankering after something realer. Of all the poses of his life, says Norman Mailer, there is only one which he utterly can't bear—"that of a nice Jewish boy from Brooklyn." Substitute Hibbing: both

Mailer and Dylan are nice Jewish boys who have grown up into virtuosos in the public manipulation of self. All of which probably sounds like a put-down, but it isn't; Dylan has simply been meeting head-on the problem that all of us face in an increasingly homogenized, riskless America. With a Howard Johnson's, now, at every interstate turn-off, it takes some searching to find out the highways that are still for gamblers. . . .

Is Bob Dylan the Greatest Poet in the United States Today?

Sandra Hochman: "I think it's wonderful that poets are becoming bards again. Since all poetry has to do with song—he is making a real contribution to our idea of what poetry can be."

John Ciardi: "My nephew (a drummer and an engaging kid who is only as mad as he has to be) would agree that Bob Dylan is a poet, but like all Bob Dylan fans I have met, he knows nothing about poetry. Neither does Bob Dylan."

John Clellon Holmes: ". . . He has the authentic mark of the bard on him, and I think it's safe to say that no one, years hence, will be able to understand just what it was like to live in this time without attending to what this astonishingly gifted young man has already achieved."

Howard Nemerov: "Mr. Dylan is not known to me. Regrets."

Hart Leavitt, teacher, Phillips Academy: "His poetry sounds like a very self-conscious imitation of Kerouac, and for an English teacher this is pretty feeble praise. My students' reaction was clear and forceful. They have lost respect for Dylan, for they think he is after publicity and the nearest buck."

English Professor, University of Vermont: "Anyone who calls Dylan 'the greatest poet in the United States today' has rocks in his head. That is such an irresponsible statement as to deserve no attention. Since his appeal (apparently) is to irresponsible teen-agers, I can't take him seriously. Dylan is for the birds—and the bird-brained."

A Princeton teen-ager: "It's the words. Either you understand him or you don't. I can't explain why he's so great, but he knows what it's *about*."

Bob Dylan Approximately

by Paul Nelson

Dylan's is a talent that evokes such a strong degree of personal participation from both his followers and detractors that he cannot be permitted so much as a random action. As a folk musician and topical songwriter, his influence on both fields was so powerful that he almost literally "exploded" them into mutations of their former selves when he progressed past them into his own highly personal, entirely subjective music. By not choosing to remain within the rigid objectivity of the former and the formalized socio-political stance of the latter, Dylan, with the glorious coming of age of his "New Music" in the album, *Highway 61 Revisited,* inadvertently and without malice rendered obsolete forever most of the urban folk song interpreters and drove the final nail into the coffin of the socially-minded, cliché-ridden topical songwriter. Suddenly, a whole new space opened up, and not much was left standing between the traditional rural folk musician and the New Music. . . .

And now we have *Blonde on Blonde,* a collection of fourteen new songs. The very title suggests the singularity and the duality we expect from Dylan. For Dylan's music of illusion and delusion—with the tramp as explorer and the clown as happy victim, where the greatest crimes are lifelessness and the inability to see oneself as a circus performer in the show of life—has always carried within it its own inherent tensions; optimism and pessimism merge and submerge amid fragmented icebergs of reality, yet both terms become finally meaningless because

Excerpted from the introduction to the songbook of *Blonde on Blonde,* 1966.

Dylan in the end truly UNDERSTANDS situations, and once one truly understands anything, then there can no longer be mere anger, no longer be moralizing, but only humor and compassion, only pity. And, ultimately, only a kind of shifting contradiction, a duality of emotion, a blonde on blonde, where all relationships can remain one, or become two, or fluctuate from between one and two.

The apparent complexity of Dylan's art should never be confused with an inability to communicate. In Dylan's verse form, the overall "theme" comes through a total picture, an entire feeling, not unlike abstraction, rather than from any particular lines which spell out a too-easily-understood message. Dylan's modern-day fables, little hip stories that both make sense and don't make sense, are in effect dabs of color on a larger canvas: cumulative, in-depth portraits of people, emotions, and events. In a Dylan song, physical objects are really no longer physical objects as such but become intellectual properties; the whole world is flattened into a plasticity that is cerebral, not physical, and we are free to float with the images in all their kinetic brilliance.

It is hard to claim too much for the man who in every sense revolutionized modern poetry, American folk music, popular music, and the whole of modern-day thought; even the strongest praise seems finally inadequate. Not many contemporary artists have the power to actually change our lives, but surely Dylan does—and has.

The Children's Crusade

by Ralph J. Gleason

One man with a dream at pleasure,
Shall go forth and conquer a crown;
And three with a new songs measure
Can trample an empire down
—Arthur O'Shaughnessy

The most serious assault on the structure of The Great Society and its predecessor, the New Frontier, comes not from the armed might of a foreign power but from a frail, slender, elusive lad, whose weapons are words and music, a burning imagination and an apocalyptic vision of the world.

His name is Bob Dylan and he sings his poetry ("I write in chains of flashing images" he once said *) on phonograph records and in concert halls and the youth of The New Frontier and The Great Society listen.

Surveys IBM-ed for super-efficiency tell us that almost 50% of the population is under 25 right now and that by 1970 the majority will be teen-agers. Certainly by 1970 the majority will have to be exposed to Bob Dylan's songs and poems, for he is the most successful songwriter of his generation (according to a publishing company representative, Dylan's song royalties for the first half of 1965 were greater than the combined royalties of such celebrated Tin Pan Alley toilers as Cole Porter, George Gershwin and Oscar Hammerstein!). Hundreds of recordings of his songs by dozens of artists flood the market. His own performances on record include 7 albums for Columbia, three of

Reprinted with permission from *Ramparts,* 1966.
* To me, December, 1965.

which are among the top selling Long Playing albums for the last half of 1965; and in addition he has had several single recordings of his own which have become hits.

Bob Dylan is a major voice in the entertainment world, greater than Sinatra in his prime and far greater than any other in his own generation.

But Dylan's voice is unique, not alone in how it sounds (though it has grown fuller in recent years and acquired resonance, it is still far from the usual standard of good voice even in unorthodox popular song) but for what it is that he is saying.

With hit recordings blaring forth from every radio, with his songs being sung by individual vocalists and played by rock 'n' roll groups everywhere, Dylan is telling the American audience (and through that audience telling the world) that it is better to make love than to make war, that the only loyalty is to oneself ("it is not he or she or them or it that you belong to") that politics are irrelevant ("you say nothin's perfect and i tell you again there are no politics") that the leadership cult of the Great Society is a fraud ("don't follow leaders, watch the parkin' meters") that the old fashioned virtues of hard work and thrift and a clean tongue are obsolete ("money doesn't talk it swears; obscenity who really cares").

He is saying, in short, that the entire system of Western society, built upon Aristotelian logic, and upon a series of economic systems from Hobbes to Marx, does not work.

And mirable dictu *what* he is saying, is getting an unbelievably intense reaction from a generation thirsting for answers other than those in the college text books.

"I have learned more from Bob Dylan than from all my classes," a teen-age high school student wrote to me after a Dylan concert. "It has made my teachers angry, but I know I am a better human being for reading Bob Dylan. I would rather write poetry now than study science," he added. "I do not know if he is the voice of my generation, I only know that he is mine," a college junior co-ed said.

Lawrence Ferlinghetti, poet, playright and publisher of the City Lights Pocket Poets Series, calls Dylan "the poet of the sixties." And like those other figures alien to the college classroom, Joseph Heller, author of *Catch-22* and C. Wright Mills, author of *The Power Elite,* Dylan is studied by the students themselves who are gradually forcing him upon the faculty.

In junior high schools all over the country in the study of contemporary poetry, students are copying down lyrics of Dylan songs from records and insisting that the class study them. A Jesuit high school in Sacramento devoted most of an English class one semester last year to the study of Dylan as poetry and the University of California, among numerous other colleges and universities, has seen students get together themselves to hold unofficial seminars on his poems. One professor, in a creative writing class, even assigned his students to attend the concert.

Dylan's attack on Western society has been attacked in turn by critics, poets and spokesmen for the Cultural Establishment. Louis Simpson, himself a prize winning poet, has said, "I don't think Bob Dylan is a poet at all; he is an entertainer—the word poet is used these days to describe practically anybody. I am not surprised, though, that American college students consider him their favorite poet, they don't know anything about poetry." Rather an ironic statement, coming from a poet who spent this college year teaching poetry to college students.

But regardless of Louis Simpson's reaction—or that of other Establishment poets, and one wag has predicted that by the time the literary magazines get around to analyzing and criticizing Dylan he'll have moved on into some other art form, like film —Dylan has already made the kind of impression upon this generation that any poet in history would have been proud to make. *His* words, not those of Pulitzer Prize winners, are quoted by students, written by them on walls and made into slogans and pasted on notebooks to demonstrate that fervor of their belief.

Louis Simpson's quote is from a *New York Times Magazine* story on Dylan in which several poets echoed Louis Simpson's dissent. "They asked the wrong poets," says Lawrence Ferlinghetti who, along with Allen Ginsberg, quite obviously considers Dylan a poet. Ferlinghetti, and critic and poet Kenneth Rexroth, have long espoused the idea of getting poetry out of the classroom and into the streets, of making the poet once again speak to the common man, of making poetry a part of the lives of the people. "It is very important to get poetry out of the hands of the squares," Rexroth once said.

And it is evident, prima facie, that Dylan has done just this, he has gotten to the youth and they are no squares. He is the first poet of that all-American artifact, the juke box, the first American poet to touch everyone, to hit all walks of life in this great sprawling society. The first poet of mass media, if you will. "I am a 38 year old housewife, mother of three teen agers, and I love the Dylan songs," reads a typical letter. And at the Bob Dylan concert in the Community Theater in Berkeley, Calif., in the fall of 1965, the first rows contained several Hells Angels, a couple of university professors, Allen Ginsberg, Lawrence Ferlinghetti, novelist Ken Kesey (*One Flew Over the Cuckoo's Nest*) and numerous artists, writers and other lesser known poets and professors.

Is Dylan a poet? The only dissent comes from those who are not moved by him. But even his advocates do not think of him as the poet sublime, at least not completely. Allen Ginsberg says Dylan is still hung up having to rhyme words and Ferlinghetti wonders if Dylan would be effective as a poet without the guitar.

But what is poetry, anyway? Malvina Reynolds, author of "Little Boxes," itself a sharp thrust at contemporary values, points out that Dylan has broken the laws of the language to make poetry "just as happened in Elizabethan England" and she feels that Dylan's merger of popular song and poetry is the first time it has come about successfully since Shakespeare's day.

"I think I understand part of why Dylan is so haunting and why he is a great poet," writes Donna Mickleson, herself a poet. "He reaches you from inside yourself . . . (Dylan) brings you to the granite outcroppings and maiden-hair ravines of your night world, shining on it a light which is sometimes a trembling candle, sometimes a torch, sometimes a naked blue neon tube—but always he makes you reach beyond the light to the wrist that holds it. And while you hold it, you tremble with him. That is why it is so painful and beautiful, too . . ." And for a definition of poetry by a poet, Auden wrote one in his "In Memory of W. B. Yeats":

For poetry makes nothing happen: it survives
In the Valley of its saying where executives
Would never want to tamper; it flows south
From ranches of isolation and the busy griefs,
Raw towns that we believe and die in; it survives,
A way of happening, a mouth.

Dylan stoutly refuses to answer questions about what he means in his songs. He says they are written to nobody in particular. "Don't put me down as a man with a message" he told a British reporter, "all I can hope to do is to sing what I'm thinking."

But then in response to the direct question whether or not his songs are about real people, and to the implication that they have subtle or symbolic meanings, Dylan says, "It's all very clear and simple to me. These songs aren't complicated to me at all. I know what I'm . . . what they're all about. There's nothing hard to figure out for me. I wouldn't write anything I can't really see. They're all about real people. I'm sure you've seen all the people in my songs—at one time or another."

Dylan thinks of songs—all songs, his own included—as pictures. He's said that numerous times in one way or another and this, coupled with his remark about writing in "chains of flashing images" is a clue to the technique he uses.

Dylan's world is a nightmare world—except for his songs of wry romance and even some of them have touches of it. The world is like a dream. "If my thought dreams could be seen, they'd probably put my head in a guillotine" he wrote. In his world are all sorts of carnival freak show figures, "Einstein disguised as Robin Hood . . . with his friend a jealous monk"; "the motorcycle black madonna two wheel gypsy queen," "Sweet Melinda, the peasants call her the goddess of doom," "Dr. Filth . . . his nurse, some local loser, she's in charge of the cyanide hole," "Mack the Finger," etc. Recurring figures in the Dylan poetry include the monk, the hunchback, the sideshow geek and clown and Napoleon. It's a gaudy, depressing, grotesquerie rivalled only by the inmates of "The Circus of Dr. Lao" or the images of Rimbaud's "Season in Hell."

For Dylan sees the world around him—and this is I suspect the core of his attraction for the young—as a world run by a vast machine and by men who are heartless men and part of that machine. He looks at this scene surrealistically, linking together his mosaics of images like a ceiling by El Greco. He sings of alienation, of the emptiness of the adult society; he is the clown, the Napoleon in rags, a Don Quixote of today riding across a neon-lighted jungle, across the moon country, past lines of empty drive-in movies showing vista-vision pictures of what's happening. The vision is apocalyptical, the images glowing, and he is articulating the realignment of priorities first heralded by the wordless revolt of the jazzmen's horns. There's something in Dylan for everybody. "You who philosophize disgrace" he screams at the law-makers in "The Lonesome Death of Hattie Carroll" (a song about the fatal beating given a Negro servant by a Maryland farmer). He sneers at the groves of academe, "the old folks' home in the college," at religion, "utopian hermit monks," Madison avenue, "grey flannel dwarfs" and "propaganda all is phony"; the war machine "With God on Our Side" and hard work "I ain't gonna work on Maggie's farm no more . . . 'sing while you slave' and I just get bored."

The new generation is a lonely one ("it's always silent where I am," Dylan said at a press conference and at another time wrote "there is no love except in silence and silence doesn't say a word") born in the shadow of the Bomb and straining to make sense out of a life governed, stratified and resting upon assumptions of another age. Dylan dramatizes this—the growing realization of the surrealism of our real world has produced the novelist-turned-reporter like Ken Kesey and Joseph Heller and James Baldwin and the reporter-turned-poet like I. F. Stone. It has also produced Dylan.

At the end of "Desolation Row," an eleven minute song on his Columbia album *Highway 61 Revisited* (Columbia CL 2389), after running through a congeries of bizarre images some of which have previously been mentioned and which include the Titanic sailing with T. S. Eliot and Ezra Pound "fighting in the captain's tower while calypso singers laugh at them and fishermen hold flowers," Dylan answers a question concerning several people, possibly those included in the song—"all those people that you mention, yes I know them, they're quite lame. I had to rearrange their faces and give them all another name."

Dylan's open use of personal references in his songs has given rise to a whole mythology of in-group stories, interpretations and meanings rivalling the interpretation of the Shakespeare sonnets. Dylan's bitter-sweet love songs, at least they are songs about women or written to women, include "It's All Over Now Baby Blue," "Don't Think Twice," "It Ain't Me Babe," "If You Gotta Go, Go Now," and "All I Really Wanna Do, Is, Baby, Be Friends With You." They begin in a slightly acid-touched romantic mood, bitter-sweet and hipster-cool and then going on into the openly accusatory "Queen Jane Approximately," "Like a Rolling Stone" and "Positively 4th Street." Some of the songs, at least, are firmly believed by many to parallel his romance with Joan Baez, the queen of the world of folk song. But then again, one wonders, how many other episodes and how many other individuals might fit? Certainly the sentiments so eloquently expressed—the truth of beauty, the necessity of freedom, the belief in the sanctity of self—fit far more than an individual romance. They speak directly to the love-hopes of the young and they speak in a language the younger understand because it is a poeticization of their own, not one based on the classics or on the a priori assumptions that cleanliness is next to godliness, work hard, love your country and love will triumph over all.

"I had to rearrange their faces and give them all another name" can work in many ways. At least one student of the Dylan literature insists that Dylan never pauses at so easy a step as merely to give another name and change a face once; he gives the same person several names and changes the points of view around over and over, like a rubber ball bouncing down hill in a wind tunnel—the movement is one way continuously but there are many points of view.

Although even the early Dylan songs, such as "Masters of War" and the great "Blowin' in the Wind" ("I wrote a song with nine questions and a group made a hit of it and so I took each question and wrote another song with it") always dealt in the grand canvas of distortion, of Goya-esque images. And perhaps there's a clue to this in something he said at a press conference in Austin, Texas.

"What folk music is, it's not depression songs and these kind of things . . . its foundations aren't *work,* its foundations aren't 'slave away' and all this. Its foundations are—except for Negro songs which are based on that and just kinda overlapped—the main body of it (folk music) is just based on myth and the bible and plague and famine and all kinds of things like that which are just nuthin' but mystery and you can see it in all the songs. Roses growing right up out of people's hearts and naked cats in bed with y'know, spears growing right out of their backs and y'know seven years of this and eight years of that and it's all really something that nobody can really touch . . ."

The magnetism that Dylan possesses for those under thirty (and remember the remark by Jack Weinberg of the Free Speech Movement—"they have a saying, in the movement, 'you can't trust anyone over thirty' ") may very well be the fact that they, too, see the world as he sees it.

"Bob Dylan says the things I feel but don't know how to say" one college student wrote me. And when these young people find someone else describing the world around them as Dylan describes it (mystically, poetically, surrealistically) they say "Yes!" and "Amen!" and "Yes!" again.

Lenny Bruce has pointed out how television has made sophisticates out of nine year old girls. At a Dylan concert in San Francisco, a young teenie-bopper, as the folk musicians call the 12, 13 and 14-year-old kids, a long-haired girl in a flowing cape, was ordered out of the backstage area by one of Dylan's entourage, a lean, longhaired man in a velvet shirt, black slim jim trousers and high Beatle boots. "You got to get out of here" he told the young girl. "Why?" she asked with the courage of irreverence this generation so openly displays, "Who are you?"

"I'm a cop" the booted character told her and the girl, pointing to his black eight inch boots, sneered "Whaaaat? With those shoes?"

So the teen-agers, the youth, the young people everywhere, joining together in an unconscious league against The Older Types, in the manner described by Colin MacInnes in "Absolute Beginners" recognize in Dylan one of their own, a spokesman for their rejection of the adult world. "Lookout kid, it's something you did, god knows when but you're doin' it again!" That line is from Dylan's "Subterranean Homesick Blues," a song that was on every juke box in the country and broadcast from every Top 40 radio station and sold half a million copies. No one under parental authority (nor any authority in loco parentis) needs to intellectualize the empathy he feels for that line. Or for: "Them that must bow down to authority that they do not respect in any degree, who despise their jobs, their destiny, speak jealously of them that are free, cultivate what they get to be nothing more than something they invest in."

One fundamental result of the acceleration of life in this technological society is to have begot a generation that is a lot smarter than its predecessors and a lot smarter than we give it credit for. And lines like Dylan's hit home immediately to the New Youth who sees all around him, everywhere from high to low position, pretense, dishonesty, absurdity, contradiction, cupidity, in fact, all the biblical sins of sloth, arrogance and greed. Dylan describes a world in which naturalness is forbidden, creativity is the enemy and beauty is assassinated. Youth, struggling to keep from growing up absurd in a land of TV commercials and highrise rapacity, sees this world and sees, too, that we adult members accept it and then they hear Dylan describe it. And when he describes it, it is either in a voice reminiscent of the juke box or in words on paper in a language they understand. Youth knows intuitively, if not empirically, that this is a true state of the nation message.

Some of Dylan's attackers insist that he offers no hope, sees nothing *but* desolation row and has no joy. Not only in his songs but in his prose outside his songs, on the backs of his albums, in his Carnegie Hall concert programs, in letters to friends, to *Broadside* magazine and in other fugitive writings, Dylan sings in words like the bards.

"Take me disappearing through the smoke rings of my mind, down the foggy ruins of time, far past the frozen leaves, the haunted, sheltered trees, out to the windy beach, far from the twisted reach of crazy sorrow" Dylan wrote in "Mr. Tambourine Man," his song which was for a while at the top of the commercial juke box hit parade. If that isn't poetry, what is? And lines from his fugitive other writings ("Some Other Kinds of Songs" he called one piece on the back of an album) persistently return to memory:

for i am runnin in a fair race
with no racetrack but the nite
an no competition but the dawn.
or
for my road is blessed
with many flowers
an the sounds of flowers
or
for all people laugh
in the same tongue
and cry
in the same tongue
or
it's just one big world of songs
an they're all on loan
if they're only turned loose t sing
lonely? ah yes
but it is the flowers an the mirrors
of flowers that now meet my
loneliness
an mine shall be a strong loneliness
dissolvin' deep
t the depths of my freedom
an that, then, shall
remain my song.

"My song" Dylan has variously described. "I try to harmonize with song the lonesome sparrow sings" he wrote at one point and, later, "my songs're written with the kettledrum in mind/a touch of any anxious color. unmentionable. obvious. and people perhaps like a soft brazilian singer . . . i have given up at making any attempt at perfection. My poems are written in a rhythm of unpoetic distortion/divided by pierced ears. false eyelashes/ substracted by people constantly torturing each other. with a melodic purring line of descriptive hollowness—seen at times thru dark sunglasses and other forms of psychic explosion, a song is anything that can walk by itself/i am called a songwriter. a poem is a naked person . . . some people say i am a poet."

But everything he does reeks of the kind of desperate honesty that characterizes the other poets he admires such as Allen Ginsberg. "The songs are insanely honest," Dylan wrote a friend * about *Another Side of Bob Dylan* (Columbia CL 2193), "not meanin t twist any heads an written only for the reason that i myself me alone wanted and needed t write them. i've conceded the fact there is no understanding of anything. at best, just winks of the eye an that is all i'm lookin for now i guess."

Dylan has been the center of bitter controversy ever since he sprang upon the music world scene in 1960. At first the argument was over the simple questions of whether or not he was a good singer and/or a good writer. Time won both of those points for him. His highly successful recording career, which began with playing the harmonica on a Carolyn Hester record for Columbia which brought him to the attention of that company's executive John Hammond, widened the controversy.

Time and *Newsweek* attacked him for changing his name from Zimmerman (in a country where the change of name was commonplace in his parents' day and despite his own sung statement "my name it means nothing, my age it means less.") and denying his parents (he brought them from Minnesota to Carnegie Hall for his first solo concert at which he also read a long tribute to Woody Guthrie). His clothing and tousled hair were criticized openly and frequently; when he flew to Puerto Rico to sing for the Columbia Recording Company convention, he was at first denied access to the hotel he was registered in because of his appearance. He provoked controversy at the Emergency Civil Liberties Union Award dinner because his friends were denied access with him to the cocktail party and because, after saying how there was a touch of Lee Oswald in all of us, he left.

Newsweek even implied "Blowin' in the Wind" was actually the work of a New Jersey high school student, even though *Broadside*, the magazine which first published Dylan, had, months before, printed a letter from that student denying that his song and Dylan's shared anything but a common name.

At the Newport Folk Music Festival of 1964 he provoked a storm of criticism, which was continued by his New York con-

* RJG.

cert later that year, by abandoning his protest songs in favor of love songs; and bitter, slightly warped though they may be, they are songs about love.

Sing Out! the national folk song magazine ran letter after letter on the subject; so did *Broadside,* culminating in an outraged howl from country and western singer Johnny Cash ("Johnny Cash, he knows where it's at," Dylan said once*), who summed it all up in the statement, "Shut up and let him sing!"

But the criticism did not stop. Devout Dylan fans even were criticized for quoting him too much! Dylan himself was continually criticized for in-group references, in his lyrics, and for turning away from the political world of issues to turn inward, into his own problems. Irwin Silber, editor of *Sing Out!,* wrote a long, impassioned open letter on this subject which provoked a storm of replies defending Dylan.

Then in the summer of 1965, again at the Newport Folk Festival and again at a New York concert (but following the hit recordings of "Subterranean Homesick Blues" by Dylan and "Mr. Tambourine Man" by the Byrds), Dylan went onstage with a rock 'n' roll band using the hated electronic amplified guitar, bass and piano. The audience booed and *Sing Out!* wrote it up as Dylan symbolically rejecting Pete Seeger.

Dylan was a bit surprised. "I didn't know what was going to happen," he said, "but well, I did this very crazy thing [coming on with an electronic rock band]. They certainly booed. I can tell you that! You could hear it all over the place. I don't know who they were, though, and I'm certain whoever it was did it twice as loud as they normally would. They kind of quieted down at Forest Hills, although they did it there too. They've done it just about all over, except in Texas, Atlanta, Boston, Minneapolis, and Ohio. They've done it a lot of places. You can't tell where the booing's going to come up. Can't tell at all. It comes up in the weirdest, strangest places and they do it in blocks and when it comes it's quite a thing in itself. I mean they must be pretty rich to be able to go someplace and boo. I couldn't afford it if I was in their shoes."

* To RJG.

The booing—which apparently has tapered off now—indicates a very real concern with what Dylan stands for and with what he does on the part of his audience. They *demand* things from him but they are beginning to realize that he is, in truth, a poet and as such cannot be "owned."

But with the very same cynicism and scepticism that Dylan speaks to, some of his teen age audience is asking today, "Has Dylan sold out?"

He certainly has made a very great deal of money; he is perhaps a millionaire, *The New York Times* quotes Columbia records as saying that. His albums and single records have been on the top of the best selling charts. His concerts fill halls everywhere. During one tour of the Pacific Coast he did a box office gross totaling almost $90,000 for nine concerts.

Allen Ginsberg, replying to a questioner about Dylan's having sold out, put the answer bluntly: "Dylan has sold out to God. That is to say, his command was to spread his beauty as wide as possible. It was an artistic challenge to see if great art can be done on a juke box. And he proved it can."

Dylan himself has had things to say about the effect of his success upon himself and his work. "I have more money," he told a press conference in Austin. "I just have a lot more money, is all." And he doesn't care about the taxes. "I have no remorse. I don't care. Uncle Sam, he's my UNCLE, he's a member of the family! Can't turn your back on a member of the family!"

"I don't know how much I make. I have no idea and I don't want to ever find out. You see a lot of people start out and they plan to try to be stars. Like they have to be stars. I mean I know a lot of these people. And they start out and they go into show business for many, many reasons. To be seen, y'know. I started out and this had nothing to do with it. It just happened. I haven't really struggled for that. It happened. You know? It happened like anything else happens. Just a happening. You don't try to figure out happenings. You dig happenings. I really have no idea. That is the truth. I always tell the truth. That is the truth."

Dylan consistently denies having sold out to the commercial interests, just as he denies having any explanation of his popularity. When one questioner asked him if, in the event he did sell out to commercial interests, what interest would it be, Dylan's straight-faced reply was "ladies garments."

Dylan has a great deal to say about the charge that he has changed his song-writing ideas, his style, or the content of his songs. "When did I make the change? That was other people writing, you didn't hear anything from me. You know I used to write a long time ago and it was almost the way I'm writing now. There's just nothing forced anymore. I don't play folk rock. I would call it, um, I like to think of it more in terms of vision music—it's mathematical music. The words are just as important as the music, there would be no music without the words." At one time Dylan said, "the albums are not important, it's the writing."* Now he says that although concerts are much more "fun" than they used to be, "the albums are the most important because it's all concise and it's easy to hear the words and everything. There's no chance of the sound interfering."

But popularity has had a deep effect on his life as it has had on any of the star figures in our culture. "I can't write in the cafeteria, everybody wants the napkin," he once complained half kidding to a friend. And then walking down the street, he objected to the fact that he couldn't go out in the streets any more without being recognized. And then later he arranged to meet the same friend † at an all night restaurant and sat in the window until the autograph seekers drove him out!

But whether Dylan does or does not admit it, he has changed style in the past year. The rock and roll band shows that and he has abandoned some of the older songs. "I wish I could write like 'Girl from the North Country' [an older song], but I can't write like that anymore. I dunno why."

When Dylan went to England last year, it marked a turning point. It was the last of his concerts without the rock and roll band. "That was the end of my older program," he says. "I knew what was going to happen all the time, y'know. I knew how many encores there was, which songs they were going to clap loudest at and all this kind of thing."

* To RJG.
† RJG.

He doesn't think of his older songs as being any less valid, though. "I just consider them something else to themselves, at another time, another dimension. It would be kind of dishonest for me to sing them now because I wouldn't really feel like singing them.

"The difference in the songs I write now, in the last year and a half, maybe two . . . the songs before the fourth record, I used to know what I wanted to say before I used to write the song. See? All the stuff which I had written before, which wasn't song, was just on a piece of toilet paper. When it comes out like that, that's the kind of stuff I never would sing because people just would not be ready for it. I just went through that other thing of writing songs until I couldn't write any more. It was just too easy and it wasn't really right. I would start out, I would know what I wanted to say before I wrote the songs and I would say it and it would never come out exactly the way I thought it would. But it touched it.

"But now I just write a song like I *know* that it's just going to be allright and I don't really know exactly what it's all about, but I do know the layers of what it's all about.

"Rolling Stone's the best song I wrote . . . I wrote Rolling Stone after England. I boiled it down, but it's all there. I had to quit after England. I had to stop and I knew I had to sing it with a band. I always sing when I write, even prose, and I heard it like that."

When he was told of high school students studying his lyrics, Dylan asked quickly if the lyrics were the old songs or the new ones. "If it's the old ones, I feel a little guilty about it. They should use the new ones, like 'Desolation Row.' I know I'm not accepted by the professors in the universities and it used to bother me, but I know now I have nothin' to live up to" * (an unconscious or conscious quote of one of his own lines in "It's Alright, Ma").

The contrast between Dylan the person and Dylan the prophet of the Doomsday Poems is startling. Thin, almost emaciated, his lips clutching a cigarette, he talks quickly and nervously in a distinctive, edgy softness, using the language of the hip street

* To RJG.

folk. His hands are cold and he seems shy and quick, like a young deer. His life is terribly complicated by the impediments of charismatic success; when he got into his dressing room in Berkeley's Community Theater, there was a girl hidden in the shower waiting for his autograph. At another hall, forced to remain in the dressing room for almost an hour until the crowd went away, he fainted.

At parties, surrounded by hordes of gate crashers, he seeks refuge in intense, rattling monologues with friends, musicians, poets, acquaintances. When a contingent of half a dozen bearded and leather-jacketed Hell's Angels came to his dressing room and sat on the floor, he invited them to visit him in New York and then, his leg swinging back and forth as he lit cigarette after cigarette and put them down half smoked, he rattled on and said over and over again, "Have you got good seats?"

Earlier, at that same concert, the Hell's Angels had sat quietly in the first rows while Joan Baez sang along with Dylan from her seat and Allen Ginsberg, when Dylan reached the line in "Gates of Eden," "the motorcycle black madonna two wheel gypsy queen," screamed it out in unison with the singer.

His pose is casualness personified, coolness, nothing matters, never get "up-tight." Yet, he spotted a quotation from a personal letter at the bottom of one article and asked the author* how he got it. At his San Francisco press conference at which he faced a horde of photographers, TV cameras and reporters, a thin, curly-haired sprite at bay in an electronic jungle, he insisted it didn't matter, he'd talk about anything, he didn't really care at all, it meant nothing to him. Yet he cut short his rehearsal with his band later that afternoon in order to get to the hotel in time to see the TV broadcast.

Interrupted in the dressing room by a photographer as he and Joan Baez were rehearsing "Chimes of Freedom" which he had just completed, Dylan was gentle and decent, never exactly refusing to pose, just not posing until the photographer left.

Before going on stage, he chats, smokes constantly and never seems like a performer. His dressing room conversation is never about box office grosses, unlike most major performers. His atti-

* RJG.

tude about money is as casual as his clothes. He had only three dollars with him one night on the town in San Francisco and when he arrived for the concert, which was a completely sold out house grossing over $10,000, he only drew $100. After another concert, when everybody expected him to come to an all night party, he was in bed asleep by midnight.

On stage, he is almost precisely the same as off. He dresses the same, though he may change boots or sometimes put on his suit of huge black and olive checks. "I come on stage the same way I go anywhere. I mean, are all these people paying to see me look neat?"

"I want to sing you a song, recognizing that there are goliaths nowadays," he said, as he prepared to sing "The Lonesome Death of Hattie Carroll," that grim description of the wanton murder of a Negro maid. "This is a true story, only the words have been changed," he said once, introducing "The Ballad of Davey Moore," which condemns the brutality of boxing. And his wry sense of humor crops up continually, sometimes he seems even to be putting himself on. "It's Halloween," he said at Carnegie Hall, "an' I've got my Bob Dylan mask on."

There's a line in one of Dylan's songs, "Like a Rolling Stone," which is very revealing. He sings, "You're invisible now, you've got no secrets to conceal." And another time he said to a questioner, "Don't these people know I expose myself every time I go on stage?" In his poem, which he read at Carnegie Hall, "Last Thoughts on Woodie Guthrie," he said the revealing, self-questioning lines "just where am I goin . . . just what am I doin on this road I'm walkin, on this trail I'm turnin . . . am I mixed up too much . . . why am I walkin . . . why am I runnin . . . What am I sayin . . . what am I knowin . . . who am I helpin . . . what am I breakin . . . what am I givin . . . what am I takin . . .?"

"The songs are what I do," he says, "what I do is write the songs and sing them. And perform them. That's what I do. The performing part of it could end, but, like I'm going to be writing these songs and singing them and I see no end, right now. That's what I do. Anything else interferes with it. Most of the time we feel like playing. That's important to me. The aftermath, whatever happens before and after is really not important to me. Just the time on the stage and the time we're singing the songs and performing them. Or really *not* performing them, even, just letting them be there."

Dylan Doomsday Poems, his apocryphal visions of the world, thunder against injustice and sing out in defense of "the confused, accused, misused, strung out ones and worse an fôr every hung up person in the whole wide universe." They include the just quoted "Chimes of Freedom" as well as "Its Alright, Ma," that bitter attack on the American Dream, a kind of verse reprise of "A Walk on the Wild Side," with its ringing lines, "make everything from toy guns that spark to flesh-colored Christs that glow in the dark. It's easy to see without looking too far that not much is really sacred" and, "even the President of the United States sometimes must have to stand naked," as well as "Gates of Eden" with its line so attractive to the young, "There are no truths outside the Gates of Eden."

"You have to vomit up everything you know. I did that, I vomited it all up and then went out and saw it all again," Dylan told a poet.* The parallel to Rimbaud is even more striking than the kinship of "Desolation Row" to "Season in Hell." Rimbaud not only was a child prodigy of poetry but, like Dylan, ran away from home again and again. "The poet makes himself a seer," Rimbaud wrote, "by a long, prodigious and rational disordering of the senses. Every form of love, of suffering, of madness; he searches himself, he consumes all the poisons in him, and keeps only their quintessences. This is an unspeakable torture during which he needs all his faith and superhuman strength and during which he becomes the great patient, the great criminal, the great accursed—and the great learned one among men. For he drives at the *unknown!* Because he has cultivated his own soul—which was rich to begin with—more than any other man! He reaches the unknown and even if, crazed, he ends up by losing the understanding of his visions, at least he has seen them! Let him die charging through these unutterable, unnameable things: other horrible workers will come: they will begin from the horizons where he has succumbed!" Then Rimbaud adds, "The poet really is the thief of fire" and "eternal art will have its function,

* Allen Ginsberg & RJG.

since poets are citizens. Poetry will no longer rhyme with action; it will be ahead of it!"

Dylan puts it slightly differently. "I am ragin'ly against absolutely everything that wants t force nature t be unnatural," he says.

This is a mystical vision. Yes, but one that has an uneasy edge of reality to it. And the New Youth is taking Dylan seriously. At an airport press conference, he noted, "something that amazed me. This 15-year-old girl, and she knew poets like William Blake and she knew his work and she was hip to all kinds of different things which people usually are not acquainted with at that age. So maybe it's just a new kind of person. A new kind of 15-year-old person. I don't know. I do know that that person is more free in the mind than 22-year-old college kids."

The strength is there in the words and the songs. The ideas cleave to the minds of the young like moss to a tree trunk. And while it rejects the values of our world, of the Great Society and the New Frontier (John Coleman, the British writer, has said that the youth are the *last* frontier), it also speaks eloquently of a world in which the sacredness of the individual is paramount. It may not turn out that way, but the New Youth's "thief of fire" limns it out for you and, if poetry is ahead of action, it will come. This is how he says it:

i can't believe that i have
t hate anybody
an when i do
it will only be out of fear
and i'll know it

i know no answers an no truth
for absolutely no soul alive
i will listen to no one
who tells me morals
there are no morals
an i dream a lot.

Dylan Hurt In Cycle Mishap

Bob Dylan, the folk singer and song writer, is under a doctor's care for injuries suffered in a motorcycle accident last Friday. A representative of Mr. Dylan said the injuries have forced the cancellation of a concert scheduled for Saturday night at the Yale Bowl in New Haven.

The Genius Who Went Underground

It's more than a year now since Bob Dylan nearly lost his life in a motorcycle accident and withdrew from the public eye.

Since then rumor has had a field day. Almost every conceivable speculation has filtered down to the folk-rock and hippie dens where Dylan's music continues to be a driving force.

The purveyors of the public Dylan—his recording company, would-be book publisher, ABC-TV with a would-be film special —have had to back and fill in the press, trying to stamp out this or that rumor and substitute an optimistic face.

For all practical purposes, Dylan, now twenty-six, has kept silent. The few things he has said or permitted to be said give little clue to when he will emerge from his retreat near Woodstock, New York, or what direction his prodigious talents will take when he does.

Dylan is a kind of quasi-underground force which is felt, and sometimes acknowledged, throughout the pop music industry and even spills over into poetry.

Dylan has changed direction at least twice and brought on himself a lot of abuse from former fans, though each time he has won over an entirely different crowd.

For a brief spell, Dylan rode the folk wave which hit one of its peaks with Joan Baez back in 1962. Then he struck out on

Reprinted from the *Chicago Tribune*, 1967.

his own, covering new ground in folk protest. Then he shocked the purists by putting rock into it.

For instance, with "Subterranean Homesick Blues" he lost some unfaithful fans, but he widened his audience to include teeny-boppers as well as the New Left, hippies, housewives and ironically, the gray flannel suit set his songs satirized.

Despite his continuing popularity, Dylan disavows his role as spokesman for this generation, a leader without a title, mapping the route to peace and brotherhood with a guitar and a headful of songs sounding like sermons.

"I don't want to write for people any more," he said a while ago. "You know, be a spokesman."

From San Francisco poet Lawrence Ferlinghetti to poet-critic Kenneth Rexroth, from bearded guru poet Allen Ginsberg to Black Mountain's Robert Creeley, Dylan is looked upon as a practicing member of the craft. Michael McClure, author of the controversial play, *The Beard,* calls Dylan's "Gates of Eden" the key to his completing a series of poems.

"He writes better poetry than I did at his age," says Ginsberg. "I'd say he's a space-age genius more than an old library poet."

Ferlinghetti calls him "higher than surreal." Seated in a North Beach cafe, he offered his view of Dylan as a poet.

"I wouldn't say he was avant-garde, certainly not in printed poetry. Dylan is doing what the Beat poets were doing ten years ago, that is, mixing poetry and jazz.

"But he has brilliant imagery and imagination. And many of his songs have crazy phrasing that any poet would be glad to have."

Ginsberg has called Dylan the most influential poet of his generation. The eminent critic Rexroth admits: "Probably the most important event in recent poetry is Bob Dylan." Says novelist John Clellon Holmes: "Dylan has the authentic mark of the bard on him. And I think it's safe to say that no one, years hence, will be able to understand just what it was like to live in this time without attending to what this astonishingly gifted young man has already achieved."

A traditional gesture of the prophet is the retreat (for instance, into the desert) and the re-emergence into public life with a new message. A good deal of what will or won't be in pop music hangs on Dylan's re-emergence and his message.

Dylan's accident occurred just after he had returned from an around-the-world trip. "We played some jobs with Bob where the music was sailing—and he was sailing," says guitarist Jamie Robbie Robertson, one member of the group that accompanied Dylan on the tour. "It turned out to be not just songs. It turned out to be a whole dynamic experience. We did it until we couldn't do it any more. We went all over the place until finally it was about ready to burst. We were so exhausted that everybody said this was a time to rest. We stopped listening to music for a year. We didn't listen to anything but what you didn't have to listen to, like opera."

Al Aronowitz
Saturday Evening Post

Scarred Bob Dylan Is Comin' Back

by Michael Iachetta

Woodstock, N. Y., May 7 (Special)—For the first time since the motorcycle accident that almost cost him his life more than nine months ago, folk music's emotionally and physically scarred Bob Dylan spoke out yesterday about life since his crackup.

"What I've been doin' mostly is seein' only a few close friends, readin' little 'bout the outside world, porin' over books by people you never heard of, thinkin' about where I'm goin', and why am I runnin', and am I mixed up too much, and what am I knowin', and what am I givin', and what am I takin'. And mainly what I've been doin' is workin' on gettin' better and makin' better music, which is what my life is all about."

In an exclusive interview—the first he has granted since his accident—Dylan flavored his words with bittersweet poetry about his record contract, his TV special, his book—and rumors that the accident had ended his career. He spoke at his mountain hideaway near this art colony about a hundred miles from New York.

He will be twenty-six on May 24. His occupation is songwriter, poet, singer and electric-guitar player. He is a hung-up middle-class kid who has put poetry on juke boxes with such songs as "Blowin' in the Wind" and "Like a Rolling Stone."

His works have been recorded by artists ranging from Lawrence Welk to the Byrds, and he is credited with starting the folk rock craze. His royalties have made him a millionaire, yet he lives like a hermit and hasn't cut a record since his accident.

Reprinted with permission from the New York *Daily News,* May 8, 1967.

Bobby goes almost into a trance as he described being thrown from the motorcycle.

"The back wheel locked, I think," he said. "I lost control, swerving from left to right. Next thing I know I was in someplace I never heard of—Middletown, I think—with my face cut up so I got some scars and my neck busted up pretty good. Just began movin' it around a month ago. New X-rays should be comin' through any day now. I know I won't be able to ride a motorcycle any more.

"But songs are in my head like they always are," said Dylan. "And they're not goin' to get written down until some things are evened up. Not until some people come forth and make up for some of the things that have happened."

As he talked, his slender fingers rubbed the new beard and mustache that make his face look strangely sensitive. A blue bandanna covered the top of his head—"Some scars on my face from the accident," he explained offhandedly.

His words indicated that the record world has left him with a few scars too.

He Has to Get Better Before He Sings Again

"Somethin' has got to be evened up is all I'm going to say," Dylan drawled. "Meanwhile, whatever is happenin' in the world is happenin' just fine without me, and I'm going to just have to get better before I do any singin' on records, but the time is right for a new record."

He says he has been working on two musical sounds described as "staccato" and "resoundin'." "The description belongs to my lead guitarist and one of my old drummers," says Dylan. "I don't use words like that, but they do the job."

He owes Columbia a record on a contract that expired not long ago. And he has been suspended for refusing to cut it. "But everything has been settled amicably and Bobby will be recording for us as soon as he is able to," said a Columbia spokesman.

Bobby doesn't seem to be in any hurry—even though MGM records has reportedly offered him a cool million to jump labels.

"What's money?" said Dylan with the nonchalance of someone who has it. "A man is a success if he gets up in the mornin' and gets to bed at night and in between he does what he wants to. What I want to do is make music."

There'll Be No Book Until It's Right

He also wanted to make a film and write a book and accepted advances to do the job, but the ABC-TV special he was working on has been canceled. "The film is finished." That's all Dylan will say. "It's different."

As for the book, "Word got around I had one when all I was doin' was writin' some things down," explained Bobby. "Editors kept makin'—what do they call it?—revisions, and makin' it wrong and it just can't be printed until it's right."

In Woodstock there is a story that Bobby's wife was following him at the time of the accident and rushed him to a doctor.

"I don't remember that," said Bobby, as always reluctant to talk about his personal life. "Lots of things I don't remember about that day."

Dylan stared for a long moment down at his gray cowboy boots. He was a gypsy-like figure in faded dungarees, lavender shirt with collar turned up to cover his neck and a purple-and-blue striped blazer. His sandy hair seemed longer and wilder than ever. He laughs at the stories that he has gone three-button Ivy and cut his hair short, but he doesn't laugh at the cruel rumors that have made the rounds from hippie haven to California to the git-fiddle mecca that is Gerde's Folk City in Greenwich Village.

The rumor mill had it that the accident had finished Bobby's career; that he was a vegetable; that he was so badly scarred he refused to come down from the top floor of his hideaway—speaking only to his friends and then only through an intercom.

Try to check the rumors in New York and all Bobby's manager, Albert Grossman, will say is that Bobby broke his neck in a motorcycle accident. "He is recovering," said Grossman, "and he is not seeing anybody."

You are left with a clicking sound and a phone receiver in your hand. So you dial Columbia Records. "We don't know where Bobby is," says a spokesman. "Somewhere in Bearsville, we think, but you'll never find him. Why waste your time?"

Maybe it is because of the anxiety in Abe Zimmerman's voice

when you call him person-to-person in Hibbing, Minn., and ask him about his son, Bobby Dylan.

Mr. Jones Doesn't Know What's Happening

"Bobby's fine," says Abe, a prosperous appliance dealer whose oldest son preferred the name of a poet to the name he was given at birth in Duluth.

"Yes, I heard about the accident," says Abe, "but Bobby's been up since then. He went to the last Cassius Clay fight. He is fine, isn't he? What does the New York office say?"

The New York office says little. So the next thing you know you are driving upstate toward a town that will create a conspiracy of silence around the mysterious Mr. Dylan.

As the one hundred miles roll away, you find yourself thinking about a line from a Dylan song, "Ballad of a Thin Man." The line is, "Something is happening here, but you don't know what it is, do you Mr. Jones?" It bothers you, as it was intended to, and you find yourself remembering the first time you met Dylan.

Even then, he shied away from talking about himself. "I'm writing about myself and that's the only way I can do it," he said, coming on like the original wandering troubador.

Mystery, Magic, Truth and the Bible

There was no mention that he had grown up as Bobby Zimmerman in the Jewish society whirl around Minneapolis-St. Paul and that he had done the three-button bit for six months as a scholarship student at the University of Minnesota. He dropped out and began hustling a buck in a coffee house called the Ten o'Clock Scholar in Dinkeytown, a small business section on the edge of campus.

There is no explaining the coffee house kick, just as there is no explaining why he began running away from home when he was 10. The cops collared him 900 miles away. Before he was 19, he had lived in Duluth, Minn., Gallup, N.M.; Cheyenne, S.D.; Phillipsburg, Kan., and finally, Hibbing, Minn.

Along the way, he taught himself to play the piano, the harmonica, the autoharp and the guitar.

He knew that he liked to write poems, and the poems became

songs that were in the air around him, and he just had to write them down before somebody else did.

"I'm tryin' to be like the medium at a seance," he explained. "There's a mystery, magic, truth, and the bible in great folk music. I can't hope to touch that, but I'm goin' to try."

In Woodstock, you run into vague answers about the whereabouts of the elusive Bob Dylan. You spend 48 hours talking to teen-agers, local merchants and the cop on the beat.

Woodstock is an artistic community and the people appreciate a man trying to do a job as best he knows how, especially when he promises not to reveal the location of Bobby's house. Finally someone lets slip the name of the man who sold the house to Dylan, and you have something to work on.

After four hours of driving up narrow mountain trails, running from watchdogs, getting stuck in the mud and winding up hopelessly lost, you get a straight answer and you are there, impressed by the brooding wealth of the mahogany-stained estate you see in front of you.

Dylan's black Cadillac limousine is in a garage off the end of the driveway and there is a miniature playground for Bobby's young son, Jesse Byron.

Snow in May: Everything's Possible

You identify yourself and ask for Dylan. "Never heard of Dylan," a voice says. "There's nobody here but my wife and child and me," says the gent at the door. "Now will you get out of here."

You leave, but as you do, another car swings in and out of the driveway. It turns out to be the house's previous owner showing the place to friends. "Is that Dylan's house?" you ask as your car blocks his on the narrow road. "Yes," he replies.

The next day it is snowing in May and you believe anything is possible, so you go back to the house and knock on the door until a figure stares out at you from behind the grating.

Bobby is standing in front of you and you are so genuinely glad to see that he is all right that you blurt out: "It's great to see you're up and around and the rumors aren't true."

He looks at your face curiously, trying to place it, and then he remembers that long-ago interview in his manager's office.

"We can't just stand here talking," he says, inviting you in for coffee.

And then he talked about life since the accident. Thin, almost emaciated, his lips clutched a cigaret. At the end of the talk, he was asked about a *News* photographer taking his picture. "I'd rather not," he said. "It's one thing facing a writer, but I have this hangup about cameras now."

BOB
DYLAN'S
GREATEST
HITS

Don't Look Back

by Richard Goldstein

"The truth is just a plain picture," says doleful Bob Dylan to a man from *Time* magazine, who answers with newsweekly non-commitment.

That is exactly what *Don't Look Back*—a running, jumping, and standing still portrait of the American rock star as a young oracle—is trying to prove. But can any movie offer a "plain picture" of the man who defined his generation with "Blowin' in the Wind," wrote its anthem in "The Times They Are a-Changin'," repudiated it with "Like a Rolling Stone," and finally commiserated with it in "Sad Eyed Lady of the Lowlands"?

With his camera tucked gingerly into armpits and forgotten corners, Donn Alan Pennebaker, who calls himself a maker of "nondocumentary" films, followed Dylan and his entourage through a three-and-a-half-week tour of England during the spring of 1965. Pennebaker shot brawls and bull sessions, put-downs and put-ons, all the frothy frenzy a pop idol experiences when he is thrust into a limelight he barely knew existed.

In 1965, Bob Dylan was still very much a folksinger, accompanying himself on a choppy guitar. His voice, far from the craggy executioner it is today, was thin and whining. English musicians "found" him on the Village coffee-house expresso belt and made him a pop celebrity. He taught them the art of the narrative line, drenched in resonant images. They taught him the value of rhythm. Out of this co-education came folk-rock and Dylan's espousal of it.

Don't Look Back shows us Bob Dylan as a young performer feeling around the edges of fame, like a chambermaid in a new mink coat. He is no visionary here but an entertainer, deeply concerned with pleasing audiences through his songs, and a bit unsure of his power as a pop conquistador.

He raves a lot, brandishing rapiers against the gentlemen of the press (Dylan's performance in these scenes is guaranteed to bring a blush to any journalist's face) but his victims from the Fourth Estate are no-account straw men and classic squares. He screams, taunts, flashes four-letter trump cards, and comes on cool enough to warm the cockles of any scenie-bopper's heart.

This veneer looks good on film. But *Don't Look Back* tries to catch another, more elusive side of Dylan. The old theory about formal interviewing is that no matter how careful the subject is to provide only formula answers to probing questions, he slips up somewhere and reveals his personality. The journalist need only wait for these moments, and underline them in his notebook. Documentary filmmakers do the same thing when shooting a profile; they sift through the poses to find the self within.

Beneath his posturing, Bob Dylan comes across in the film as a young man suspicious of everything that happens to him, but anxious to have it happen anyway. He pores over the papers, reading the outrageous conclusions reporters have reached from his cryptic press conferences. "Anarchist!", he muses, dumbfounded at this new title, but dazzled all the same. "It must have taken them a long time to think that one up . . . Give the anarchist a cigarette."

Before his concerts, he runs his fingers tensely across a piano keyboard. He combs his hair before a mirror, straightens his harmonica, and finally leaps toward the spotlight like a challenger, about to enter a hostile ring. Throughout the film he jokes about Donovan, who had been considered an English Dylan before he gave up denim jackets and discovered art nouveau. Dylan first sees the name in a fan sheet. "Who's this Donovan?" he sniffs. The line comes up again and again until the two finally meet at a party. Donovan picks up a guitar and sings an innocuous ditty. Dylan responds with his darkly passionate "It's

All Over Now, Baby Blue." He doesn't say much about it after that, but we know from the corners of his mouth that Donovan is no competition, and that Dylan is relieved.

Dylan is an inveterate chart watcher, barely concealing his delight at finding "Subterranean Homesick Blues" in the English Top Ten. He meets his British fans, rocking nervously on his boot heels, and bristling just a bit when they tell him to stick to folk. Explaining his new rock sound, he tells a cluster of girls: "I have to give some work to my friends."

Not the least significant aspect of *Don't Look Back,* to a pop historian anyway, is the glimpse it offers of Bob Dylan contemplating the world of pop music from outside. *Bringing It All Back Home*—the crucial album in which Dylan fused folk and rock for the first time—had just been released when *Don't Look Back* was filmed. He is fascinated by pop musicians and their accoutrements. He marvels at the selection of electric guitars in a store window. The scene in which Dylan meets a small-time Merseyside combo is crucial; they praise his lyrics, assuring him: "We try to tell our audience to listen to the words, not the . . ." But Dylan interrupts with questions about their instruments and sound.

His uncertain embrace of rock and its public is brilliantly conveyed in *Don't Look Back.* But the certainty with which we leave the theater thinking we have finally, utterly met Bob, is deceptive. For Pennebaker and his crew caught Dylan in England a few months before American fans did at the Newport Festival and Forest Hills. Unlike English audiences nurtured on the rock beat, Dylan's American followers thought they knew what a folksinger was and what he wasn't. When their idol brought out an electric combo, they were outraged. When he dared perform rock that was not parody, they booed and threw things at the stage.

It is said that after the Newport debacle, he cried. But Pennebaker was not present to film that side of Bob Dylan, or the isolation and bitterness that followed. His next album, *Highway 61 Revisited,* was an ode to those feelings. It burst with violent, stinging venom. Its image-blossoms snapped shut when approached for meaning. On all his subjects, he heaped a passionate, surreal scorn. Where he once declared, "The times they are a-changin'," he now hissed: "Something is happening and you don't know what it is, do you, Mr. Jones?"

Don't Look Back is a finely wrought antique which offers no insight into Bob Dylan in 1967. Since his marriage, and a subsequent motorcycle accident, he has been in virtual isolation, and his forthcoming album will give us only selective clues to what is going on in Bob Dylan's head.

Today, he is Shakespeare and Judy Garland to my generation. We trust what he tells us. But his flagrant *mysterioso*—even if it is sincere—evokes hungry demands for at least a penetrating glimpse of the oracle-star. *Don't Look Back* satisfies that hunger. We watch him leaping about before the camera in hand-held innocence. He is noble, he is nervous, he is—does one dare to use this word in the psychedelic sixties—sensitive?

But is he? *Don't Look Back* offers only guesses, but they are persuasive indeed. The dialogue sounds spontaneous, the scenes look utterly unstaged. The bobbing, wobbling camera convinces us, as no newsreel could, that we can smell the venom on Bob Dylan's tongue. This is the danger in cinema verité, as well as its greatest virtue. In the Hollywood fiction—film, where the camera stands still and the actors emote against throbbing strings, we know we are seeing a studio product which is at most only emotionally real. But the tricks involved in making a verité film are invisible if they work. Though it was edited from twenty hours of raw film down to ninety minutes, *Don't Look Back* seems to tell it like it was. And though the footage is two years old, its chief impact is in its impression of immediacy.

Don't Look Back is blessed with the spontaneous and untapped comic talent of Dylan himself. His timing is beautiful to watch, especially in the put-downs. The Caruso bit (he claims he is as good a singer because "I can hold my breath three times as long") is a gem. But Pennebaker's camera is almost too willing to play cinematic straight man. Without a program, you can hardly tell the vaudeville from the verité.

Don't Look Back poses the same problem for its audience that the New Journalism presents to its readers. With realism heightened by novelistic technique, how do you tell fact from formula? This credibility gap between medium and message is furthered here by presence of Dylan's manager, Albert Grossman, as the movie's producer. It is a bad omen when an artist's manager produces a film about his client. At worst *Don't Look Back* could have been a commercial. With Grossman's presence felt during the crucial cutting and editing this film is at best a commissioned portrait. It's an artistic job, but still a bit flattering around the edges.

We should continue to be impressed with verité technique—especially when it is presented with the taste and skill of *Don't Look Back*. But we must be wary of it as well. After all, it is only a version of the truth.

The Guthrie Concert

by Lillian Roxon

HERALD SYDNEY HERALD SYDNEY

NYR SUPP553/YA
HERALD SYDNEY
FOR HERALD SATURDAY PAGE
EXROXON NEW YORK
DYLAN ONE

THERE HAS NEVER BEEN AN EVENING QUITE LIKE IT BEFORE AND THERE PROBABLY WILL NEVER BE ONE QUITE LIKE IT AGAIN. IT WAS A NIGHT FOR APPLAUDING SO HARD THAT PALMS BECAME BRUISED, A NIGHT OF STANDING OVATIONS AND THUNDEROUS FOOT STAMPINGS, A NIGHT OF OVERWHELMING EMOTIONS AND CHEEKS AWASH WITH TEARS.

THE OCCASION WAS A BENEFIT CONCERT AT CARNEGIE HALL ON JANUARY 20 TO HONOR WOODY GUTHRIE, FOLK POET, AUTHOR, MUSICIAN, WRITER OF MORE THAN A THOUSAND SONGS AND SINGER OF THEM IN A HARSH GRATING VOICE THAT MIGHT NOT BE KNOWN OUTSIDE FOLK CIRCLES HAD IT NOT INSPIRED SCORES OF MORE COMMERCIALLY SUCCESSFUL IMITATORS, NOT THE LEAST BEING BOB DYLAN.

DYLAN WAS THERE, OF COURSE, AND THAT, ALONE, MADE THE EVENING HISTORIC. IT WAS HIS FIRST APPEARANCE IN PUBLIC SINCE HIS

For the Sydney *Morning Herald*, January, 1968.

ACCIDENT SEVENTEEN MONTHS AGO AND WHEN THAT PIECE OF NEWS GOT OUT, TICKETS WENT OFF LIKE ROCKETS, PRICES DOUBLING, TRIPLING AND QUADRUPLING ON THE BLACK MARKET.

BUT DYLAN WAS JUST THE ICING N THE TASTIEST FOK CAKE EVER CONCOCTED. THE EVENING PRODUCED BY THE DYNAMIC HAROLD LEVENTHAL SHIMMERED WITH SUPERSTARS AND SUPERTALENT.

(MORE)

NYR SUPP554/YA
HERALD SYDNEY
FOR HERALD SATURDAY PAGE
DYLAN TWO

THERE THEY ALL WERE, THE FOLK ARISTOCRACY, ON STAGE TOGETHER, TO THE DELIGHT OF THE AUDIENCE, FOR THE WHOLE EVENING, SINGING TOGETHER, SITTING TOGETHER, ACCOMPANYING EACH OTHER ON GUITARS, BANJOS AND MOUTH ORGANS, A MILLION DOLLAR HOOTENANNY.

(MORE)

NYR SUPP555/YA
HERALD SYDNEY
FOR HERALD SATURDAY PAGE
DYLAN THREE

FIRST JUDY COLLINS, LONG HAIRED, SHINY EYED, A ROSE AT HER THROAT, A GUITAR IN HER HAND; PETE SEEGER, STILL, AS WOODY GUTHRIE ONCE CALLED HIM, A STRINGBEAN KID, WITH CHECKED SHIRT AND TRUSTY BANJO; WOODY'S SON, ARLO, PALE, ETHEREAL IN A PURPLE JACKET AND A LONG CURLY LOUIS XVI HAIRDO; TOM PAXTON, MOUSTACHIOD AND IN SPLENDID VOICE; RICHIE HAVENS, A LEAN NEGRO IN RIMLESS HIPPIE GLASSES; JACK ELLIOTT IN COWBOY HAT, LOOKING AS HE ALWAYS HAS, A LITTLE LIKE GUTHRIE; ODETTA, MASSIVE, MONUMENTAL LIKE A BROWN

EARTH GODDESS; AND IN THE MIDDLE THERE, SO QUIETLY AND UNOBTRUSIVELY THAT IT TOOK A WHOLE FIVE MINUTES FOR THE AUDIENCE TO RECOGNISE HIM, BOB DYLAN, HIS ONCE HUGE HEAD OF HAIR NOW NEATLY SHORN, HIS FACE TIGHT AND TANNED AND ALTERED NOT SO MUCY BY A NEW TRIM BEARD OR BY WHAT SEEMED LIKE A LITTLE POST-ACCIDENT SURGERY, BUT BY A WHOLE NEW EXPRESSION, NOT THE FAMILIAR ONE OF REBELLION AND CONFUSION, BUT ONE OF PEACE AND TRANQUILITY.

THAT ARRAY UP THERE. IT WAS ALMOST MORE THAN THE AUDIENCE COULD BEAR.

GUTHRIE, WHO DIED LAST OCTOBER, HAS WRITTEN A THOUSAND SONGS AND A STAGGERING AMOUNT OF PROSE. WHAT THE AUDIENCE GOT TO HEAR FOR THREE INCREDIBLE HOURS WAS A SORT OF ANTHOLOGY OF THE BEST OF BOTH. NARRATION READ BY ACTORS ROBERT RYAN AND WILL GEER, AND THIRTY SONGS THE EIGHT SINGERS TOOK TURNS WITH.

(MORE)

NYR SUPP556/YA
HERALD SYDNEY
FOR HERALD SATURDAY PAGE
DYLAN FOUR

ALTHOUGH THE NAME OF THIS OKLAHOMA FOLK POET, "THE RUSTY VOICED HOMER" OF THE DEPRESSION IS NOT AS FAMILIAR AS IT DESERVES TO BE, HIS SONGS ARE.

IN AUSTRALIA, I REMEMBER, GUTHRIE WAS THE FIRST OF THE FOLK NAMES, ALONG WITH PETE SEEGER AND LEADBELLY, TO BE REVERED AND LONG BEFORE THE 1956 FOLK BOOM, A SURE WAY TO FILL YOUR HOUSE ON A COLD SUNDAY AFTERNOON WAS TO ANNOUNCE YOU HAD SOMEHOW GOT HOLD OF ONE OF WOODY'S RECORDS. AND IT WAS WOODY'S SONGS, "UNION

MAID", "SO LONG IT'S BEEN GOOD TO KNOW YOU", "REUBEN JAMES" AND "DO-RE-ME," THAT PEOPLE SANG DRUNKENLY AND SENTIMENTALLY AT STUDENT PARTIES.

HEARING PETER SEEGER AND JUDY COLLINS SINGING TOGETHER "YOU CAN'T SCARE ME, I'M STICKIN' TO THE UNION" OR BOB DYLAN AND ODETTA IN "THIS TRAIN IS BOUND FOR GLORY" BROUGHT BACK MEMORIES OF A SCORE OF FUND-RAISING PARTIES AT SYDNEY'S IRONWORKERS HALL.

GUTHRIE'S WIDOW, HER EYES RED, BUT HER FACE BEAMING WITH HAPPINESS, SAID SHE STILL GOT LOTS OF MAIL FROM AUSTRALIA. THERE WAS ALWAYS SOMETHING VERY AUSTRALIAN ABOUT WODDY'S DUSTBOWL SONGS AND HIS AMERICAN "ANTHEM" "THIS LAND IS YOUR LAND" WAS A LOVELY SONG TO SING RIPPING ALONG PRINCE'S HIGHWAY ON THE BACK OF A TRUCK LOOKING OUT AT THE GUM TREES AND THE MOUNTAINS.

(MORE)

•

NYR SUPP557/YA
HERALD SYDNEY
FOR HERALD SATURDAY PAGE
DYLAN FIVE

IT WAS DURING "THIS LAND IS YOUR LAND" THE GRAND FINALE, THAT THE TEARS REALLY FLOWED AND THE APPLAUSE SOUNDED AS IF IT WOULD NEVER END.

MANY PEOPLE, I THINK, CAME BECAUSE OF DYLAN AND THE CHANCE TO SEE EIGHT OF THE COUNTRY'S BIG FOLK NAMES ON ONE PROGRAMME. BUT THE APPLAUSE AND THE TEARS WERE FOR WOODY WHOSE PERSONALITY AND FORCE THE EVENING OF WORDS AND MUSIC SLOWLY UNFOLDED.

BY THE END, EVEN THE PEOPLE WHO CAME JUST FOR DYLAN, KNEW THAT WITHOUT WOODY THERE

•

WOULD HAVE BEEN NO DYLAN, NO ODETTA, NO PETE SEEGER, NO JUDY COLLINS—OR NOT, AT LEAST, THE WAY WE NOW KNOW THEM.

DYLAN FIRST CAME TO NEW YORK FROM INNESOTA BECAUSE HE WANTED TO MEET WOODY. WOODY WAS THEN ALREADY IN HSOSPITAL FIGHTING HIS THIRTEEN-YEAR-OLD FIGHT AGAINST HUNTINGTON'S DISEASE.

WHEN DYLAN FIRST STARTED SINGING, HE DID WHAT MANY YOUNG FOLK SINGERS OF THAT TIME DID, NAMELY MODELLED HIMSELF ALMOST ENTIRELY ON WOODY. UP AT FOK CITY, THEY SIGHED AND DISMISSED HIM AS JUST ANOTHER GUTHRIE FREAK. NO ONE IN THOSE DAYS WOULD FOR A MINUTE HAVE BELIEVED HE WOULD GO ON TO WORLD FAME, BECOME A LEGENDARY NAME IN HIS OWN RIGHT AND SIGN A RECORDING CONTRACT FOR TWO MILLION DOLLARS, LET ALONE REVOLUTIONISE THE WHOLE POPULAR MUSIC SCENE.

(MORE)

NYR SUPP558/YA
HERALD SYDNEY
FOR HERALD SATURDAY PAGE
DYLAN SIX

TO THIS DAY THERE IS STILL SOME BITTERNESS IN FOLK CIRCLES THAT "BOBBY" MADE THE BIG TIME WHILE WOODY, FROM WHOM SO MUCH HAD COME, LANGUISHED UNKNOWN IN HOSPITAL.

BUT "BOBBY" WAS ONLY ONE OF MANY WHO LIKE JUDY COLLINS AND JOAN BAEZ WERE THERE WHEN THE TIME WAS RIGHT, WHEN THE WORLD WAS READY TO ACCEPT FOLK ON A COMMERCIAL BASIS.

IN THE WAKE OF THE BOOM THEY SET OFF, PETE SEEGER WHO HAD BEEN SINGING THE SAME SONGS FOR YEARS, MADE A DRAMATIC COMEBACK SO THAT TODAY HE MAKES THE SORT OF MONEY HE DESERVED TO MAKE ALL ALONG.

AGAIN, IN THESE DAYS WHEN PROTEST HAS FINALLY BECOME FASHIONABLE, AND BLACKLISTS ARE OUT, THE POLITICAL VIEWS THAT SEEMED SO EXTREME TO THE GENERAL PUBLIC IN WOODY'S DAY ARE NOW CONSIDERED ENTIRELY ACCEPTABLE. PETE SEEGER IS NO LONGER BLACKLISTED OFF THE AIR, JUDY COLLINS CAN MARCH ON WASHINGTON, BOB DYLAN CAN BERATE THE MASTERS OF WAR AND JOAN BAEZ CAN REFUSE TO PAY TAXES.

WHAT "BOBBY" GOT FROM WOODY, HE HAS GIVEN BACK A THOUSANDFOLD IN GETTING FOLK MUSIC ACCEPTED BY MORE THAN A SMALL HANDFUL.

(MORE)

NYR SUPP559/YA
HERALD SYDNEY
FOR HERALD SATURDAY PAGE
DYLAN SEVEN

AND THE PROCESS WHICH SEEMS TO HAVE BEEN COMPLETED, HAS, IN FACT, JUST BEGUN, AS DYLAN HAS VERY DRAMATICALLY DEMONSTRATED WITH HIS NEW RECORD ALBUM, THE FIRST SINCE HIS AUGUST 1966 ACCIDENT.

HERE IN THE NEW RECORD IS A COMPLETELY FOLK MOOD, NONE OF THE ELECTRICAL INSTRUMENTS THAT MARKED HIS TRANSITION TO ROCK, JUST GENTLE UNAMPLIFIED GUITARS, DRUMS, PIANO AND HIS OWN HARMONICA.

THAT A RECORD OF SUCH SIMPLICITY COULD BE A RUNWAY BEST SELLER WAS UNTHINKABLE UNTIL DYLAN SPRANG THE SURPRISE HIMSELF. NOW HE HAS OPENED THE WAY FOR A WHOLE LOT MORE GENTLE MUSIC.

WOODY, FOR ONCE, COULD REALLY MAKE IT TODAY IN TIN PAN ALLEY. ANOTHER REVOLUTION IS ON ITS WAY AND ALREADY THE NEW YORK TIMES' CRITIC ROBERT SHELTON HAS PREDICTED A MASSIVE REVIVAL OF GUTHRIE MATERIAL—

ESPECIALLY OF HIS 700 OR SO STILL UNPUBLISHED SONGS.

AS FOR DYLAN, WELL, IT WAS CLEAR THAT WOODY AND NO ONE ELSE, WAS THE STAR OF THE EVENING, AND WITHOUT DYLAN THERE, IT STILL WOULD HAVE BEEN A NIGHT OF NIGHTS AND INFINITELY MOVING.

(MORE)

NYR SUPP560/YA
HERALD SYDNEY
FOR HERALD SATURDAY PAGE
DYLAN EIGHT

BUT SOMEHOW HIS PRESENCE, SO CHANGED, SERENE, SMILING, ODDLY RESPECTABLE IN HIS GRAY SUIT AND OPEN NECKED BLUE SHIRT, WAS THE CROWNING TOUCH.

HE WAS ALIVE AND WELL, AFTER ALL, DESPITE RUMORS TO THE CONTRARY, AND WHEN HE CLOSED THE FIRST HALF WITH THREE GUTHRIE SONGS, ARRANGED ROCKABILLY STYLE ACCOMPANIED BY A RINKY-TINK PIANO, DRUMS, TWO NON-ELECTRIC GUITARS (ONE HIS OWN) AND ONLY ELECTRIC ONE, YOU SAW HE WAS IN THE FINEST OF VOICE AND SPIRITS AND HAD NEVER BEEN BETTER.

THE LONG REST AFTER THE ACCIDENT, THE MARRIAGE TO A YOUNG SLIM DARK HAIRED GIRL WHO RESEMBLES JOAN BAEZ, THE BIRTH OF TWO CHILDREN, THE TRANQUILITY OF HIS COUNTRY HIDEOUT IN WOODSTOCK, ALL HAVE COMBINED TO PRODUCE A NEW GENTLER, MORE MATURE DYLAN. THE OLD TENSIONS AND ANGERS SEEM GONE FOR EVER.

HE COULD HAVE MADE HIS COMEBACK AT HIS OWN BIG CONCERT, OF COURSE, AND SOLD OUT EVERY TICKET AT GOD KNOWS HOW MUCH. AND HIS WILY MANAGER, ALBERT GROSSMAN, WAS PROBABLY PLANNING IT THAT WAY IN HIS OWN

GOOD TIME. BUT WHEN THE IDEA OF THE GUTHRIE CONCERTS CAME UP, IT WAS BOBBY HIMSELF WHO WANTED TO APPEAR TO PAY TRIBUTE TO THIS MAN WHO HAD SO INSPIRED HIM.

(MORE)

NYR SUPP561XYA
HERALD SYDNEY
FOR HERALD SATURDAY PAGE
DYLAN NINE LAST

IT WAS A BEAUTIFUL AND MOVING EVENING FOR MANY YEARS REASONS, NOT THE LEAST BEING THE IMPECCABLE PRODUCTION AND STAGING, BUT WHEN THE CARDS WERE DOWN, WHAT MADE IT REALLY SPECIAL, AND WHAT MADE IT APPROPRIATE FOR DYLAN TO STAGE HIS COMEBACK UNDER ITS AUSPICES, WAS THE FEELING IT GAVE THAT GUTHRIE'S SPIRIT LIVED ON AND WOULD CONTINUE TO DO SO.

ALREADY THERE ARE THOSE WHO ARE GETTING FROM DYLAN WHAT DYLAN GOT FROM GUTHRIE. ALL DYLAN'S SUCCESS MEANS IS THAT MORE PEOPLE ARE GETTING IT, THAT THE POETRY IS OUT OF THE SONG BOOKS AND THE FOLK CLUBS, INTO THE JUKEBOXES AND TELEVISION SETS.

THESE DAYS ROUND TIN PAN ALLEY WAY THERE'S A LOT OF BEAUTIFUL MUSIC AROUND. YOU CAN BE CYNICAL AND SAY SHREWD MERCHANDISING OF DYLAN MADE IT POSSIBLE. PERHAPS.

BY DYLAN'S PRESENCE AT THE GUTHRIE CONCERT BROUGHT HOME ONE IMPORTANT POINT, AND THAT WAS THAT IT WAS NO LONGER NECESSARY TO BY CYNICAL. WOODY'S PEOPLE, DYLAN, JUDY COLLINS, ODETTA, WERE RICH AND FAMOUS BUT THEIR SONGS WERE STILL BEAUTIFUL. THE "GOODIES" WERE WINNING WITHOUT SELLING OUT. IT SAID A LOT FOR THE FUTURE.

ENDS FILED 21930

Dylan

by Ellen Willis

Nearly two years ago, Bob Dylan had a motorcycle accident. Reports of his condition were vague and he dropped out of sight. Publication of his book, *Tarantula,* was postponed indefinitely. New records appeared, but they were from his last album, *Blonde on Blonde.* Gruesome rumors circulated: Dylan was dead; he was badly disfigured; he was paralyzed; he was insane. The cataclysm his audience was always expecting seemed to have arrived. Phil Ochs had predicted that Dylan might someday be assassinated by a fan. Pete Seeger believed Dylan could become the country's greatest troubadour, if he didn't explode. Alan Lomax had once remarked that Dylan might develop into a great poet of the times, unless he killed himself first. Now, images of James Dean filled the news vacuum. As months passed, reflex apprehension turned to suspense, then irritation: had we been put on again? We had. Friends began to admit, with smiles, that they'd seen Bobby; he was rewriting his book, he was about to sign a contract with MGM Records. The new rumor was that the accident had been a cover for retreat. After *Blonde on Blonde*, his intensive foray into the pop demi-monde, Dylan needed time to replenish his imagination. According to a less romantic version, he was keeping quiet till his contracts expired.

The confusion was typical. Not since Rimbaud said "*I* is another" has an artist been so obsessed with escaping identity.

His masks hidden by other masks, Dylan is the celebrity-stalker's ultimate antagonist. The original disparity between his public pose as rootless wanderer with Southwestern drawl and the private facts of home and middle-class family and high school diploma in Hibbing, Minn., was a commonplace subterfuge, the kind that pays reporters' salaries. It hardly showed his talent for elusiveness; what it probably showed was naïveté. But his attitude toward himself as a public personality was always clear. On an early recording, he used the eloquent pseudonym, "Blind Boy Grunt." "Dylan" is itself a pseudonym, possibly inspired by Dylan Thomas (a story Dylan now denies), possibly by a real or imaginary uncle named Dillon, who might or might not be the "Las Vegas dealer" Dylan once claimed was his only living relative.

In six years, Dylan's stance has evolved from proletarian assertiveness to anarchist angst to pop detachment. At each stage he has made himself harder to follow, provoked howls of execration from those left behind, and attracted an ever-larger, more demanding audience. He has reacted with growing hostility to the possessiveness of his audience and its shock troops, the journalists, the professional categorizers. His baroque press conference inventions are extensions of his work, full of imaginative truth and virtually devoid of information. The classic Dylan interview appeared in *Playboy*, where Nat Hentoff, like a housewife dusting her furniture while a tornado wrecks the house, pursued the homely fact through exchanges like: "Do you have any unfulfilled ambitions?" "Well, I guess I've always wanted to be Anthony Quinn in *La Strada*. . . . I guess I've always wanted to be Brigitte Bardot, too; but I don't really want to think about *that* too much."

Dylan's refusal to be known is not simply a celebrity's ploy, but a passion that has shaped his work. As his songs have become more introspective, the introspections have become more impersonal, the confidences of a no-man without past or future. Bob Dylan as identifiable *persona* has been disappearing into his songs, which is what he wants. This terrifies his audiences. They could accept a consistent image—roving minstrel, poet of alienation, spokesman for youth—in lieu of the "real" Bob Dylan. But his progressive self-annihilation cannot be contained in a game of let's pretend, and it conjures up nightmares of madness, mutilation, death.

The nightmares are chimerical; there is a continuing self, the Bobby Dylan friends describe as shy and defensive, hyped up, careless of his health, a bit scared by fame, unmaterialistic but shrewd about money, a professional absorbed in his craft. Dylan's songs bear the stigmata of an authentic middle-class adolescence; his eye for detail, sense of humor, and skill at evoking the archetypal sexual skirmishes show that some part of him is of as well as in the world. As further evidence, he has a wife, son and house in Woodstock, N.Y. Instead of an image, Dylan has created a magic theater in which the public gets lost willy-nilly. Yet he is more—or less—than the sum of his illusions.

Many people hate Bob Dylan because they hate being fooled. Illusion is fine, if quarantined and diagnosed as mild; otherwise it is potentially humiliating (is he laughing at me? conning me out of my money?). Some still discount Dylan as merely a popular culture hero (how can a teen-age idol be a serious artist—at most, perhaps, a serious demagogue). But the most tempting answer—forget his public presence, listen to his songs—won't do. For Dylan has exploited his image as a vehicle for artistic statement. The same is true of Andy Warhol and, to a lesser degree, of the Beatles and Allen Ginsberg. (In contrast, James Dean and Marilyn Monroe were creatures, not masters of their images.) The tenacity of the modern publicity apparatus often makes artists' personalities more familiar than their work, while its pervasiveness obscures the work of those who can't or won't be personalities. If there is an audience for images, artists will inevitably use the image as a medium—and some images are more original, more compelling, more relevant than others. Dylan has self-consciously explored the possibilities of mass communication just as the pop artists explored the possibilities of mass production. In the same sense that pop art is about commodities, Dylan's art is about celebrity.

This is not to deny the intrinsic value of Dylan's songs. Everyone interested in folk and popular music agrees on their importance, if not their merit. As composer, interpreter, most of all as lyricist, Dylan has made a revolution. He expanded folk idiom into a rich, figurative language, grafted literary and philosophical subtleties onto the protest song, revitalized folk vision by rejecting proletarian and ethnic sentimentality, then all but destroyed pure folk as a contemporary form by merging it with pop. Since then rock-and-roll, which was already in the midst of a creative flowering dominated by British rock and Motown, has been transformed. Songwriters have raided folk music as never before for new sounds, new images, new subject matter. Dylan's innovative lyrics have been enthusiastically imitated. The folk music lovers who managed to evolve with him, the connoisseurs of pop, the bohemian fringe of the literary community, the turned-on searchers after absolute experience and of course teen-agers consider him a genius, a prophet. Folk purists and political radicals, who were inspired by his earlier material, cry betrayal with a vehemence that acknowledges his gifts.

Yet many of Dylan's fans—especially ex-fans—miss the point. Dylan is no apostle of the electronic age. Rather, he is a fifth-columnist from the past, shaped by personal and political nonconformity, by blues and modern poetry. He has imposed his commitment to individual freedom (and its obverse, isolation) on the hip passivity of pop culture, his literacy on an illiterate music. He has used the publicity machine to demonstrate his belief in privacy. His songs and public role are guides to survival in the world of the image, the cool, and the high. And in coming to terms with that world, he has forced it to come to terms with him.

II

By 1960, the folk music revival that began in the fifties had expanded into an all-inclusive smorgasbord, with kitschy imitation-folk groups at one end, resurrected cigarbox guitarists and Ozark balladeers at the other. Of music that pretended to ethnic authenticity, the most popular was folk blues—Leadbelly, Sonny Terry and Brownie McGhee, Lightnin' Hopkins. The response to blues was in part a tribute to the ascendancy of rock-and-roll—Negro rhythms had affected the consciousness of every teenager in the fifties. But blues, unlike rock, was free of identification with the dominant society. Its sexuality and rebelliousness were undiluted, and it was about people, not teen-agers. Besides, the Negro, always a dual symbol of suffering and life-force, was gaining new political importance, and folk blues expressed the restlessness of activists, bohemians, declassé intellectuals. Since younger black performers were not interested in preserving a genre they had abandoned for more distinctly urban forms, white city singers tried to fill the gap. Patronized unmercifully by blues purists, the best of them did not simply approximate Negro sounds but evoked personal pain and disenchantment with white culture.

At the same time, there was a surge of folk composing. The Weavers, in the vanguard of the revival, had popularized the iconoclastic ballads and talking blues of Woody Guthrie, chronicler of the dust bowl and depression, the open road, the unions, the common man as intrepid endurer. Pete Seeger, the Weavers' lead singer in the early days and the most prestigious folk musician in the country, had recorded albums of topical songs from the thirties and forties. With the emergence of the civil rights movement, freedom songs, some new, some updated spirituals and union chants, began coming out of the South. Northern musicians began to write and perform their own material, mainly variations on the hard-traveling theme and polemics against racism, the bomb and middle-class conformity. Guthrie was their godfather, Seeger their guru, California songwriter Malvina Reynolds their older sister. Later, they were to acquire an angel—Joan Baez, who would record their songs and sing them at racial demonstrations and peace rallies; an organ—*Broadside,* a mimeographed magazine founded in 1962; and a sachem—Bob Dylan.

Gerde's Folk City, an unassuming, unbohemian cabaret in Greenwich Village, was the folk fan's chief New York hangout. On Monday, hootenanny night, blues interpreters like Dave Van Ronk, bluegrass groups like the Greenbriar Boys, the new topical songwriters—Tom Paxton, Phil Ochs, Len Chandler—would stop in and perform. Established singers came because Gerde's was part of the scene, because they enjoyed playing to the aficionados who gathered after midnight. The young ones came for a showcase and for contact with musicians they admired.

When Bob Dylan first showed up at Gerde's in the spring of 1961, fresh-skinned and baby-faced and wearing a schoolboy's corduroy cap, the manager asked him for proof of age. He was nineteen, only recently arrived in New York. Skinny, nervous, manic, the bohemian patina of jeans and boots, scruffy hair, hip jargon and hitchhiking mileage barely settled on nice Bobby Zimmerman, he had been trying to catch on at the coffeehouses. His material and style were a cud of half-digested influences: Guthrie cum Elliott; Blind Lemon Jefferson cum Leadbelly cum Van Ronk; the hillbilly sounds of Hank Williams and Jimmie Rodgers; the rock-and-roll of Chuck Berry and Elvis Presley. He was constantly writing new songs. On stage, he varied poignancy with clownishness. His interpretations of traditional songs—especially blues—were pretentious, and his harsh, flat voice kept slipping over the edge of plaintiveness into strident self-pity. But he shone as a comedian, charming audiences with Charlie Chaplin routines, playing with his hair and cap, burlesquing his own mannerisms, and simply enjoying himself. His specialty was composing lightly sardonic talking blues—chants to a bass run guitar accompaniment, a favorite vehicle of Woody Guthrie's: "Them Communists were all around/ in the air and on the ground/ . . . I run down most hurriedly/ and joined the John Birch society."

That fall, *New York Times* folk music critic Robert Shelton visited Gerde's and gave Dylan an enthusiastic review. Columbia Records signed him and released a mediocre first album in February, 1962. It contained only two Dylan compositions, both non-political. Dylan began publishing his topical songs in *Broadside*. Like his contemporaries, he was more propagandist than artist, his syntax often barbarous, his diction crude. Even so, his work stood out—it contained the most graphic descriptions of racial atrocities. But Dylan also had a gentler mood. Road songs like "Song to Woody" strove—not too successfully—for Guthrie's expressive understatement and simple, traditional sound.

In May, 1962, *Broadside* published a new Dylan song:

> How many roads must a man walk down before you
> call him a man?

How many seas must a white dove sail before she sleeps in the sand?
How many times must the cannonballs fly before they're forever banned?
The answer, my friend, is blowin' in the wind, the answer is blowin' in the wind.*

Set to a melody adopted from a spiritual, "Blowin' in the Wind" combined indignation with Guthriesque simplicity and added a touch of original imagery. It received little circulation until nearly a year later, when Peter, Paul and Mary heard Dylan sing it at a coffeehouse. Their recording of the song sold a million copies, inspired more than 50 other versions, and established topical song as the most important development of the folk revival. The relative subtlety of the lyric made the topical movement aesthetically self-conscious. It did not drive out direct political statements—Dylan himself continued to write them—but it set a standard impossible to ignore, and topical songs began to show more wit, more craftsmanship, more variety.

"Blowin' in the Wind" was included in Dylan's second album, *The Freewheelin' Bob Dylan,* which appeared in May, 1963. This time, nearly all the songs were his own; five had political themes. It was an extraordinary record. The influences had coalesced; the voice, unmusical as ever, had found an evocative range somewhere between abrasion and sentimentality; the lyrics (except for "Masters of War," a simplistic diatribe against munitions-makers) were vibrant and pithy. The album contained what may still be Dylan's best song—"It's A Hard Rain's a-Gonna Fall," a vivid evocation of nuclear apocalypse that owed much to Allen Ginsberg's Biblical rhetoric and declamatory style. Its theme was modern, its spirit ancient. At first hearing, most of the *Freewheelin'* songs sounded less revolutionary than they were: so skillfully had Dylan distilled the forms and moods of traditional music that his originality took time to register.

Freewheelin' illuminated Dylan's America—or rather two Americas. "Hard Rain" confronted the underside, "where the executioner's face is always well-hidden," "where black is the color and none is the number," a world of deserted diamond

* Copyright © M. Witmark & Sons, 1962.

highways, incipient tidal waves, clowns crying in alleys, children armed with guns and swords, "10,000 whisperin and nobody listenin" and occasional portents of redemption: "I met a young girl, she gave me a rainbow." The satirical "Talking World War III Blues" toured the country's surface: hot dog stands, parking meters, Cadillacs, rock-and-roll singers, telephone operators, cool females, officious doctors. Dylan's moral outrage coexisted with a grudging affection for American society and its foibles. If there was "Masters of War," there was also "I shall Be Free"; "My telephone rang, it would not stop, it was President Kennedy callin me up./ He said my friend Bob what do we need to make this country grow I said my friend John, Brigitte Bardot."

For a time, the outrage predominated. Dylan's output of bitter protest increased and his humor receded. He was still learning from Woody Guthrie, but he often substituted despair for Guthrie's resilience: his finest ballads chronicled the disintegration of an unemployed miner's family; the killing of a Negro maid, punished by a six-month sentence; the extremity of a penniless farmer who shot himself, his wife, and five kids. At the same time, his prophetic songs discarded the pessimism of "Hard Rain" for triumph in "The Times They Are a-Changin'" and vindictiveness in "When the Ship Comes In": "Then they'll raise their hands, say we'll meet all your demands and we'll shout from the bow, your days are numbered."

It was Dylan's year. Stimulated by the wide acceptance of his work, inspired by his ideas and images, topical songwriters became more and more prolific. Dylan songs were recorded by dozens of folk singers, notably Joan Baez (at whom he had once sneered, "She's still singing about Mary Hamilton. Where's that at?"). No folk concert was complete without "Hard Rain," or "Don't Think Twice," or a protest song from Dylan's third album, *The Times They Are A-Changin'*. The college folk crowd imitated Dylan; civil rights workers took heart from him; masochistic journalists lionized him. And in the attenuated versions of Peter, Paul and Mary, the Chad Mitchell Trio, even Lawrence Welk, his songs reached the fraternity house and the suburb.

Then Dylan yanked the rug: he renounced political protest. He put out an album of personal songs, and in one of them, "My Back Pages," scoffed at his previous moral absolutism. His refrain—"Ah, but I was so much older then, I'm younger than that now"—seemed a slap at the thirties left. And the song contained scraps of uncomfortably private imagery—hints of aesthetic escapism?

Folk devotees were shocked at Dylan's apostasy. Folk music and social protest have always fed on each other, and the current revival had been political all along. For children of depression activists growing up in the Eisenhower slough, folk music was a way of keeping the faith. When they converged on the Weavers' Town Hall hootenannies, they came as the anti-McCarthy resistance, pilgrims to the thirties shrine. The Weavers were blacklisted for alleged Communist connections; Pete Seeger had been *there,* singing for the unions, for the Spanish Republic. It didn't matter what they sang—in the atmosphere of conspiratorial sympathy that permeated those performances even "Greensleeves" had radical overtones. Later, as the left revived, folk singing became a badge of involvement, an expression of solidarity, and most important, a history-in-the-raw of struggle. Now, Dylan's defection threatened the last aesthetically respectable haven for believers in proletarian art.

Dylan had written personal songs before, but they were songs that accepted folk conventions. Narrative in impulse, nostalgic but restless in mood, their central image the road and its imperative, they complemented his protest songs: here was an outlaw, unable to settle for one place, one girl, a merely private life, committed to that symbolic journey. His new songs were more psychological, limning characters and relationships. They substituted ambition for the artless perfection of his best early songs: "It Ain't Me, Babe," a gloss on the spiritual possessiveness of woman, took three stanzas to say what "Don't Think Twice, It's All Right" had suggested in a few phrases: "I'm thinkin and wonderin, walkin down the road/ I once loved a woman, a child and I'm told/ gave her my heart but she wanted my soul." Dylan's language was opening up—doves sleeping in the sand were one thing, "crimson flames tied through my ears" quite another. And his tone was changing; in his love songs, ingenuousness began to yield to self-possession, the spontaneity of the road to the gamesmanship of the city. They were transitional songs, full of half-realized ideas; having rejected the role of people's bard, Dylan had yet to find a new niche.

III

In retrospect, Dylan's break with the topical song movement seemed inevitable. He had modeled himself on Woody Guthrie, whose incessant traveling was an emotional as well as economic necessity, whose commitment to radical politics was rooted in an individualism as compulsive as Dylan's own. But Guthrie had had to organize or submit; Dylan had other choices. For Guthrie, the road was habitat; for Dylan, metaphor. The closing of the iron mines had done to Hibbing what drought had done to Guthrie's Oklahoma, but while Guthrie had been a victim, Dylan was a bystander. A voluntary refugee from middle-class life, more aesthete than activist, he had less in common with the left than with literary rebels—Blake, Whitman, Rimbaud, Crane, Ginsberg.

The beauty of "Hard Rain" was that it exploited poetry while remaining a folk lyric, simple, repetitive, seemingly uncontrived. Now Dylan became self-consciously poetic, adopting a neo-beat style loaded with images. Though he had rejected the traditional political categories, his new posture was if anything more scornful of the social order than before. "It's Alright, Ma (I'm Only Bleeding)" attacked both the "human gods" who "make everything from toy guns that spark to flesh-colored Christs that glow in the dark" and their acquiescent victim, who "gargles in the rat-race choir." "Gates of Eden," like "Hard Rain," descended into a surreal nether-world, the menace this time a psychic bomb, the revolt of repressed instinct: "The motorcycle black madonna two-wheeled gypsy queen/ and her silver-studded phantom cause the gray flannel dwarf to scream." As poetry these songs were overrated—*Howl* had said it all much better—and they were unmusical, near-chants, declaimed to a monotonous guitar strum. Yet the perfunctory music made the bohemian commonplaces work—made them fresh. Perhaps it was the context: though few people realized it yet, the civil rights movement was losing its moral force; the Vietnam juggernaut was becoming the personal concern of every draft-age man;

a new generation of bohemians, more expansive and less cynical than the beats, was about to blossom. The time was right for a reaffirmation of individual revolt.

But Dylan had also been exposed to a very different vision: in May, 1964, he had toured an England transformed by mod fashion and the unprecedented excitement over the Beatles and the Rolling Stones. When his new record came out the following spring, its title was *Bringing It All Back Home*. On the album jacket, a chiaroscuro Dylan, bright face emerging from ominous shadows, stared accusingly at the viewer. In black suit and striped shirt, he perched on a long divan, hugging a cat, behind him a modish, blank-faced beauty in scarlet lounging pajamas. The room, wreathed in light and dominated by a baroque mantelpiece, abounded with artifacts—*Time,* a movie magazine, a fallout shelter sign, folk and pop records (including earlier Dylan), a portrait, a candlestick, a few mysterious objects obscured by a halo.

Most of side one was devoted to "Gates of Eden" and "It's Alright, Ma." But the most arresting cut on the side was "Mr. Tambourine Man," a hymn to the psychedelic quest: "take me disappearing through the smoke-rings of my mind/ down the foggy ruins of time/ . . . take me on a trip upon your magic swirling ship." Drug-oriented bohemians loved it; it was another step away from the sobersided politicals. It was also more like a folk song than anything Dylan had written since giving up politics, a spiritual road song with lilting, singable melody.

The other side was rock-and-roll, Dylan on electric guitar and piano backed by a five-man band. It was not hard rock. There was no over-dubbing, and Dylan played his amplified guitar folk-style. But the beat was there, and the sound, if not overwhelming, was big enough to muffle some of the lyrics. These dispensed a new kind of folk wisdom. Chaos had become a condition, like the weather, not to analyze or prophesy but to gripe about, cope with, dodge: "Look out, kid, it's somethin you did/ God knows when but you're doin it again." The message was pay attention to what's happening: "Don't follow leaders, watch the parkin meters."

One rock song, "Subterranean Homesick Blues," was released as a single. As Dylan's pop debut it was a modest success, hovering halfway up the *Cash Box* and *Billboard* charts. That summer, Dylan cut "Like a Rolling Stone," the most scurrilous and—with its powerful beat—the most dramatic in a long line of non-love songs:

> You used to ride on the chrome horse with your
> diplomat
> who carried on his shoulder a Siamese cat
> ain't it hard when you discovered that he wasn't really
> where it's at
> after he took from you everything he could steal.*

It was a number one hit, as "Blowin' in the Wind" had been two years before—only now it was Dylan's own expressive snarl coming over radio and jukebox.

"Rolling Stone" opened Dylan's first all-rock album, *Highway 61 Revisited.* More polished but less daring than *Bringing It All Back Home,* the album reworked familiar motifs. The title song, which depicted the highway as junkyard, temple, and arena for war, was Dylan's best face-of-America commentary since "Talking World War III Blues." The witty and scarifying "Ballad of a Thin Man," which derided the rationalist bewildered by the instinctual revolt, was an updated "Times They Are a-Changin'," with battle lines redrawn according to pop morality. Dylan did not hail the breakdown of sanity he described but merely kept his cool, mocking Mr. Jones (the pop equivalent of Mr. Charlie) for committing squareness: "The sword-swallower he comes up to you and then he kneels/ . . . and he says here is your throat back, thanks for the loan/ and something is happening but you don't know what it is, do you, Mr. Jones?" "Desolation Row" was Dylan's final tribute to the götterdämmerung strain in modern literature—an eleven-minute freak show whose cast of losers, goons and ghosts wandered around in a miasma of sexual repression and latent violence underscored by the electronic beat: "Einstein disguised as Robin Hood . . ./ passed this way an hour ago with his friend, a jealous monk/ now he looked so immaculately frightful as he bummed a cigarette/ then he went off sniffing drainpipes and reciting the alphabet."

The violent hostility of traditionalists to Dylan's rock-and-roll made the uproar over "My Back Pages" seem mild. Not only orthodox leftists but bohemian radicals called him a sellout and a phony. At the July, 1965 Newport Folk Festival, he appeared with his electric guitar and was booed off the stage. Defiantly, Dylan exacerbated the furor, insisting on his contempt for message songs and his indifference to causes, refusing to agonize over his wealth or his taxes ("Uncle Sam, he's my *uncle!* Can't turn your back on a member of the family!"). In one notorious interview, he claimed he had written topical songs only to get published in *Broadside* and attract attention. Many former fans took the bait. Actually, Dylan's work still bristled with messages; his "opportunism" had absorbed three years of his life and produced the finest extensions of traditional music since Guthrie. But the purists believed in it because they wanted to. Their passion told less about Dylan than about their own peculiar compound of aristocratic and proletarian sensitivities.

Pure folk sound and idiom, in theory the expression of ordinary people, had become the province of middle-class dissidents who identified with the Common Man but whose attitude toward common men resembled that of White Russian expatriates toward the communized peasants. For them popular music—especially rock-and-roll—symbolized the displacement of the true folk by the mass. Rock was not created by the people but purveyed by the communications industry. The performer was incidental to engineer and publicity man. The beat was moronic, the lyrics banal teen-age trivia.

These were half-truths. From the beginning, there was a bottom-up as well as top-down movement in rock-and-roll: neighborhood kids formed groups and wrote songs; country singers adopted a rhythm-and-blues beat. Rock took a mechanized, acquisitive society for granted, yet in its own way it was protest music, uniting teen-agers against adults' lack of sympathy with youthful energy and love and sex. The mediocrity of most performers only made rock more "authentic"—anyone could sing it—and one of the few remaining vindications of the American dream—any kid from the slums might become a millionaire. (The best singers, of course, were fine interpreters; Elvis Presley and Chuck Berry did not have golden voices, but neither did Leadbelly or Woody Guthrie.) Rock-and-roll was further from the grass roots than traditional music, but closer than any other kind of pop. If the *realvolk* did not recognize this, the average adult did, and condemned the music for its adolescent surliness and its sexuality, covert in the lyrics, overt in the beat and in the intense response to idols.

But it remained for the British renaissance to prove that the mainstream of mass culture could produce folk music—that is, anti-establishment music. The Beatles, commercial without apology, delighted in the Americanized decadence of their environment. Yet their enthusiasm was subversive—they endorsed the reality of the culture, not its official myths. The Stones were iconoclastic in a different way: deliberately ugly, blatantly erotic, they exuded contempt for the public while making a fortune. Their cynicism, like Leadbelly's violence or Charlie Parker's heroin, was part of their charisma: unlike traditional folk singers, they could cheerfully censor their lyrics for Ed Sullivan without seeming domesticated—the effect was more as if they had paraded a sign saying "Blank CBS." British rock was far superior to most early rock-and-roll. Times had changed: electronic techniques were more sophisticated, radio stations and record companies less squeamish about sexual candor, and teen culture was merging into a more mature, less superficial youth culture with semi-bohemian tastes. Most important, the British groups successfully assimilated Negro music, neither vitiating rhythm-and-blues nor imitating it, but refining it to reflect their own milieu—white, lower-class, urban, technological, materialistic, tough-minded.

Most folk fans—even those with no intrinsic objections to rock, who had perhaps listened to it when they were teen-agers and not obliged to be serious—assumed that commercial exploitation automatically gutted music. Yet the Rolling Stones were creating as valid blues as any folk singers, black or white. After *Bringing It All Back Home*, the contradiction could no longer be ignored, and those not irrevocably committed to the traditional folk ethos saw the point. Phil Ochs praised *Highway 61;* Joan Baez cut a rock-and-roll record; more and more folk singers began to use electronic instruments. Folk-rock generated an unaccustomed accord between the folk and pop worlds. In *Crawdaddy!*, Richard Fariña lauded "this shift away from open-road-protest-flat-pick-style to more Nashville-Motown-Thameside, with the strong implication that some of us had been listening to the A.M. radio." Malvina Reynolds pronounced the new rock-and-roll "a wonder and delight." By November, 1966, folk-rock had received the final imprimatur—Pete Seeger recorded an album backed by three members of the Blues Project.

Folk-rock was never a form, but a simple-minded inspiration responsible for all sorts of hybrids. At first it was mostly rock versions of Dylan folk songs, social protest rock, and generational trauma rock, a weekend-hippie version of the classic formula, children against parents. Then, self-styled musical poets Simon and Garfunkel began imitating Dylan's apocalyptic songs ("People bowed and prayed/ to the neon god they made/ . . . the words of the prophets are written on a subway wall"), starting a trend to elaborate and, too often, sophomoric lyrics. The Lovin' Spoonful invented the "good-time sound," a varying mixture of rock, blues, jug and old pop. Donovan wrote medieval fantasies and pop collages like "Sunshine Superman" and "Mellow Yellow." And there was acid-rock, the music of new bohemia.

Psychedelic music, like folk-rock, was a catch-all label; it described a variety of products shaped by folk, British rock, Chicago blues, jazz, Indian music. Psychedelic lyrics, heavily influenced by Dylanesque imagery, used the conventions of the romantic pop song to express sexual and mystical rather than sentimental love and focused on the trip—especially the flight—the way folk music focused on the road. The Byrds, who had started folk-rock moving with their hit record of "Mr. Tambourine Man," launched the California psychedelic sound with "Eight Miles High," which picked up on the Beatles' experiments with Indian instrumentation and was ostensibly about flying over London airport (it was banned anyway by right-thinking disc-jockeys). Though the Byrds were from Los Angeles, the scene soon shifted north, and a proliferation of underground rock groups—some, like Jefferson Airplane, the Grateful Dead, and Country Joe and the Fish, quickly surfaced—made San Francisco the new center of avant-garde pop, superseding Britain.

The California groups came closest to making the term folk-rock say something. For hippie culture, bastard of the beat generation out of pop, was much like a folk culture; oral, naive, communal, its aphorisms ("Make love, not war," "turn on, tune in, drop out") intuited, not rationalized. Pop and beat, thesis and antithesis of the affluent society, contained elements of synthesis: both movements rejected intellect for sensation, politics for art, and Ginsberg and Kerouac glorified a grass-roots America that included supermarkets and cars as well as mountains and apple pie. The hippies simplified the beats' utopian anarchism and substituted psychedelic drugs for Zen and yoga; they also shared the pop enthusiasm for technology and the rainbow surface of affluence—their music was rock, their style mod. Like Dylan, they bridged old culture and new—they were still idealists—and they idolized him. But he did not consider himself their spokesman. At 25, he was too old ("How can I be the voice of their generation? I'm not their generation") and, though he did not admit it publicly, too well-read. While "Mr. Tambourine Man" was becoming the hippie anthem, he was saying "LSD is for mad, hateful people" and making fun of drugs in "Memphis Blues Again." Dylan was really at cross-purposes with the hippies. They were trying to embody pop sensibility in a folk culture. He was trying to comprehend pop culture with—at bottom—a folk sensibility.

IV

It is a truism among Dylan's admirers that he is a poet using rock-and-roll to spread his art: as Jack Newfield put it in the *Village Voice*, "If Whitman were alive today, he too would be playing an electric guitar." This misrepresentation has only served to discredit Dylan among intellectuals and draw predictable sniping from conscientious B-student poets like Louis Simpson and John Ciardi. Dylan has a lavish verbal imagination and a brilliant sense of irony, and many of his images—especially on the two *Blonde on Blonde* records—are memorable. But poetry also requires economy, coherence and discrimination, and Dylan has perpetrated prolix verses, horrendous grammar, tangled phrases, silly metaphors, embarrassing clichés, muddled thought; at times he seems to believe one good image deserves five others, and he relies too much on rhyme. His chief literary virtue—sensitivity to psychological nuance—belongs to fiction more than poetry. His skill at creating character has made good lyrics out of terrible poetry, as in the pre-rock "Ballad in Plain D," whose portraits of the singer, his girl and her family redeem lines like: "With unseen consciousness I possessed in my grip/ a magnificent mantelpiece though its heart being chipped."

Dylan is not always undisciplined. As early as *Freewheelin'*, it was clear that he could control his material when he cared to. But his disciplines are song-writing and acting, not poetry; his words fit the needs of music and performance, not an intrinsic pattern. Words or rhymes that seem gratuitous in print often make good musical sense, and Dylan's voice, an extraordinary interpreter of emotion though (or more likely because) it is almost devoid of melody, makes vague lines clear. Dylan's music is not inspired. His melodies and arrangements are derivative, and his one technical accomplishment, a vivacious, evocative harmonica, does not approach the virtuosity of a Sonny Terry. His strength as a musician is his formidable eclecticism combined with a talent for choosing the right music to go with a given lyric. The result is a unity of sound and word that eludes most of his imitators.

Dylan is effective only when exploiting this unity, which is why his free verse album notes are interesting mainly as autobiography (or mythology) and why *Tarantula* is unlikely to be a masterpiece. When critics call Dylan a poet, they really mean visionary. Because the poet is the paradigmatic seer, it is conventional to talk about the film poet, the jazz poet. Dylan is verbal, which makes the label even more tempting. But it evades an important truth—the new visionaries are not poets. Dylan is specifically pessimistic about the future of literature. Far from Desolation Row, "The Titanic sails at dawn/ . . . Ezra Pound and T. S. Eliot fighting in the captain's towers/ while calypso singers laugh at them and fishermen hold flowers." The infamous Mr. Jones, with his pencil in his hand, his eyes in his pocket and his nose on the ground, is a literary man. With the rock songs on *Bringing It All Back Home,* Dylan began trying to create an alternative to poetry. If Whitman were alive today, he might be playing electric guitar; then again, he might be writing advertising copy.

In May, 1966, Dylan recorded *Blonde on Blonde,* a double album cut in Nashville with local musicians. Formally, it was his finest achievement since *Freewheelin',* but while the appeal of the *Freewheelin'* songs was the illusion of spontaneous folk expression, the songs from *Blonde on Blonde* were clearly artifacts, lovingly and carefully made. The music was rock and Nashville country, with a sprinkling of blues runs and English-ballad arpeggios. Thematically, the album was a unity. It explored the sub-world pop was creating, an exotic milieu of velvet doors and scorpions, cool sex ("I saw you makin love with him,/ you forgot to close the garage door"), zany fashions ("it balances on your head just like a mattress balances on a bottle of wine,/ your brand-new leopard-skin pill-box hat"), strange potions ("it strangled up my mind,/ now people just get uglier and I have no sense of time"), neurotic women ("she's like all the rest/ with her fog, her amphetamine, and her pearls").

The songs did not preach: Dylan was no longer rebel but seismograph, registering his emotions—fascination, confusion, pity, annoyance, exuberance, anguish—with sardonic lucidity. Only once, in "Just Like a Woman," did his culture shock get out of control: "I can't stay in here/ ain't it clear/ that I just can't fit/ . . . please don't let on that you knew me when/ I was hungry, and it was your world." Many of the songs were about child-women, bitchy, unreliable, sometimes vulnerable, usually one step ahead: "I told you as you clawed out my eyes/ I never really meant to do you any harm." But there were also goddesses like Johanna and the mercury-mouthed, silken-fleshed Sad-Eyed Lady of the Lowlands, Beatrices of pop who shed not merely light but kaleidoscopic images: "these visions of Johanna are now all that remain."

The fashionable, sybaritic denizens of *Blonde on Blonde* are the sort of people despised by radicals as apologists for the system. Yet in accepting the surface that system has produced, they subvert its assumptions. Conservative and utopian ideologues agree that man must understand and control his environment; the questions are how, and for whose benefit. But pop culture defines man as a receiver of stimuli, his environment as sensory patterns to be enjoyed, not interpreted (literature and philosophy are irrelevant) or acted upon (politics is irrelevant). "If you want to understand me, look at my surface," says Andy Warhol. And "I like my paintings because anybody can do them." The bureaucrat defends standardization because it makes a complex society manageable. Yet he thinks of himself as an individualist, and finds the idea of mass-produced, mechanized art incomprehensible, threatening—or a put-on. The pop artist looks at mass culture naively and sees beauty in its regular patterns; like an anthropologist exhibiting Indian basket-weaving, Warhol shows us our folk art—soup cans. His message—the Emperor has no clothes, but that's all right, in fact it's beautiful—takes acceptance of image for essence to its logical extreme. *Blonde on Blonde* is about this love of surface.

Dylan's sensitivity to pop comes straight out of his folk background. Both folk and pop mentalities are leery of abstractions, and Dylan's appreciation of surface detail represents Guthriesque common sense—to Dylan, a television commercial was always a television commercial as well as a symbol of alienation. From the first, a basic pragmatism tempered his commitment to the passionate excesses of the revolutionist and the *poète-maudit* and set him apart from hipster heroes like James Dean. Like the beats, who admired the total revolt of the hipster from a safe distance, Dylan is essentially non-violent. Any vengefulness in his songs is either impersonal or funny, like the threats of a little boy to beat up the bad guys; more often, he is the bemused butt of slapstick cruelty. "I've got a woman, she's so mean/ sticks my boots in the washing machine/ sticks me with buckshot when I'm nude/ puts bubble gum in my food."

Dylan's basic rapport with reality has also saved him from the excesses of pop, kept him from merging, Warhol-like, into his public surface. *John Wesley Harding*, released after twenty months of silence, shows that Dylan is still intact in spirit as well as body. The songs are more impersonal—and in a way more inscrutable—than ever, yet the human being behind them has never seemed less mysterious. For they reveal Dylan not as the protean embodiment of some collective nerve, but as an alert artist responding to challenge from his peers. Dylan's first rock-and-roll songs were his reaction to the changes in life-style the new rock represented; *John Wesley Harding* is a reaction to the music itself as it has evolved since his accident. The album is comprehensible only in this context.

As Dylan's recovery advanced, he began making the papers again. He signed a new contract with Columbia—the defection to MGM never came off—and the company announced that he was recording. Dylan was still revered, his near-mythic status only solidified by his long absence from the scene. But whether he could come back as an active performer was another question. It was reported that he had listened to the first few cuts of *Sgt. Pepper* and snapped "Turn that off"; perhaps the new developments in rock had left him behind. On the other hand, perhaps he was leaving rock behind. Many of Dylan's associates—notably Tom Wilson, his former A&R man—had always insisted that Dylan was much more sophisticated musically than he let on. And in May, a New York *Daily News* reporter quoted Dylan as saying he was at work on "two new sounds."

Ever since the emergence of the Late Beatles and the New Beach Boys, the "serious" rock groups had been producing albums that said, in effect, "Can you top this?" The competition extended to elaborate album covers and titles. By Christmas, the Stones had won the prize—*Their Satanic Majesties Request,* with its 3-D cover, was almost a parody of the whole art-rock phenomenon. How was Dylan going to top *that?* Everyone waited for a revolutionary masterpiece or an extravagant flop. What they got was *John Wesley Harding* in a plain gray jacket with a polaroid snapshot of Dylan and three Indians in the country. The first sound to greet the eager listener was the strumming of an acoustic guitar. The first line of the first song was "John Wesley Harding was a friend to the poor." Dylan had done it again.

The new melodies are absurdly simple, even for Dylan; the only instruments backing his guitar, piano and harmonica are a bass, a drum, and in two songs an extra guitar; the rock beat has faded out and the country and English ballad strains now dominate. The titles are all as straight as "John Wesley Harding": most are taken from the first lines of the songs. The lyrics are not only simple but understated in a way that shows Dylan has learned a trick or two from Lennon-McCartney, and they are folk lyrics. Or more precisely, affectionate comments on folk lyrics—the album is not a reversion to his early work but a kind of hymn to it. Nearly all the songs play with the clichés of folk music. The title song, for instance, seems at first hearing to be a second-rate "Jesse James" or "Pretty Boy Floyd." It starts out with all the catch phrases about the benevolent outlaw, then goes into the story: "It was down in Cheney County the time they talk about/With his lady by his side he took a stand." But the next line goes right out of it again: "And soon the situation was all but straightened out." You never learn what happened in Cheney County or why it wasn't *entirely* straightened out, and the song ends with more stock lines about the bandit's elusiveness and the helplessness of the law. It is not about John Wesley Harding, but about a familiar formula: and this, friends, is how you write the generic outlaw song.

Several of the songs are folk-style fantasies. "Frankie Lee and Judas Priest" is both a folk-ballad (based on another stock situation, the gambler on the road) and one of Dylan's surrealist dream songs; "As I Walked Out One Morning" describes a run-in with an Arthurian enchantress as if she were a revenue agent or the farmer's daughter. This juxtaposition of the conventional and the fantastic produces an unsettling gnomic effect, enhanced in some cases by truncated endings—in "The Drifter's Escape," the drifter's trial for some unknown offense ends abruptly when lightning strikes the courthouse, and he gets away in the confusion; "All Along the Watchtower" ends with a beginning, "Two riders are approaching, the wind began to howl." The aura of the uncanny that these songs create is probably what Dylan meant when he remarked, years ago, that folk songs grew out of mysteries.

But some of the album is sheer fun, especially "Down Along the Cove," a jaunty blues banged out on the piano, and "I'll Be Your Baby Tonight," a thirties-type pop tune that rhymes "moon" with "spoon" for the benefit of those pundits who are always crowing over the demise of "Tin Pan Alley pap." And "Dear Landlord," the best cut musically, is further evidence that Dylan has—well, the only word for it is mellowed:

Dear landlord, please don't dismiss my case
I'm not about to argue, I'm not about to move to
no other place
Now each of us has his own special gift and you know
this was meant to be true
And if you don't underestimate me I won't
underestimate you.*

In the end, what this album is about is Dylan's reconciliation with his past, with ordinary people, and even—warily, ambivalently—with his arch-enemies, the landlords of the world.

Of course, being Bob Dylan, he has turned this reconciliation into a rebellion. His sudden removal of the mask—see, it's me, a songwriter, I just want to write nice songs—and the apparent step backward could be as traumatic for the public as his previous metamorphoses; Dylan is still in the business of shaking us up. *John Wesley Harding* does not measure up to *Blonde on Blonde*. It is basically a tour de force. But it serves its purpose, which is to liberate Dylan—and the rest of us—from the *Sgt. Pepper* straitjacket. Dylan is free now to work on his own terms. It would be foolish to predict what he will do next. But hopefully he will remain a mediator, using the language of pop to transcend it. If the gap between past and present continues to widen, such mediation may be crucial. In a communications crisis, the true prophets are the translators.

* Copyright © Dwarf Music, 1967.

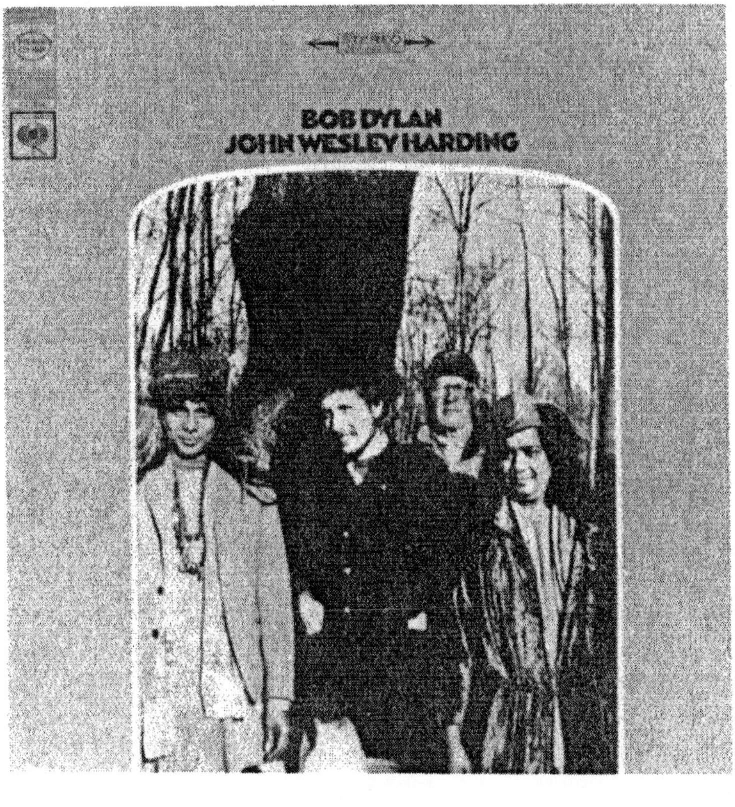
BOB DYLAN
JOHN WESLEY HARDING

Dylan Is Back

by Hubert Saal

"I won't be giving any concerts for a while," declared Bob Dylan. "I'm not compelled to do it now. I went around the world a couple of times. But I didn't have anything else to do then." So the hunger of an adoring public, famished by Dylan's eighteen-month retirement after his near-fatal motorcycle accident in 1966, is feasting on his new record, *John Wesley Harding.*

It has broken all Dylan records, its sales already verging on half a million and the gold disk that it took Dylan's three previous albums a year to achieve. In a month it has leapfrogged up the Billboard hit parade to No. 2, eclipsing the Rolling Stones and challenging the front-running Beatles.

Each Dylan album mapped new directions, alienating or delighting old admirers, enlisting armies of fresh recruits. In *Another Side of Dylan* he turned deaf ears to the protest idiom to which he had contributed such classics as "Blowin' in the Wind" and "The Times They Are A-Changin'." And then, when he exchanged his acoustical guitar for electric, used a rock beat and invented a form called folk rock and such songs as "Like a Rolling Stone," the folk purists called him "traitor." "It's just development," Dylan says. "We're always changing. You use new imagination and you get a new look."

'G': John Wesley Harding is no exception. Dylan likes change so much he even added a "g" to the name of the legendary Texas desperado. A few people have suggested that Dylan was trying to make up for all the g's he's dropped while singing his

songs, but when asked he replied, "No, that's just the way the name always sounded to me."

The obvious change in the new album is Dylan's return to the acoustical guitar and his train-wail harmonica. "I was always with the traditional song," Dylan says, "I just used electricity to wrap it up in. Probably I wasn't ready yet to make it simple. It's more complicated playing an electric guitar because you're five or ten feet away from the sound and you strain for things that you don't have to when the sound is right next to your body. Anyway it's the song itself that matters, not the sound of the song."

Craft: The simplicity and brevity of most of the songs in the new album happily reverse the tangled, surrealistic prolixity that characterizes such previous songs as "Desolation Row" and "Sad-Eyed Lady of the Lowlands." The new songs are carefully crafted, the imagery vivid and direct, the language concise, the rhymes often consonantly sophisticated. But concision inspires its own enigmas, demanding that the listener fill in between the lines—and sometimes provide the ending to a narrative ballad. "I Dreamed I Saw St. Augustine" burns with fervent evangelism, and, "All Along the Watchtower" mixes the symbolic, the pedestrian and the mystic to present a vision of irresistible evil.

An unusual quality of the new album is its fervent morality. Three of the songs actually end preaching a moral. "A song is moral just by being a song," Dylan comments. "We're all moralists. We all believe the same things in the same places." But Dylan's morality here is no longer concerned with specific causes, individual victims or, as in "The Gates of Eden" or "It's Alright, Ma (I'm Only Bleeding)," with unrelieved pessimism. Rather it is more philosophical, insisting in "The Wicked Messenger" and "I Pity the Poor Immigrant" on a fundamentalist approach to good and evil.

The two love songs that end the album reveal a new sexual maturity in Dylan. In earlier love songs, women are usually portrayed as selfish, fickle and even contemptible. But now he shows an adult and mutual tenderness. At the same time he gives the songs an amusing added dimension by slyly playing with love words that apply as easily to mother and son as to lovers. The simple, witty, lovely "I'll Be Your Baby Tonight" begins "Close your eyes/close the door/you don't have to worry any more/I'll be your baby tonight" and ends "Do not fear/ bring that bottle over here/I'll be your baby tonight."

Poet: In a rare interview, a slender smiling and bearded Bob Dylan, who wears octagonal-shaped rimless Ben Franklin glasses, expressed a surprising attitude toward his songs, which accounted in part for the obscurity surrounding so many of his lyrics. "I only look at them musically," he said, in a soft, Midwestern drawl. "I only look at them as things to sing. It's the music that the words are sung to that's important. I write the songs because I need something to sing." He elaborated. "It's the difference between the words on paper and the song. The song disappears into the air, the paper stays. They have little in common. A great poet, like Wallace Stevens, doesn't necessarily make a great singer. But a great singer always—like Billie Holiday—makes a great poet."

Dylan appeared much more concerned with his performance of the songs themselves. "I could have sung each of them better. I'm not exactly dissatisfied but I'm just not about to brag about the performance. In writing songs I have one great trouble. I'm lazy. I wish I could but you're not going to find me sitting down at the piano every morning. Either it comes or doesn't. Of course some songs, like 'Restless Farewell,' I've written just to fill up an album. And there are songs in which I made up a whole verse just to get to another verse."

He didn't do this in *John Wesley Harding*. "It holds together better. I've always tried to get simple. I haven't always succeeded. But here I took more care in the writing. In *Blonde on Blonde* I wrote out all the songs in the studio. The musicians played cards, I wrote out a song, we'd do it, they'd go back to their game and I'd write out another song." He wasn't composing on the spot but merely writing down songs he had carried around in his head for some time.

Confusion: Dylan prefers Nashville, where the new album was recorded, to New York. "I've cut seven albums in New York. You have to put up with all that taxicab nonsense and that big-city confusion which disables you a lot. It's always cold and you can't go outside when you want, you get a boxed-in feeling. And, though New York has top-quality people, musicians sure know how to play in Nashville."

Dylan's dislike of being boxed-in apparently accounts for his seclusion in Woodstock, N.Y. Since his recovery from the motorcycle accident, he's made only one brief appearance at a memorial concert for Woody Guthrie at Carnegie Hall, where he received a hero's ovation. Shying at personal questions, he would only say about the accident: "I stared at the ceiling for a few months. But since I've often sat around staring at ceilings, it didn't bother me much. I haven't been in retreat. I'm a country boy myself, and you have to be let alone to really accomplish anything. The reason I wasn't recording was some confusion over the contract." (Columbia Records suspended Dylan and he was reportedly offered $1 million by M-G-M to switch companies. He didn't. "It was just some misunderstanding between the parties," he said.)

Wife: Dylan's current reluctance to give concerts has nothing to do with the accident from which he appears fully recovered. "I have more responsibilities now," he says. They include a wife and at least one child. Asked how long he had been married, Dylan said: "If you ask me or my wife we'd say eternity, but if you ask somebody else he'd probably say three or four years." How many children does he have? "Some," he replied.

He was more communicative about the book he's writing, which is not the long-delayed *Tarantula*. "You see," he said, "that was an opportunity for me to write a book rather than a book I wanted to write. I just put down all these words and sent them off to my publishers and they'd send back the galleys, and I'd be so embarrassed at the nonsense I'd written I'd change the whole thing. And all the time they had 100,000 orders." He shook his head in wonder. "Why, that is an audience for lots of writers' dreams. The trouble with it, it had no story. I'd been reading all these trash books, works suffering from sex and excitement and foolish things which only happen in a man's mind."

Hits: "I've discovered," Dylan continued, "that there are many many ways to write a story. Sensationalism isn't the way. Now I do have a story, the way Charlie Chaplin would think of it. It's all in here," he said, clutching the sides of his head. He hoped that the new book could be ready by July. Publication of *Tarantula* is indefinitely postponed.

Dylan's innocent approach to writing is both touching and oddly persuasive. His way with words is indisputable, from the frequently effective poems on his record jacket to the songs themselves, so many wonderful songs that it's amazing that he is just twenty-six years old. What is encouraging is the evidence supplied by his new album. A few songs are weak. None of them can match the incandescence of "Blowin' in the Wind" or "A Hard Rain's A-Gonna Fall." But the album displays Dylan the craftsman, the artist, who if he smacked no towering home runs, got a few extra base hits and got on base nearly every time. "I used to think," he says, "that myself and my songs were the same thing. But I don't believe that any more. There's myself and there's my song, which I hope is everybody's song."

John Wesley Harding

by Jon Landau

White rock is moving in a single direction at this time. The trend is unmistakably toward the redefinition of the musical structures that have been identified with it during its existence as a recognizable musical idiom. Bob Dylan alone stands outside this development. He alone moves in circles, not lines. Or at least Dylan is the only major artist in the field whose circularity has become evident. For the space between *Bob Dylan* and *John Wesley Harding* is that between birth and rebirth, not that between beginning and end. Unlike the Beatles, whose basic identity has been totally altered in the space between *Meet the Beatles* and *Magical Mystery Tour,* Dylan achieves a continuity through growth seldom found in the development of a popular artist. (Although the Beatles may bring it all back home yet.)

This continuity was more evident in the progression of Dylan's first seven albums than it is on his latest, *JWH*. The source of that continuity was derived from every facet of his recordings: the continuity of his use of the blues, his humor and, especially, his reliance on the melodramatic and the mythical. Musically, continuity has been sustained by the self-imposed limits he has placed on the structure of his melodies, his guitar style and his almost static use of the harmonica. (John Lennon gave that up after *Hard Day's Night.*) With the advent of *JWH* Dylan has totally redefined himself by breaking with much that was consistently in evidence on the albums immediately preceding this one. And the breaks with the past that he has made here

Reprinted with permission from *Crawdaddy!*, 1968.

are of greater import than any of his earlier breaks with his own past—such as the shift away from pure self-accompaniment. Yet the major break I wish to discuss—Dylan's abandonment of myths and melodrama that dominated all of his earlier albums—evidences Dylan's growth as an artist and when fully understood heightens the sense of continuity one can derive from his entire career. It is a break which allows Dylan to get more in touch with himself and with his audience.

The myth to which I refer has certainly not been a static one. Dylan has redefined it with each successive album, including *JWH,* namely, Bob Dylan, a moderate man, is a qualitatively different kind of myth than all the previous ones Dylan has created about himself. And to really understand its importance one has to look at his development from the beginning to see how Dylan has used myth, how he has defined his myth at each successive stage in his career and how, on *JWH,* he completely shatters the vestiges of the myths that had dominated all of his previous recordings.

The Dylan process began with a folk-singer stance. On his first album, *Bob Dylan,* he defined himself as a son of Woody Guthrie. Obviously the image was only skin deep. The comparison between Guthrie and Dylan was an incongruity from the very beginning—yet Dylan did his best to come on like the comparison was real. In a most un-Guthrie-like gesture, Dylan's first subject emerges on the album as "death." The album ended with "See That My Grave Is Kept Clean," which is an inherently melodramatic selection for ending an album and an inherently absurd one for anybody but Blind Lemon Jefferson to have recorded. While Dylan seems to have wanted to live up to his image very much he had already been overinfluenced by the urban folk-types' concern with bigness and overstatement. The self-consciousness which separates this type of artist from a Woody Guthrie unfortunately fell very heavily on Dylan even on his earliest work. Even on the lovely "Song to Woody" the attempt at understatement at the end of the song simply magnifies the feeling of overstatement that Dylan's vocal mannerisms impart to the song. In fact, the obvious affectations illustrate that for all his folk antiquarian and eclectic impulses the earliest Dylan was uncomfortable with his material. It doesn't seem to say enough to satisfy him. Most of his interpretations are really whole new songs like his "Freight Train Blues," which has nothing to do with Roy Acuff's version. The overall feel of the album is a tension between Dylan and his material, Dylan's need to impose his own drama on the drama of the originals. The resulting attempts at saying something important, something big, will contain the seeds of the Dylan myth of the creative genius, the artist as a totally free man and the totally self-reliant and unique individual.

The fact that Dylan did choose to create his style out of the sources of the past, however, cannot be overlooked, for his antiquarianism, his love of the simple, has a tendency to reassert itself at times you least expect it throughout his career. And his consistent use of the blues—the folk style he has been most at home with and most competent at—shows that his feel for music never gets too far ahead of his sense of the past.

The transition from folk singer to folk writer and in turn to folk prophet is the substance of *Freewheelin'* and *The Times They Are A-Changin'*, and it is in these two works that Dylan's myth and melodrama define themselves. In this regard a song like "Masters of War" is most revealing. It is, of course, a song of deep hatred and it illustrates Dylan's polarizing and dualistic tendencies. The Masters are on one side and he is on the other. Neither his own righteousness (as the first person of the song) nor their wickedness is ever questioned. Not only does he end up by wishing the death of his enemies but he wants to bury them himself and then stand over their graves until he's sure that they're dead. What is jarring here is not Dylan's political judgments—they are unobjectionable by themselves—but the unreality of Dylan's response to this situation. He is creating an abstraction, a stereotype, upon which he can justify his hatred, not the other way around. His response is not to someone he knows, but to someone he imagines, and the only possible result is a mythical picture of his subject and his feelings. The overstatement and the overkill of the imagery and narrative of the song strain the credibility of even those fully in agreement with the political implications of the song. The entire conception suffers from its one-dimensionality. Yet it was a dimension that Dylan could put his finger on very well indeed. His vocal style, his droning guitar, the charisma of his performance, elevated the song to a very high level of kitsch. There is a "touchability" and a monomania that give the work great power, not unlike the power of a demagogue. Yet it never goes beyond the boundaries of Dylan creating a myth and becoming its prophet.

I am not unaware of the fact that there was more than "Masters of War" on *Freewheelin'*. It is obvious that songs of this type constitute only a fraction of Dylan's work, even on this particular album. However, I do think it the most revealing strain to look at for purposes of comparison with *JWH* for reasons that will become evident shortly. There is, in fact, a continuing tension between Dylan's continually evolving mythical view of himself and society and his own desire to get outside of it. Hence, "Corrina, Corrina" falls completely outside the frame of reference I am using to discuss Dylan's early work. But "Don't think Twice," which on the surface seems very little like "Masters of War," is lyrically really not so different. Dylan casts himself in the same light, with reference to his subjects, i.e., above them. Also, his lack of sympathy for the girl, the totalness of the putdown, the necessity to come right out and say it, the lack of subtlety, are all characteristics of Dylan's one-dimensional myth-making. It's just that in "Don't Think Twice" the beauty of Dylan's vocal-guitar-harmonica performance doesn't really say what the words do, and, in fact, really transforms the verbal meaning of the song into something much deeper and much less coarse.

Nor is all of this myth talk to criticize the early Dylan—an irrelevant function at best. Dylan created a myth that already existed. In a very real sense we could call it the myth of the adolescent, the myth of self-righteousness, the myth of our own purity. Dylan was the only one on the scene who had the self-awareness, charisma, talent, imagination and lack of repression to give structure to this world view. This would tend to explain why he attracted the following he did, in contrast to his numerous and minor contemporaries. Beyond that, we can say that Dylan was not only able to put his finger on the world view, but he was, unlike some of his adulators, never satisfied with what he created for very long. He has always had an unrelenting capacity to grow, a capacity which is too great to sustain any particular myth for too long, or for him to lose control of it. Part of his genius—a word not to be used lightly—is certainly his capacity to always remain one step ahead of the game.

When we come to *The Times They Are A-Changin'* the myth is unquestionably the dominating force, and this album, along with *Highway 61,* is the one which is most dominated by Dylan's melodramatic and stereotyping tendencies. The imagery on *Times* goes back to the grand myth, Christianity. The song "Times" parrots the New Testament "the first will be last," and thereby gives expression to Dylan's new verbal love, the apocalypse. Dylan's apocalyptic vision manifests itself throughout the album. First, there is his religious optimism: the times are changing. An inevitable, unquestionable change. An inexorable change. That is the feeling that the almost droning guitar and Dylan's voice impart to the lyrics. The change is also to be all-encompassing. And then the specific, biblical imagery: "rattle your walls," "beyond your command," "first one now will later be last" and "the curse it is cast." This Dylan could have been preaching in the church where Otis Redding learned how to sing. Again, there is the lack of subtlety, the all-encompassing nature of the vision, the lack of self-doubt.

Even more so than the title song of the album, "When the Ships Come In" showed off the apocalyptic myth of this Dylan. The entire imagery is biblical: "Pharaoh's tomb," "the foes will rise," the use of the ship itself as an image and the concluding wish that the foes will drown. Shades of "Masters of War." This song is truly frightening in its righteous zeal. It is vengeful in the Old Testament sense of the word. It is the work of a profoundly religious mentality, but Bob Dylan didn't have to go any farther than the good old USA to get into this kind of religion. And if this wasn't enough, Dylan ends this album with "Restless Farewell." It is hard to conceive of what could follow Dylan's vision of destruction, but "Restless Farewell" does the trick. After having sold his audience on the impending revolution Dylan tried to tell them that he is not really a prophet, that he cherishes his freedom, that he wishes to stand alone, that he will bid them all farewell and not give a damn. That desire, combined with the self-pitying last verse of the song, offers very strong parallels with a self-destructiveness not uncommon to messianism of any kind. Yet one can't help but feel listening to the album in retrospect that Dylan himself realizes that his apocalypse in a quasipolitical setting has played itself out. It has degenerated into a Hollywood production—into pure kitsch—and Dylan, seeing that, tries to break with it on his next album—unsuccessfully.

In the poems on the back of *Another Side of Bob Dylan*, Dylan shows his sensitivity to the fact that he has backed himself into an artistic corner and that he now wants out. The problem with the myth of the apocalypse is that there is no place you can go with it. Jesus promised he would come again—a promise that never actually materialized. What could Dylan promise after telling us of the time when the good will win and the bad shall lose. It *clearly* was time to de-escalate and on the surface that is what it appears Dylan did. With this de-escalation Dylan's political-minded enthusiasts began to feel sold out. What they of course failed to realize was that Bob Dylan never was political. He was simply acting out a religious allegory on the political landscape of contemporary America. His primary concerns were on the face of it moral, and moral in a religious, Jewish, Christian sense. If he had lived fifteen hundred years ago he would probably have been a Talmudic moralist, and two thousand years ago an apostle or savior. What happens on *Another Side* is that Dylan begins to discard the political landscape, but retains the mannerisms, style and content of an essentially one-dimensional moralist.

Only now he is a poet instead of a prophet. There are attempts at understatement, subtlety and depth, like on "Spanish Harlem Incident," just as on *Times* there had been the jarringly out of place "One Too Many Mornings" and the pre-apocalyptic "Spanish Boots." Yet Dylan has at best only begun to pick up the pieces of reality. "I Don't Believe You" was his first real rock'n'roll song and was a pure delight, giving off the kind of charm and cuteness Dylan is so capable of and uses so rarely. Another brilliant example is "If You Got to Go Now, Go Now" the best recording of which was done by Manfred Mann. He should record it with a band someday, if he wants to. "My Back Pages," with its denouncement of the old myth, shows Dylan's vast capacity at self-analysis and criticism and his ability to be honest with both himself and his audience. Yet the advances remain on the surface. Dylan still sounds like he is singing about the apocalypse—and Dylan's voice always tells us so much more than his words. Even when he renounces the fantasies of the past in "My Back Pages," he creates new ones in "It Ain't Me, Babe." And the "Chimes of Freedom" shows that his love of the majestic, big, epic type of material is an all but permanent side of Bob Dylan. How many artists would come right out and say they are singing for "every hungup person in the whole universe"? Yet, for all its obviousness, the album had undeniable power, especially when it first came out. The fact that we were buying the records shows where we all were at. There seems to be all the signs of the search for the constant, static truth. And just as on *Times*, after Dylan completely wins his audience over he ends on a note of rejection—"It Ain't Me, Babe."

When Bob Dylan switched to an electrified sound the furor that ensued was indicative of the emotional investment so many of his fans had put in him. I was at Forest Hills for his first really electric concert, and the response he evoked from those who six months earlier had thought him a semi-deity showed the frightening possibilities Dylan possessed as "spokesman for his generation." The absurd thing of course is the fact that ten months after the hostility and the boos, these same people found themselves standing in line to buy *Blonde on Blonde*. As usual it was just that he was a little too far ahead of the game.

The reason why Dylan switched to electrified instrumentation is fairly obvious. He had simply exhausted all the possibilities of his guitar-harmonica accompaniment. In that his brilliant melodic sense is essentially limited in its range, Dylan undoubtedly found that by adding a band he could extend his range without having to transcend the limitations of his compositional abilities. In addition, perhaps he had gotten a little tired of the lone-man-against-the-world image. Maybe he just liked the company.

Bringing It All Back Home had the electrified sound. But, interestingly, with the exception of one cut, they were all blues. I think it reasonable to say that a very strong side of Dylan had already recognized the ultimate vacuity of the previous stances. The blues side of this album was another attempt to de-escalate. However, de-escalate or not, Dylan has never been able to get too far away from high seriousness. Consequently we got side two, which contains some of Dylan's best serious songs prior to *JWH*. The two particularly arresting numbers were "Mr. Tambourine Man" and "It's Alright, Ma," both notable because they clearly take Dylan beyond the one dimension of his earlier seriousness. The multilevelness and diversity of imagery in "Mr. Tambourine Man" is comparatively innovative. The simplicity of Dylan's requests, the lack of uptightness and the artistic perspective with which this song was both written and performed, the fact that the Byrds could do it justice by performing it in the cyclical, unmelodramatic style, all this points up the fact that this song is a break with Dylan's chain of dialectical myth, his polarizing tendencies.

"It's Alright, Ma" does exactly the opposite. It is the ultimate statement of the earlier myth, only this time the depth of Dylan's vision created a reality that transcends the purely mythical quality of something like "Chimes of Freedom." The polarity is there but voiced so honestly and with such brilliance and sense of awareness of where both Dylan and this country are at, that the song is totally credible. Hence, on *Bringing It All Back Home,* we get the ultimate dialectic within a dialectic: Dylan himself has become polarized between an aesthetically brilliant statement of what all his past work has led to, and an aesthetically brilliant attempt to transcend the limitations of the self-created myth. And as on the previous two albums, he ends on a note of rejection with "Baby Blue." The resolution of the conflict in Dylan's work, to the extent that there has been one, is quite delayed, and on *Highway 61* the old myth reasserts itself, although in a somewhat disguised manner. In a sense this disguise is embodied in the brilliant accompaniment that dominates the album as well as in Dylan's superb vocal work. Dylan is one of the finest singers of rock-and-roll who ever lived—the truest slogan that Columbia's PR people have ever come up with is the "Nobody sings Dylan like Dylan" thing—and it is on this album that his abilities as a vocalist begin to come into full bloom. He is truly at home with the band (the instrumental work on the previous album was really not very good at all), and when he sings a beautiful song like "It Takes A Lot to Laugh, It Takes A Train to Cry," he can be really relaxed and drive the thing home. (The song itself impresses me as being a superior statement of the "Don't Think Twice," "It Ain't Me, Babe" theme.)

Despite the musical virtues contained on this album compared to previous ones, there are some real problems. Dylan's basic antipathy and hostility to all kinds of people has multiplied itself many times over and the most powerful works on this album are flat-out putdowns. On the back of this album it is he who seems intent on wiping out things, not unlike what he was trying to do in "Masters of War." "Like a Rolling Stone" is of course a putdown most likely the best Dylan ever wrote. What is annoying about it to me is its self-righteousness, its willingness to judge others without judging oneself, the proselytizing in disguise for Dylan's own way of life. Let me hasten to add, apropos Dylan's particular genius, that the structure of the song, his vocal performance and the instrumental arrangement are perfectly suited to communicating his hostility. The first two lines of each verse have an ascending chord progression of c-d-minor-E-minor-F-G. Each line moves straight up in a perfect creation of a melodramatic feeling. And the cry of "aah" before the fourth verse is simply brilliant vocal work. It is Dylan's genius again that no matter where he is at he has the power to make you feel it and to pull you along, perhaps because none of us is so far removed from where he is at that we can't grasp what it is he is trying to communicate.

The bitterness of "Like a Rolling Stone" is magnified still further in "Ballad of a Thin Man." Dylan's mood in this instance can be characterized as one of overkill. When he sang "Only A Pawn In Their Game," he seemed to have realized that sometimes even the most guilty are not the most guilty, that they are a product of situations created by people other than themselves. In this song he wants to blame Mr. Jones for things that aren't his fault and the result is, to me, an embarrassingly hateful putdown of unreal and wholly fictitious entity. It is a meaningless attack on forces which Dylan doesn't really understand at this point, or forces that he simply can't control. At the other end, however, "Desolation Row" must be counted a logical extension of the "It's Alright, Ma" mode and is a fantastic achievement. Those two songs taken together, in fact, give us a fantastically real picture of the good old U.S.A. 1968. This Dylan is infinitely more political than the earlier one, and in a much more real way. Yet what Dylan himself says about where he was at this time should not be overlooked. He wrote on the back of the record involvement was lifelessness. Most of the songs on the album show that he really meant it.

And then came *Blonde on Blonde* and involvement was no longer the enemy and all of a sudden Dylan was writing about love again. The only other album where this theme had been central was *Another Side* and there it was still tied to Dylan's religious, epic style and was as unreal as everything else during that phase. On *Blonde on Blonde* Dylan shows phenomenal abilities in the area of love songs. His selection of Charlie McCoy's Nashville band to accompany was an act of genius. Those musicians showed themselves capable of the kind of fluid yet structured sound that Dylan utilized so brilliantly when just performing alone. While at times this fluidity seems to be excessive to the point of liquidness, resulting in the observation that the sound is not unlike Muzak in its overall effect, what is overlooked in this insight is Dylan's contribution to the total sound. For the purpose of this instrumental fluidity is simply to give Dylan a point of reference against which he can create a genuine artistic tension. (Nobody has ever said Dylan's voice reminds them of Muzak.) The smoothness of the band is a perfect counterweight to Dylan's toughness. The height of this type of interaction is reached on the chorus of "Memphis Blues Again," in which Dylan gives us "Oh, mama, could this really be the end," over the perfectly symmetrical organ-drum sound. It should be recalled how nicely Kenneth Buttrey shatters the fluidity at the end of the line. A most un-Muzak-like gesture.

On the whole this is instrumentally Dylan's finest pre-*JWH* album, and his own performance is beautifully relaxed, controlled and yet soulful. The hostility is vastly reduced. He is smiling again and not the cynical smile of *Highway 61*, either. "Rainy Day Women, #12 & #35" really did set the tone for this work. I was particularly taken with the richness and complexity of "Visions of Johanna," perhaps the high point of the album (especially Dylan's vocal and the drumming), and the power of "Sooner or Later." About this last number there is great reliance on the clichés of "Like a Rolling Stone" but the impact is vastly different. Because on *Highway 61* he could put down involvement and on this cut he could sing "I really did try to get close to you." Or elsewhere, "You break just like a little girl."

Concurrently with this verbal opening up by Dylan, there is a striking revitalization of his blues style on "Obviously Five Believers," possibly his best blues performance. The vocal here is truly the entire message and on this cut we are listening to a genuine blues artist.

One of the most pleasing things about *Blonde on Blonde* is that by shifting the focus from the impossible epics of earlier works to subjects which were closer to himself personally Dylan was able to create a more powerful and lasting artistic tension than he ever was out of things like "With God On Our Side." The tension of a painfully real work like "Visions of Johanna" is infinitely more pervasive and lasting than that of the earlier work because, whereas "With God On Our Side" becomes less real with successive listenings, "Vision" becomes more so. And anyway, if you don't like what he is saying, you can just move your mind over to those musicians and to just Dylan's vocal. For the Dylan of *Blonde on Blonde* is in many ways a performer, a musician before he is a lyricist, and his actual performance as a singer on this album is one of the most brilliant rock performances ever recorded.

With *Blonde on Blonde* Dylan was well on the way to closing the first cycle in his artistic development, the journey from folk singer to rock star, which took him five years to accomplish. In that time he explored and eventually exhausted the artistic potential of his recurring stances as prophet and polarizer, teller of truths, moralist and creator of epics. The originator of the eight-minute rock song, the arch foe of all authority, the extreme resistance to involvement (he did end three albums in succession with songs indicating as much), the stance of the self-reliant artist, in fact, the entire metamorphosis, from "Song to Woody" to "Ballad of a Thin Man," had come to an end. His first recording after the interim of a sixteen-month absence is a thoroughly startling redirection for him, and justifies being called a new birth of his artistic potential, for it is clearly the beginning of a new Dylan myth—the myth of the moderate man. The new myth is the product of an adult Dylan. The essentially adolescent quest for certain truths, static imagery, finality and the underlying hostile world view which allowed him to create his compelling but ultimately unsatisfying visions have been superseded. We will get no more "When the Ships Come In," "It's Alright, Ma," "Chimes of Freedom" or "Like a Rolling Stone" from Bob Dylan. For whatever the virtues of these works, they have been abandoned along with their faults in favor of "a whole other level."

John Wesley Harding is a profoundly egotistical album. For an album to be released amidst *Sgt. Pepper, Their Satanic Majesties Request, Strange Days* and *After Bathing At Baxter's,* somebody must have had a lot of confidence in what he was doing. Hence the first noteworthy fact about this album is its essential lack of insecurity. Dylan seems to feel no need to respond to the predominant trends in pop music at all. And he is the only major pop artist about whom this can be said. The Dylan of *John Wesley Harding* is a truly independent artist who doesn't feel responsible to anyone else, whether they be fans or his contemporaries. It is implicit, in fact, in his rejection of the formal basis of a rock band on this album that Dylan does not accept what is happening in pop music at the moment.

Of course Dylan's independence from much of what passes for the scene these days is not the product of deliberate intent but simply the result of a fundamentally different level of awareness of what is going on all around us. He appears to be one of the few intellectuals making popular music at this time and he doesn't appear to be interested in the same bill of goods that everyone else is. I doubt whether Bob Dylan would have ever pushed a Maharishi Mahesh Yogi on us. Rather, what I hear on this album is two things. The first is a fundamentally American artistic statement. That is to say that Dylan's influences and sources are primarily peculiar to American culture. The second thing is that out of his identity being tied to what is happening in this country, Dylan manifests a profound awareness of the war and how it is affecting all of us. This doesn't mean that I think any of the particular songs are about the war or that any of the songs are protests over it. All I mean to say is that Dylan has felt the war, that there is an awareness of it contained within the mood of the albums as a whole. (The only other recent pop album that strikes me in the same way is *The Notorious Byrd Brothers.*) Dylan's songs acknowledge the war in the same way that songs like "Magical Mystery Tour" and "Fool on the Hill" ignore it. They acknowledge it by attempting to be real, by attempting to not speak falsely and by playing fewer games than ever before. Bob Dylan, 1968, could not write a song analogous to "Magical Mystery Tour" just because he knows too much.

The Dylan of *JWH* is profoundly moral. Of course Dylan has always been a moralist; on this album the nature of his moralizing is drastically altered. In the past his judgments were the inevitable results of unreal, stereotyped depictions of good against bad. They were the kitsch moralisms of young America —pop moralizing at its best. The type of moral judgments Dylan is making on this album are really more of a prudential kind of wisdom which is the outgrowth of very real narratives that avoid one-dimensional stereotyping of the past. "Don't go mistaking paradise for the home across the road" is a form of moral advice, a moral suggestion, not a final answer or an exaggerated dividing up of what is good and what is bad as on *The Times They Are A-Changin'*. The same is true of the earnest plea that "If you don't underestimate me, I won't underestimate you."

This difference in the quality of Dylan's moral outlook is shown in the difference in vocal style he now uses to communicate his lyrics. In the past Dylan's vocal style has been a perfect vehicle for the melodramatic myths of his youth. On this transitional album he redefines his vocal style more than he ever has before. There is genuine understatement, there is an attempt at expressing different moods through different styles and there is an attempt to be honest without affecting honesty. He doesn't always succeed—some of his singing is painfully awkward, as on "I Pity the Poor Immigrant"—yet he is really trying to do things differently and it is good to hear it. His two best vocal performances on this album, "All Along the Watchtower" and "I'll Be Your Baby Tonight," reflect a vocal sophistication and honesty you won't hear anywhere else these days. Dylan's charisma, timing and coloration, when functioning at their best, transcend just about anything.

To round out his own performance vocally he again chose Charlie McCoy and Kenneth Buttrey to accompany him. Buttrey is a great drummer, especially for Dylan, and McCoy's bass playing is without flaw. It must astound people that these two crackers (that's what McCoy calls his new band) have just been floating around Nashville spending their talents on studio sessions. And then somebody tells us that this is the way that all those Nashville cats play.

What I see on *JWH,* then, is a Dylan prepared to confront reality without many of the crutches of the past, with a new flexibility to vocal style and musicians who can sustain that flexibility, and a Dylan with a lyrical sense that is unafraid to judge but that judges differently and more responsibly than before. He achieves a genuine detachment from his work that allows him to do several things at once without seeming to contradict himself. On this album he is above all a musician, a singer first, and in looking at how these overall characteristics manifest themselves on the particular songs of the album, it will help us to look especially at how Dylan is using his voice.

The four songs on the record I want to talk about are "All Along the Watchtower," "Dear Landlord," "Along the Cove" and "I'll Be Your Baby Tonight." The first lends itself to a certain amount of interpretation, but ultimately one is prevented from coming up with anything too concrete due to the lyrics' incongruities, if one confines oneself to just the lyrics. Rather than see the song as something to be interpreted, I tend to see it as an evocation of a mood, a mood created primarily by the way Dylan sings his words. Suppose he sang "There must be some way out of here" softly, in ¾ time. Supposing he was laughing while he sang it. That would change the meaning, such as there may be, drastically. But now suppose he scatted in place of using words, and that he did the scatting precisely as he sings the words. You'd probably respond quite similarly, except your response would be less specific due to the lack of words to focus on. That is, I think that the line "There must be some way out of here" is a great line to sing in the tone of voice Dylan uses, not the other way round.

Of course the words give you a good alternative way at getting to what it is he is singing about. They can be the same kind of tip-off that the card in *Don't Look Back* reading "Dig Yourself" was. It's just that I think it more natural to respond first to the music and then to the words when one is listening to a song, and I think that is in fact what most people probably do.

Or, finally, to put it another way, in *Don't Look Back* Dylan tells the *Time* man that he is as good a singer as Caruso. And, in fact, Dylan is comparable to an opera singer because at his best he is using his voice to say things for him and is not just relying on verbal levels of meaning. On some songs he could probably sing the whole thing in French and it wouldn't be that much harder to understand him. Just like you can understand the Beatles when they sing "I Wanna Hold Your Hand" in German.

All of which is not to say that the lyrics are of no importance. Particular lines in "All Along the Watchtower" give tremendous focus to the emotive qualities of the vocal. Lines like "life is but a joke," "you and I have been through that," "let us not speak falsely" and, of course, the opening line. The overall impression that I get is of a kind of updated "My Back Pages" in which Dylan is trying to communicate his realization that life is not a joke, that the hour is getting late, that unlike the earlier stages of his career, perhaps recently he hasn't been serious enough. The overwhelming feeling is that of immediacy, but a controlled immediacy—it is not, for example, desperation. Perhaps the one word to use is forceful.

"Dear Landlord" is similarly given a recognizable layer of meaning which is in turn obscured somewhat by incongruent images. And again, more striking than the words in and of themselves is Dylan's interpretative powers as a vocalist. While the landlord has been thought to represent all manner of authority—everyone from his manager to the government—that type of speculation is unimportant. What is important is Dylan's attitude toward the subject. He is not out for blood, yet at the same time he isn't willing to give in. He is empathetic but realistic. "If you don't underestimate me I won't underestimate you." I will recognize you but you are going to have to deal with me. This is a truly incredible transformation in attitude when seen in contrast with "Ballad of a Thin Man." The role of the vocal is totally complementary to the verbal level of meaning. What I particularly dig is the firmness in Dylan's voice. No reliance on exaggerated mannerisms but a simple and direct statement. Also, the melodic structure of the song is one of the most sophisticated Dylan has ever devised and his piano playing is quite incisive and competent.

Dylan's greater reliance on vocal style is most evidenced in the last two songs on the album, both of which are singer's songs. In "Down Along the Cove" and "I'll Be Your Baby Tonight" he has given us very little to interpret verbally, possibly because he wants to make himself perfectly explicit, and possibly because he wants his singing to do his talking for him.

"Down Along the Cove" is a blues without the artifacts we have come to expect from white blues: no Mike Bloomfield. The words border on cuteness but basically there is no real barrier between Dylan's voice and our response to it. The need for words at this point is more habit than anything else. "Lord have mercy, sure is good to see you coming today," "Down along the cove I spied my little bundle of joy," and "Everyone knows we're in love, yes they understand," clichés all of them, but given new life in the act of Dylan's singing them. It just feels so right that after all the bigness Dylan should wind up writing and feeling something so simple and so basic. The marvelous demonstrativeness with which he renders the vocal lines is just perfect.

And then "I'll Be Your Baby Tonight" and we go from the blues to c&w without even thinking about it: the bridge is perfectly crossed. And again we are given clichés which aren't clichés and that fantastically expressive voice. This song shows Dylan's absolute mastery of the sources of his music. The break in which he sings "You won't regret it" is so like rock-and-roll and so much more than we have come to expect, so much more personal. There is an easiness and a relaxed quality to it all that is coupled with a realization that he really means it that is virtually cathartic. Such a simple performance, yet so subtle and so complex. And, please note, this album ends on a note of acceptance in marked contrast to the three albums that ended with "Restless Farewell," "It Ain't Me, Babe" and "Baby Blue."

What we are forced to see on *JWH* is Bob Dylan growing up. In every possible respect. On this album Dylan's songs are no longer just him, they are separate identities which exist apart from their author. And we see Dylan moving toward an identity of himself as a classical artist, not as just a pop artist. He sees the distinction himself and is willing to accept it. I think we are also beginning to see a Dylan who is prepared more than ever before to accept uncertainty, to give up the search for the finite, a Dylan who no longer feels that each of his songs must tell us everything he knows. He is prepared to look at the pieces of reality, and let the miller tell his tale.

As a musician we can see him as he sees himself—seriously. It isn't all just something he does so that we will hear his words. He seems to realize that on a record his musical performance has always been, and will always be, pre-eminent, and he is prepared to utilize his fantastic talents as a vocalist to their fullest, even though he hasn't begun to approach his potential in this area.

At both levels he seems determined to search for authenticity, which is perhaps what was most often lacking in his earlier work. And to the extent that he is able to approach that state of being able to create without the aid of the earlier myths, to the extent that he can sustain an identity of being a "moderate man"—which he certainly does on *JWH*—to that extent he will come much closer to approaching the tradition of the genuine folk-artists whom Dylan modeled his career after in the beginning. With the reduction in the need for a self-conscious stance, he has made the first step toward becoming a very real kind of modern folk singer, for when I hear Dylan now, and this is of course simply my own response to what is happening on *JWH,* I am reminded of Woody Guthrie and of Robert Johnson. And the Bob Dylan of *JWH* may bear more in common with either of those men than he does with anyone else who is performing in April of 1968.

Conversations with Bob Dylan

by John Cohen & Happy Traum

The following was transcribed from three separate interviews, taped by John Cohen in June and July of 1968. The participants are Bob Dylan, John Cohen, and Happy Traum.

JOHN: I didn't realize how good that film was, when I saw it last.

BOB: You thought it was good?

J.: It wasn't finished—I liked it because of that. But I didn't see *Don't Look Back.*

B.: It's just as well. The difference between the two would be in the editing . . . the eye. Mr. Pennebaker's eye put together *Don't Look Back,* whereas someone else's eye put together this film which you saw.

J.: Wasn't one of the "eyes" involved yours?

B.: Not entirely. Don't forget, Mr. Pennebaker shot all the film, and Mr. Alk was under direction from him. The (edited) cut was under the direction of, well . . . I was one of them. What we had to work with was not what you would conceive of if you were going shooting a film. What we were trying to do is to make a logical story out of this newsreel-type footage . . . to make a story which consisted of stars and starlets who were taking the roles of other people, just like a normal movie would do. We were trying to do the same thing with this footage. That's not what anyone else had in mind, but that is what myself and Mr. Alk had in mind. And we were very limited because the film was not shot by us, but by the eye, and we had come upon this decision to do this only after everything else

Reprinted with permission from *Sing Out!,* October–November, 1968.

failed. And in everything else failing, the film had been cut just to nothing. So we took it and tried to do it this way because it was a new method and it was new to us, and we were hoping to discover something. And we did. People might see it and say it's just a big mess. Well, it might seem like a mess, but it's not. It starts with a half hour of footage there, that is clean; the film is sloppy and it looks like a lot of cutting in it, thirty second cuts to ten second cuts. But what we tried to do was to construct a stage and an environment, taking it out and putting it together like a puzzle. And we did, that's the strange part about it. Now if we had the opportunity to re-shoot the camera under this procedure, we could really make a wonderful film.

J.: I liked this quality of having things that would normally not be used, that would be discarded, suddenly put together in such a way . . .

B.: Well, we had to do that because it's all we had. The reason it didn't get seen was that the program (TV) folded, and by the time we handed it in, they had already a state-wide search begun to confiscate the film, because it was the property of ABC. So we were a little pressured here and there. What you saw was a rough work print.

J.: What I liked was that the trip had such wildness, such insanity, it looked to me like things could only get worse, they couldn't get better while you were on such a thing. As the film built up, everything seemed to contribute to that. The nature of the crowds, the nature of the reporters . . . I don't know if it was the film, or if it was where we were sitting when we saw it, but . . . well I'm sure one person is capable of being both things . . .

B.: The subject and the director?

J.: . . . Or the editor.

B.: Well the editor and director were two different people.

J.: Let's say the subject and one of the editors was the same person.

B.: Well, you have a lot of major films where the subject himself might be the director. Marlon Brando. Charlie Chaplin. Frank Black.

J.: But the nature of the person in the film . . . maybe to you that wasn't so wild.

B.: I can imagine something a lot wilder . . . maybe not on a singing tour, but as a film. On the screen, what do you say is wild, and what do you say when wildness turns into chaos? Cecil B. DeMille made *Samson and Delilah* . . . that's pretty wild.

J.: But that was a stage set . . . I had the feeling that your film was really happening. You didn't set up the reporters, . . . well, that girl who maybe jumps out the window, and maybe doesn't . . . it's hard to draw the line where play leaves off.

B.: It's hard to do a tour, and in the after hours make a movie. What we were doing was to try to fulfill this contract, to make a television show, and the only time I had to do it was when I was on tour, because I was on tour all the time.

J.: I never saw you perform when you were touring with an electric band, except the last time I saw you which was at Newport, in 1965, when the public first became fully aware of what you'd been writing and thinking. But by the time this movie was shot in England, why you were really flying . . . your hands going all over, above the mouth harp . . . I got the feeling that you don't necessarily have to predetermine these things, that they grow by themselves. When reporters ask such questions, and audiences scream at nothing, it invites you to become something that you didn't necessarily intend to be.

B.: That's true, but I know quite a few people who accept it as a challenge. I used to see people who'd take off their tie and dangle it over the first row, and it would be almost hypnotic. P. J. Probie used to do that, there are people who actually invite it, who actually enjoy being pulled, you know . . . it's something having to do with contact. It's very athletic in a way.

J.: I take that film as very different from the new record you made . . . it might be opposite sides of the same coin. I think it's great, that in the period of three years, you can be the same person who did both.

B.: Well, you can do anything if it's your job. When I was touring, it was my line of work, to go out there and deliver those songs. You must accept that in some way. There's very little you can do about it. The only other thing to do is not do it. But you certainly can't tell what's going to happen when you go on the stage, because the audiences are so different.

Years ago the audience used to be of one nature, but that's not true anymore.

J.: You talked of it in the past—that *was* your job. But is it necessarily now your job?

B.: It is in a way. I like to play music on the stage, I expect to be playing music endlessly. So this period of time now isn't important to me; I know I'm going to be performing again, it's just a matter of the right time. And I'll have different material—so there'll be a change there.

J.: I recall a conversation we had in 1962 . . . I don't know if I was seeing something, or wishing something on you—but I had just come back from Kentucky and you showed me "Hard Rain," at Gerde's or upstairs from the Gaslight . . .

B.: I believe at the time, you were wondering how it fit into music. How I was going to sing it.

J.: That was my initial reaction. That's really ancient history now because a whole aesthetic, a whole other approach has come into music since then, to make it very possible to sing that kind of song.

B.: Yes, that's right.

J.: Before then it wasn't so possible. The question I asked you on seeing this stream of words was, if you were going to write things like that, then why do you need Woody Guthrie? How about Rimbaud? And you didn't know Rimbaud . . . yet.

B.: No, not until a few years ago.

J.: Back then, you and Allen Ginsberg met.

B.: Al Aronowitz, a reporter from the *Saturday Evening Post*, introduced me to Allen Ginsberg and his friend Peter Orlofsky, above a book store on 8th Street, in the fall of '64 or '65. I'd heard his name for many years. At that time these two fellas had just gotten back from a trip to India. Their knapsacks were in the corner and they were cooking dinner at the time. I saw him again at Washington Square, at a party . . .

J.: At that time, for you, was there a stronger leaning towards poetry, and the kind of thing that Allen had dealt with? . . . as opposed to what Woody had dealt with.

B.: Well, the language which they were writing, you could read off the paper, and somehow it would begin some kind of tune in your mind. I don't really know what it was, but you could see it was possible to do more than what . . . not more . . . something different than what Woody and people like Aunt Molly Jackson and Jim Garland did. The subject matter of all their songs wasn't really accurate for me; I could see that they'd written thousands of songs, but it was all with the same heartfelt subject matter. . . whereas that subject matter did not exist then, and I knew it. There was a sort of semi-feeling of it existing, but as you looked around at the people, it didn't really exist the way it probably existed back then, there was no real movement, there was only organized movement. There wasn't any type of movement which was a day by day, liveable movement. When the subject matter wasn't there anymore for me, the only thing that was there was the style. The idea of this type of song which you can live with in some kind of way, which you don't feel embarrassed twenty minutes after you've sung it; that type of song where you don't have to question yourself . . . where you're just wasting your time.

J.: I don't know which was the cart and which was the horse, but people were asking about your music (and Phil Ochs' and others'), "Is this stuff poetry or is this song?"

B.: Yes, well you always have people asking questions.

J.: What I'm trying to get at is whether you were reading a lot then, books, literature? Were your thoughts outside of music?

B.: No, my mind was with the music. I tried to read, but I usually would lay the book down. I never have been a fast reader. My thoughts weren't about reading, no . . . they were just about that feeling that was in the air. I tried to somehow get a hold of that, and write that down, and using my muscial training to sort of guide it by, and in the end, have something I could do for a living.

J.: Training!

B.: Yes, training. You have to have some. I can remember traveling through towns, and if somebody played the guitar, that's who you went to see. You didn't necessarily go to meet them, you just went necessarily to watch them, listen to them, and if possible, learn how to do something . . . whatever he was doing. And usually at that time it was quite a selfish type of thing. You could see the people, and if you knew you could do what they were doing, with just a little practice, and you were looking for something else, you could just move on. But when it was down at the bottom, everyone played the guitar, when you knew that they knew more than you, well, you just had to listen to everybody. It wasn't necessarily a song; it was technique and style, and tricks and all those combinations which go together—which I certainly spent a lot of hours just trying to do what other people have been doing. That's what I mean by training.

J.: It's hard for me, because this is an interview and can't be just a conversation . . . like the tape recorder is a third element . . . I can't just say to your face that you did something great, that I admire you . . .

B.: Well in my mind, let me tell you John, I can see a thousand people who I think are great, but I've given up mentioning any names anymore. Every time I tell somebody who I think is pretty good, they just shrug their shoulders . . . and so I now do the same thing. Take a fellow like Doc Watson, the fellow can play the guitar with such ability . . . just like water running. Now where do you place somebody like that in this current flow of music? Now he doesn't use any tricks. But that has to do with age, I imagine, like how long he lives.

J.: I think it's also got to do with the age he comes from, he doesn't come from yours or mine.

B.: No, but I'm a firm believer in the longer you live, the better you get.

J.: But Doc is different from you and me. I know people who hate your voice. They can't stand that sound, that kind of singing, that grating. The existence of your voice and people like you, like Roscoe Holcomb, it challenges their very existence. They can't conceive of that voice in the same breath as their own lives.

B.: Well my voice is one thing, but someone actually having hate for Roscoe Holcomb's voice, that beautiful high tenor, I can't see that. What's the difference between Roscoe Holcomb's voice and Bill Monroe's?

J.: I don't think Bill likes Roscoe's voice. Bill sings with such control. Roscoe's voice is so uncontrolled.

B.: Well Bill Monroe is most likely one of the best, but

Roscoe does have a certain untamed sense of control which also makes him one of the best.

J.: I don't think Doc Watson's voice and your voice are compatible, it doesn't bother me.

B.: No, no . . . maybe some day, though.

J.: I'd like to talk about the material in the songs.

B.: All right.

J.: Well, I mean your music is fine, it's complete . . . but what I'm asking about is the development of your thoughts . . . which could be called "words." That's why I was asking about poetry and literature. Where do these things come upon a person? Maybe nobody asks you that.

B.: No, nobody does, but . . . who said that, it wasn't Benjamin Franklin, it was somebody else. No, I think it was Benjamin Franklin. He said (I'm not quoting it right) something like, "For a man to be—(something or other)—at ease, he must not tell all he knows, nor say all he sees." Whoever said that certainly I don't think was trying to cover up anything.

J.: I once got a fortune cookie that said "Clear water hides nothing. . . ." Three or four years ago, there was an interview with you in *Playboy*. One particular thought stuck with me. You said it was very important that Barbara Allen had a rose grow out of her head, and that a girl could become a swan.

B.: That's for all those people who say, "Why do you write all these songs about mystery and magic and Biblical intonations? Why do you do all that? Folk music doesn't have any of that." There's no answer for a question like that, because the people who ask them are just wrong.

J.: They say that folk music doesn't have this quality. Does rock and roll music have it?

B.: Well, I don't know what rock and roll music is supposed to represent. It isn't that defined as a music. Rock and roll is dance music, perhaps an extension of the blues forms. It's live music; nowadays they have these big speakers, and they play it so loud that it might seem live. But it's got rhythm . . . I mean if you're riding in your car, rock and roll stations playing, you can sort of get into that rhythm for three minutes—and you lose three minutes. It's all gone by and you don't have to think about anything. And it's got a nice place; in a way this place is not necessarily in every road you turn, it's just pleasant music.

J.: You're part of it aren't you? Or it's part of you.

B.: Well music is a part of me, yes.

J.: From what I saw in that film, you were really in it.

B.: I was in it because it's what I've always done. I was trying to make the two things go together when I was on those concerts. I played the first half acoustically, second half with a band, somehow thinking that it was going to be two kinds of music.

J.: So acoustic would mean "folk" and band would mean "rock and roll' at that moment?

B.: Yes, rock and roll is working music. You have to work at it. You just can't sit down in a chair and play rock and roll music. You can do that with a certain kind of blues music, you can sit down and play it . . . you may have to lean forward a little.

J.: Like a ballad, or one of your "dreams"?

B.: Yes, you can think about it, you don't necessarily have to be in action to think about it. Rock and roll is hard to visualize unless you're actually doing it . . . . Actually too, we're talking about something which is for the most part just a commercial item; it's like boats and brooms, it's like hardware, people sell it, so that's what we're talking about. In the other sense of the way which you'd think about it, it's impossible.

J.: But the kids who are getting into it today, they don't want to sell brooms.

B.: It's an interesting field . . . .

(aside to daughter)

Hello, did you just get home? Well maybe you better ask mamma. How was school? You learn anything? Well that's good. "My shoes hurt right here." Well, we'll see what we can do about it.

J.: Could we talk about your new record *John Wesley Harding?*

B.: There were three sessions: September, October and December, so it's not even a year old. I know that the concepts are imbedded now, whereas before that record I was just trying to see all of which I could do, trying to structure this and that. Every record was more or less for impact. Why, I did one song on a whole side of an album! It could happen to anybody. One just doesn't think of those things though, when one sees that other things can be done. It was spontaneously brought out, all those seven record albums. It was generously done, the material was all there. Now, I like to think that I can do it better, on my own terms, and I'll do whatever it is I can do. I used to slight it off all the time. I used to get a good phrase or a verse, and then have to carry it to write something off the top of the head and stick it in the middle, to lead this into that. Now as I hear all the old material that was done, I can see the whole thing. I can't see how to perfect it, but I can see what I've done. Now I can go from line to line, whereas yesterday it was from thought to thought. Then of course, there are times you just pick up an instrument—something will come, like a tune or some kind of wild line will come into your head and you'll develop that. If it's a tune on the piano or guitar—you'll just uuuuuhhhh (hum) whatever it brings out in the voice, you'll write those words down. And they might not mean anything to you at all, and you just go on, and that will be what happens. Now I don't do that any more. If I do it, I just keep it for myself. So I have a big lineup of songs which I'll never use. On the new record, it's more concise. Here I am not interested in taking up that much of anybody's time.

J.: That's why I gave you Kafka's *Parables and Paradoxes*, because those stories really get to the heart of the matter, and yet you can never really decipher them.

B.: Yes, but the only parables I know are the Biblical parables. I've seen others. Khalil Gibran perhaps . . . . It has a funny aspect to it—you certainly wouldn't find it in the Bible—this type of soul. Now Mr. Kafka comes off a little closer to that. Gibran, the words are all mighty but the strength is turned into that of a contrary direction. There used to be this disc jockey, Rosko. I don't recall his last name. Sometimes at night, the radio would be on and Rosko would be reciting this poetry of Khalil Gibran. It was a radiant feeling, coming across it on the radio. His voice was that of the inner voice in the night.

J.: When did you read the Bible parables?

B.: I have always read the Bible, though not necessarily always the parables.

J.: I don't think you're the kind who goes to the hotel, where the Gideons leave a Bible, and you pick it up.

B.: Well, you never know.

J.: What about Blake, did you ever read . . . ?

B.: I have tried. Same with Dante, and Rilke. I understand what's there, it's just that the connection sometimes does not connect . . . Blake did come up with some bold lines though . . .

J.: A feeling I got from watching the film—which I hadn't considered much before folk music and rock and roll got so mixed together—is about this personal thing of put ons, as a personal relationship. Like with the press, they ask such idiotic questions that they are answered by put ons.

B.: The only thing there, is that that becomes a game in itself. The only way to not get involved in that is not to do it, because it'll happen every time. It even happens with the housewives who might be asked certain questions.

J.: It's become a way of imparting information. Like someone will come with an idea, a whole thesis, and then they'll ask, "Is this so?" and you might not have thought of it before, but you can crawl on top of it.

B.: It's this question and answer business, I can't see the importance of it. There's so many reporters now. That's an occupation in itself. You don't have to be any good at it at all. You get to go to fancy places. It's all on somebody else.

J.: Ridiculous questions get ridiculous answers, and the ridiculous response becomes the great moment.

B.: Yes, well you have to be able to do that now. I don't know who started that, but it happens to everybody.

J.: I wouldn't have mentioned it, but to me, you've moved away from it . . . gotten beyond it.

B.: I don't know if I've gotten beyond it. I just don't do it any more, because that's what you end up doing. You end up wondering what you're doing.

J.: Hey. In the film, was that John Lennon with you in the

car, where you're holding your head? He was saying something funny, but it was more than that . . . it was thoughtful.

B.: He said "Money". . . .

J.: Do you see the Beatles when you go there or they come here? There seems to be a mutual respect between your musics —without one dominating the other.

B.: I see them here and there.

J.: I fear that many of the creative young musicians today may look back at themselves ten years from now and say "We were just under the tent of the Beatles." But you're not.

B.: Well, what they do . . . they work much more with the studio equipment, they take advantage of the new sound inventions of the past year or two. Whereas I don't know anything about it. I just do the songs, and sing them and that's all.

J.: Do you think they are more British or International?

B.: They're British I suppose, but you can't say they've carried on with their poetic legacy, whereas the Incredible String Band who wrote this "October Song" . . . that was quite good.

J.: As a finished thing—or did it reach you?

B.: As a finished song it's quite good.

J.: Is there much music now that you hear, that reaches you?

B.: Those old songs reach me. I don't hear them as often as I used to. But like this other week, I heard on the radio Buell Kazee and he reached me. There's a lot . . . Scrapper Blackwell, Leroy Carr, Jack Dupree, Lonnie Johnson, James Ferris, Jelly Roll Morton, Buddy Bolden, Ian and Sylvia, Benny Fergusen, Tom Rush, Charlie Pride, Porter Wagoner, The Clancy Brothers and Tommy Makem . . . . Everything reaches me in one way or another.

J.: How do you view the music business?

B.: I don't exactly view it at all. Hearing it and doing it, I'll take part in that—but talking about . . . there's not much I can contribute to it.

J.: I recall in *Billboard,* a full page ad of you with electric guitar like in the movie . . . .

B.: Sure, I was doing that.

J.: I'm interested how you talk of it in the past tense, as if you don't know what's coming next.

B.: Well, I don't in a sense . . . but I've been toying with some ridiculous ideas—just so strange and foreign to me, as a month ago. Now some of the ideas—I'll tell you about them—after we shut off this tape recorder.

J.: I was pleased that you know the music of Dillard Chandler, and that you were familiar with some unaccompanied ballads on a New Lost City Ramblers record. Do you think you'll ever try to write like a ballad?

B.: Yes, I hope so. Tom Paxton just did one called "The Cardinal," quite interesting . . . it's very clean . . . sings it unaccompanied. The thing about the ballad is that you have to be conscious of the width of it at all times, in order to write one. You could take a true story, write it up as a ballad, or you can write it up in three verses. The difference would be, what are you singing it for, what is it to be used for. The uses of a ballad have changed to such a degree. When they were singing years ago, it would be as entertainment . . . a fellow could sit down and sing a song for a half hour, and everybody could listen, and you could form opinions. You'd be waiting to see how it ended, what happened to this person or that person. It would be like going to a movie. But now we have movies, so why does someone want to sit around for a half hour listening to a ballad? Unless the story was of such a nature that you couldn't find it in a movie. And after you heard it, it would have to be good enough so that you could sing it again tomorrow night, and people would be listening to hear the story again. It's because they want to hear the story, not because they want to check out the singer's pants. Because they would have a conscious knowledge of how the story felt and they would be a part of that feeling . . . like they would want to feel it again, so to speak.

J.: It must be terrific to try to write within those dimensions.

B.: Well once you set it up in your mind, you don't have to think about it any more. If it wants to come, it will come.

J.: Take a song like the "Wicked Messenger." Does that fit?

B.: In a sense, but the ballad form isn't there. Well, the scope is there actually, but in a more compressed sense. The scope opens up, just by a few little tricks. I know why it opens up, but in a ballad in the true sense, it wouldn't open up that way. It does not reach the proportions I had intended for it.

J.: Have you ever written a ballad?

B.: I believe on my second record album, *Boots of Spanish Leather.*

J.: Then most of the songs on *John Wesley Harding,* you don't consider as ballads.

B.: Well I do, but not in the traditional sense. I haven't fulfilled the balladeer's job. A balladeer can sit down and sing three ballads for an hour and a half. See, on the album, you have to think about it after you hear it, that's what takes up the time, but with a ballad, you don't necessarily have to think about it after you hear it, it can all unfold to you. These melodies on the *John Wesley Harding* album lack this traditional sense of time. As with the third verse of the "Wicked Messenger," which opens it up, and then the time schedule takes a jump and soon the song becomes wider. One realizes that when one hears it, but one might have to adapt to it. But we are not hearing anything that isn't there; anything we can imagine is really there. The same thing is true of the song "All Along the Watchtower," which opens up in a slightly different way, in a stranger way, for here we have the cycle of events working in a rather reverse order.

J.: One suggested interpretation of "Dear Landlord" is that you wrote it to bring out the line "each one has his own special gift" . . . .

B.: I don't know about that. These songs might lay around in your head for two or three years, and you're always writing about something previous. You learn to do that, so that the song would not tend to be a reaction, something contemporary would make it a reaction. I don't know what it seems to explain any more than anyone else. But you always have to consider that I would write the song for somebody else. He might say something, or behave in a certain manner, or come right out and offer information like that. And if it's striking enough, it might find an opening. And don't forget now John I'll tell you another discovery I've made. When the songs are done by anybody on a record, on a strange level the songs are done for somebody, about somebody and to somebody. Usually that person is the somebody who is singing that song. Hear all the records which have ever been made and it kinda comes down to that after a while.

J.: Could you talk about where you were going when you first started out from home?

B.: As I think about it, it's confusing to me to think of how I reached whatever place this is. I tend not to wonder about it anyway. It's true, I have no goal so to speak. I don't have any more intentions than you do.

J.: I intend to do my work.

B.: Yes, me too, and to make the work interesting enough, in order to keep doing it.

That's what has kept it up so far. I really can't do it if it's not interesting. My intention would be not to think about it, not to speak about it, or remember any of it that might tend to block it up somehow. I've discovered this from the past anyway. There was one thing I tried to do which wasn't a good idea for me. I tried to write another "Mr. Tambourine Man." It's the only song I tried to write "another one." But after enough going at it, it just began bothering me, so I dropped it. I don't do that anymore.

J.: A danger of such a position is that you can be accused of only living in the present. People will say you're just living for the minute—with no plan and no care for the past.

B.: I have more memories for the past than for the future. I wouldn't think about the future. I would only have expectations, and they'd all be very good. For the past I just have those memories. We were just talking of this "past" business the other night. Say this room is empty now, except with just myself. Now you enter the room, but you're bound to leave, and when you do, what's to guarantee that you've even been in this room. But yet you were in this room, if I want to reconstruct it, sit here for the rest of the day . . . if I take enough notes while you are in the room, I could probably sit here for a week, with you in the room . . . something like that anyway.

J.: It's elusive. Anyway, back to the thought of "each one has his own special gift."

B.: That would be . . . just a fact.

J.: But if everybody felt it, perhaps the American army wouldn't be so capable of killing, and Kennedy might not be killed—King might not be killed.

B.: But we're talking now about things which have always happened since the beginning of time, the specific name or deed isn't any different than that which has happened previous to this. Progress hasn't contributed anything but changing face . . . and changing situations of money, wealth . . . that's not progress really. Progress for disease—that's progress . . . but putting in a new highway through a backyard is getting rid of the old things.

J.: The real progress each person makes is not going outwards, but going inwards. I have the feeling that a change has come over you . . . you seem to have discovered that same idea.

B.: Well, the songs are a funny thing. If I didn't have the recording contract and I didn't have to fulfill a certain amount of records, I don't really know if I'd write down another song as long as I lived. I'm just content enough to play just anything I know. But seeing as how I do have this contract, I figure my obligation is to fill it, not in just recording songs, but the best songs I can possibly record. Believe me, look around. I don't care if I record my own songs, but I can't sometimes find enough songs to put on an album, so then I've got to do it all with my songs. I didn't want to record this last album. I was going to do a whole album of other people's songs, but I couldn't find enough. The song has to be of a certain quality for me to sing and put on a record. One aspect it would have to have is that it didn't repeat itself. I shy away from those songs which repeat phrases, bars and verses, bridges . . . so right there it leaves out about nine-tenths of all the contemporary material being written, and the folk songs are just about the only ones with a chorus like "Ruben's Train." I don't know, maybe then too I'm just too lazy to look hard enough.

J.: Do you consider that there's been a change of pace in your life over the past three years?

B.: "Change of pace" if you mean what I was doing before. I was touring for a couple of years. That's a fast pace, plus we were doing a whole show, no other acts. It's pretty straining to do a show like that, plus a lot of really unhealthy situations rise up. I was just going out there performing these songs. Everyone else was having a good time. Right now I don't think about it anymore. I did it, and I did it enough to know that there must be something else to do.

J.: In a way, you had the opportunity to move into it and move out of it at your own choice.

B.: It wasn't my own choice. I was more or less being pushed into it—pushed in and carried out.

(enter Happy Traum)

H.: Has anyone picked up on your new approach—like on the album, clear songs and very personal, as opposed to the psychedelic sounds?

B.: I don't know.

H.: What do you know?

B.: What I do know is that I put myself out of the songs. I'm not in the songs anymore, I'm just there singing them, and I'm not personally connected with them. I write them all now at a different time than when I record them. It used to be, if I would sing, I'd get a verse and go on and wait for it to come out as the music was there, and sure enough, something would come out, but in the end, I would be deluded in those songs. Besides singing them, I'd be in there acting them out—just pulling them off. Now I have enough time to write the song and not think about being in it. Just write it for somebody else to sing, then do it—like an acetate. At the moment, people are singing a simpler song. It's possible in Nashville to do that.

J.: I heard "Blowin' in the Wind" played on the radio after the most recent assassination.

B.: By who?

J.: It was Muzak style . . . music to console yourself by.

B.: Airplane style.

J.: Do you think you'll ever get a job playing for Muzak? The best musicians do that work, Bob.

B.: Well I'd give it a try if they ask.

J.: No one calls you into the studio to "Lay down some music," as they say.

B.: Before I did the new album, I was waiting to meet someone who would figure out what they would want me to do. Does anybody want any songs written about anything? Could Bob be commissioned, by anybody? Nobody came up with anything, so I went ahead and did something else.

J.: For a while a number of years ago, the songs you were writing, and that others were writing along similar lines, were played a lot on popular radio. Today it's not completely disappeared, but it certainly is going in some other direction.

B.: You just about have to cut something tailor-made for the popular radio. You can't do it with just half a mind. You must be conscious of what you're involved in. I get over-anxious when I hear myself on the radio, anyway. I don't mind the record album, but it's the record company, my A & R man, Bob Johnston—he would pick out what's to be played on the radio.

H.: Did you ever make a song just to be a single?

B.: Yes I did. But it wasn't very amusing because it took me away from the album. The album commands a different sort of attention than a single does. Singles just pile up and pile up; they're only good for the present. The trend in the old days was that unless you had a hit single, you couldn't do very well with an album. And when you had that album, you just filled it up. But now albums are very important.

J.: You've tried movies and books . . .

B.: In both cases, in shallow water.

J.: In that book of photographs of you that was published, when I finished looking at it, I came away knowing not one bit more than when I started.

B.: Yes, well what can you know about anybody? Book or photographs, they don't tell you too much about a person.

H.: For years now, people have been analyzing and pulling apart your songs. People take lines out of context and use them to illustrate points, like on "Quinn, the Eskimo" . . . I've heard some kids say that Quinn is the "bringer of drugs." Whatever you meant doesn't matter . . . the kids say "Dylan is really into this drug thing . . . when the drugs come, everybody is happy." This kind of thing is always happening with all your songs.

B.: Well, that's not my concern.

J.: Many of the songs have set up conditions where people can read whatever they want into them.

H.: People pull them apart and analyze them.

B.: It's not every one who does that—just a certain kind. People I come in contact with don't have any questions.

H.: Perhaps that's come back lately in the very spontaneous art, in the whole multi-media kind of thing. Response to impulses . . . you can't respond any other way.

J.: I think it's to anyone's favor that they can follow what's on their own mind, what comes from within them, rather than getting swept up in all these other possibilities . . . which might be just a reaction against the analytic approach anyway. There is another way . . . someone might just follow his inner course . . . without being unaware of what is going on. Bob, how do you respond to multi-media?

B.: When you say multi-media, would that be like the clothes stores?

J.: Never having been to one, I'll say yes.

B.: I've never been to one either.

H.: It's also stage presentations where music, dance, lights and the rest are jumbled together, piled on the viewer, where all the senses are used.

J.: In that context of multi-media, where are you?

B.: Well I'm a very simple man. I take one, maybe two . . . too much just confuses me. I just can't master confusion. If I don't know what's happening and everyone who goes and tells me just says that they don't know what happened any more than I do, and they were there, then I'd say that I didn't know where we were.

H.: Do you feel the same way about the psychedelic sound on records?

B.: No, I don't.

H.: A lot of the music today is not only very loud and very fast, but it's structured in such a way that a lot of instruments are playing at once, with a lot of distortion.

B.: That's fine. A lot of people are playing it.

H.: You seem to have made a conscious effort away from that on your last record.

B.: It was a conscious effort just to begin again. It wasn't a conscious effort to go in a certain direction, but rather like put up or shut up, so-to-speak. So that's all.

J.: I see that picture of Muhammad Ali here. Do you know him?

B.: No, I've seen him perform a few times.

H.: Do you follow the fights?

B.: Not any more. When he came down to Bleecker Street to read his poetry, you would have wished you were there.

J.: He really made a point that lasted afterwards—beyond that someone got conked.

H.: Not being particularly interested in fighting, what impressed me is how he stayed true to himself—his own stand as a human being was more important to himself than the championship.

J.: Could you talk about some of the diverse elements which go into making up one of your songs, using a song from which you have some distance?

B.: Well, there's not much we could talk about—that's the strange aspect about the whole thing. There's nothing you can see. I wouldn't know where to begin.

J.: Take a song like "I Pity The Poor Immigrant." There might have been a germ that started it.

B.: Yes, the first line.

J.: What experience might have triggered that? Like you kicked the cat who ran away, who said "Ouch!" which reminded you of an immigrant.

B.: To tell the truth, I have no idea how it comes into my mind.

J.: You've said there was a person usually in it.

B.: Well, we're all in it. They're not any specific people . . . say, someone kicks the cat, and cat writes a song about it. It might seem that way, during some of the songs, and in some of the poetry that's being passed around now-a-days. But it's not really that way.

J.: You said that often a song is written for a certain person.

B.: That's for a person, not about him. You know, you might sometimes be with someone who's got no song to sing, and I believe you can help someone out, that's the extent of it really.

J.: Well, "Quinn the Eskimo" wasn't that way.

B.: You see, it's all grown so serious, the writing-song business. It's not that serious. The songs don't painfully come out. They come out in a trick or two, or from something you might overhear. I'm just like any other songwriter, you pick up the things that are given to you. "Quinn the Eskimo," I can't remember how that came about. I know the phrase came about, I believe someone was just talking about Quinn, the Eskimo.

J.: Someone told me there was once a movie with Anthony Quinn playing an Eskimo. Did you know of that?

B.: I didn't see the movie.

J.: But that could have triggered it.

B.: Of course.

J.: This makes a lot of sense, in the sense that you can travel down a road, and see two signs advertising separate things, but where two words come together, it will make a new meaning which will trigger off something.

B.: Well, what the songwriter does, is just connect the ends. The ends that he sees are the ones that are given to him and he connects them.

H.: It seems that people are bombarded all the time with random thoughts and outside impulses, and it takes the songwriter to pick something out and create a song out of them.

B.: It's like this painter who lives around here—he paints the area in a radius of twenty miles, he paints bright strong pictures. He might take a barn from twenty miles away, and hook it up with a brook right next door, then with a car ten miles away, and with the sky on some certain day, and the light on the trees from another certain day. A person passing by will be painted alongside someone ten miles away. And in the end he'll have this composite picture of something which you can't say exists in his mind. It's not that he started off willfully painting this picture from all his experience . . . That's more or less what I do.

J.: Which and where is Highway 61?

B.: I knew at one time, but at this time it seems so far away I wouldn't even attempt it. It's out there, it's a dividing line.

J.: Is it a physical Highway 61?

B.: Oh yes, it goes from where I used to live . . . I used to live related to that highway. It ran right through my home town in Minnesota. I travelled it for a long period of time actually. It goes down the middle of the country, sort of southwest.

J.: I think there is an old blues about Highway 61.

B.: Same highway, lot of famous people came off that highway.

J.: Can you keep contact with the young audiences who perhaps buy most of your records?

B.: That's a vague notion, that one must keep contact with a certain illusion of people which are sort of undefinable. The most you can do is satisfy yourself. If you satisfy yourself then you don't have to worry about remembering anything. If you don't satisfy yourself, and you don't know why you're doing what you do, you begin to lose contact. If you're doing it for *them* instead of you, you're likely not in contact with them. You can't pretend you're in contact with something you're not. I don't really know who I'm in contact with, but I don't think it's important.

J.: Well, on the airplanes, they have these seven channels of stereo, and your music is marked as "for the kids" rather than anywhere else, and it sort of bothered me. Do you have a chance to meet the kids?

B.: I always like to meet the kids.

J.: Do you get a chance?

B.: Not so much when I'm touring as when I'm not touring. When you're touring, you don't get a chance to meet anybody. I've just been meeting people again in the last few years.

J.: It's a strange phenomenon, for you reach them the most when you are on tour yet you can't reach them at all.

B.: Well yes, but the next time I go out, it's going to be a little bit more understandable. Next time out, my hopes are to play the music in a different way.

H.: How can you get around the problems you encountered last time?

B.: I'm not really aware of those problems. I know they exist because it was very straining, and that's not the way work should be. But it's a situation that's pretty much all over . . . the screaming. Even some musician like Jimi Hendrix gets people seeing him who aren't coming there to scream—they're coming to hear him.

H.: Do you see any way you can approach your music in a public way, that would give a different perspective to an audience?

B.: Yes. Just playing the songs. See, the last time we went out, we made too much of a production of the songs. They were all longer, they were all my own songs, not too much thought had gone into the program, it just evolved itself from when I was playing single.

J.: And the film we've been discussing, is that a fair summary of that kind of a tour?

B.: Yes it was. I hope people get a chance to see that film.

J.: Why do you think your music appeals to American Indians?

B.: I would hope that it appeals to everybody.

J.: I know suburban people who can't stand it.

B.: Well, I wish there was more I could do about that.

J.: We just heard your record being played at an elegant store in New York City, as the background for people shopping.

H.: Pete Seeger told me the *John Wesley Harding* album is great to skate to. He said some records are good to skate to and some aren't, and that's a good one.

B.: I'm awfully glad he feels that way about it.

J.: What is your relationship to student groups, or black militants, like the kids at Columbia or at Berkeley?

B.: If I met them at all, I would meet them individually; I have no special relationship to any group.

J.: Do you follow these events, even from a distance, like reading a newspaper?

B.: Just like anyone else. I know just as much about it as the lady across the street does, and she probably knows quite a bit. Just reading the papers, talking to the neighbors, and so forth.

J.: These groups feel more about you than they do about that lady next door.

B.: I can assure you I feel the same thing. There are people who are involved in it and people who are not. You see, to be involved, you just about have to be there, I couldn't think about it any other way.

J.: Someone like Pete Seeger, who is different from all of us in this room, he reaches out.

B.: But how much of a part of it is he?

H.: Do you forsee a time when you're going to have to take some kind of a position?

B.: No.

H.: You don't think that events will ever reach you?

B.: It's not that events won't reach me, it's more a case of what I, myself would reach for. The decisions I would have to make are my own decisions, just like anyone else has to make his own. It doesn't necessarily mean that any position must be taken.

J.: Although I asked it, this is not really the kind of question I'm really concerned with. After all, if someone asked me, I could only say I do what I can, I sing my own music, and if they like to hear it, well, fine.

B.: Yes, but I don't know . . . . What was the question again? You must define it better.

H.: I think that every day we get closer to having to make a choice.

B.: How so?

H.: I think that events of the world are getting closer to us, they're as close as the nearest ghetto.

B.: Where's the nearest ghetto?

H.: Maybe down the block. Events are moving on a mass scale.

B.: What events?

H.: War, racial problems, violence in the streets.

J.: Here's a funny aspect; we're talking like this here, but in a strange way, Bob has gone further than you or I in getting into such places. I just heard from Izzy Young that the songs they were singing at Resurrection City were "Blowing In The Wind" and "The Times They Are Changing." So, in a sense by maintaining his own individual position, Bob and his songs are in the ghetto, and the people there are singing them—to them they mean action.

H.: Well, the kids at Columbia University are taking a particular stand on what they see as the existing evils. They're trying to overcome the people ruling them, and there are powerful people who are running the show. They can be called the establishment, and they are the same people who make the wars, that build the missiles, that manufacture the instruments of death.

B.: Well, that's just the way the world is going.

H.: The students are trying to make it go another way.

B.: Well, I'm for the students of course, they're going to be taking over the world. The people who they're fighting are old people, old ideas. They don't have to fight, they can sit back and wait.

H.: The old ideas have the guns, though.

J.: Perhaps the challenge is to make sure that the young minds growing up remain open enough so that they don't become the establishment they are fighting.

B.: You read about these rebels in the cartoons, people who were rebels in the twenties, in the thirties, and they have children who are rebels, and they forget that they were rebels. Do you think that those who are rioting today have to hold their kids back from doing the same thing?

J.: Are your day-to-day contacts among the artists, crusaders, businessmen or lumberjacks?

B.: Among the artists and lumberjacks.

J.: Crusaders?

B.: Well, you mean the people who are going from here to there, the men in long brown robes and little ivy twines on the head? I know quite a few crusaders but don't have much contact with them.

J.: How about leaders of the student groups? Did you know Malcolm X, or the kids from SNCC?

B.: I used to know some of them.

J.: Social crusaders, someone like Norman Mailer.

B.: No.

J.: What about businessmen?

B.: I get a lot of visitors and see a lot of people, and who's a businessman? I'm sure a whole lot of businessmen have passed by the past few hours, but my recollection really isn't that brilliant.

J.: Does your management serve as a buffer in translating your artistic works into business?

B.: I'm just thankful that my management serves. Every artist must have one these days.

J.: Would you talk of any of the positive things that drugs have to offer, how they might have affected your work?

B.: I wouldn't think they have anything to offer. I'm speaking about drugs in the everyday sense of the word. From my own experience they would have nothing positive to offer, but I'm not speaking for anyone else. Someone else might see them offering a great deal.

J.: But in the way of insights or new combinations, it never affected you that way?

B.: No, you get those same insights over a period of time anyway.

J.: For a while you were working on a book, they gave it a name *Tarantula*. Have you tried any other writing since then, or did you learn anything from the experience of trying?

B.: Yes, I do have a book in me, it'll be out sometime. Macmillan will publish it.

J.: Did you learn from the one you did reject?

B.: I learned not to do a book like that. That book was the kind of thing where the contract comes in before the book is written, so you have to fulfill the contract.

J.: In thinking over this interview thus far, it seems like that has happened to you several times over the recent years, not necessarily of your choosing.

B.: Yes, that's true. But it happens to other people and they come through. Dostoevsky did it, he had a weekly number of words to get in. I understand Frederick Murrey does it, and John Updike must . . . For someone else it might be exactly what they always had wished.

J.: In trying to write it, was it a difficulty of structure or concept?

B.: No, there was no difficulty in writing it at all. It just wasn't a book, it was just a nuisance. It didn't have that certain quality which now I think a book should have. It didn't have any structure at all, it was just one flow. It flowed for ninety pages.

J.: I'm thinking of a parallel. You know some of those old crazy talking blues? They go on where just the last phrase of a sentence connects up to the next sentence, but the two thoughts aren't related. "Slipping up and down the mantle piece, feet in a bucket of grease, hunting matches, etc." Did it go that way?

B.: More or less. They were short little lines, nothing within a big framework. I couldn't even conceive of doing anything in a big framework at that time. I was doing something else.

H.: Do you think future writings will use the poetic form of the novel?

B.: I think it will have everything in it.

J.: Listening to the car radio, I heard that you have a song on the country music stations, "I'll Be Your Baby Tonight." I can't remember the singer's name, but I understand that Burl Ives has also recorded it.

B.: A lot of people record them, they always do a good job.

J.: When did you first hear Burl Ives?

B.: I first heard Burl Ives when I was knee-high to a grasshopper.

J.: Was that folk music to you when you first heard it?

B.: Yes, I guess everybody's heard those old Burl Ives records on Decca, with a picture of him in a striped T-shirt, holding a guitar up to his ear, just wailing.

J.: Did you know that his first recordings were for Moe Asch (of Folkways records)? Alan Lomax had brought him in. Who made the first recordings you are on?

B.: I recorded with Big Joe Williams.

J.: Where did this Blind Boy Grunt thing come in?

B.: Someone told me to come down 'cause they were doing some kind of an album. So I was there and singing this song, and it only had a couple of verses and that's all, so someone in the control booth said "Do some more." I said well, there is no more, I can't sing any more. The fellow says "If you can't sing, GRUNT." So I said "Grunt?" Then someone else sitting at a desk to my left says, "What name shall I put down on this record?" and I said, "Grunt." She said "Just Grunt?" Then the fellow in the control booth said "Grunt." Somebody came in the door then and said "Was that Blind Boy Grunt?" and the lady at the desk said "Yes it was."

J.: Was this Moe Asch and Marion Distler?

B.: It could have been.

J.: My last question is really a rehash of one aspect we've

already discussed; at the moment, your songs aren't as socially or politically applicable as they were earlier.

B.: As they were earlier? Could it be that they are just as social and political, only that no one cares to . . . let's start with the question again. (J. repeats question) Probably that is because no one cares to see it the way I'm seeing it now, whereas before, I saw it the way they saw it.

H.: You hear a lot about the word "engaged" artists. Painters, filmmakers, actors, they're actively involved in current events, through their art.

B.: Well, even Michelangelo though . . .

H.: Many artists feel that at this particular time in history, they can't just do their thing without regarding the larger scale around them.

B.: The thing is, if you can get the scales around you in whatever you create, that's nice. If you physically have to go out there and experience it time and time again you're talking about something else.

H.: Probably the most pressing thing going on in a political sense, is the war. Now I'm not saying any artist or group of artists can change the course of the war, but they still feel it their responsibility to say something.

B.: I know some very good artists who are for the war.

H.: Well I'm just talking about the ones who are against it.

B.: That's like what I'm talking about; it's for or against the war. That really doesn't exist. It's not for or against the war. I'm speaking of a certain painter, and he's all for the war. He's just about ready to go over there himself. And I can comprehend him.

H.: Why can't you argue with him?

B.: I can see what goes into his paintings, and why should I?

H.: I don't understand how that relates to whether a position should be taken.

B.: Well, there's nothing for us to talk about really.

J.: Someone just told me that the poet and artist William Blake harboured Tom Paine when it was dangerous to do so. Yet Blake's artistic production was mystical and introspective.

H.: Well, he separated his work from his other activity. My

feeling is that with a person who is for the war and ready to go over there, I don't think it would be possible for you and him to share the same basic values.

B.: I've known him a long time, he's a gentleman and I admire him, he's a friend of mine. People just have their views. Anyway, how do you know I'm not, as you say, for the war?

J.: Is this comparable? I was working on a fireplace with an old local stone mason last summer, while running off to sing at the New Politics Convention. When I returned I was chopping rocks with him, and he says, "All the trouble today is caused by people like Martin Luther King." Now I respect that man, not for his comments on Dr. King, but for his work with stone, his outlook on his craft, and on work and life, in the terms he see it. It is a dilemma.

H.: I think it is the easy way out, to say that. You have to feel strongly about your own ideas, even if you can respect someone else for their ideas. (to Bob) I don't feel there is that much difference between your work now and your earlier work. I can see a continuity of ideas, although they're not politically as black and white as they once were. "Masters of War" was a pretty black and white song. It wasn't too equivocal. You took a stand.

B.: That was an easy thing to do. There were thousands and thousands of people just wanting that song, so I wrote it up. What I'm doing now isn't more difficult, but I no longer have the capacity to feed this force which is needing all these songs. I know the force exists but my insight has turned into something else. I might meet one person now, and the same thing can happen between that one person (and myself) that used to happen between thousands.

J.: This leads right to the last statement on my interview list: On your latest album, the focus has become more on the individual, axioms and ideas about living, rather than about society's doings or indictments of groups of people. In other words, it's more of how one individual is to act.

B.: Yes, in a way . . . in a way. I would imagine that's just the way we grow.

Dylan's Country Pie

by Hubert Saal

Raspberry, strawberry, lemon and lime,
What do I care?
Blueberry, apple, cherry, pumpkin and plum.
Call me for dinner, honey, I'll be there.

These lines from "Country Pie," one of the ten songs on Bob Dylan's new Columbia album, *Nashville Skyline,* are a kind of declaration of independence, just as the song itself, with its country lyrics and jaunty Nashville sound, illustrates the character of the new record. When Dylan talks of eating pies, all kinds, he means writing songs, all kinds. And when he goes on in the song to say "Ain't runnin' any race," he seems to be rejecting the musical direction his many admirers have chosen for him in the past or would choose for him in the future.

Like almost every Dylan album, *Nashville Skyline* is full of surprises, perhaps even more than *Another Side of Bob Dylan* in 1964, in which he half turned away from topical protests like "Blowin' in the Wind," or the shock of 1965's *Bringing It All Back Home,* when he fused folk and rock and electrified both his instruments and his audience, or last year's *John Wesley Harding,* in which Dylan switched to a series of narrative ballads, simple, mournful and mystical.

This new album is country Dylan, a collection of unaffected and highly tuneful love songs, riding comfortable cushioned on the Nashville sound, which sometimes, as in "To Be Alone With You" or "One More Night," is pure Country and Western, but which for the most part is just a relaxed get-together of expert musicians who seem to know each other's—and Dylan's—moves as if they were playing at the Grand Ole Opry.

Blend: And just to make his point clear, Dylan starts the album off in a duet with the great country singer Johnny Cash, singing an old Dylan song called "Girl From the North Country." The blend of Dylan's light voice and Cash's melodious baritone is as rough in texture and as unassuming as if they happened to meet on the street and burst into song. As a matter of fact, they almost did. When Dylan was asked how this duet with Cash came about, his first reply was, "He happened to be in Nashville at the time." His follow-up was: "It's a great privilege to sing with Johnny Cash."

The great charm of the album is in the variety of pretty songs and the ways Dylan, both as composer and performer, has found to exploit subtle differences on a deliberately limited emotional and verbal scale. In the oddly syncopated "Lay Lady Lay," in the mocking musical figures of the plaintive "Tell Me That It Isn't True" and in the bluesy "Tonight I'll Be Staying Here With You," each melody is distinct and distinctive, the rhythms varied and complex, the music delicately and expressively colored. "Peggy Day" is almost a pastiche of the '30s; its rhythms recall "swing," and Dylan sings with the kind of lighthearted showmanship that used to come from college bandstands. And if in the songs the words are plain and direct, they do not lack for cunning: "Love to spend the night with Peggy Day," and later, "Love to spend the day with Peggy Night."

"Inner Me": Bob Dylan is still staying pretty much out of public sight in Woodstock, N. Y., although he confesses that plans for public appearances are afoot. He expects to appear on Johnny Cash's television show this summer: "Fair is fair," says Dylan. In his diffident way, he is apparently pleased with his new album. "These are the type of songs that I always felt like writing when I've been alone to do so," he says. "The songs reflect more of the inner me than the songs of the past. They're more to my base than, say *John Wesley Harding*. There I felt everyone expected me to be a poet so that's what I tried to be. But the smallest line in this new album means more to me than some of the songs on any of the previous albums I've made."

The base that Dylan refers to is the musicians and the music he knew before he came to New York. "The people who shaped my style were performers like Elvis Presley, Buddy Holly, Hank Thompson." He sank back on his couch recalling the earlier years, out of which came "Blowin' in the Wind," "A Hard Rain's A-Gonna Fall" and "The Times They Are A-Changin'." "Those songs were all written in the New York atmosphere. I'd never have written any of them—or sung them the way I did—if I hadn't been sitting around listening to performers in New York cafes and the talk in all the dingy parlors. When I got to New York it was obvious that something was going on—folk music—and I did my best to learn and play it. I was just there at the right time with pen in hand. I suppose there was some ambition in what I did. But I tried to make the songs genuine."

Among the things that Dylan was willing to say pleased him on the new record were the venturesomeness of the music, the extra and unusual guitar chording, the growing melodic nature of his songs. "I admire the spirit to the music," he says. "It's got a good spirit." Good? "Yes, like a good door, a good house, a good car, a good road, a good girl. I feel like writing a whole lot more of them too."

H.S.

Joan Baez On Dylan

"I always wanted to do an album of Dylan songs," she said, munching a tuna fish sandwich in a sunny San Francisco kitchen. "Whether or not he decides to join forces with the human race, he's a genius. Something of Bobby will survive in history; some of the songs that will survive are on this record. But it doesn't matter which songs you choose, when someone is that much of a mystic and a genius, you have to get an insight from listening to anything he's written." Her admiration for Dylan is not exactly boundless, though. "As a person, I just can't sing his nasty, hateful ugly songs; I can appreciate the honesty of them, and melodically they're good, but I can't sing them."

She went to Nashville, where Dylan recorded *John Wesley Harding,* and used some of the same studio musicians, the legendary Nashville cats ("Nashville cats play clean as country water/ Nashville cats play wild as mountain dew," sings John Sebastian). "They're real pokerfaced, don't show anything. At first I couldn't tell what they were thinking. Then one night we all went out to dinner, and they said they'd been really surprised by me. 'We expected you to be just like Dylan—a slob,' they said, 'but you're real ladylike,' and one of them told me he hadn't recognized me until we started singing because he thought I'd be wearing motorcycle boots."

Interviewed by Susan Lydon

Bob Dylan Meets the Revolution

by Tom Smucker

At the SDS National Convention in June, the written statement of one of the factions there was titled with a line from Bob Dylan's "Subterranean Homesick Blues":

You don't need a weatherman to tell which way the wind blows and sub(con?)sequently this group, who now controls the National Office of SDS (and is currently the most flamboyant of all the factions) is called "Weatherman."

At this point in the history of the Movement, everyone, from White Panthers to Socialist Scholars, is talking about relating to the white working class, one way or another, and it was interesting to me that one of the leading factions in the Movement would title their explanation of how to do this with a line from *Bob Dylan's First Rock and Roll Top Forty Hit.*

There has been a history of connections, separations, identities and anxieties between Bob Dylan and political people. It began with the early-middle sixties, when he was king of the topical protest song. Then he went Rock, and at the time, many considered that selling out. As the concept of Folk-Rock, Acid-Rock, etc. got assimilated, he then came out with *John Wesley Harding*, which seemed a return to the discredited folk-song simplistic world-view. And most recently, at a time when many liberals and radicals were waiting for a Revolutionary-Rock album from the number one prophet, he comes out with *Nashville Skyline*. It's about *love*, there is no anger in it, and it's cast in the reactionary, Wallace-for-President, traditionally repressed cultural form of Country Music.

Reprinted with permission from *Fusion*, Oct. 31, 1969.

So it was interesting to me, at this time, that a leading faction of the largest white radical organization would choose a line from a song that at one time was considered the final symbol of Bob Dylan's degeneracy and co-optation. And from a type of music embodying certain attitudes that Dylan himself is no longer associated with.

In the early sixties, due to many factors I don't exactly understand, having something to do with Post WWII America, the breakdown of the socializing forces of schooling, affluence, the Cold War, and the beginnings of the Black Revolt as a vital semi-alternative, some white kids began: 1) listening to black music on the radio, and/or eventually their own derivative of that: Rock and Roll; 2) participating in what was called then The Civil Rights Movements.

Along with this, because of the paranoia created by the anti-communism and conformity of the Cold War, the more self-conscious aspects of this protest among whites, in an attempt to identify with the people, but not with America, found its solution in Folk Music. Remember? Folkies liked the Folk, but not the Masses.

This form of music reached its limits, being based on a tradition that essentially had ended, or was judged ended when it became electro-citi-mass-mediad; and this milieu of people began to see that its protest could not be embodied by the Black Protest . . .

This is when Dylan left Folk Music, sort of, when the English, using American idioms to express *their* alienation were able to return our culture to us as a slightly more hip semicultural alternative to the Civil Rights-Altruistic-Folk Music-Purist bag.

Dylan picked up on this in several forms, and it's interesting to note that it is at this point that his language becomes allegorical to the point of being incomprehensible. Because it seems to me now that that whole world, which is decadent or dying today, was always based on a complex agreement with reality. The Pop world was maintained at a distance from the real world that it commented on (although it was always close enough to comment, unlike the consciously isolated Folk Music world), and Pop people, which we all were then to some extent, viewed themselves as representations of bits and pieces of the middle-class corruption they had abandoned, or the victims of that corruption they identified with. Thus it was necessary for Dylan to use so many images in his work that weren't literal, because he was helping create that world which never existed except as the struggle of our imagination, for a brief while, to separate itself from its middle-class origins.

After the original realization of the morality and altruism of Folk Music, and the collapse of that alternative forever with the advent of Black Power, the next step was the acceptance of chaos—*Highway 61 Revisited,* including its bitter put-down and delineation of outsiders (Mr. Jones) and its evil chortle towards the girl who thought she could avoid the chaos and didn't—"Like a Rolling Stone." But after the acceptance of that rootlessness, there is nowhere to go but masquerade and mind games.

White kids had learned that they weren't black, but that didn't mean they wanted to go back. So you had Rock and the constellation of cultural forms around it. And the slow acceptance of many political people to the idea of Rock as a Revolutionary Life Style, the creation of an Alternate Culture-Community.

Which unfortunately could not survive. That is today's lesson. Politically-Economically you can talk about the impossibility for liberation as long as everyone is forced to tie into that corrupt whorehouse of economic relationships we have called Capitalism. You can talk about the totality of the oppression caused by the system, and about the connection between the consciousness and economic arrangements between (and over people).

Anecdote-wise you can point out how Pot is still illegal, Nixon president, Good People in jail, and how the War goes on regardless of how people feel. And point out all the pricks and big-time egos with long hair, tripping, grooving . . .

And looking at Dylan you can see how after *Highway 61 Revisited, Blonde On Blonde* (a two record set!), appeared as the ultimate achievement, a formal commentary on the detached, exotic world that was being created then (partially by the record itself)—but how the existence of that world was limited by its angry origins and detached attitude.

Of course it wasn't exactly clear, you know. And so when

Dylan finally released an album after his long disappearance, in that long ago time when people were still wondering *what* could top *Sgt. Pepper,* and Rock as Art, it *was* surprising that his record was so acoustic, so folky, so subdued, and really so anguished.

To me, *John Wesley Harding* shows Dylan trying to struggle out of the straight-jacket created by his earlier records, and all of our earlier cultural-political attitudes.

The straight-jacket was this: a conception of an alternate culture and attitude without any real base, once the graft to the black movement was removed—based on a youth put-down of an outside world what could only last as long as the child/adult division could be maintained. In other words, what do you do when *you* have kids? A culture that saw itself, after *Sgt. Pepper,* either becoming a new establishment and aristocracy, or changing direction. And particularly in the case of Dylan, an attitude heavy on self-righteousness and individualism to the point of chaos. Old Dylan songs, always praised for their frankness, were also almost always about the intrigues and dangers of sexual relationships. An attitude that could not sustain a man for life. (Take a tip from one who tri-i-i-i-ed.)

The straight-jacket for The Movement was similar. The conception of The Movement as a set of people with alternative ideas could only go so far before it realised that its success depended on its incorporation in the *majority* of Americans, not on its opposition to them. Its anger at America and Americans could only pay off for a while. Ultimately that approach would mean its repression at the hands of the majority, or its disintegration at its lack of growth.

The straight-jacket manifested itself in the following ways:

1) Bob Dylan's Motorcycle Crash and Disappearance

2) Lots of crummy over-produced Art-Rock records and Art-Rock concepts

3) a general decline of enthusiasm about Rock

4) The Movement understanding that it must become a white working class Movement to succeed

5) the disintegration of SDS into factions with different understandings of how this must be done

The agony of the Movement at this point is Dylan's agony,

although each takes place in different spheres. On *John Wesley Harding* he goes through it, trying to disconnect the half-false distinctions made on his earlier records. "There must be someway out of here," dig? Arriving at new definitions of his relationship to Landlords, Folk-Myths, and Women. I think people don't understand "Dear Landlord," which is not an accommodation with the Landlord, but an explanation of the necessary relationship. Earlier Dylan (and earlier me, and earlier you) was more excited by the realization that LANDLORDS WERE BAD.

He's arriving at the point of *pitying* the poor immigrant, 'way beyond the original morally ironic statement of separation from good-guy-immigrant myths in "With God On Our Side."

And to me it's no mistake that at the very end of the album there are two slightly C&W songs, both about love.

Because the problem of sustaining yourself involves the problem of sustaining yourself with people, sexually maybe most significantly, and sustaining yourself too with THE PEOPLE.

And the only popular musical form that exists as some form of expression of current people culture in America is Country and Western music. Folk Music as we knew it in Greenwich Village Night Clubs was the expression of Artistocratic Pro-Prole Culture, as the Movement once was. Rock has become, when it transcends its teenager reality, the expression of a semi-elitist alternative culture (dig Woodstock). Country music, although identifiable with a specific poor-wasp ethnic framework, in fact seems to be the one non-middle-class musical form that speaks for working people.

And, incidentally, it flows in and out of the History of Rock, and vice versa, as a musical influence. Remember Don and Phil, Conway, Jerry Lee, and Brenda? Country Artists all.

The cultural idea of sustaining Bob Dylan's career and the future of Rock and Roll beyond teenagerism in Country Music contains contradictions and problems. It's a very traditional form in many ways. And it's a form that bears the brunt of a lot of middle-class scorn.

But that is the only place to go, man, and beyond the distintegration of SDS, and the difference in Dylan's albums there is only one hope for maintaining the continuity of either. And that is disappearing into America, which is the beginning of a very scary trip.

But I think *Nashville Skyline* has already shown a few things.

First of all, the fact that the number one hip-rock-poet goes to honky Nashville to record, and RECORDED HIS FIRST DUET ON HIS OWN ALBUM EVER WITH JOHNNY CASH, has automatically made Nashville, Country Music, and Johnny Cash human to a whole milieu that would have thought otherwise last year.

This has neither made Johnny Cash a hippie nor Bob Dylan a Country and Western Artist, but I think it has lent new respectability to both. On the level of Pop-Symbolism-Star-Gossip Dylan concretely has exhibited a shift of sensibilities.

The fact that his first TV appearance (and first "public" appearance in a while) was on Cash's show in Nashville, and the fact that he was so modest, to the point some people mistook it for incompetence, demonstrates on a celebrity level the correct approach to take towards relating to the masses, as they say.

The fact that his first live appearance was at the Isle of Wight, England's Transatlantic Woodstock, also shows, however, that an interest in Country and Western music does not make millions of alienated middle-class kids or the forces that created them disappear.

Some observations about *Nashville Skyline:*

It's the first album on which Dylan sings with continuous affection about sex, and about women. On it his formally frank, paranoid visions of insane social and sexual relationships are replaced completely with positive or at least light-hearted ones. On it love seems to be presented as the reward for work. The question of how are you going to earn your bread if you aren't going to work on Maggie's farm no more is reformulated. And work is mentioned for the first time as an actual fact of life.

And so on.

There is a time, frequently, after a Dylan album when people wonder whether he has sold out. Then they decide that the album really is *good,* and decide that he knows where it's at musically but wonder whether *they* have sold out for liking it. Or whether they should worry. And then a long time later it all fits into place.

Well, it isn't a long time later yet, and I think Dylan is so good he can never be totally understood until a long time later and I'm not going to try now. I think one thing this article can do is show how Dylan's political significance is as great as ever, although the startling manifestations of this significance aren't all apparent now.

And if there are no "political" songs in the old sense, that in itself is political. We are beyond the point now where rhetoric comes from singers. That was back when Dylan, and Baez, and Peter, Paul and Mary led the March on Washington. Going back now, we won't be led by singers. Marching to the seat of power with a petition is different than thinking about SEIZING STATE POWER.

But that won't be done either if we don't understand our own music, and our own prophets. Bob Dylan is one. Is Johnny Cash another?

The "I Wanna Be With You If You Wanna Be With Me" Fiction Interview

by Michael March

Summer 66 and the world destroyed Dylan. Not on some rocky road/highway 61. Neck broken by harmonica holder cycling through village. Somewhere back in 65, maybe at Forest Hills, the crowd devoured his image while masturbating itself. But Dylan still exists hidden in Woodstock, New York with wealth, wife, and piano. Stoned with Clapton one night, we visited. What remains is a residue of recollections.

Q. Like why don't you come out?

A. The image. The image. Wearing a wig was a bad scene. All those people screaming and amphetamine. And where it's at. Grossman wanted me to ball Baby Jane Holzer for press.

Q. With protrusions and pearls . . .

A. And chinese flutes.

Now I must compose and ship in supermarkets. The broken neck covered my tripping out. Man, those fuckin' gigs. England. A roomed life with wall to wall jokes. And people clawing to get inside of me and my shoes when all I know is the farmer's daughter.

Q. What about your appearance at the Guthrie Memorial Concert?

A. What about it. The man was a genius. What I did was for him and no one else.

But everybody gets so excited. "He's wearing a suit," rehearses the audience . . .

Q. And the band . . .

Reprinted with permission from *Fusion*, October 31, 1969.

A. Friends. We just play together cause we're friends.

Q. What about Baez?

A. Haven't seen her in two years—doesn't like my voice or somethin'. Electricity scares her. Morbid lyrics scares her. So she sings in the same pitch—records my songs cause she's too scared to record her own. In the old days. Beautiful. Used to wipe herself with an American flag after doin' it. Sure, I still love her even though she's straddled on peace an some punk ex-resident-from-college-kid. Yeh, and the way she drops acid lying naked on ole Fats Domino records.

Q. Love was a four-letter word in *Don't Look Back.*

A. Right, man. Four years ago in some dogshit farce. When I was developing as an international noise. "Subterranean Homesick Blues" hit fourteen while posing for Pennebaker who positioned himself for the networks and the show-must-go-on hype and Grossman's contractual constipation. Making me peeking through a keyhole down upon my knees . . .

Q. And the electric transformation?

A. In Minnesota at seventeen when I played fo' food an local ball I was into rock. Cut "Mixed-up Confusion" in '62 with electric backup. So for like three years I sang caruso—hitting all the notes and holding my breath three times as long until "Like a Rolling Stone."

I was electric on the '65 European tour. Filmed me and the band doin' a little for another film called *Nine Below Zero*—don't think it'll be released though.

Q. Why?

A. Look, I always wanted to be Little Richard. If ya don't believe me, look in my ole high-school yearbook. I used to stand there with a piano and scream and everybody laughed at the amps. I came to New York an' got into folk cause that's what was man. I wrote what people wanted an' Grossman created the image with all this stuff about my leavin' home and stuff. Suddenly people were doin' me—I had the bread an' fame so like I reverted to high-school-eleventh grade to be exact. And there was me in this movie screaming in the Olympia in Paris and Grossman said cut the tracks but wait a few takes on the image, Bobbie.

Q. You've always been aware of your image and public taste.

Was your Woodstock seclusion just another bit to gather the tribes?

A. I knew it was time to stop, that's all. Someday I may be hung as a thief.

Q. You're not copping out politically?

A. I say what I have to, man. The artist is the most political figure in society because he stands outside. *John Wesley Harding* is religious and political—besides, they're both the same. "Where another man's life might begin that's exactly where mine ends."

Q. "He was never known to make a foolish move."

A. So "don't go mistaking paradise for that home across the road." Let's take that again. "All Along The Watchtower" contains an encapsulated "Desolation Row" in science fiction terms. "There must be some way out of here said the joker to the thief." What's political man? Sorry I can't do that William Zan Zinger stuff anymore. Besides, none of them along the line know what any of it is worth. Everybody wants to be inside my shoes and I'm married with three kids—where the fuck is Nashville in space?

Q. But as a poet you must realize that people associate your musical thoughts with their existence. They want . . .

A. Did I hear product or me? They've pirated the basement tape, xeroxed *Tarantula*, and made me cut my hair off. But there's about eighty cuts that they ain't gonna hear because Columbia won't release 'em. Right now I'm into my existence and it feels good.

Q. Has your voice changed? On *Nashville Skyline* it's higher and smoother . . .

A. That's because I'm higher and smoother.

Q. I mean . . .

A. "Music is so much less than what you are." O.K.?

Bob Dylan and "The Great White Wonder"

"Dylan translates everything into a strange, fearful, unified dirge. His voice is altogether unique—black and country at once, as though he were on the brink of some improbable fusion . . ."

by William C. Woods

The double-barreled "underground" Dylan disc is hardly big news at this point, which is just as well. Because what it calls for is less a record review than a considered response to the—forgive this—cultural artifact that it is.

Happily if heavily named *The Great White Wonder,* this pirated collection of music that spans the decade with blurry reminders of its creator's career has now moved from the FM rock stations on both coasts to people's record collections, where it will occupy a place of some esteem.

Ignoring the ethical question posed by a pirate record, we can cut the problem of Great White Wonder into three parts: sound quality, intrinsic value of the music, and historical importance.

The last is self-evident. This album is as significant as Stephen Hero, Hemingway's poems, or a Charlie Parker master. But the other two parts of the problem are tougher.

Take quality. Jamie Robbie Robertson—songwriter and lead guitarist for the Band, and a long-time Dylan friend and backup man—has remarked: "This bootleg record is a tape of a tape of a tape of a dub of a tape of a dub that was actually recorded in the basement of Big Pink." (Unlike *Music From Big Pink* itself, incidentally).

That would make it a sixth generation dub, which should mean a beggar's banquet of surface noise, high and low frequency loss, and general disaster. In fact, the quality is surprisingly good—not professional, obviously, because these songs were recorded off vintage TV sets and in people's hovels and hotel rooms on old gear.

But it's usable; if your system has decent filters and balancing capacity, it's very usable indeed. Then too, there is a wide range in the sound quality. The newest song—"Livin' The Blues," taken right off last summer's Johnny Cash premiere—is clear as a bell; most of the 1961 songs (demos for Columbia?) are passably clean; the songs done with the Band are, regrettably, pretty muddy.

At last report, your money will be 13 bucks. For that, you get two discs with white labels in white slipcases inside a white cover. Virgin stuff. Whether this impressive void of information is designed to protect the producers or enhance the mystery of their product, it leaves questions that will remain unanswered until Dylan makes his own statement about the record.

Are Al Kooper and Mike Bloomfield really wailing in the background? Is that Pete Seeger asking the mechanical questions Dylan fields so nicely? ("Bob, do you make up a song before breakfast every day, or before supper?" "Naw, I don't make up a song like that . . . in fact, sometimes I can go two weeks without making up a song . . . but I wrote five songs last night.") No matter. Once more, it's words and music by Bob Dylan, and that brings us to the second item, the worth of this album as a thing-in-itself.

That worth is considerable, but it is hard to separate from the historical overlap. For the material in the album is, if not a microcosm of Dylan's development, a convincing survey of the major stages of his career.

Great White Wonder is topheavy with early Dylan, the artist as a young man under the shadow of Woody Guthrie and the thumb of his own uncertainty. His thought may be Platonic ("the song was there before me"), but his message is straight from folk's more tired treasure-trove: "Baby Please Don't Go," "Dink's Song," "Ramblin' Round." It all sounds like stuff edited out of his first album, which may be exactly what it is.

The single Cash show cut is the sole amplification of present-day Dylan. It is an easy, up-beat country blues of no great distinction.

But the real meat of the album lies in the handful of songs recorded with the Band—vexing, troublesome, fascinating, transition Dylan. Music that merits close attention.

Some of these songs appeared on the Band's first album, *Music From Big Pink*—"I Shall Be Released," "Tears of Rage," "Wheels on Fire"—and one number, "The Mighty Quinn," was a big hit for Manfred Mann. But only this album gives us the composer working out his own songs in his own way, and the effect—even through the static—is electric.

Dylan translates everything into a strange, fearful, unified dirge. His voice is altogether unique—black and country at once, as though he were on the brink of some improbable fusion that might speak not only of a new music, but of a new world. And in less familiar songs, he goes digging for images of the void that echo the long wasteland take-out of "Desolation Row." In "Too Much of Nothing," for example, he uses oxymoron—a seventeenth-century device he remains fond of—to give a short giddy image central to his thought:

> In a hail of confusion
> We cannot mark the soul
> For when there's too much of nothing
> No one has control

And elsewhere you may trip over a line that has fed two other major pieces: "Well this Arabian doctor comes in and gives me a shot but wouldn't tell what it was that I got." There are other clues. "Open The Door, Richard" comprehensively sketches Dylan's relationship to his art and its audience:

> Take care of all of your memories, said Nick
> For you cannot relive them
> And remember when you're out there tryin' to heal
> the sick
> That you must always first forgive them

In a sense, this piecemeal pop criticism is offensive, because the Dylan of *Nashville Skyline* has opened a more spacious scene.

But it is indispensable, because Dylan does not purvey music to ride elevators by, and to dig him is, above all, to dig into him. *The Great White Wonder,* outlaw though it is, is now an irreplaceable part of that archeology of the finest songwriter of our time.

Dylan In England: Trauma Or Triumph?

by Nik Cohn

Bob Dylan's appearance at the Isle of Wight pop festival last weekend was his first major concert in three years and probably the most traumatic convulsion that English rock has ever been put through. Two hundred thousand people waited three days to see him, sleeping in an improvised shanty town called Desolation Row; the population of the island hid from him, peeping out at his disciples from behind their curtains; the English press gave him an estimated quarter of a million words; the flower of the English rock aristocracy, three Beatles and three Rolling Stones among them, crouched at his feet in the press enclosure, herded together like sheep; and Dylan himself took away upwards of $80,000 for one hour's work.

The idea behind all this was that the Isle of Wight would go down as England's answer to the 1967 Monterey Festival, a final expression of love, peace and flowers. It didn't work out like that. It was, in fact, a fiasco.

The background was romantic enough. A few months ago, three local brothers named Foulks, all in their early twenties, suddenly decided that they wanted Dylan for their festival and they tracked him like Mounties.

The obstacles were considerable. None of the Foulks brothers had much previous experience in promotion and they met with a comprehensive squelch from Dylan's office. Still, they persevered; they kept writing, kept calling, kept hassling. Finally, they made a special film on the island and all its splendors, sending it to Dylan direct. Exhausted, he gave in.

By any standards, this was a triumph. The only trouble was the brothers didn't carry it through. Having set up a perfect pitch, they messed it up with lack of planning. For a start, they built their arena much too small, so that everyone got squashed in like sardines. Then there weren't enough good supporting acts, enough food stalls or even enough latrines.

Most important, there weren't enough diversions. A gaggle of poetry readings, a giant phallic balloon and a communal foam bath during which one couple made love. Spread across three days, it was pretty slow stuff.

By the second day, therefore, the festival was already sunk deep in apathy. When The Who arrived by helicopter, sweeping down backstage in a puff of smoke, they caused not a ripple. Dirty and hungry and exhausted, the audience sat like 200,000 suet puddings, applauding politely at everything.

Things didn't finally begin to warm up until Tom Paxton appeared on the afternoon of the third day. Paxton is a straight folk singer—he doesn't ham much—but he's been around and he's a trouper. Coming after Blodwyn Pig and Gary Farr, he seemed like genius and, for the first time, people began to cheer.

Next there was Richie Havens, a black singer-guitarist with a good curdled voice and a bottomless box of bull. "Outa sight," he told us. "You're all beautiful. You're all groovy. Outa sight. You're all beautiful because you're people. And people are. And people are people are people, period. Outa sight."

Predictably, this went down like a storm and there was more cheering. By this time, it was 8 o'clock and Dylan was due any minute. But the Foulks brothers had overfilled the press enclosure and journalists kept fainting. Accordingly, the whole show was stopped while we were sorted out. This took 90 minutes and, by the end, we were the most hated minority in the island's history.

Bottles and beer cans and rotten fruit rained down on us, clods of earth and half-eaten sandwiches. I was hit on the neck by an apple core, clonked on the head by a blunt instrument and, finally, wandering too close to a barrier, I was spat upon. Love, peace and flowers.

Finally, around 10:30, Dylan's backing group, The Band, came out and did a warm-up set. They were terrific. Their harmonies half-country, half-gospel and the beat good hard rock, they made the endless succession of English bands that had gone before seem like so much Mickey Mouse.

Then Dylan came out. He was a tubby little man. He wore a white suit, he had a curly beard and he didn't just walk, he ambled. Where once he'd been all angles and neuroses, he now seemed almost cozy.

He sounded good. Most of the time, he worked in the style of his last album, *Nashville Skyline*, meaning that he was deep-toned and lazy and romantic. His voice had lost its whine, his lyrics had lost their sting. Even his old anguished monologues, like "Like A Rolling Stone" and "Positively 4th Street" and "It Ain't Me, Babe," sounded mellow now. Almost too much so, in fact: after a few numbers, he got a touch monotonous and his audience, which had started out ecstatic, wound up merely appreciative.

Still, he was impressive. No longer a prophet, he was magnetic just the same. On this night he overdid his cool, speaking just five sentences and messing about interminably between each number. Even so, he had it—he was a showbiz presence in the grand tradition.

After an hour, Dylan finished. He did just one encore then disappeared and, if he'd been less than apocalyptic, most everyone seemed content.

They didn't stay that way. Milling about in the fields, the crowd shoved furiously in opposite directions and got nowhere. There were bonfires everywhere and the latrines stank.

In the nearest town, 20,000 kids slept on the pavements, waiting for ferries back to the mainland. Myself, I cut off down a side road and curled up in a ditch. It was a very cold night and loudspeaker announcements kept drifting through to me: "Let's hear it for the Foulks brothers," the man said, "without whom none of this could have happened."

Dylan is small and frail, a large-eyed nocturnal animal, with a thin, almost whiney voice. Offstage he looks quite unimpressive, with none of the magnetism of his quiet stage performances. He mumbles as he speaks, scarcely moving his lips, says very little, and seems unwilling or unable to express himself articulately except through his songs. People have eagerly categorised him. The young chose him as their symbol, but what strikes some observers most about him is his coldness, alienation, and sardonic detachment. Once, asked if he was married, he answered: 'I was born married 45 years ago.' Asked why he wore dark glasses, he said: 'I'm a very sick person. I have mercuryesque eyes. And another thing, my toe-nails don't fit.'

From the *London Observer*, 1969.

The Rolling Stone Interview: Dylan

by Jann Wenner

They say Bob Dylan is the most secretive and elusive person in the entire rock and roll substructure, but after doing this interview, I think it would be closer to the point to say that Dylan, like John Wesley Harding, was "never known to make a foolish move."

The preparations for the interview illustrates this well. About 18 months ago, I first started writing Bob letters asking for an interview, suggesting the conditions and questions and reasons for it. Then, a little over a year ago, the night before I left New York, a message came from the hotel operator that a "Mr. Dillon" had called.

Two months later, I met Bob for the first time at another hotel in New York: . . . he casually strolled in wearing a sheepskin outfit, leather boots, very well put together but not too tall, y'understand. It was 10 A.M. in the morning, and I rolled out of bed stark naked—sleep that way, y'understand—and we talked for half an hour about doing an interview, what it was for, why it was necessary. Bob was feeling out the situation, making sure it would be cool.

That meeting was in the late fall of 1968. It took eight months—until the end of June this year—to finally get the interview The meantime was covered with a lot of phone calls, near misses in New York City, Bob's trips to California which didn't take place, and a lot of waiting and waiting for that right time when we were both ready for the show.

The interview took place on a Thursday afternoon in New York City at my hotel, right around the corner from the funeral home where Judy Garland was being inspected by ten thousand people, who formed lines around several city blocks. We were removed from all that activity, but somehow it seemed appropriate enough that Judy Garland's funeral coincided with the interview.

Bob was very cautious in everything he said, and took a long time between questions to phrase exactly what he wanted to say, nothing more and sometimes a little less. When I wasn't really satisfied with his answers, I asked questions another way, later. But Bob was hip.

Rather than edit the interview into tight chunks and long answers, I asked Sheryl to transcribe the tapes with all the pauses, asides and laughs left in. So, much of the time, it's not what is said, but how it is said, and I think you will dig it more just as it went down.

To bring us up to date after all that, August through September was spent trying to get Baron together with Bob to get some new photographs of him, in a natural, non-performance situation. But it proved fruitless. Perhaps if we had had another six months to work on getting the photographs, but Bob was simply not to be rushed or pushed into something he really didn't feel like doing at the time. ("I'll have Baron meet you in New York tomorrow." "Well, tomorrow I might be in Tucson, Arizona," "Baron will fly to Tucson," etc.)

The photographs we have used are from rehearsals for the Johnny Cash show and from the Isle of Wight, ones you probably have not seen yet, and some photos of Bob from a long time ago. Bob promised that we would get together soon to take some photos, and if we do, you'll see them as soon as we get them. But don't hold your breath.

Meantime, here's the interview.

When do you think you're gonna go on the road?

November . . . possibly December.

What kind of dates do you think you'll play—concerts? Big stadiums or small concert halls?

I'll play medium-sized halls.

What thoughts do you have on the kind of back-up you're going to use?

Well, we'll keep it real simple, you know . . . drums . . . bass . . . second guitar . . . organ . . . piano. Possibly some horns. Maybe some background voices.

Girls? Like the Raylettes?

We could use some girls.

Do you have any particular musicians in mind at this time?

To go out on the road? Well, I always have some in mind. I'd like to know a little bit more about what I'm gonna do. You see, when I discover what I'm gonna do, then I can figure out what kind of sound I want.

I'd probably use . . . I'd want the best band around, you know?

Are you going to use studio musicians or use some already existing band?

I don't know . . . you see, it involves putting other people on the bill, full-time. I'd only probably use the Band again . . . if I went around.

And they'd do the first half of the show?

. . . Sure . . . sure . . .

Are you thinking of bringing any other artists with you?

Well, every so often we do think about that. (Laughter) We certainly do. I was thinking about maybe introducing Marvin Rainwater or Slim Whitman to "my audience."

Have you been in touch with either of them?

No. . . no.

What did you think when you saw yourself on the Cash show?

(Laughs) Oh, I'd never see that . . . I can't stand to see myself on television. No.

Did you dig doing it?

I dig doing it, yeah. Well, you know, television isn't like anything else . . . it's also like the movie business, you know, where they call you and then you just sit around. So by the time you finally do something, you have to do it three or four times, and usually all the spirit's gone.

You didn't watch it on TV?

(Laughs) I *did* watch it on TV . . . just because I wanted to see Johnny. I didn't realize they slowed Doug Kershaw down, too. They slowed his song down to . . . his song was like this . . . (taps out steady beat) . . . and they slowed him down to . . . (taps slow rhythm) . . . you know?

Just by slowing down the tape?

They just slowed him down. I don't know how. I don't know what happened. I think the band slowed him down or something, but boy he was slowed down. During rehearsals and just sitting around, he played these songs . . . the way we was going at it, maybe 3/4 time, and they slowed him down to about 3/8 time, you know?

Did you have any difficulty working with the TV people doing something like that?

O no, no, they're wonderful people . . . they really are. It was by far the most enjoyable television program I've ever done. I don't do television just because you get yourself in such a mess . . . so I don't do it.

You told me once that you were going to do a TV special?

That's what I'm talking about.

In Hollywood?

No, I'm talking about CBS.

In New York?

Well, we don't know that yet. They don't have in mind exactly what they would like. They kind of leave it wide open, so we're trying to close the gap now.

What do you have in mind for it?

Oh, I just have some free-form type thing in mind. A lot of music.

Presenting other artists?

Sure . . . I don't mind. I don't know who, but . . .

Why haven't you worked in so long?

Well, uh . . . I do work.

I mean on the road.

On the road . . . I don't know, working on the road . . . Well, Jann, I'll tell ya—I was on the road for almost five years. It wore me down. I was on drugs, a lot of things. A lot of things just to keep going, you know? And I don't want to live that way anymore. And uh . . . I'm just waiting for a better time—you know what I mean?

What would you do that would make the tour that you're thinking about doing different from the ones you did do?

Well, I'd like to slow down the pace a little. The one I did do . . . the next show's gonna be a lot different from the last show. The last show, during the first half, of which there was about an hour, I only did maybe six songs. My songs were long, *long* songs. But that's why I had to start dealing with a lot of different methods of keeping myself awake, alert . . . because I had to remember all the words to those songs. I've written 'em for the road, you know. So I'll be doing all these songs on the road. They're gonna sound a lot better than they do on record. My songs always sound a lot better in person than they do on the record.

Why?

Well, I don't know why. They just do.

On Nashville Skyline*—who does the arrangements? The studio musicians, or . . .*

Boy, I wish you could've come along the last time we made an album. You'd probably enjoyed it . . . 'cause you see right there, you know how it's done. We just take a song; I play it and everyone else just sort of fills in behind it. No sooner you got that done, and at the same time you're doing that, there's someone in the control booth who's turning all those dials to where the proper sound is coming in . . . and then it's done. Just like that.

Just out of rehearsing it? It'll be a take?

Well, maybe we'll take about two times.

Were there any songs on Nashville Skyline *that took longer to take?*

I don't know . . . I don't think so. There's a movie out now, called *Midnight Cowboy.* You know the song on the album, "Lay Lady Lay"? Well, I wrote that song for that movie. These producers, they wanted some music for their movie. This was last summer. And this fellow there asked me, you know, if I could do some music for their movie. So I came up with that song. By the time I came up with it, though it was too late. (Laughs) It's the same old story all the time. It's just too late . . . so I kept the song and recorded it.

There's something going on with Easy Rider*—you wrote the lyrics for a song that Roger McGuinn wrote the music for, or something? Something . . . writing a song for* Easy Rider, *the Peter Fonda film? Were you involved in that at all?*

They used some of my music in it. They used a song of the Band's too. They also used Steppenwolf music. I don't know anything more about it than that.

Do you know which song of yours they used?

"It's Alright, Ma"—but they had Roger McGuinn singing it.

Have you been approached to write music for any other movies?

Uh-hum.

Considering any of them?

Unh-unh.

Why? Scripts?

Ummmm . . . I don't know. I just can't seem to keep my mind on it. I can't keep my mind on the movie. I had a script awhile ago, that was called *Zachariah and the Seven Cowboys.* (Laughs) That was some script. Every line in it was taken out of the Bible. And just thrown together. Then there was another one, called *The Impossible Toy.* Have you seen that? (Laughs) Let's see, what else? Ummm . . . no, I'm not planning on doing any music for movies.

When are you going to do another record?

You mean when am I going to *put out* an album?

Have you done *another record?*

No . . . not exactly. I was going to try and have another one out by the fall.

Is it done in Nashville again?

Well, we . . . I think so . . . I mean it's . . . seems to be as good a place as any.

What first got you involved with or attracted you to the musicians at the Columbia studios.

Nashville? Well we always used them since *Blonde on Blonde.* Well we didn't use Pete on *Blonde on Blonde.*

What was Joe South like to work with?

Joe South? Well he was quiet. He didn't say too much. I always did like him though.

Do you like his record?

I love his records.

That album, Introspect?

Um-hmm. I always enjoyed his guitar-playing. Ever since I heard him.

Does he have any solos on Blonde on Blonde?

Um-hmm. Yes he does. He has a . . . he's playing a high guitar lick on . . . well, if you named me the songs, I could tell you which one it was, but it's catchin' my mind at the moment. He was playing . . . he played a big, I believe it was a Gretsch, guitar—one of those Chet Atkins models. That's the guitar he played it on.

"Absolutely Sweet Marie"?

Yeah, it could've been that one. Or "Just Like A Woman" . . . one of those. Boy he just . . . he played so pretty.

On Nashville Skyline, *do you have any song on that that you particularly dig? Above the others.*

Uh . . . "Tonight I'll be Staying Here With You." I like "Tell Me That It Isn't True," although it came out completely different than I'd written it. It came out real slow and mellow. I had it written as sort of a jerky, kind of polka-type thing. I wrote it in F. I wrote a lot of songs on this new album in F. That's what gives it kind of a new sound. They're all in F . . . not all of them, but quite a few. There's not many on that album that aren't in F. So you see I had those chords . . . which gives it a certain sound. I try to be a little different on every album.

I'm sure you read the review of Nashville Skyline. *Everybody remarks on the change of your singing style . . .*

Well Jann, I'll tell you something. There's not too much of a change in my singing style, but I'll tell you something which is true . . . I stopped smoking. When I stopped smoking, my voice changed . . . so drastically, I couldn't believe it myself. That's true. I tell you, you stop smoking those cigarettes (Laughter) . . . and you'll be able to sing like Caruso.

How many songs did you go into Nashville Skyline *with?*

I went in with uhh . . . the first time I went into the studio I had, I think, four songs. I pulled that instrumental one out . . . I needed some songs with an instrumental . . . then Johnny came in and did a song with me. Then I wrote one in the motel . . . then pretty soon the whole album started fillin' in together, and we had an album. I mean, we didn't go down with that in mind. That's why I wish you were there . . . you could've really seen it happen. It just manipulated out of nothing.

How many songs did you do with Johnny?

Well, we did quite a few. We just sat down and started doing some songs . . . but you know how those things are. You get into a room with someone, you start playing and singing, and you sort of forget after a while what you're there for. (Laughs)

You must have a lotta songs with him on tape . . . are you thinking of putting out a collection of them ?

Well I'm not, no. But you usually have to leave those things in the hands of the producers.

Is there one afoot?

A tape?

No, an album.

No . . . not that I know of. If there was an album, I believe that we would both have to go back into the studio and record some more songs.

There's not enough there already . . . or it's just not good enough?

Well, it's uhh . . . what it comes down to is a choice of material. If they wanted an album—a joint album—they could probably get a lot more material with a broader range on it. If we went there with actually certain songs in mind to do . . . see, that didn't happen last time.

How did you make the change . . . or why did you make the change, of producers, from Tom Wilson to Bob Johnston?

Well, I can't remember, Jann. I can't remember . . . all I know is that I was out recording one day, and Tom had always been there—I had no reason to think he wasn't going to be there—and I looked up one day and Bob was there. (Laughs)

There's been some articles on Wilson and he says that he's the one that gave you the rock and roll sound . . . and started you doing rock and roll. Is that true?

Did he say that? Well, if he said it . . . (Laughs) more power to him. (Laughs) He did to a certain extent. That is true. He did. He had a sound in mind.

Have you ever thought of doing an album . . . a very arranged, very orchestrated album, you know, with chicks and . . . ?

Gee, I've thought of it . . . I think about it once in a while. Yeah.

You think you might do one?

I do whatever comes naturally. I'd like to do an album like that. You mean using my own material and stuff.

Yeah, using your own material but with vocal background and . . . ?

I'd like to do it. Who wouldn't?

When did you make the change from John Hammond . . . or what caused the change from John Hammond?

John Hammond. He signed me in 1960. He signed me to Columbia Records. I think he produced my first album. I think he produced my second album, too.

And Tom Wilson was also working at Columbia at the time?

He was . . . you know, I don't recall how that happened . . . or why that switch took place. I remember at one time I was about to record for Don Law. You know Don Law? I was about to record for Don Law, but I never did. I met Don Law in New York, in 1962 . . . and again recently, last year when I did the *John Wesley Harding* album, I met him down in the studio. He came in . . . he's a great producer. He produced many of the earlier records for Columbia and also for labels which they had before—Okeh and stuff like that. I believe he did the Robert Johnston records.

What did you do in the year between Blonde on Blonde *and* John Wesley Harding?

Well I was on tour part of that time . . . Australia, Sweden . . . an overseas tour. Then I came back . . . and in the spring of that year, I was scheduled to go out—it was one month off, I had a one-month vacation—I was gonna go back on the road again in July. *Blonde on Blonde* was up on the charts at this time. At that time I had a dreadful motorcycle accident . . . which put me away for awhile . . . and I still didn't sense the importance of that accident till at least a year after that. I realized that it was a *real* accident. I mean I thought that I was just gonna get up and go back to doing what I was doing before . . . but I couldn't do it anymore.

What did I do during that year? I helped work on a film . . . which was supposed to be aired on *Stage 67*, a television show which isn't on anymore . . . I don't think it was on for very long.

What change? Well, it . . . it limited me. It's hard to speak about the change, you know? It's not the type of change that one can put into words . . . besides the physical change. I had a busted vertebrae; neck vertebrae. And there's really not much to talk about. I don't want to talk about it.

Laying low for a year . . . you must have had time to think. That was the ABC-TV show? What happened to the tapes of that? How come that never got shown?

Well, I could make an attempt to answer that, but . . . (Laughs) . . . I think my manager could probably answer it a lot better.

I don't think he answers too many questions.

Doesn't he? He doesn't answer questions? Well he's a nice guy. He'll usually talk to you if you show some enthusiasm for what you're talking about.

So what happened to the tapes?

You mean that film? As far as I know, it will be sold . . . or a deal will be made, for its sale. That's what I'm *told.* But you see, Jann, I don't hold these movie people in too high a position. You know this movie, *Don't Look Back?* Well, that splashed my face all over the world, that movie *Don't Look Back.* I didn't get a *penny* from that movie, you know . . . so when people say why don't you go out and work and why don't you do this and why don't you do that, people don't know *half* of what a lot of these producers and people, lawyers . . . they don't know the half of those stories. I'm an easy-going kind of fellow, you know . . . I forgive and forget. I like to think that way. But I'm not interested in finding out anymore about any film.

Did you like Don't Look Back?

I'd like it a lot more if I got paid for it. (Laughter)

There was supposed to be another film that Pennebaker shot —I don't know when or where—maybe it was the ABC film . . .

That was *it.* Sure it was. That's the one you're talking about.

Is it a good one?

Well, we cut it fast on the eye. It's fast on the eye. I'd have to let you see it for yourself, to think about if it's a good one. For me, it's too fast for the eye . . . but there are quite a few people who say it's *really* good. Johnny Cash is in it. John Lennon's in it. The Band's in it. Who else . . . a lot of different people from the European capitals of the world are in it.

Princes and princesses? (Laughs)

Well not princesses, (laughs) but presidents (laughs) and people like that.

What is the nature of your acquaintance with John Lennon?

Oh, I always love to see John. Always. He's a wonderful fellow . . . and I always like to see him.

He said that the first time that you met, in New York, after one of the concerts or something like that, it was a very uptight situation.

It probably was, yes. Like, you know how it used to be for them. They couldn't go out of their room. They used to tell me you could hardly get in to see them. There used to be people surrounding them, not only in the streets, but in the corridors in the hotel. I should say it was uptight.

How often have you seen them subsequently?

Well, I haven't seen them too much recently.

What do you think of the bed-ins for Peace? Him and Yoko.

Well, you know . . . everybody's doing what they can do. I don't mind what he does, really . . . I always like to see him.

Do you read the current critics? The music critics, so-called "rock and roll writers?"

Well I try to keep up. I try to keep up-to-date . . . I realize I don't do a very good job in keeping up to date, but I try to. I don't know half the groups that are playing around now. I don't know half of what I should.

Are there any that you've seen that you dig?

Well I haven't seen *any*.

I mean like Traffic, and . . .

See, I never saw Traffic . . . I never even saw Cream. I feel bad about those things, but what can I do?

See them? (Laughs)

Well, I can't now. I'm going to see this new group, called *Blind Faith*. I'm going to make it my *duty* to go see them . . . 'cause they'll probably be *gone* (laughter) in another year or so. So I'd better get up there quick and see them.

Do you like Stevie Winwood singing ?

Oh sure, sure . . . Stevie Winwood, he came to see us in

Manchester. Last time we were in Manchester . . . that was 1966. Or was it Birmingham? His brother—he's got a brother named Muff—Muff took us all out to see a haunted house, outside of Manchester, or Birmingham, one of those two. Or was it Newcastle? Something like that. We went out to see a haunted house, where a man and his dog was to have burned up in the 13th century. Boy, that place was spooky. That's the last time I saw Stevie Winwood.

Have you been listening to his . . . have you heard the Traffic records? The stuff that he's been doing lately?

I heard them doing "Gimmie Some Lovin'"; I love *that.* I didn't get all the names . . . after that. I seem to recall hearing a Traffic record. I know I've heard the Traffic . . . the group, Traffic, on the radio. I've heard that.

Have you heard the San Francisco bands?

Jefferson Airplane? Quicksilver Messenger Service? Yeah, I've heard them. The Grateful Dead.

Do you like them?

Yeah, sure do.

Is there anything happening on the current rock and roll scene that strikes you as good?

Yeah, I heard a record by Johnny Thunder. It's called "I'm Alive." Never heard it either, huh? Well, I can't believe it. Everyone I've talked to, I've asked them if they've heard that record.

Is it on the radio right now?

I don't know. I heard it on the radio a month ago, two months ago . . . three months ago. It was one of the most powerful records *I've* ever heard. It's called "I'm Alive." By Johnny Thunder. Well, it was that sentiment, truly expressed. That's the most I can say . . . if you heard the record, you'd know what I mean. But that's about all . . .

Do you like the stuff that Ray Stevens is doing?

Oh, I've always liked Ray Stevens. Sure.

Have you had occasion to go to Memphis, you know, when you're down there . . . or Muscle Shoals or Pensacola, any of the great musical centers of the South?

No, I've never been in any of the recording studios there.

Have you ever met Ray Stevens?

Uh, I've been in the same building with Ray Stevens. He was behind another door . . . but I've never met him; I've never shook his hand. No.

I don't want to get nosy or get into your personal life . . . but there was a series recently in the Village Voice, about your growing up, living, and going to high school. Did you read that series?

Yeah I did. At least, I read some of it.

Was it accurate?

Well, it was accurate as far as this fellow who was writing it . . . this fellow . . . I wouldn't have read it if I thought . . . he was using me to write his story. So I feel a little unusual in this case, 'cause I can see through this writer's aims. But as far as liking it or disliking it, I didn't do neither of those things. I mean it's just publicity from where I am. So if they want to spend six or seven issues writing about me (laughs) . . . as long as they get it right, you know, as long as they get it in there, I can't complain.

You must have some feelings about picking up a newspaper that has a hundred thousand circulation and seeing that some guy's gone and talked to your parents and your cousins, and uncles . . .

Well, the one thing I did . . . I don't like the way this writer talked about my father who has passed away. I didn't dig him talking about my father and using his name. Now that's the only thing about the article I didn't dig. But that boy has got some lessons to learn.

What did he say?

That don't matter what he said. He didn't have no right to speak about my father, who has passed away. If he wants to do a story on me, that's fine. I don't care what he wants to say about me. But to uhh . . . I got the feeling that he was taking advantage of some good people that I used to know and he was making *fun* of a lot of things. I got the feeling he was making fun of quite a *few* things . . . this fellow, Toby. You know what I mean, Jann? Soooo . . . we'll just let that stand as it is . . . for now.

I've gone through all the collected articles that have appeared, all the early ones and Columbia records' biographies, that's got the story about running away from home at 11 and 12 and 13-one-half . . . why did you put out that story?

I didn't put out *any* of those stories!

Well, it's the standard Bob Dylan biography . . .

Well, you know how it is, Jann . . . If you're sittin' in a room, and you have to have something done . . . I remember once, I was playing at Town Hall, and the producer of it came over with that biography . . . you know, I'm a *songwriter*, I'm not a biography writer, and I need a little help with these things.

So if I'm sitting in a room with some people, and I say "Come on now, I need some help; gimme a biography," so there might be three or four people maybe they'll come up with something, come up with a biography. So we put it down, it reads well, and the producer of the concert is satisfied. In fact, he even gets a kick out of it. You dig what I mean?

But in actuality, this thing wasn't written for hundreds of thousands of people . . . it was just a little game for whoever was going in there and getting a ticket, you know, they get one of these things too. That's just show business. So you do that, and pretty soon you've got a million people who get it on the side. You know? They start thinkin' that it's written all for them. And it's *not* written for them—it was written for someone who bought the ticket to the concert. You got all these other people taking it too seriously. Do you know what I mean? So a lot of things have been blown out of proportion.

At the time when all your records were out, and you were working and everybody was writing stories about you, you let that become your story . . . you sort of covered up your parents, and your old friends . . . you sort of kept people away from them . . .

Did I?

Well, that was the impression it gave . . .

Jann, you know, my best friends . . . you're talking about old friends, and best friends . . . if you want to go by those standards, I haven't seen my best friends for over 15 years. You know what I mean?

I'm not in the business of covering anything up. If I was from New Jersey, I could make an effort to show people my old neighborhood. If I was from Baltimore, same thing. Well, I'm from the Midwest. Boy, that's two different worlds.

This whole East Coast . . . there are a few similarities between the East Coast and the Midwest and, of course, the people are similar, but it's a big jump. So, I came out of the Midwest, but I'm not interested in leading anybody back there. That's not my game.

Why do you choose to live in the East?

Well, because we're nearer New York now. We don't choose anything . . . we just go with the wind. That's it.

Most people who become successful in records, especially artists, start wondering at some point about whether they're becoming businessmen, taking care of contracts, and making money . . . did you ever get that?

Yeah, I certainly did. I'd love to become a businessman. (Laughs) Love it. Love it.

What do you think of the music business?

I'd love to become a businessman in the music business.

Doing what?

Well, doing that same thing that other businessmen are doing . . . talking about recording, publishing, producing . . .

Have you ever wanted to produce an album for some other artist?

I have.

Which one?

Uhh . . . it's been a long time. I can't even remember which one. I saw somebody once, it was down in the Village. Anyway . . .

Are there any artists around today that you'd like to produce?

Well, there was some talk about producing Burt Lancaster doing the hymn "I Saw St. Augustine" . . .

Well, the movie business being what it is . . . going back to reviews that you've gotten for various albums; everybody has a lot of strange interpretations and decisions . . . have you ever read any criticisms about that that you liked or thought was accurate—or possibly got close to what you were trying to do?

Mmmmm . . . I can't say that I have. I don't recall. Like I say, Jann, I don't keep up with it as much as I should.

At the time when Highway 61 *and* Bringing It All Back Home *were coming out . . . do you remember anything from them?*

Do you?

Yeah, the liner notes.

What did you like about those liner notes?

I think they were very groovy. They explained what was going on in the album, and how the album came to be recorded, and how it all came to be said. Why didn't you publish Tarantula?

Why? Well . . . it's a long story. It begins with when I suddenly began to sell quite a few records, and a certain amount of publicity began to be carried in all the major news magazines about this "rising young star." Well, this industry being what it is, book companies began sending me contracts, *because* I was doing interviews before and after concerts, and reporters would say things like "What else do you write?" And I would say, "Well, I don't write much of anything else." And they would say, "Oh, come on. You must write other things. Tell us something else. Do you write books?" And I'd say, "Sure, I write books."

After the publishers saw that I wrote books, they began to send me contracts . . . Doubleday, Macmillan, Hill and Range (laughter) . . . we took the biggest one, and then owed them a book. You follow me?

But there was no book. We just took the biggest contract. Why? I don't know. Why I *did*, I don't know. Why I was *told* to do it, I don't know. Anyway, I owed them a book.

So I sat down, and said "Wow, I've done many things before, it's not so hard to write a book." So I sat down and wrote them a book in the hotel rooms and different places, plus I got a lot of other papers laying around that other people had written, so I threw it all together in a week and sent it to them.

Well, it wasn't long after that when I got it back to proofread it. I got it back and I said "My gosh, did I write this? I'm not gonna have this out." Do you know what I mean? "I'm not gonna put this out. The folks back home just aren't going to understand this at all." I said, "Well, I have to do some corrections on this," I told them, and set about correcting it. I told them I was improving it.

Boy, they were hungry for this book. They didn't care what it was. They just wanted . . . people up there were saying "Boy, that's the second James Joyce," and "Jack Kerouac again" and they were saying "Homer revisited" . . . and they were all just talking through their heads.

They just wanted to sell *books*, that's all they wanted to do. It wasn't about anything . . . and I knew that—I figured they *had* to know that, they were in the business of it. I knew that, and I was just nobody. If I knew it, where were they at? They were just playing with me. My book.

So I wrote a new book. I figured I was satisfied with it and I sent that in. Wow, they looked at that and said "Well, that's another book." And I said, "Well, but it's better." And they said, "Okay, we'll print this." So they printed that up and sent that back to proofread it. So I proofread it—I just looked at the first paragraph—and knew I just couldn't let that stand. So I took the whole thing with me on tour. I was going to rewrite it all. Carried a typewriter around . . . around the world. Trying to meet this deadline which they'd given me to put this book out. They just backed me into a corner. A lot of invisible people. So finally, I had a deadline on it, and was working on it, before my motorcycle accident. And I was studying all kinds of different prints and how I wanted them to print the book, by this time. I also was studying a lot of other poets at this time . . . I had books which I figured could lead me somewhere . . . and I was using a little bit from everything.

But still, it wasn't any book; it was just to satisfy the publishers who wanted to print something that we had a contract for. Follow me? So eventually, I had my motorcycle accident and that just got me out of the whole thing, 'cause I didn't care anymore. As it stands now, Jann, I could write a book. But I'm gonna write it first, and then give it to them. You know what I mean?

Do you have any particular subject in mind, or plan, for a book?

Do you?

For yours or mine?

(Laughs) For any of them.

What writers today do you dig? Like who would you read if you were writing a book? Mailer?

All of them. There's something to be learned from them all.

What about the poets? You once said something about Smokey Robinson . . .

I didn't mean Smokey Robinson, I meant Arthur Rimbaud. I don't know how I could've gotten Smokey Robinson mixed up with Arthur Rimbaud. (Laughter) But I did.

Do you see Allen Ginsberg much?

Not at all. Not at all.

Do you think he had any influence on your songwriting at all?

I think he did at a certain period. That period of . . . "Desolation Row," that kind of New York type period, when all the songs were just "city songs." His poetry is city poetry. Sounds like the city.

Before, you were talking about touring and using drugs. During that period of songs like "Mr. Tambourine Man" and "Baby Blue," which a lot of writers have connected to the drug experience, not in the sense of them being "psychedelic music," or drug songs, but having come out of the drug experience.

How so?

In terms of perceptions. A level of perceptions . . . awareness of the songs . . .

Awareness of the *minute*. You mean that?

An awareness of the mind.

I would say so.

Did taking drugs influence the songs?

No, not the writing of them, but it did keep me up there to pump 'em out.

Why did you leave the city and city songs for the country and country songs?

The country songs?

The songs . . . you were talking about "Highway 61" being a song of the city, and songs of New York City . . .

What was on the album?

Highway 61? *"Desolation Row," "Queen Jane"* . . .

Well, it was also what the audience wanted to hear, too . . .

don't forget that. When you play every night in front of an audience you know what they want to hear. It's easier to write songs then. You know what I'm talking about?

Who do you think your current audience is? Who do you think you're selling records to? What kind of people?

Well, I don't know. When I go out on the road, I'll find out, won't I?

Did you get any indication of that from who showed up in the audience in Nashville?

No, they were just people. Just people. I find every audience more or less the same, although you can have a certain attachment or disattachment for one because it may be bigger or smaller. But . . . people are just people.

Many people—writers, college students, college writers—all felt tremendously affected by your music and what you're saying in the lyrics.

Did they?

Sure. They felt it had a particular relevance to their lives . . . I mean, you must be aware of the way that people come on to you.

Not entirely. Why don't you explain to me.

I guess if you reduce it to its simplest terms, the expectation of your audience—the portion of your audience that I'm familiar with—feels that you have the answer.

What answer?

Like from the film, Don't Look Back*—people asking you "Why? What is it? Where is it?" People are tremendously hung-up on what you write and what you say, tremendously hung-up. Do you react to that at all? Do you feel responsible to those people?*

I don't want to make anybody *worry* about it . . . but boy, if I could ease someone's mind, I'd be the first one to do it. I want to lighten every load. Straighten out every burden. I don't want anybody to be hung-up . . . (laughs) especially over *me*, or anything *I* do. That's not the point at all.

Let me put it in another way . . . what I'm getting at is that you're an extremely important figure in music and an extremely important figure in the experience of growing up today. Whether you put yourself in that position or not, you're in that position. And you must have thought about it . . . and I'm curious to know what you think about that . . .

What would I think about it? What can I do?

You wonder if you're really that person.

What person?

A great "youth leader" . . .

If I thought I was that person, wouldn't I be out there doing it? Wouldn't I be, if I was meant to do that, wouldn't I be doing it? I don't have to hold back. This Maharishi, he thinks that—right? He's out there doing it. If I thought that, I'd be out there doing it. Don't you . . . you agree, right? So obviously, I don't think *that.*

What do you feel about unwillingly occupying that position?

I can see that position filled by someone else . . . not by . . . the position you're speaking of . . . I play music, man. I write songs. I have a certain balance about things, and I believe there should be an order to everything. Underneath it all. I believe, also, that there are people trained for this job that you're talking about—"youth leader" type of thing, you know? I mean, there must be people *trained* to do this type of work. And I'm just one person, doing what I do. Trying to get along . . . staying out of people's hair, that's all.

You've been also a tremendous influence on a lot of musicians and writers, they're very obviously affected by your style, the way you do things . . .

Who?

Well, somebody like Phil Ochs, for example . . . a lot of people like that.

Phil Ochs, uh . . . was around the same time I was, I remember when he came to town. He had his . . . he was doing his "Stand Tall Billy Sol" type songs. I mean, he had it then. I think he made it, there being a certain amount of momentum—he *pushed*—from being on the scene. But he did bring his own thing in, when he came in. He didn't—as *some* people come in as a dishwasher to dig some sounds and suddenly put down the broom, and pick up the guitar. You know what I mean?

I'm thinking also of other singers, of people who were singing before and playing the guitar.

Do you see any influence in the Motown? All those things that the Motown records are doing now? Like "Runaway Child" and those kind of things. I mean, Motown wasn't doing those kind of records a few years ago, were they? What do you think they're doing, Jann? Are they really sincere and all that kind of thing?

I think they're sincere about making good records, and they're going to sell a lot of them. I dig that. Do you like the Motown records?

Well, yeah . . . I like them . . .

Do you like the ones today better than the ones that they were doing before?

Oh, I have always liked the Motown records. Always. But because I like them so much, I see that change.

Have you got anything to do with that change?

Have I? Not that I know of.

Do you think that you've played any role in the change of popular music in the last four years?

I hope not. (Laughs)

Well, a lot of people say you have.

(Laughs) Well, you know, I'm not one to argue. (Laughs)

There's a lot of talk about you and Albert Grossman, your relationship with Albert Grossman, and whether he's going to continue to manage you.

Well . . . as far as I know, things will remain the same, until the length of our contract. And if we don't sign another contract, or if he does not have a hand in producing my next concerts or have a hand in any of my next work, it's only because he's too busy. 'Cause he's got so many acts now . . . it's so hard for him to be in all places all the time. I mean you know, it's the old story . . . you can't be in two places at once. That old story. You know what I mean ?

When does your contract with him expire?

Sometime this year.

You were supposed to leave Columbia and sign with MGM? A million dollars . . . what happened to that?

It . . . went up in smoke.

Did you want a new label?

I didn't, no.

Who did?

I believe my advisors.

I take it you haven't had any recent trouble with Columbia, like you used to have in the beginning . . .

No . . . no.

Do you know approximately how many songs that you've recorded that have not been released? Like songs left over from recording John Wesley Harding *or* Blonde on Blonde? *Do you have any idea how many?*

Well, we try to use them all. There may be a few lying around.

What do you think was the best song, popular song, to come out last year?

Uhh . . . I like that one . . . of Creedence Clearwater Revival—"Rolling On the River"?

Any others?

George Jones had one called "Small Town Laboring Man."

You've been very reluctant to talk to reporters, the press and so on . . . why is that?

Why would you think?

Well, I know why you won't go on those things.

Well, if you know why, *you tell 'em* . . . 'cause I find it hard to talk about. People don't understand how the press works. People don't understand that the press, they just use you to sell papers. And, in a certain way, that's not *bad* . . . but when they misquote you all the time, and when they just use you to fill in some story. And when you read it after, it isn't *anything* the way you pictured it happening. Well, anyhow, it hurts. It hurts because you think you were just played for a fool. And the more hurts you get, the less you want to do it. Ain't that correct?

Were there any writers that you met that you liked? That you felt did good jobs? Wrote accurate stories . . .

On what?

On you. For instance, I remember two big pieces—one was in The New Yorker, *by Nat Hentoff . . .*

Yeah, I like 'em. I like that. In a way, I like 'em all, whether I feel bad about 'em or not, in a way I like 'em all. I seldom get a kick out of them, Jann, but . . . I mean, I just can't be spending my time reading what people write. (Laughter) I don't know anybody who can, do you?

Do you set aside a certain amount of time during the day to . . . how much of the day do you think about songwriting and playing the guitar?

Well, I try to get it when it comes. I play the guitar wherever I find one. But I try to write the song when it comes. I try to get it all . . . 'cause if you don't get it all, you're not gonna get it. So the best kinds of songs you can write are in motel rooms and cars . . . places which are all temporary. 'Cause you're forced to do it. Rather, it lets you go into it.

You go into your kitchen and try to write a song, and you can't write a song—I know people who do this—I know some songwriters who go to work every day, at 8:30 and come home at 5:00. And usually bring something back . . . I mean, that's legal too. It just depends on . . . how you do it. Me, I don't have those kind of things known to me yet, so I just get 'em when they come. And when they don't come, I don't try for it.

There's been a lot of artists who have done your songs . . . songs that you have released and songs that you haven't released. Have you written any songs lately for any other artists to do, specifically for that artist? Or any of your old songs.

I wrote "To Be Alone with You"—that's on *Nashville Skyline*—I wrote it for Jerry Lee Lewis. The one on *Nashville Skyline.* (Laughter) He was down there when we were listening to the playbacks, and he came in. He was recording an album next door. He listened to it . . . I think we sent him a dub.

"Peggy Day"—I kind of had the Mills Brothers in mind when I did that one. (Laughter)

Have you approached them yet?

(Laughter)

No, unfortunately, I haven't.

During what period of time did you write the songs on Nashville Skyline? *During the month before you went to do it or . . .*

Yeah, about a month before we did it. That's why it seemed to be all connected.

You're going to do your next album in Nashville?

I don't know, Jann. I don't know where I'm gonna be doing the next album. Sometimes I envy the Beatles . . . they just go down to the studio, and play around . . . I mean, you're bound to get a record. You know what I mean? Bound to get a record. Their studio is just a drive away . . . boy, I'd have an album out every month. I mean, how could you not?

Have you ever thought about getting four- or eight-track equipment up where you live?

Well, everyone's talking about that now. But it's just talk as far as I know. I would come to New York if I wanted to use the studio, because it's all here . . . if you need a good engineer, or if you need a song, or somebody to record it, an artist . . . whereas some place like up in the country there, in the mountains, you could get a studio in, but that doesn't guarantee you anything else but the studio. You can get violin players, cello players, you can get dramatic readers . . . you can get anybody at the drop of a hat, in New York City. I imagine it's that way over in London, where the Beatles make their records. Anything they want to put on their record, they just call up and it's there. I'd like to be in that position.

What do you look for when you make a record . . . I mean, what qualities, do you judge it by when you hear it played back?

Ummmm . . . for the spirit. I like to hear a good lick once in a while. Maybe it's the spirit . . . don't you think so? I mean, if the spirit's not there, it don't matter how good a song it is or . . .

What do you think of the current rock and roll groups doing all the country music?

Well, once again, it really doesn't matter what kind of music they do, just so long as people are making music. That's a good sign. There are certainly more people around making music than there was when I was growing up. I know that.

Do you find any that are particularly good—country rock, or merely rock and roll bands, doing country material, using steel guitars?

As long as it sounds good . . .

Do any particular one of those groups appeal to you?

Who . . . who are in those groups?

Oh, Flying Burrito Brothers . . .

Boy, I love them . . . the Flying Burrito Brothers, unh-huh. I've always known Chris, you know, from when he was in the

Byrds. And he's always been a fine musician. Their records knocked me out. (Laughs) That poor little hippie boy on his way to town . . . (Laughs)

What about the Byrds . . . they did a country album . . .

Sweetheart? Well, they had a distinctive sound, the Byrds . . . they usually were hanging in there . . .

Of all the versions of "This Wheel's On Fire," which do you like the best?

Uh . . . the Band's. Who else did it?

Julie Driscoll . . . the Byrds did it.

I remember hearing the Julie Driscoll one . . . I don't remember hearing the Byrds.

What was the origin of that collection of songs, of that tape?

The origin of it? What do you mean?

Where was that done?

Well that was done out in . . . out in somebody's basement. Just a basement tape. It was just for . . .

Did you do most, did you write most of those songs, those demos, for yourself?

Right.

And then decide against them?

No, they weren't demos for myself, they were demos of the songs. I was being PUSHED again . . . into coming up with some songs. So, you know . . . you know how those things go.

Do you have any artists in mind for any of those particular songs?

No. They were just fun to do. That's all. They were a kick to do. Fact, I'd do it all again. You know . . . that's really the way to do a recording—in a peaceful, relaxed setting—in somebody's basement. With the windows open . . . and a dog lying on the floor.

Let me explain something about this interview. If you give one magazine an interview, then the other magazine wants an interview. If you give one to one, then the other one wants one. So pretty soon, you're in the interview business . . . you're just giving interviews. Well, as you know, this can really get you down. Doing nothing but giving interviews.

So the only way you can do it is to give press conferences. But you see, you have to have something to give a press conference about. Follow me? So that's why I don't give interviews. There's no mysterious reason to it, there's nothing organized behind it . . . it's just that if you give an interview to one magazine, then another one'll get mad.

Why have you chosen to do this interview?

'Cause this is a *music paper.* Why would I want to give an interview to *Look* magazine? Tell me, why?

I don't know . . . to sell records.

To sell records, I could do it. Right. But I have a gold record *without* doing it, do you understand me? Well, if I had to sell records, I'd be out there giving interviews to everybody. Don't you see? Mr. Clive Davis, he was president of Columbia Records, and he said he wouldn't be surprised if this last album sold a million units. Without giving *one* interview. Now you tell me. Jann, why am I going to go out and give an interview?

To get hassled . . .

Why would I want to go out and get hassled? If they're gonna pay me, I mean . . . who wants to do *that.* I don't.

Do you have any idea how much money your publishing has brought in over the last five years?

Well, now, that's difficult to answer because my songs are divided up into three, no, four companies. So there you have it. There you have it right there.

Which companies?

Well, I've got songs with Leeds Music. I've got songs with Witmark Music. I've got a bunch of songs with Dwarf Music. I've got songs in Big Sky Music. So you see, my songs are divided up, so . . .

Do you own Big Sky Music wholly yourself?

It's my company. I chose to start this company.

If you put all the estimated income from those four companies together, or estimated gross income from publishing from those, it must be a considerable . . .

Not as much as the Beatles.

Yeah, but other than the Beatles?

Not as much as those writers from Motown.

Other than the writers from Motown . . .

You know there are many more musical organizations than

me. They've top staffs of writers bringing in more money than you can dream of.

What songwriters do you like? Do you like any of the teams like Holland, Dozier, Holland or Hayes and Porter . . .

Yeh, I do. I know that fellow—what's his name, Isaac Hayes? —he does a real nice song called "The Other Woman." I believe that's the title to it. It's on his album. I think it's on his new one. I don't believe he wrote it, though.

Otis Redding was playing at the Whiskey A Go Go, a coupla years ago. You came in and talked to Otis. What was that all about?

He was gonna do "Just Like A Woman." I played him a dub of it. I think he mighta cut it for a demo . . . I don't think he ever recorded it, though. He was a fine man.

Why did you think "Just Like A Woman" would be a good song for him to do?

Well I didn't necessarily think it was a good song for him to do, but he asked me if I had any material. It just so happened that I had the dubs from my new album. So we went over and played it. I think he took a dub . . . that was the first and only time I ever met him.

I take it that you dug Otis real well. Are there any other soul singers that you dig as much as Otis?

You mean rhythm and blues pop? Well, you know I've always liked Mavis Staples ever since she was a little girl. She's always been my favorite . . . she's always had my favorite voice.

Have you heard their new Stax album?

I heard one of those . . . the ones they're doing with other people. Yeah, I heard that, that one that Pop Staples did. (Laughs) It's ridiculous. Oh, Steve Cropper did do a nice song on that album . . . that he wrote, called "Water."

On his own album?

No, not on his own album. On the *Jammed Together* album. I find it interesting seeing . . . Mr. Staples being referred to as "Pop." (Laughter)

Have you heard the Steve Cropper solo album?

Yeah, I heard that too.

Do you like that?

Sure, I've always dug Steve Cropper . . . his guitar playing. Ever since the first Booker T. record. I heard that back in the Midwest. Yeah, everybody was playing like him.

What records of Otis' did you dig?

I've got one that contained that song where he was born in a tent by the river—(hums and sings) "A Change Is Gonna Come." Yeah, I like that one.

What is your day-to-day life like?

Hmmmm . . . there's no way I could explain that to you, Jann. Every day is different. Depends on what I'm doing.

Do you paint a lot?

Well, I may be fiddling around with the car or I may be painting a boat, or . . . possibly washing the window. I just do what has to be done. I play a lot of music, when there's a call in . . . I'm always trying to put shows together, which never come about. I don't know what it is, but sometimes we get together and I say, "Okay, let's take six songs and do 'em in, let's say, 40 minutes . . . we got 'em in, let's say, 40 minutes . . . we got a stopwatch timing 'em. But I mean nothing happens to it. We could do anything with it, but I mean . . .

Boy, I hurried . . . I hurried for a long time. I'm sorry I did. All the time you're hurrying, you're not really as aware as you should be. You're trying to make things happen instead of just letting it happen. You follow me?

That's the awkwardness of this interview.

Well, I don't find anything awkward about it. I think it's going great.

The purpose of any interview is to let the person who's being interviewed unload his head.

Well, that's what I'm doing.

And trying to draw that out is . . .

Boy, that's a good . . . that'd be a great title for a song. "Unload my head. Going down to the store . . . going down to the corner to unload my head." I'm gonna write that up when I get back. (Laughter) "Going to Tallahassee to unload my head."

What do you think can happen with your career as a singer?

What are the possibilities?

Go on the road, continue to make records . . . for instance, do you foresee continuing to make records?

If they're enjoyable. I'm going to have to receive a certain amount of enjoyment out of my work pretty soon. I'd like to keep a little closer to the studios than I am now. It's awful hard for me to make records when I've got to go 4,000 miles away, you know? Like I say, when you do have these companies around who're just there to serve . . .

Are you thinking of moving to Nashville? I mean that would be . . .

Well, if I moved to Nashville, I'd still have to book studio time, wouldn't I?

But still, you'd have the accessibility of the session men and the engineers . . .

That's true. But I'd have to do everything with that same sound, wouldn't I? I couldn't really use a variety of techniques.

Can you see a time when you would stop making records?

Well, let's put it this way: making a record isn't any more than just recording a song, for me. Well, that's what it's been up 'til now. Not necessarily going into the studio for any other reason than to record a song. So, if I was to stop writing songs, I would stop recording. Or let's say, if I was to stop singing, I guess I would stop recording. But I don't foresee that. I'll be recording, 'cause that's a way for me to unload my head.

You said in one of your songs on Highway 61 *. . . "I need a dump truck, mama, to unload my head." Do you still need a dump truck or something? (Laughter)*

What album was that?

It was on Highway 61. *What I'm trying to ask is what are the changes that have gone on between the time you did* Highway 61 *and* Nashville Skyline *or* John Wesley Harding?

The changes. I don't think I know exactly what you mean.

How has life changed for you? Your approach to . . . your view of what you do . . .

Not much. I'm still the same person. I'm still uhh . . . going at it in the same old way. Doing the same old thing.

Do you think you've settled down, and slowed down?

I *hope* so. I was going at a tremendous speed . . . at the time of my *Blonde on Blonde* album, I was going at a tremendous speed.

How did you make the change? The motorcycle accident?

I just took what came. That's how I made the changes. I took what came.

What do they come from?

What was what coming from? Well, they come from the same sources that everybody else's do. I don't know if it comes from within oneself anymore than it comes from without oneself. Or outside of oneself. Don't you see what I mean? Maybe the inside and the outside are both the same. I don't know. But, I feel it just like everyone else. What's that old line—there's a line from one of those old songs out . . . "I can recognize it in others, I can feel it in myself." You can't say that's from the inside or the outside, it's like *both.*

What people do you think from the outside have influenced a change?

Uhh . . . what change are you talking about?

The change from Highway 61 *to* Nashville Skyline . . .

I'm not probably as aware of that change as you are, because I haven't listened to that album *Highway 61* . . . I'd probably do myself a lot of good going back and listening to it. I'm not aware of that change. I probably could pinpoint it right down if I heard that album but I haven't heard it for quite a while.

Are there any old albums that you do listen to?

Well, I don't sit around and listen to my records, if that's what you mean.

Like picking up a high school yearbook, and just . . .

Oh, I love to do that . . . every once in a while. That's the way I listen to my records—every once in a while. Every once in a while I say "Well, I'd like to see that fellow again."

Are there any albums or tracks from the albums that you think now were particularly good?

On any of my old albums? Uhh . . . As songs or as performances?

Songs.

Oh yeah, quite a few.

Which ones?

Well, if I was performing now . . . if I was making personal appearances, you would know which ones, because I would play them. You know? But I don't know which ones I'd play now. I'd have to pick and choose. Certainly couldn't play 'em all.

Thinking about the titles on Bringing It All Back Home.

I like "Maggie's Farm." I always liked "Highway 61 Revisited." I always liked that song. "Mr. Tambourine Man" and "Blowing in the Wind" and "Girl From the North Country" and "Boots of Spanish Leather" and "Times They Are A-Changing" . . . I liked "Ramona" . . .

Where did you write "Desolation Row"? Where were you when you wrote that?

I was in the back of a taxi-cab.

In New York?

Yeah.

During the period where you were recording songs with a rock and roll accompaniment, with a full-scale electric band, of those rock and roll songs that you did, which do you like?

The best rock and roll songs . . . which ones are there?

Uhh . . . "Like a Rolling Stone" . . .

Yeah, I probably liked that the best.

And that was the Tom Wilson record . . . how come you never worked with that collection of musicians again?

Well, Michael Bloomfield, he was touring with Paul Butterfield at that time . . . and I could only get 'em when I could. So I wouldn't wait on Michael Bloomfield to make my records. He sure does play good, though. I missed having him there, but what could you do?

In talking about the songs as performance, *which of the* performances *that you did, that were recorded . . .*

I like "Like a Rolling Stone" . . . I can hear it now, now that you've mentioned it. I like that sound. You mean, which recorded performances?

Yeah, I mean in your performance *of the song . . .*

Oh . . . I like some of them on the last record, but I don't know, I tend to close up in the studio. After I've . . . I could never get enough presence on me. Never really did sound like me, to me.

On Nashville Skyline, *you see a lot of echo, and a lot of limiting. What made you decide to alter your voice technically and use those kind of studio tricks? Rather than doing it more or less flat.*

Well, how would you have liked it better? Would you have liked it flat?

I dig the echo.

I do too. I dig the echo myself. That's why . . . we did it that way. The old records *do* sound flat. I mean there's just a flatness to them, they're like two-dimensional. Isn't that right? Well in this day and age, there's no reason to make records like that.

"Nashville Skyline Rag" was that a jam that took place in a studio, or did you write the lyrics before? . . .

Ummm . . . I had that little melody quite a while before I recorded it.

There's a cat named Alan Weberman who writes in the East Village Other. *He calls himself the world's leading Dylanologist. You know him?*

No . . . oh, yes, I did. Is this the guy who tears up all my songs? Well, he oughta take a rest. He's way off. I saw something he wrote about "All Along the Watchtower," and boy, let me tell you, this boy's *off*. Not only did he create some type of fantasy—he had Allen Ginsberg in there—he couldn't even hear the words to the song right. He didn't hear the song right. Can you *believe* that? I mean this fellow couldn't hear the words . . . or something. I bet he's a hard working fellow, though. I bet he really does a good job if he could find something to do but it's too bad it's just my songs, 'cause I don't know really if there's enough material in my songs to sustain someone who is really out to do a big job. You understand what I mean?

I mean a fellow like that would be much better off writing about Tolstoy, or Dostoevsky, or Freud . . . doing a really big analysis of somebody who has countless volumes of writings. But here's me, just a few records out. Somebody devoting so much time to those few records, when there's such a wealth of material that hasn't even been touched yet, or hasn't even been heard or read . . . that escapes me. Does it escape you?

I understand putting time into it, but I read this, in this *East Village Other;* I read it . . . and it was clever. And I got a kick out of reading it (laughter) on some level, but I didn't want to think anybody was taking it too seriously. You follow me?

He's just representative of thousands of people who do *take it seriously.*

Well, that's their own business. Why don't I put it that way. That's their business and his business. But . . . I'm the source of that and I don't know if it's my business or not, but I'm the source of it. You understand? So I see it a little differently than all of them do.

People in your audience, they obviously take it very seriously, and they look to you for something . . .

Well, I wouldn't be where I am today without them. So, I owe them . . . my music, which I would be playing for them.

Does the intensity of some of the response annoy you?

No. No, I rather enjoy it.

I'm trying to get back to the thing about being a symbol of youth culture, being a spokesman for youth culture . . . what're your opinions or thoughts on that? At some point you pick up the paper or the magazine and find out that this is happening and you know that you're considered like this. That people are watching you for that . . . and you've got to say to yourself, "Am I hung-up?"

Well, not any more than anybody else is, who performs in public. I mean, everyone has his following.

What do you think your following is like?

Well, I think there are all kinds . . . I imagine they're . . . you would probably know just as much about that as I would. You know, they're all kinds of people. I remember when I use to do concerts, you couldn't pin 'em down. All the road managers and the sound equipment carriers, and even the truck drivers would notice how different the audiences were, in terms of individual people. How different they . . . like sometimes I might have a concert and all the same kind of people show up, I mean, what does that mean?

Did you vote for President?

We got down to the polls too late. (Laughter)

People are always asking about what does this song mean and what does that song mean, and a lot of them seem to be based on some real person, just like any kind of fiction, you expect . . . are there any songs that you can relate to particular people, as having inspired the song?

Not now I can't.

What do you tell somebody who says, 'What is 'Leopard-Skin Pill-box Hat' about?"

It's just about that. I think that's something I mighta taken out of the newspaper. Mighta seen a picture of one in a department store window. There's really no more to it than that. I know it can get blown up into some kind of illusion. But in reality, it's no more than that. Just a leopard skin pillbox. That's all.

How did you come in contact with the Band?

Well. There used to be this young lady that worked up at Al Grossman's office—her name was Mary Martin, she's from Canada. And she was a rather persevering soul, as she hurried around the office on her job; she was a secretary; did secretarial work, and knew all the bands and all the singers from Canada. She was from Canada. Anyway, I needed a group to play electric songs.

Where did you hear them play?

Oh, I never did hear them play. I think the group I wanted was Jim Burton and Joe Osborne. I wanted Jim Burton and Joe Osborne to play bass, and Mickey Jones. I knew Mickey Jones, he was playing with Johnny Rivers. They were all in California, though. And there was some difficulty in making that group connect. One of them didn't want to fly, and Mickey couldn't make it immediately, and I think Jim Burton was playing with a television group at that time.

He used to play with Ricky Nelson?

Oh, I think this was after that. He was playing with a group called the Shindogs, and they were on television. So he was doing that job. Anyway, that was the way it stood, and Mary Martin kept pushing this group who were out in New Jersey—I think they were in Elizabeth, New Jersey or Hartford, Connecticut, or some town close to around New York. She was pushing them, and she had two of the fellows come up to the office, so we could meet. And it was no more . . . no more, no less. I just asked them if they could do it and they said they could. (Laughs) These two said they could. And that was how it started. Easy enough, you know.

How come you never made an album with them?

We tried. We cut a couple sides in the old New York Columbia studies. We cut two or three and right after "Positively 4th Street," we cut some singles and they didn't really get off the ground. You oughta hear 'em. You know, you could find 'em. They didn't get off the ground. They didn't even make it on the charts.

Consequently, I've not been back on the charts since the singles. I never did much care for singles, 'cause you have to pay so much attention to them. Unless you make your whole album full of singles. You have to make them separately. So I didn't really think about them too much that way.

But, playing with the Band was a natural thing. We have a real different sound. Real different. But it wasn't like anything heard. I heard one of the records recently . . . it was on a jukebox. "Please Crawl Out Your Window."

That was one of them? What were the others?

There were some more songs out of that same session . . . "Sooner or Later"—that was on *Blonde on Blonde*. That's one of my favorite songs.

What role did you play in the Big Pink *album, the album they made by themselves.*

Well, I didn't do anything on that album. They did that with John Simon.

Did you play piano on it or anything?

No.

What kind of sound did you hear when you went in to make John Wesley Harding?

I heard the sound that Gordon Lightfoot was getting, with Charlie McCoy and Kenny Buttrey. I'd used Charlie and Kenny both before, and I figured if he could get that sound, I could. But we couldn't get it. (Laughs) It was an attempt to get it, but it didn't come off. We got a different sound. . . . I don't know what you'd call that . . . it's a muffled sound.

There used to be a lot of friction in the control booth, on these records I used to make. I didn't know about it, I wasn't aware of them until recently. Somebody would want to put limiters on this and somebody would want to put an echo on that, someone else would have some other idea. And myself, I don't know anything about any of this. So I just have to leave it up in the air. In someone else's hands.

The friction was between the engineer and the producer . . .

No, the managers and the advisors and the agents.

Do you usually have sessions at which all these people are there, or do you prefer to close them up?

Well, sometimes there's a whole lot of people. Sometimes you can't even move there's so many people . . . other times, there's no one. Just the musicians.

Which is more comfortable for you?

Well, it's much more comfortable when there's . . . oh, I don't know, I could have it both ways. Depends what kind of song I'm gonna do. I might do a song where I *want* all those people around. Then I do another song, and have to shut the lights off, you know?

Was "Sad-Eyed Lady of the Lowlands" originally planned as a whole side?

That song is an example of a song . . . it started out as just a little thing, "Sad-Eyed Lady of the Lowlands," but I got carried away, somewhere along the line. I just sat down at a table and started writing. At the session itself. And I just got carried away with the whole thing . . . I just started writing and I couldn't stop. After a period of time, I forgot what it was all about, and I started trying to get back to the beginning. (Laughs) Yeah.

Did you plan to go down and make a double record set?

No. Those things just happen when you have the material.

Do you like that album?

Blonde on Blonde? Yeah. But like I always think that a double set could be made into a single album. But I dug *Blonde on Blonde* and the Beatles thing. They are like huge collections of songs. But a real great record can usually be compacted down . . . although the Beatles have that album, and *Blonde on Blonde* . . . I'm glad that there's two sides, that there's that much . . .

How long did that take to record?

Blonde on Blonde? Well I cut it in between. I was touring and I was doing it whenever I got a chance to get into the studio. So it was in the works for awhile. I could only do maybe two or three songs at a time.

How long did John Wesley Harding *take?*

You mean how many sessions? That took three sessions, but

we did them in a month. The first two sessions were maybe three weeks to a month apart, and the second one was about two weeks from the third.

John Wesley Harding—*why did you call the album that?*

Well, I called it that because I had that song, "John Wesley Harding." It didn't mean anything to me. I called it that, Jann, 'cause I had the song "John Wesley Harding," which started out to be a long ballad. I was gonna write a ballad on . . . like maybe one of those old cowboy . . . you know, a real long ballad. But in the middle of the second verse, I got tired. I had a tune, and I didn't want to waste the tune, it was a nice little melody, so I just wrote a quick third verse, and I recorded that.

But it was a silly little song (Laughs) . . . I mean, it's not a commercial song, in any kind of sense. At least, *I* don't think it is. It was the one song on the album which didn't seem to fit in. And I had it placed here and there, and I didn't know what I was gonna call the album anyway. No one else had any ideas either. I placed it last and I placed it in the middle somewhere, but it didn't seem to work. So somehow that idea came up to just put it first and get done with it right away, and that way when it comes up, no one'll . . . you know, if someone's listening to "All Along the Watchtower" and that comes up, and they'll say, "Wow, what's that?" (Laughs)

You knew that cowboy . . .

I knew people were gonna be brought down when they heard that, and say "Wow, what's that?" You know a lot of people said that to me, but I knew it in front. I knew people were gonna listen to that song and say that they didn't understand what was going on, but they would've singled that song out later, if we hadn't called the album *John Wesley Harding* and placed so much importance on that, for people to start wondering about it . . . if that hadn't been done, that song would've come up and people would have said it was a throw-away song. You know, and it would have probably got in the way of some other songs.

See, I try very hard to keep my songs from interfering with each other. That's all I'm trying to do. Place 'em all out on the disc. Sometimes it's really annoying to me when I listen to all these dubs; I listen to one, and then I put on another one, and the one I heard before is still on my mind. I'm trying to keep away from that.

Why did you choose the name of the outlaw John Wesley Harding?

Well, it fits in tempo. Fits right in tempo. Just what I had at hand.

What other titles did you have for the album?

Not for that one. That was the only title that come up for that one. But for the *Nashville Skyline* one, the title came up *John Wesley Harding, Volume II.* We were gonna do that . . . the record company wanted to call the album *Love Is All There Is.* I didn't see anything wrong with it, but it sounded a a little spooky to me . . .

What about Blonde on Blonde?

Well, that title came up when . . . I don't even recall how exactly it came up, but I do know it was all in good faith. It has to do with just the word. I don't know who thought of that. *I* certainly didn't.

Of all the albums as albums, excluding your recent ones, which one do you think was the most successful in what it was trying to do? Which was the most fully realized, for you?

I think the second one. The second album I made.

Why?

Well, I got a chance to . . . I felt real good about doing an album with my own material. My own material and I picked a little on it, picked the guitar, and it was a *big* Gibson—I felt real accomplished on that. "Don't Think Twice." Got a chance to do some of that. Got a chance to play in open tuning . . . "Oxford Town," I believe that's on that album. That's open tuning. I got a chance to do talking blues. I got a chance to do ballads, like "Girl From the North Country." It's just because it had more variety. I felt good at that.

Of the electric ones, which do you prefer?

Well, sound-wise, I prefer this last one. 'Cause it's got the sound. See, I'm listening for sound now.

As a collection of songs?

Songs? Well, this last album maybe means more to me, 'cause

I did undertake something. In a certain sense. And . . . there's a certain pride in that.

It was more premeditated than the others? I mean, you knew what you were gonna go after?

Right.

Where did the name Nashville Skyline . . .

Well, I always like to tie the name of the album in with some song. Or if not some song, some kind of general feeling. I think that just about fit because it was less in the way, and less specific than any of the other ones there.

Certainly couldn't call the album *Lay Lady Lay.* I wouldn't have wanted to call it that, although that name was brought up. It didn't get my vote, but it was brought up. *Peggy Day—Lay Peggy Day,* that was brought up. A lot of things were brought up. *Tonight I'll Be Staying Here with Peggy Day.* That's another one. Some of the names just didn't seem to fit. *Girl From the North Country.* That was another title which didn't really seem to fit. Picture me on the front holding a guitar and *Girl From the North Country* printed on top. (Laughs) *Tell Me That It Isn't Peggy Day.* I don't know who thought of that one.

What general thing was happening that made you want to start working with the Band, rather than working solo?

I only worked solo, because there wasn't much going on. There wasn't. There were established people around . . . yeah, The Four Seasons . . . there were quite a few other established acts. But I worked alone because it was easier to. Plus, everyone else I knew was working alone, writing and singing. There wasn't much opportunity for groups or bands then; there wasn't. You know that.

When did you decide to get one together, like that? You played at Forest Hills, that was where you first appeared with a band? Why did you feel the time had come?

To do what? Well, because I could *pay* a backing group now. See, I didn't want to use a backing group unless I could pay them.

Do you ever get a chance to work frequently with the Band? In the country.

Work? Well, *work* is something else. Sure, we're always running over old material. We're always playing, running over old material. Testing out this and that.

What do you see yourself as—a poet, a singer, a rock and roll star, married man . . .

All of those. I see myself as it all. Married man, poet, singer, songwriter, custodian, gatekeeper . . . all of it. I'll be it all. I feel "confined" when I have to choose one or the other. Don't you?

You're obligated to do one album a year?

Yes.

Is that all you want to do?

No, I'd like to do more. I would do dozens of them if I could be near the studio. I've been just lazy, Jann. I've been just getting by, so I haven't really thought too much about putting out anything really new and different.

You've heard the Joan Baez album of all your songs . . .

Yeah, I did . . . I generally like everything she does.

Are there any particular artists that you like to see do your songs?

Yeah, Elvis Presley. I liked Elvis Presley. Elvis Presley recorded a song of mine. That's the one recording I treasure the most . . . it was called "Tomorrow Is A Long Time." I wrote it but never recorded it.

Which album is that on?

Kismet.

I'm not familiar with it at all.

He did it with just guitar.

"I heard *New Morning*, and I just couldn't take the fact that he still hadn't learned how to play the harmonica or how to sing. His mark of distinction was his intensity and funkiness. And when he was really on, it didn't matter that he couldn't sing or play—he was so present. Now he's like a ghost of his former self, and it drives me up the wall. I don't know where the real Bob Dylan went, but I don't believe this one, I haven't since *Nashville Skyline*. I don't know what happened to him, but something did—and he disappeared. He stopped being a rebel and started being a nice guy, a family man. He don't fool me, man."

Country Joe McDonald, in *Rolling Stone*,
May 27, 1971.

"Then there's the unreported deaths of Dylan and Lou Reed, both of them dead TO THIS WORLD but for very different reasons. Bob is just a stiff, pure and simple, he's been that way since the mishap with the bike. . . ."

Richard Meltzer, in *No-one Waved Goodbye*
edited by Robert Somma, 1971.

It's Dr. Bob Dylan now. Though he is the most reclusive figure in rock today, Dylan showed up at Princeton University last week to receive an honorary doctorate "as one of the most creative popular musicians of the last decade." Dylan did not make a speech.

From *Time*, July 22, 1970.

Consumer Guide: Self-Portrait by Robert Christgau

Bob Dylan: *Self-Portrait* (Columbia). C plus. Jon Landau wrote to suggest I give this a D, but that's pique. Conceptually, this is a brilliant album which is organized, I think, by two central ideas. First, that "self" is most accurately defined (and depicted) in terms of the artifacts—in this case, pop tunes and folk songs claimed as personal property and semi-spontaneous renderings of past creations frozen for posterity on a piece of tape and (perhaps) even a couple of songs one has written oneself—to which one responds. Second, that the people's music is the music people like, Mantovani strings and all. But in order for a concept to work it has to be supported musically—that is, you have to listen. I don't know anyone, even vociferous supporters of this album, who plays more than one side at a time. I don't listen to it at all. The singing is not consistently good, though it has its moments, and the production—for which I blame Bob Johnston, though Dylan has to be listed as a co-conspirator—ranges from indifferent to awful. It is possible to use strings and soprano choruses well, but Johnston has never demonstrated the knack. Other points: it's overpriced, the cover art is lousy, and it sounds good on WMCA. For further elucidation, see Greil Marcus's farewell piece in *Rolling Stone*.

Bob Dylan and the Poetry of Salvation

by Steven Goldberg

> Now I wish I could write you a melody so plain,
> That could hold you, dear lady, from going insane,
> That could ease you and cool you and cease the pain
> Of your useless and pointless knowledge.*

We don't have many wise men left, you know. We have seen our incredible competence and our surfeit of intelligence lead us only to loneliness and rationalization. We are able to be so much, yet we are so little able to understand what it is we are supposed to be. We are learning to run faster and faster. Into the abyss. And we are leaving behind the few who might give us a hint of what to do when we get there.

Like the rest of us, Bob Dylan faces a universe that science discovers to be more and more a deterministic unity no part of which has meaning without reference to every other part. To the dispossessed this universe seems to be inhabited not by free agents in a world of free will, but by the living, irrelevant effects of an infinite number of causes. To a man who yearns for meaning, the thought that life is merely playing out directions imprinted before birth, or given in childhood, or decreed by an alien society, is intolerable unless it is a part of a master plan. The songs of Bob Dylan, a few of them, speak of such a master plan.

Bob Dylan is a mystic. His importance lies not in the perversion of his words into a politicism he ridicules as irrelevant or in the symbols that once filled the lesser social protest songs of

* "Tombstone Blues," © M. Witmark and Sons, 1965.

his late adolescence. His only relevance is that, in a world which has lost faith that it is infused with godliness, he sings of a transcendent reality that makes it all make sense again.

The mystical experience is, by its very nature, indescribable. Dylan's genius is that he is able to give us some clues. I can merely attempt to state a few of the implications of mysticism in an effort to indicate the basic underpinning of Dylan's songs.

The mystic has always seen what science is now beginning to see: all distinction is illusory. Man's mental dissection of reality into different things, even the very separation of his mind into thoughts, results from his viewing only an artificial division of the One. With this in mind, one can appreciate that the mystical truth that "life is pain" is not in the slightest nihilistic, but an acknowledgment that all the separate joys that this world has to offer contain the basic pain of our seeming separation from the One. The mystical experience, in which all separations fuse into the infinite unity as all colors fuse into white, is a reunification with the One. Only in the life which is illuminated by the afterglow of such an experience is there the possibility of salvation. I believe that such an experience pervades all that Dylan has written since 1964.

Salvation means many things in Dylan's songs. On one level it is the conquest of guilt, ambition, impatience, and all the other obsessive states of egotistic confusion in which we set ourselves apart from the natural flow of things. On another it is the supremely free flight of the will. On still another it is faith, an acceptance of a transcendent, omnipresent godhead without which we are lost.

This is why Dylan merits our most serious attention. For he stands at the vortex: when the philosophical, psychological, and scientific lines of thought are followed to the point where each becomes a cul-de-sac, as logic without faith eventually must, Dylan is there to sing his songs. Perhaps it is only in a time like ours that anyone will listen. For a man who sees his life as satisfactorily defined by the terms of his society will have no need to roam that border area which, while it does hold his salvation, also threatens him with madness. The cynic and the atheist, who see such a need as escapist rationalization, fail to see that necessity is also the mother of discovery. We have all always been out on the street, but it is only at a time like this that any great number of us are sufficiently troubled to realize it.

The Dylan songs that are most commonly discussed are the early ramblings such as "Blowin' in the Wind" and "The Times They Are A-Changin'," whose simplemindedness allows instant comprehension. It was not until 1964, when he wrote "Lay Down Your Weary Tune" and "My Back Pages," that Dylan gave indication that he was about ready to discard the security which one can find in symbols. Where he had formerly seen his own identity in the terms of the civil rights struggle, he now ridicules professors who teach that "liberty is just equality in school" and continues:

> Yes, my guards stood hard when abstract threats
> Too noble to neglect,
> Deceived me into thinking
> I had something to protect.
> Good and bad, I defined these terms
> Quite clear, no doubt, somehow—
> Ah, but I was so much older then;
> I'm younger than that now.*

It was at this point that Dylan was preparing to become an artist in the Zen sense; he was searching for the courage to release his grasp on all the layers of distinctions that give us meaning, but, by virtue of their inevitably setting us apart from the life-flow, preclude our salvation. All such distinctions, from petty jealousies and arbitrary cultural values to the massive, but ultimately irrelevant, confusions engendered by psychological problems, all the endless repetitions that those without faith grasp in order to avoid their own existence—all of these had to be released. The strength, the faith, necessary for this release was to be a major theme of Dylan's for the next three years. In "Mr. Tambourine Man," an invocation to his muse, he seeks the last bit of will necessary for such strength:

> Take me on a trip upon your magic swerlin' ship.
> My senses have been stripped, my hands can't feel to
> grip.

* "My Back Pages," © M. Witmark and Sons, 1964.

My toes too numb to step, wait only for my boot heels
To be wandering.
I'm ready to go anywhere, I'm ready for to fade,
Into my own parade, cast your dancin' spell my way,
I promise to go under it.*

Having summed up the courage to deal with his vision, Dylan is now able to expose the myriad confusions which offer us security at the expense of freedom. His declaration (in "It's Alright, Ma") that "I got nothing, Ma, to live up to" is a rejection of others' inevitably futile attempts to impose a source of meaning on him. This line has been misinterpreted, I believe, as a condemnation of a society without values (values which are relative and irrelevant to ultimate meaning) by some and used as a basis for a psychological criticism of Dylan's work by others. This latter approach may conceivably offer some interesting insights, both of the obvious possible psychoanalytic correlates of the mystical experience and of Dylan's own compelling psychological perceptions. As Walter Kaufman would say, these are merely different snapshots of the same journey. However, Dylan's vision is particularly fragile and one must take care not to destroy it with a lethal reductionism.

In "Gates of Eden" Dylan is well into his own parade. He has found his mystical fixed point and is attempting to illuminate it. As is the case with the other songs on *Bringing It All Back Home,* Dylan's vision has developed at a far more rapid rate than his talent. As a result, his cosmology is stated more concretely (if less poetically) than in his later songs. In "Gates of Eden" Dylan's kinship to Blake becomes apparent. Like Blake, Dylan relegates experience to eternal subordination to innocence:

The kingdoms of experience
In the precious winds they rot,
While paupers change possessions
Each one wishing for what the other has got.
And the princess and the prince discuss
What's real and what is not.
It doesn't matter inside The Gates of Eden.†

* "Mr. Tambourine Man," © M. Witmark and Sons, 1964.
† "Gates of Eden," © M. Witmark and Sons, 1965.

It is interesting to compare this to Blake's "Auguries of Innocence":

> We are led to Believe a Lie
> When we see not Thro' the Eye
> Which was Born in a Night to perish in a Night
> When the soul Slept in Beams of Light.
> God Appears & God is Light
> To those poor Souls who dwell in Night,
> But does a Human Form Display
> To those who Dwell in Realms of day.

Dylan's conception of a transcendence that flows through man is similar to Blake's, and the compassion it generates is later to suffuse Dylan's work with a humanity it lacks at this point. For now Dylan is struggling to express his newly-discovered Oceanus. D. T. Suzuki has written:

> Our consciousness is nothing but an insignificant floating piece of island in the Oceanus encircling the earth. But it is through this little fragment of land that we can look out to the immense expanse of the unconscious itself; the feeling of it is all that we can have, but this feeling is not a small thing, because it is by means of this feeling that we can realize that our fragmentary existence gains its full significance, and thus that we can rest assured that we are not living in vain.*

This is the Eden of which Dylan sings. It is, of course, possible that even those readers who accept all that has been said thus far will conclude that Dylan does indeed speak of a godhead, yet is no more a poet than are the many philosophers who have spoken of being and existence in such an excruciatingly unpoetic way that descriptions of the unfathomable are rendered virtually unreadable. Those who are particularly concerned with a separation of form and content are most likely to look unfavorably upon Dylan's poetry. It is difficult to imagine, however, any poet more capable of speaking to his given time than is Dylan, or a time more in need of someone capable of speaking to it.

With respect to form, Dylan faces the same problems that

* *Zen Buddhism and Psychoanalysis* by Erich Fromm, D. T. Suzuki, and Richard De Martino, Harper and Row, 1960.

face all artists. His creations must give form and order to apparent chaos. In an attempt to catch the tune of a universal melody, mere awareness of the melody is not enough. For we all possess the potential to hear the tune; many of us do hear it, but are incapable of communicating even a hint of its beauty. Only a supreme talent can hope to translate the experience into art. It is not enough for the poet or the composer merely to relay random sounds, for such sounds have beauty only in their universal context. The artist must create a new form on a smaller scale that, if it will not mirror the holy chord, will at least provide harmony for it. Dylan is like the chess grand master; there is *one* correct way to play chess, but this way is far too complicated for any person or computer to comprehend. So the master does not attempt merely to extract a few moves from a plan he can know of but cannot understand; he creates his own imperfect form in order to suggest a chord that can only be sensed.

Dylan does not teach, neither does he proselytize. At most he merely affirms the existence of The Way. His effect is limited, of course, by the inherent inadequacy of words which precludes the possiblity of total communication of the mystical experience. It is further limited by the fact that, while we are all capable of salvation, it is a relatively rare man who is an embodiment of the particular complex of psyche, intelligence, sensitivity, courage, and coincidence from which the mystical experience and salvation can erupt. Dylan can effect only the last; "take what you have gathered from coincidence," he tells Baby Blue. At most all that any artist or prophet can hope for is to ignite our faith. Dylan, perhaps more than any other contemporary poet, is capable of the words that can ignite this faith. If language's impotence is in its inability to convey the melody of the universe, its strength is its power to reproduce the harmonics at least of that infinitely beautiful melody.

By the time Dylan wrote the songs that were to appear on his next album, *Highway 61 Revisited,* his talent was rapidly achieving parity with his vision. He now felt more at home with that vision and was less obsessed with detailing its every aspect. This enabled him to return partially to the subject of man. About the only redeeming virtue of Dylan's pre-visionary songs had been an attractive empathy toward the outsider. While Dylan was not to achieve the complete suffusion of vision with compassion until *John Wesley Harding,* in *Highway 61 Revisited* he did begin to feel that the eternally incommunicable nature of the religious experience did not render human contact irrelevant. If his attentions were not loving, at least he was attempting to reconcile man's existence with his vision. In "Like a Rolling Stone" he developed a conceit that had appeared in seminal form in "It's All Over Now, Baby Blue." "Like a Rolling Stone," which is probably Dylan's finest song and most certainly his quintessential work, is addressed to a victim who has spent a lifetime being successfully seduced by the temptations that enable one to avoid facing his own existence. Dylan plays the fool, the "juggler," the "clown," "Napoleon in rags," who—like numerous literary fools before him—is discovered by the mocking victim to be the bearer of truth. To the Oriental, the fool is easily discernible as the Master whose path to truth is paved with riddle and paradox. Perhaps the Occidental most comparable to the fool is the psychoanalyst whose maddening silence is well known to the victims who come to him. In any case, the victim, imprisoned in the ego straitjacket that has been his only source of meaning, is not quick to release his protective ball and chain:

> You said you'd never compromise
> With the mystery tramp,
> But now you realize
> He's not selling any alibis
> As you stare into the vacuum of his eyes
> And say "do you want to
> Make a deal?" •

There are no deals. Standing naked, knowing that all that came before is irrelevant, Miss Lonely is still not capable of the ultimate honesty which is required for her salvation. She cannot be honest because she lacks the courage to manifest the will to discard the rationalizations that imprison her and the diversions that allow her to avoid the knowledge of her imprisonment. Dylan later will write, "to live outside the law you

• "Like a Rolling Stone," © M. Witmark and Sons, 1965.

must be honest"; when one surrenders the limited, arbitrary, relative societal values which define life for most men, pretense will not suffice.* It is with perhaps a bit too much bitterness, a bitterness which is to plague Dylan in his search for peace, that he ridicules Miss Lonely:

You used to be so amused
At Napoleon in rags and the language that he used.
Go to him now, he calls you, you can't refuse
When you ain't got nothing you got nothing to lose.
You're invisible now, you got no secrets
To conceal.

How does it feel, ah, how does it feel
To be on your own
With no direction home,
Like a complete unknown
Like a rolling stone.†

Bitterness surfaced in all its virulence in "Positively 4th Street," a song written at this time but excluded from the album. On one level this song may have been an attack on a critic who decried Dylan's dismissal of the relevance of politics. More importantly, I think that Dylan's bitterness arose from his having to face the most basic spiritual conflict: having seen the vision, how does one either live a life which flows naturally from that vision or resign himself to the impossibility of such a life? This song is not all bitterness, however; Dylan's refusal to accept another man's problems is not lack of compassion, but a reiteration of the ultimately irrelevant nature of those problems and the impossibility of any man's being the source of another's courage.

There is more of brilliance on *Highway 61 Revisited*. In "Ballad of a Thin Man" Dylan lays aside his usual reticence about the use of sexual imagery (he once derided obscenity on the grounds that all propaganda is phony) when he utilizes

* "And just how far would you like to go in?" he asked and the three kings all looked at each other. "Not too far but just far enough so's we can say that we've been there . . ." (from Dylan's liner notes on *John Wesley Harding*).

† "Like a Rolling Stone," © M. Witmark and Sons, 1965.

a homosexual encounter in order to deal with man's search for realization. "Desolation Row" is a denunciation of intellectual word-mongering as a road to salvation. It is this song's cornucopia of imagery that is primarily responsible for what is, I believe, the common misconception that Dylan is a symbolist. Words are already symbols; to force Dylan's phrases of rough-hewn delicacy further into the stultifying context of symbolism is to render them totally incapable of bridging the gap between word and essence.

It is only when one realizes he has been out on the street that the faith which precedes salvation becomes necessary and possible. The journey home to peace can begin only in the cobwebbed room of suicidal meaninglessness that is Desolation Row.

Dylan's poetic talents are at their zenith in *Blonde on Blonde*. Vision overwhelms him less than before, and he concentrates on finding peace through the kinds of women he has always loved: women of silent wisdom, women who are artists of life, women who neither argue nor judge, but accept the flow of things.

Dylan had suggested the premise of this album in "Queen Jane Approximately" on *Highway 61 Revisited.* As in many of the songs on *Blonde on Blonde,* here one finds not only Dylan's ever-present sense of irony and humor, but also his use of overlapping levels of meanings. As one enters this song more and more deeply he becomes aware first of its concern with the fashionable ennui that periodically affects us all, then its representation of disgust with oneself and the games he thinks he must play, and—finally—its subtle description of the endless repetition to which so many of us chain ourselves.

"Visions of Johanna," an incandescently beautiful song, and "Memphis Blues Again," which is also on *Blonde on Blonde,* fuse all the themes discussed so far and indicate Dylan's imminent discovery that the mystical experience must give way to a life infused with mysticism and compassion lest even the mystical experience be perverted into an excuse for evasion.

> In the empty lot where the ladies play blind man's
>   bluff with the keychain

And the all-night girls, they whisper of escapades out
 on the "D" train
We can hear the night watchman click his flashlight,
Ask himself if it's him or them that's insane,
Louise—she's alright—she's just near,
She's delicate and seems like veneer,
But she just makes it all too concise, and too clear
That Johanna's not here.
The ghost of electricity
Howls in the bones of her face
Where these visions of Johanna
Have now taken my place.

Inside the museums
Infinity goes up on trial
Voices echo this is what
Salvation must be like
After awhile.*

There are no "messages" in Dylan's songs, neither is there ideology. The flight of a supreme imagination, the ability to tap into the highest levels of truth, preclude the artist's accepting the simplistic artificiality that is necessary for ideology's goal of widespread acceptance. If an artist is capable of no greater vision than the rest of us, then of what value is he? By imprisoning Dylan's songs in a context of political ideology we play the barbarian as surely as if we were to hammer Rodin's *Thinker* into a huge metal peace symbol. Dylan may well be upset by contemporary America; on one level "Tears of Rage" would seem to indicate this. Much of Dylan's anger, however, is directed not at any political entity (politics must forever play a secondary role in his universe) but at the young themselves—many of whom have used his words to avoid fighting the battles of their own existences. It is ironic, but not surprising, that Weatherman, a group of individuals who channel their own confusions into violence, take their name from the song of a man who ridicules all forms of escape through symbol and evasion.

In itself, Dylan's political philosophy is irrelevant; he sees

* "Visions of Johanna," © Dwarf Music, 1966.

both philosophy and politics as evasive concern with the repetition of cause and effect that can never lead one to the Light which shines within him. Indeed, Dylan ridicules all codes and moralities that claim holy sanction. His vision concerns the God within and without.

It is quite conceivable, therefore, that, when he bothers with politics at all, Dylan's political outlook is conservative. His emphasis on personal, as opposed to societal, salvation could very possibly leave him feeling most at home with a political philosophy that emphasizes the individual's right to be left alone to his own search for God. *John Wesley Harding* appeared at a time when the indescribable revulsion felt by the young toward Lyndon Johnson was at its zenith; yet, in a time of ornate, kaleidoscopic record covers, *John Wesley Harding* had an Americana cover. Dylan's declaration that he was not about to argue or to move contrasted with the student rage that was asserting itself. If Dylan does tend toward conservatism, it is because conservatism, at least theoretically, mirrors his distrust of political routes to salvation.

In *John Wesley Harding* Dylan reiterates his belief that compassion is the only secular manifestation of the religious experience; any code which demands more than pure compassion is generated in the imperfection of experience and does not flow only from a vision of God. Indeed, while change in Dylan's universe is the natural state of things, impatience to implement change is the supreme form of egotism, the ultimate vanity: it is an individual's setting himself apart from the flow. Preoccupation with the methodology of change, like any magnification of one small aspect of the flow of life, implies a ceaseless intellectualization which precludes a possibility of the religious experience.

John Wesley Harding is not a political philosophy and our attempting to view it as such is to drain it of the wisdom it has to offer. This album is Dylan's supreme work; it is his solution to the seeming contradiction of vision and life. His vision continues to preclude a political path to salvation, but finally overcomes the exclusion of humanity that had plagued his previous visionary songs. The mere existence of Dylan's songs had indicated the problem: if other men were totally irrelevant—if God could be experienced, but the experience was totally incommunicable—then Dylan's songs would have been silent psalms read to deaf sinners. In this album, the creative manifestation of a life infused with God, gentleness and compassion replace bitterness and cynicism. Where once there was confusion, now there is peace. Dylan has paid his dues. He has discovered that the realization that life is not in vain can be attained only by an act of faith; only when one accepts the flow of life can he manifest the will to overcome the confusion and vanity which tear him apart. To the children of Pirandello, drowning in their ennui and their relativism, Dylan sings:

> "There must be some way out of here,"
> Said the joker to the thief,
> "There's too much confusion,
> I can't get no relief."
> "Businessmen, they drink my wine, plowmen dig my
> earth,
> None of them along the line
> Know what any of it is worth."
>
> "No reason to get excited," the thief, he kindly spoke,
> "There's many here among us
> Who feel that life is but a joke.
> But, you and I, we've been through that,
> And this is not our fate,
> So, let us not talk falsely now,
> The hour is getting late." *

The only way in which any of us can hope to play the thief, can ignite the faith of another and rob him of his confusion, is through love and compassion. For better or worse, all wisdom is eventually distilled into a few lines; even the unfathomable mysteries of the Bible must finally reside in the compassion of the Golden Rule. Dylan concludes "Dear Landlord" with a prayer for true compassion.

Perhaps it is inevitable that, sooner or later, there will be a falling out between Dylan (with his emphasis on wisdom and the acceptance that it generates) and his public (with its desire

* "All Along the Watchtower," © Dwarf Music, 1968.

for the passion and change that political objectives demand). I must admit to skepticism concerning how many of Dylan's youthful followers have even the vaguest conception of what he is singing about. Many look no deeper than the level of his very fine rock music, while others are merely in the market for political slogans. However, contemporary technology enables Dylan's songs to be disseminated to an incredibly large number of people. No doubt many of them are at least aware that Dylan is sending out clues. Dylan's art is capable of igniting their faith. In any age that is a considerable artistic achievement; in the lonely world of the contemporary young it would seem almost a miracle.

I hope that these observations have served as invitation. One discusses Dylan's poetry with the knowledge that his observation affects his subject just as the physicist's affects his. Dylan has warned us of the danger:

> At dawn my lover comes to me
> And tells me of her dreams,
> With no attempt to shovel the glimpse
> Into the ditch of what each one means.
> At times I think there are no words,
> But these to tell what's true,
> And there are no truths outside the Gates of Eden.*

There is no denying that Dylan's work subsequent to *Nashville Skyline* does not soar to the heights Dylan navigated in the songs discussed in this essay. Perhaps this is the unavoidable price one must pay when his growth forces him to surrender the confusions which drove him to new artistic heights. Much later Dylan, a poet who had dealt directly with the most complex and profound questions facing man, is to write:

> Build me a cabin in Utah,
> Marry me a wife,
> Catch rainbow trout,
> Have a bunch of kids who call me "pa,"
> That must be what it's all about.†

* "Gates of Eden," © M. Witmark and Sons, 1965.
† "Sign on the Window," © Big Sky Music, 1970.

Indeed, it is apparent even in *Nashville Skyline* that Dylan is surrendering the surrogate joys of genius for the emotional joys of the maturity which genius must pursue in vain. *Nashville Skyline* can be seen in all its clarity only in the light of all that came before. Perhaps this is a failure of the work; certainly one would think so if he insists that any great work of art must stand alone. Alone, *Nashville Skyline* is a tightly-written, cleverly executed series of clichés that would seem to be merely a collection of nice songs written by a Dylan who has gotten a bit mentally plump. As the final step in Dylan's search for God, however, it is a lovely paean, Dylan's acknowledgment of the joy of a life suffused with compassion and God. If this does not make the album particularly illuminating for the man who is unaware of Dylan's cosmology, to others it is evidence that Dylan has finally been able to bring it all back home. He has heard the universal melody through the galaxies of chaos and has found that the galaxies were a part of the melody. The essence that Dylan had discovered and explored is a part of him at last. There will be no more bitterness, no more intellectualization, no more explanation. There will be only Dylan's existence and the joyous songs which flow naturally from it.

Dylan Meets Weberman

A Dylan Interview Conducted by A. J. Weberman, Dylanologist & Minister of Defense, Dylan Liberation Front

by (of course) *A. J. Weberman, Dylanologist*

Preface

The following interview is actually a series of conversations I had with Dylan in early January 1971. Since D wouldn't let me record them, I had to reconstruct them through my recollections. When I showed Bob what I had come up with, he said, "There's lies in there & that's sneaky shit talkin to a cat, then writing about it." We corrected my errors over the phone & D gave me some direct quotes (I recorded the phone call & have included parts of it). I think I caught the leap of D's bound to some extent.

NOTE
D stands for Dylan
CB stands for current bag

I was really fucking hassled the day I met Dylan. Pigs. Heavy shit. I was goin fucking crazy. I made it to the D class that I teach each week at the Alternate U & gave a shirt rap & then said—"Tonight's the field trip to D's pad." About fifty of us headed down 6th Ave. towards MacDougal St. When we got to 4th St. I pointed out the pad D lived in from 62–64 and tried to explain how it related to D's single—POSITIVELY FOURTH STREET—but this drunk wouldn't let me get a word in edgewise. We continued to march & picked up a couple of street kids along the way (that's the dangerous part about doing something like this—like I could trust the people in my class, but these kids were full of undirected violence). Soon

Reprinted with permission from the *East Village Other*, January 19, 1971.

we were all standing in front of D's. I began to yell, HEY BOBBY PLEASE CRAWL OUT YOUR WINDOW. Someone else screamed—OPEN THE DOOR BOBBY. The lights started to go on and off and one of D's kids came to the window & started playing with his blocks on the sill, building sort of a wall against us. We stopped yelling. I invited the class into D's lobby in order to show them where D "came down into the lobby to make a small call out" but by this time the class had split into two groups—the hardcore Dylan Liberationists were with me in the hall, while the people with groupie tendencies were standing across the street. Then Eric Williams (DLF) said —"Hey man, I saw someone look out from on top of the stairs for a flash." Dylan was home!

We went outside & I decided to go thru D's garbage with the class, & so they formed a circle around me. David Peel (DLF) pointed out that his garbage bags were green, like his money. My "Garbage Article" had already come out so there was nothing of interest to be found, but we did the thing anyway. Then one of the street kids decided he was gonna enter D's thru a window. I was explaining what we'd do to him if he tried it (I wasn't ready for an illegal demo—yet) when Sharon (DLF—groupie tendencies) comes over and says: "There's someone standing across the street who looks JUST LIKE DYLAN." "Holy shit," I thought. "What the fuck am I going to do? D's caught me red-handed going thru his garbage. He's gonna be pissed off . . . he may get violent. I may have to beat the shit out of that slimy bootlicker here and now." I looked up and saw Bob standing directly across the street from me—he was dressed in denim, wearing rimless glasses, & it looked like smoke was coming out of his head. I just stood there. David Peel came over and pushed me forward. It was like High Noon. "Do not forsake me oh my Dylanology." I eventually walked over to D, who looked like a cross between someone in his "current bag" and a Talmudic scholar, and said, "How are you, man?" "Turn off the tape recorder" (I had one with me & I did). Then D said, "Al, why'd ye bring all these people around my house for?" "It's a field trip for my Dylan class, man . . . but actually it's a demonstration against you and all you've come to represent in rock music." "Alan, let's go talk about this," and he took me by the arm (I knew that very instant he meant to do me harm) & he started putting on the pressure and I had no other choice except but for to go. "Cool it man," I yelled, "that fuckin hurts—no violence—unless you want to fight it out here and now." "Al, did you ever write anything about my Karate? Ever write anything about my race & stuff it in my mailbox?" "I knew you took Karate but I never wrote anything about it . . . your race . . . ?" "What race are you, Alan?" "The human race." "And what race were yer parents?" "Well, they considered themselves Jewish, I guess." "You sure you never wrote anything about my race?" "No, man, it ain't yer race I object to, it's yer politics and lifestyle." "Well, I didn't think ya would, Al." "Hey Bob, what do you do with all your money?" "It all goes to Kibbutzim in Israel and Far Rockaway." "But you were one of the first Jews to put down Israel." "Where?" "In the liner notes to ANOTHER SIDE OF D." "Don't remember! . . . You know, Al, you've been in the city too long, the city does something to your thinking—I know how it is."

D sat down on this stoop a few blocks from his pad and we continued the conversation—"What about your cb, Bobby?" He denied it and did something that would make people believe he was telling the truth. But not A.J. Like he says—"We'll fly over the ocean JUST AS THEY SUSPECT" ("Fly over ocean" is a metaphor for D's cb from other contexts). Later on he told me—"Everyone's been asking me about your writing" THE RUMOR. "The man in Dylan would do nearly any task when asked for compensation . . ." just give him his current bag. "From my TOES up to my HEELS" Dig what I mean.

Somewhat taken aback by D's willingness to cooperate, I told him—"Man, but there's all this evidence in your poetry—I could stand here for hours and hours running it all down . . . and then there's all the songs written to you by other poets in yer own language putting you down for your cb." "Al, you've got to keep in mind that my poetry doesn't reflect the way I'm feeling, now, it's like years behind." "Well, bullshit . . ."

So we talked. D said he didn't dig the Panthers because of their position on the Mideast situation—"Little Israel versus all those . . ." I started to explain to D how the Panthers believed that everyone has a right to live: Jews, Arabs AND Palestinian refugees, when this kid from my class come over and says he wants to talk to D. I told him that was cool but to wait until we got done . . . I had something important to say to Bob & I didn't know if I'd ever see him again. (I was seizing the time.) So the punk says—"You're full of shit and so is Dylanology." So I grabbed him by the collar & screamed SPLIT, ASSHOLE! He left but as he was going he yelled out in gradeschool intonation—WEBERMAN'S BOOTLEGGING TARANTULA (D's suppressed novel). Dylan said I only had half of the book—the other half was out in Calif.—& that I should never worry about running out of things to interpret. He said he was gonna invite me up to Woodstock a couple of months ago. I asked, "How come you didn't, how come I had to have a demonstration in front of yer house to get you to negotiate . . . you know how dedicated I am & how well I know your work." "I know, Al, and one day we'll go for a ride together and I'll interpret all my poems for ya." "We ain't goin down by the docks, are we?" "No . . . Al, you scared my tenants yelling like that." "Sorry, man, I didn't mean to grag yer innocent people into it . . . dig like these radical freaks were staying over at The Archives & I told them where you were at & they thought about trashing your place but I told them DON'T DO IT . . . it ain't fair to Dylan's kids." "Al, I know a lot of people who want to hurt you, especially after that 'Garbage' thing—you know, all these college kids come to my garbage & take some of it back to their dorms—you wouldn't like these kids either . . ." "Get a garbage compacter and I'll come around and pick it up once a week." "I don't like machines . . . no, that's not true." "Bob, you wouldn't have me offed, would you?" "You scared?" "Sure I am, this is an oligarchy, the more money you have the more power." "I wouldn't do it, Al, don't worry, it's too late anyway." "I didn't think so, man, it would be like GM offing Nader, but if you do, you BETTER do a good job."

I went on & gave D a rap against Imperialism, Racism & Sexism (he didn't seem like he was listening) and then I told him that NASHVILLE SKYLINE sucked while SELF PORTRAIT was a stone rip-off since many people bought it, played it once, and stuck it on their shelf. Neither album related to objective reality. Dylan responded quietly—"Well, there were 2 good songs on S.P., DAYS OF FORTY-NINE and KOPPER KETTLE . . . and without those 2 lps they'd be no NEW MORNING, anyway I'm just starting to get back on my feet as far as my music goes . . . Al, do you use Amphetamine?" "No, man, the reason I have so much energy is because I'm tuned in to the life force that's trying to assert itself here on earth—I'M ALIVE MAN." "Why worry so much about earth when there's . . ." "What do you want me to worry about: if Mars invades us?" "What drugs do you use, Al?" "Just reefer & caffeine, and you?" "No drugs." "BULLSHIT!" Although I must admit that D's eyes looked normal almost every time we met. "Well, so long, Al, you're an interesting fellow, see you in a few weeks." I gave him the power handshake & he split.

When I got home I was fucking wasted. I was rapping with Harvey, a lawyer friend, when the phone rang—"Hello Al, this is Bob." Suddenly the telephone began to look like my record player. "Want to come over and visit me tomorrow?" "That's like asking a strung-out junkie if he wants a fix." "Al, I wanted to thank you for helping me sell a lot of records—your articles have helped to keep it going." "Yeah, that's one aspect of Dylanology I don't dig . . . but I may cancel it out soon." "Al, do you have a driver's license?" "No, never learned to drive." "Too bad, I know of this chauffeur's job that's open." "Are you trying to buy me out, man? STOP RIGHT HERE. It's im-fucking-possible." "No, no, I wasn't trying to buy you out, I just wanted you to see me from another seat, you've been on the streets too long." "Hey Bob, you know that song CHAMPAGNE, ILLINOIS you wrote and gave to Carl Perkins?" "Yeah, I figured Carl needed a song." "He needed something, anyway, why not write a song called CARBONDALE, ILL. cause that's where the pigs just murdered this black man who was gonna testify against them . . ." Dylan remained silent. "You there?" "Call ye tomorrow." I hung up.

The next day he called me & told me to come over to his midtown studio with a tape deck & an amplifier if I wanted to hear some rare D tapes cause all he had at the studio was a record player. My old lady, Ann, helped me take the stuff uptown & then split cause D said he wanted to see me alone. D began—"I've seen you around a lot, Al." "Bob, let's set up the equipment, okay?" I went over to the speaker and asked him to disconnect it & he started unscrewing the terminal with no lead on it. "Let me do it, man," & I did the thing. (This little bit of play acting and the riff about not having a tape recorder in his studio was a clever ploy designed to convince me D wasn't into recording conversations, but I didn't go for it & maintained my cool when it came to saying self-incriminating things.)

We began—"What do you think of Tim Leary?" Dylan asked. "I think he's great—like he was into revolution all along but felt he could attract a lot of the middle class by talking about it in mystical terms. He's a national hero of Woodstock Nation. What do you think?" "I don't follow politics." "How come I found newspaper in yer garbage—every day?" "It's not my garbage—everyone in my building—we mix all the garbage together." "Sure ye do! . . . hey man, I'll tell you something about yer politics—they're fucking genocidal—cause I talk to a lot of people when I'm out on the streets selling TARANTULA and most of the people I talk to got the impression from that SING OUT! interview that you support the war in Vietnam." "I only did that to get back at the freaks who wouldn't leave me alone & let me do my thing up in Woodstock—every five minutes there was someone at my door. I mean this fame thing got out of hand. I never expected to become this famous. I DON'T DIG IT. Everywhere I go—man, even if I go to some small town somewhere—a bunch of freaks always manage to find me and then they go apeshit." "Get a long-haired wig, they'd never recognize you." "Why don't you buy me one, Al . . ." "Hey man, how come you associated yourself with Cash—that lackey was so conservative at that time you did things together that Nixon later invited him to sing at the White House & Cash still goes out of his way to praise Nixon's genocidal policies at his concerts." "I've heard Cash since I was a kid . . . I love him." "Bob, yer so fucking conservative lately, I'm surprised Nixon didn't invite you to sing fer him." "I am too, man." "Man, almost all the other rock people put you down in their songs—in yer own language—for yer politics." "They're just using my phrasing."

"No, man, they understand what you're saying the same way I do—from studying yer poetry."

"Why don't you ask them about it?" "Man, they'd deny it cause it's a secret language & cause of the controversial nature of you cb which they sing about—anyway it's poetry & its up to the listener or critic to figure it out." "I deny it's happening and so do they." "Hey, Dylan man, all of you can deny your asses off, but as long as ya don't come up with another system that's more consistent, makes more sense, etc., MINE STANDS, DIG?" "NO."

"And, man, if you really believe in yer current bag and want to continue to remain in it, how come you copped-out on yourself in your poetry? And the poetry is simple enough that many people understand it. Isn't that indicative of a contradiction in yer personality?" Now I had Dylan going. He suddenly became very depressed and didn't say anything. He looked hurt. I almost felt sorry for him. "Hey Bob, you okay, man? Like a lot of these cats are full of shit—putting you down for not doing anything when they don't do shit themselves." "Remember, Al, I'm not like them. . . . not fresh out of college . . . " "Man, you've been telling everyone my interpretations are 'way off' . . . let's hear you interpret one of your songs, then I'll interpret it and we'll see whose interpretation is better . . . how about TONIGHT I'LL BE STAYING WITH YOU?" "Okay, but I feel stupid . . . Throw my ticket out the window . . . so we were down in Nashville and the train was leaving and I didn't want to go so I said . . . " "Hey man, didn't you once sing 'You hand in your money' for the line 'You hand in your ticket' (from MR. JONES) at a concert in England?" "Yeah." So doesn't ticket symbolize money?" "A ticket is anything you want it to be." "You mean your symbolism isn't consistent?" "It's as consistent as me." "So isn't it money?" "It could be." Dylan then changed the subject—"You sure you didn't write any letters about my race?" "No, man, how many times do I have to tell you . . . like every letter I ever wrote you was on Dylan Archives stationery—was that?" "Yes, I got it right here." He couldn't find it. (Since "letter" symbolizes "article" in D's symbology, he may have been referring to part of my *EVO* "garbage article," where, after finding cards and thank-you notes from D's family, I wrote—"Good to see Dylan is still a Zimmerman." What I meant by that was, "Good to see D still associates with middle class, lames like his straight relatives." It was a riff in the Lenny Bruce LIMA OHIO & John Lennon "don't believe in Zimmerman" tradition & not antisemitic.)

"Did you ever write a song to me?" "Absolutely not." "How about Dear Landlord, or was that to Grossman?" "Grossman wasn't in my mind when I wrote it. Only later when people pointed out the song may have been written for Grossman I thought it could have been . . . it's an abstract song . . . sure as hell wasn't written for you . . . I wasn't aware of you then." "Does Albert still act in your behalf?" "No."

Throughout our conversation the phone rang constantly, and at one point someone came to the door and handed D a fan letter and a book of poems. He read the fan letter right then and there and handed me the book—"Take a look at it—tell me what you think—advise me—you're a knowledgeable cat and I could use some advice—even on politics." "Bullshit." "I should have a book of my poems out in two years & a book containing all my songs should be out soon & I'm planning to release that song you have a rare tape of—SHE'S YOUR LOVER NOW—as a single." "Bullshit . . . what do you think about my work, man?" "Your approach is sincere." "You know, if I lived in another age I might have been a Talmudic scholar." "So would I." "I guess so—you say I'm 'sincere.' Why didn't you say that in the *Rolling Stone* interview instead of saying I was 'way-off'?" "I'm thru with that. The only reason I gave them an interview was because they hounded me for years." "Do you follow the rock criticism scene closely?" "No." "How come I found all those rock papers in yer garbage?" "I only read them when Al Kooper brings them over . . . wanna hear a tape?" He played one cut—it was D singing DON'T YE TELL HENRY, a song the band often does at concerts—this lent support to my theory that D ghosts for the band. "We got a better fidelity version of this tape back in the Archives." Then D offered me all this stuff that would help my "career" as a rock critic; I could sit in on recording sessions, he hinted I could call him up & get info on his new records thusly making my review "straight from the horse's mouth" so to speak. I kind of got the feeling that I'd get all these privileges if I behaved. FUCK THAT SHIT. "Want to see the rest of the studio?" We walked into this room filled with the band's instruments and D's paintings. They were these impressionistic abysslike things. "What do you think of my paintings?" "Stick to poetry." "I paint what's on my mind." "Yeah, empty." For the first time D laughed—IT TAKES A LOT to make Dylan LAUGH—but he could relate to emptiness. Then I decided to lay it on the line—"Dylan, you've got to live up to your responsibility as a culture hero—

you're DYLAN, man, every freak has a soft spot in their heart for ya, they love ya, you're DYLAN, DYLAN, DYLAN." "I'm not Dylan, you're Dylan." "I know, you're some other man, right?" We went back into the front of the studio—"Want some records, Al?" "No, I get them for free from the record companies." "Want a rare picture of me?" "I told you we got all that shit back in the Archives . . . getting back to the subject at hand, did you ever think that maybe your wealth has corrupted you—you once said that the more of a stake you have in the system the more conservative one becomes—'Relationships of ownership they whisper in the sings," etc. And man, you used the struggle of black people for a decent life to make you famous, remember BLOWIN IN THE WIND and you ripped the blacks for their music—YOU OWE THEM QUITE A BIT—any truth to what I'm saying, man?" "Could be." Then I began to tell Bob why I feel the way I do about 3rd World Liberation & went into a riff about my visit with a very poor cat in Mexico. "Let's write a song together about your trip & we'll split the royalties." "Send my cut to Caesar Chavez, man." "So you just tell me what happened to you and I'll do the writing." "I was down in Progresso, in the Yucatan, & I stayed with this laborer, a typical third world scene, poverty, famine, disease—like being born into a nitemare—prolonged death agony—anyway, the cat became a 'bracero'—rhymes with sombrero." "And this cat thought the communists were 'little people'—he was brainwashed—his pad was next to a garbage dump. Now we got to convince Amerikans—thru this song—that they should support wars of national liberation." Dylan came up with a song that went like this—"Down in Progresso a bracero lived in a sombrero full of espresso." "What the fuck is this, man? No one is ever gonna be convinced of anything when you write that abstractly." "That's my thing, Al."

"Know anything about the other books being written about me?" "Well, Robert Shelton, Tony Scaduto and Toby Thompson are doing books. I know Tony. He says he's goin around talkin to all yer old friends (Jack Elliot, the McKenzies, etc.) and yer old lovers (Suzie Rottello, Joanie Baez, etc.) collecting 'information' about you—he said he would have studied yer lyrics but he knew he couldn't get permission to reprint them." "That's not the reason—he could have never figured them out

—he'll only come up with rumors." "He did a pretty good job, tho."

"Man, I think you're a fucking reactionary. You don't use your influence to save lives. Look at all the death around us. Look what just happened in Pakistan—that was the result of capitalism—the people were so poor they couldn't cope with a natural disaster." "I wonder why the good Lord wanted all those people to die?" "You don't believe in God . . . !" "I sure do . . . " "But how about WITH GOD ON OUR SIDE . . . Did ya believe in God then?" "I must have then too."

"How about using some of your five million dollars to save lives?" "I don't have that much." "Bullshit, I got inside info, you multi millionaire PIG. Anyway, you were a self proclaimed millionaire in '65. And you never do any benefits. Then there's your apolitical lyrics—everyone who heard NASHVILLE SKYLINE said—'Dylan's in a mellow head; he's singing about love.' You cut your hair, you only help apolitical rock people with their careers—you're a punk and me and the DLF are going to do a number on you. We got some shit planned that gonna blow your mind. Not only that, but everyone in rock with a political consciousness is gonna come down on you. Lennon has started already by calling you Zimmerman; McGuinn just put you down." "Where?" "In Creem." "How?" "By saying you write BALLAD OF EASY RIDER even tho you told him not to." "What? Well, I want to know who's gonna do this (getting angry) cause I'm not gonna take it. I'm gonna get them. I'm gonna get them. They'll never get out of it. Too bad for them . . . punks!" "Hey Bob, why not show the people your heart's in the right place and do a benefit for John Sinclair?" "I'm not about to help Sinclair by doing a concert, nor am I about to do any concerts at this time, man." "All you got to do is show up and plunk your guitar a little and a hundred thousand freaks will come out of their pads and go anywhere you are . . . " "Sorry, Al, I can't do it. But I will write a song about political prisoners on my next album . . . " "I don't want any promises for nine months later, I WANT TO SEE SOME ACTION NOW . . . see, Bob, you set the trends in rock and if you become like a human being a lot of other performers will go along . . ."

"Al, a lot of the things you do aren't on the up and up. You 'tap' phones, and ya go thru garbage like a pig." "But I didn't sell the garbage to LIFE MAGAZINE." "You must get money for your articles." "I'm not like you man, I send em all out fer free . . . everything should be free . . . money equals slavery. I'm proud I do it." "No reason not to be, but Al, I'm gonna write a song about you." "I could use the publicity." "That's one reason why I wouldn't . . . but I got a good song called PIG." "I can't take that seriously coming from you, multi-millionaire who hoards his bread. No matter how you cut it, when you have all that bread and most people in the world have shit, you're the enemy—THE PIG. Bobby, you're just another capitalist, but instead of producing cars, guns, etc., you produce culture." "That's something." "Sure it is . . . 'Blue moon, you left me standing alone' . . ." "Al, if I was a kid growing up I'd have to look out for you . . . I'd keep my eyes open for you. I'd make sure whatever street I went down I'd have to stand on the other side of the street when you came down, man. Al, why don't you get a guitar and put some of this energy to good use?" "But there's a need for someone like myself—no one else is doing the thing." "But yer so extreme . . . " "Thanks." "Off on one end—there's no one balancing the other end . . . " "How about lame rock critics . . . " "They're in the middle . . . " "Hey Bob, they all say I'm full of shit, Griel Mucus, Richie Goldstein, Christgau . . . they're all CORRUPT."

The sun had set & Dylan's wife had called him for dinner on the phone a couple of times. Bob gave me his phone number and asked me to call him when I'm on the radio or if something comes up. "Ever hear me on the radio, Bob?" "Just a couple of times on Alex Bennett's Show—I dug it when he asked you if you had any personal messages for me. What do you think of Bob Fass?" "He's a revolutionary brother but he don't dig it when I attack you cause you were an old friend of his." "Well, Al, so long, and one more thing—you're not going to get into my life." "Why?" "If you do I might gain a soul." "Is that a threat?"

Talking to Dylan was like talking to a ghost. The old Dylan, full of ideas and stories was gone, replaced with a shell. It was also like talking to a con-man who was really conning himself. I know D's still into his cb & he was trying to cool me out by using his charisma & offering me his "friendship." Trying to co-opt me & the DLF but we will fight on—till we win.

FREE BOB DYLAN

POWER TO THE PEOPLE

TARANTULA
BOB DYLAN

Tarantula

by Robert Christgau

The official appearance of Bob Dylan's *Tarantula* is not a literary event because Dylan is not a literary figure. Literature comes in books, and Dylan does not intend his most important work to be read. If he evei did, his withdrawal of these pieces from publication five years ago indicates that he changed his mind. Of course, it's possible that he's changed his mind again—with Dylan, you never know. Most likely, however, his very elusiveness is what the unexpected availability of this book is really about. The pursuit of the great public artist by his great audience has been a pervasive theme of his career, and the bootleg versions of *Tarantula* hawked on the street and under the counter by self-appointed Dylanologists and hip rip-off artists were simply a variation on that theme. For Dylan to permit the release of the book now (at a non-rip-off price, it should be noted) is to acknowledge the loss of a battle in his never-ending war for privacy. Quite simply, his hand has been forced by his fans. He is a book-writer now, like it or not.

To assert that Dylan doesn't belong in the history of literature is not to dismiss him from the history of artistic communication, or of language. Quite the contrary. A songwriter does not use language as a poet or novelist does because he chooses his words to fit into some larger, more sensual effect, an artist who elects to work in a mass medium communicates in a different way from one who doesn't and must be judged according to his own means, purposes, and referents. That much ought to be obvious. I would also argue, however, that Dylan's choices not only merit their own critical canons but must be recognized as incisive responses to modernism's cul-de-sac, in which all the arts, especially literature, suffer from self-perpetuating intellectualism and elitism.

What makes this all so confusing is that Dylan's fame and influence are based on his literary talents and pretensions. Just for fun, I might suggest that Dylan is no greater artist than Chuck Berry or Hank Williams, but only Dylan could have become the culture hero of a decade of matriculating college classes. Even at first, when Dylan's best songs were mostly acute genre pieces, he was believed to embody transcendent artistic virtues. The standard example was "Blowin' in the Wind," which interspersed straightforward political questions with metaphorical ones, always concluding: "The answer, my friend, is blowin' in the wind, the answer is blowin' in the wind." The song's "poetic" language, effective in musical and emotive context even though it appears hackneyed on the page, captured listeners sympathetic to its apparent assumptions and inspired much unfortunate image-mongering, but in retrospect we notice the ambivalence of the title—can the answer be plucked from the air or does it flutter out of reach?

Dylan may not have been aware he was equivocating when he wrote the song, but that doesn't matter. Equivocation was inherent in his choice of method. Like most of his confreres in the folk movement, Dylan got his world-view from the listless civil-rights and ban-the-bomb radicalism of the late 50s but was forced to find his heroes elsewhere, among the avant-garde artists who helped young post-conformists define for themselves their separation from their fellow citizens. Once Dylan found the ambition to use those artists as his own exemplars, he had to come to terms with their characteristic perspective—namely, irony. Sure enough, in "My Back Pages" (1964), he was renouncing politics with a nice ironic flourish—"I was so much older then, I'm younger than that now." Moreover, the same song signalled his debut as a poetaster with a portentously clumsy opening line: "Crimson flames tied through my ears, growing high and mighty traps."

Between early 1964 and mid-1966—a period that includes the

four albums from *Another Side of Bob Dylan* to *Blonde on Blonde* and the switch from acoustic to electric music—Dylan became a superstar. Pioneers of youth bohemia seized upon his grotesque, sardonic renderings of America as experienced by a native alien and elevated Dylan into their poet laureate. In response, professional defenders of poetry declared themselves appalled by his barbaric verbosity. Indeed, many of us, even while we were astonished, enlightened, and amused by Dylan's sporadic eloquence, knew why John Ciardi wasn't. But we didn't care, not just because Dylan's songs existed in an aural and cultural context that escaped the Ciardis, but because we sensed that the awkwardness and overstatement that marred his verse were appropriate to a populist medium. No one was explicit about this at the time, however, least of all Dylan, whose ambitions were literary as well as musical and whose relationship to his ever-expanding audience was qualified by the fascination with an arcane elite to which his songs testified.

Tarantula is a product of this period; in fact, Dylan fans who want a precise sense of what the book is about need only refer to the liner notes of *Highway 61 Revisited.* The basic technique is right there: the vague story, peopled with historical (Paul Sargent) and fabulous or pseudonymous (the Cream Judge, Savage Rose) characters, punctuated with dots and dashes and seasoned with striking but enigmatic asides, all capped off with a fictitious letter having no obvious connection to what has preceded. That's all, folks. The book is a concatenation of similar pieces. Most of them seem unconnected, although a few characters, notably someone named Aretha, do recur. The only literary precedent that comes to mind is *Naked Lunch,* but in a more general way the book is reminiscent of a lot of literature because it's an effort to read it. Unless you happen to believe in Dylan, I question whether it's worth the effort, and don't call me a philistine—it was Bob Dylan who got me asking such questions in the first place.

For the strangest aspect of Dylan's middle period is that although it was unquestionably his literary pretensions that fanaticized his admirers and transformed the craft (or art) of songwriting, Dylan's relationship to literature as a discipline was always ambivalent. In fact, even to call it ambivalent is to point up the confusion—it was actually downright hostile. From *Tarantula:* "wally replies that he is on his way down a pole & asks the man if he sees any relationship between doris day & tarzan? the man says 'no, but i have some james baldwin and hemingway books' 'not good enough' says wally." From the notes to *Bringing It All Back Home:* "my poems are written in a rhythm of unpoetic distortion." Dylan borrowed techniques from literature—most prominently allusion, ambiguity, symbolism, and fantasy—and he obviously loved language, but he despised the gentility with which it was supposed to be tailored. His songs do seem derivative, but (like *Tarantula*) they don't derive from anyone in particular. Obvious parallels, or "influences"—Blake, Whitman, Rimbaud, Celine—share only his approach and identity: the Great Vulgarian, the Magnificent Phonus Balonus. He wrote like a word-drunk undergraduate who had berserked himself into genius, the jumbled culture of the war baby—from da Vinci to comic strips, from T. S. Eliot to Charlie Rich—his only tradition. His famous surrealism owes as much to Chuck Berry as to Breton or even Corso, and even though his imagery broadened the horizons of songwriting, it was only a background for the endless stream of epigrams—which songwriters call good lines—flowing into out language, some already clichés ("The times they are a-changin'," "You know something's happening, but you don't know what it is"), others still the property of an extensive, self-informed subculture ("Stuck inside of Mobile with the Memphis blues again," "Don't follow leaders, watch the parking meters"). Dylan may be a poor poet, but he is a first-class wit.

But such talk accedes to the temptation of placing Dylan's work in a page context, always a mistake. Literature may have engendered the Dylan mystique, but rock and roll nurtured it. We remember those lines because we've heard them over and over again, often not really listening, but absorbing the rhythm of unpoetic distortion just the same. *Tarantula* may contain similar gems, but we'll never know they're there, because *Tarantula* will never be an album. The wonderful letters, the funny bits, as well as the dreary, vaguely interesting stuff and the failed doomsday rhetoric—all will go. Aretha Franklin's continuing presence through the book is a portent of why, for shortly after

Tarantula and *Blonde on Blonde,* Dylan made another switch by abandoning the verbal play (and excess) of his long songs for brief, specifically pop works. For a while, it appeared that this meant a total abandonment of the complexity of his vision, but his latest album, *New Morning,* makes clear that it is only a condensation. More and more, Dylan affirms the value of the popular and the sensual over the verbal. This book will find its way into A. J. Weberman's Dylan concordance and doubtless become a cult item, but it is a throwback. Buy his records.

BOB
DYLAN'S
GREATEST
HITS
VOL.II

Even a poet as *now* as Dylan has two kinds of female character in his imagery—the sad-eyed lady of the lowlands, the girl from the north country, who is inviolate and inviolable, *to kalos,* and the others who are human, confused and contemptible. This crude version of romanticism . . .

Germaine Greer, *The Female Eunuch*

There's no way you can get me to *expose* Bob Dylan—there's nothing to expose. Anybody with any sensibility can see that like any great artist he's naked in his art, man—and that's all there is to say.

Bob Neuwirth, in *Rolling Stone,*
August 19, 1971

Decay turns me off. I'll die first before I decay.

Bob Dylan, to Jules Siegel,
Saturday Evening Post,
July 30, 1966

Bob Dylan: Freedom and Responsibility

by Wilfrid Mellers

In a sense Bob Dylan is the most traditional artist in the pop field since he leaves us in no doubt that he is concerned with self-expression and communication. A youth of the American mid-west, he early opted out both from college and from the superfices of the American Way of Life; or rather he returned to a primitive American folk-culture in order to deflate a civilization which to him, as to many young people, seemed moribund. Strictly speaking he was not, even in his early days, a folk singer, since all his material was notated; none the less, he used folk techniques, and almost all his material was his own. Moreover, like a true folk artist he dealt in rock-bottom reality rather than in escape.

While Dylan's originality is his strength, his art *has* roots, and these are a strength also. Primarily, one looks to the words, since the significance of early Dylan is inseparable from his articulateness. The basic source is the traditional folk ballad, both in its British origins and in its American permutations. Closely allied to the ballad are children's rhymes, British and American; Negro blues poetry; the Bible, the mythology of which permeates the American mid-west; and runic verses of all kinds, reminding us of, and possibly even including, the lyrical poems of Blake.

Dylan's musical sources are both white and black. Most fundamental is the American transmutation of British ballad style. In the world of the "poor white," the grand modal themes survive, but the line becomes harder, tighter, the rhythm more cabined and confined in the metres of hymnody. Complementarily the vocal production of a singer such as Sarah Ogan Gunning, from the Kentucky Mining area, becomes at once pinched and lacerating. The poor white had, however, his resilience: which found outlet in his instrumental playing rather than in his singing. On banjo, guitar or mouthorgan a Hobart Smith could create a music unsubtle in line (for the old flexible modality is banished in favour of a simple harmonic diatonicism): yet jauntily virtuosic in its command of instrumental resource. The happiness is eupeptic, even if also a bit euphoric: for the shutting out of pain involves a wilful hardening of sensibility.

The contrast with black folk music is pointed; and although Dylan is white, it is significant that in his art black and white sources are inextricably linked. Most basic among his black roots is the Negro holler—the unaccompanied, usually pentatonic, ululation which the black man chants to the empty fields. Scarcely less primitive is the talking blues which cannot aspire to song: the Negro mumbles to himself whilst vamping an accompaniment on guitar or piano. A performer such as Fred Macdowell often combines the holler (close to the savage's "tumbling strain") with spoken incantation; and will further explore antiphony between the "aloneness" of such a personal testament in the spoken word and the "togetherness" of public involvement in a tribal beat.

All these sources, black and white, came together in the music of the man Dylan acknowledges as his master—Woody Guthrie. When Guthrie performs a song such as "It Was Sad When That Great Ship Went Down" it's scarcely possible to separate elements that derive from Negro blues, white ballad, American hymn, country-western banjo and harmonica music, circus song and music-hall number. Although not himself a Negro, Guthrie had every right to exploit sources that sprang from people dispossessed, alienated, persecuted. On the face of it, it seems odd that the music of today's affluent young should derive from similar roots. The development of Dylan's art may, however, provide both explanation and justification.

Bob Dylan, like Beethoven and the Beatles, has three periods: which correspond to an evolution towards music and a maturing of sensibility. In the first period the young mind and senses are preoccupied with the world OUTSIDE, which is regarded as at once separate and hostile: so that most of the songs are in some sense protest. In many songs of this phase music is minimal. Thus "Talking World War III Blues" has NO tune, no lyricism; the words are spoken against a rudimentary blues sequence on guitar, and the piece differs from a Negro talking blues mainly in that the words are sophisticated, acid in their comment on the plight of modern man, yet with a touch of fantasticality that distances the experience. The songs proper in the early period fall roughly into three types. The first is narrative, based on the American mutation of British balladry. A fine example is the "Ballad of Hollis Brown," which tells a (true) story of a poor-white farmer in South Dakota who, maddened by poverty, shoots himself and his family. The music could hardly be more primitive, more deprived, counteracting the flashes of poetic metaphor in the verse: for it consists of an almost pre-pentatonic reiterated incantation, supported by an unchanging ostinato of tonic and dominant chords on guitar. Dylan sings the four-note incantation in a pinched, rasping vocal sonority, with painful elongation of vowel sounds: a cross between the production of a Sarah Gunning and a Fred Macdowell. Musically, nothing happens in the song, except for a slight agitation of the guitar figuration in the penultimate stanza; yet the numbing vocal line, the nagging instrumental rhythm, serve an imaginative purpose. The song tells us it's possible to GO ON, at whatever level of rock-bottom fortitude. If seven people are dead on a South Dakota farm, somewhere seven new people are born; and Dylan's dead-pan, throw-away delivery of this statement leaves it open to us to interpret it as optimism or despair.

In the second type of song protest hits back by way of satire and (sometimes) lyricism. "With God On Our Side" recounts American military history with savage humour; and unlike "Hollis Brown" it *has* a tune (related to the hill-billy waltz) which is memorable if not affecting. Despite the bitterness of the words, their wit and the tune's memorability make the song affirmative, even comic.

Because such songs are positive in total effect, they tie up with the third type of song from the early period, wherein satire is transcended into the apocalyptic. In these songs both words and tune are often a permutation of real folk sources. "A Hard Rain's A-Gonna Fall" is a recreation of the ballad of Lord Rendal. The poetic imagery has a genuine affinity with runic folk verse and there are lines of visionary splendour that recall Bunyan and Blake. The incremental treatment of the original tune is preserved, but the modality of the melody is translated into a diatonic hillbilly waltz.

Interestingly enough, these apocalyptic songs often spring from topical and local events: "Who killed Davey Moore?" for instance, deals with a real and specific human situation, but makes out of it an experience as universal as the Cockrobin rhyme it transmutes. Not surprisingly, it was these visionary songs that provided the transition from Dylan's first to his second period, wherein the drama turns within the mind. Whereas his first phase had been a kind of anti-liturgy, exorcising the devil in an unlyrical, even at times unmusical, rasping, cawing and talking style, raucous and rancid: the evolution from protest to acceptance is also a move towards lyricism and music. "It's all right, ma, I'm only bleedin'" is a turning-point. Basically it's a talking blues, to which is added a pentatonic lyrical refrain accompanied by a rudimentary guitar ostinato similar to that in "Hollis Brown." This time, however, the innocent pentatonic lyricism of the refrain gets the better both of the nagging ostinato and of the talk. The music fulfils the words: despite the horrors abroad, the bleedin' and sighin' and dyin', it IS all right; and the mother figure can be addressed comically yet without contempt. It's interesting that there are more Negroid elements in this song than in the others so far discussed. Out of the black rhythmic flexibility and the ambiguous blue thirds comes the hint of a NEW WORLD.

As Dylan explores within the mind, the key-songs of his second period contain the complementary poles of DREAM and NIGHTMARE. "Mr. Tambourine Man" is the first great Dylan tune, no longer definable in term of sources, though it has something in common with celtic folksong and American hillbilly, if little in common with the Negro blues. Far from being socially committed, it looks as though it might be an escape song, and is so, in that a tambourine man is a peddler of pot. Yet Dylan says he's "not sleepy," even though there ain't no place he's going to; and his pied piper myth encourages us to follow the unconscious where spontaneously it may lead us. This is subtly suggested by the wavery refrain and by the irregularity of both verbal and musical clauses, which pile or float up like smoke rings. As the rings unfurl, we are liberated: so the song turns out to be about recharging our spiritual batteries today in order to find life again tomorrow. The song is unexpectedly disturbing because its mythology plumbs unexpectedly deep.

But going back to the world of instinct means accepting everything that the mind contains; the Edenic dream of "Mr. Tambourine Man" couldn't be valid if Dylan hadn't also faced up to the mind's darker depths. So the great dream-songs are complemented by the songs of nightmare; and significantly, whereas "Mr. Tambourine Man" is folky, countrified, with natural guitar, "Ballad of a Thin Man" is in city-blues style, late Chicago vintage, with driving rhythm and electrophonic amplification. When Dylan first turned from folk guitar to the pop group's electronic media he was branded as traitor by folk purists, even though he'd never in fact been a folk singer. Their objection was frivolous: for a folk-pop artist, wanting to communicate with thousands, has no choice but to use the media his environment offers him; and may do so the more potently when these media may be used to turn the tables. This fine modal tune can embrace both the subtlest harmonic ellipsis and the spooky electronic gibberings: so that although Mr. Jones (who is the respectable Man in the Street and probably you and I) is witheringly demolished, the melody's breadth preserves something like compassion. Dylan is no longer outside his victim; the nightmare is both without and within: and the dark thread inherent in melody, harmony and the driving pulse is poles removed from the self righteous arrogance of the early protest songs.

So in his second phase Bob Dylan has turned from the world without to the world within; and has expressed this by complementary songs of dream and of nightmare. In the double album *Blonde on Blonde*—which provides a transition to his third period—dream and nightmare have become almost indistinguishable. All the songs would seem to be concerned with the drug experience and the rediscovery of identity; and the verses contain a fair proportion of what looks like "automatic" writing by free association. This release of "consciousness" leads to further musical enrichment; and "Sad Eyed Lady of the Lowlands" stands with "Mr. Tambourine Man" as perhaps the most insidiously haunting pop song of our time. It's impossible to tell from the verses whether the Lady is a creature of dream or nightmare; but she's beyond good and evil, as the cant phrase has it, only in the sense that the simple, hypnotic, even corny waltz tune contains, in its unexpected elongations of line, both fulfilment and regret. Mysteriously, the song also effaces Time. Though chronometrically it lasts nearly twenty minutes, it enters a mythological once-upon-a-time where the clock doesn't tick. The concluding harmonica solo is the most moving of all Dylan's evocations of Eden by way of this country instrument: perhaps because the Sad-Eyed Lady so equivocates between dream and nightmare, and because the harmonica seems the lonesomer against the resonance of electric, rather than natural, guitar.

Dylan's third period is initiated with *John Wesley Harding*, for me his finest disc thus far. The songs' maturity comes from their fusion of the social commitment of the early phase with the commitment to the inner life manifest in the second period; the public and private manners become one, in a style that is all song. While the words have gained undertones and overtones from Dylan's submission to dream and nightmare, they're now always meaningful, if not unambiguously so. Complementarily, the tunes are more complex in organization; and the interrelationship of line, rhythm and harmony powerfully "incarnates" the words. A relatively simple example is "Dear Landlord" in which the music directly expresses the equivocation of the title. Though we all know that landlords must be wicked and the adjective "dear" ironic, we end up feeling a wry compassion: the reason being partly melodic (the tune, lingering almost caressingly on the "dear," combines an upward aspiring tenderness with strength)—and partly harmonic (the sudden change, at the top of the phrase, from the triad of C to that of E is a revelation—our ears open in a tragi-comic wonder, if not dismay, at the realisation that Dylan and landlord might learn to accept one another).

There's a comparable effect in a song explicitly about isolation, "All Along the Watchtower." One can hardly speak of humour in reference to this grandly swinging tune and thrusting rhythm; but the sudden harmonic ellipsis offers what T. S. Eliot once called a "recognition of other modes of experience that may be possible," so that the song's severity acquires too a quality that might be called pathos. Still subtler is a number like "I Dreamed I Saw St. Augustine" which, since it concerns guilt, is more aware of human fallibility. The tune opens in narrow compass, with a modal flavour and flatly subdominant-tending harmony; yet the almost trancelike melody lowers into release: an effect which Dylan couldn't have achieved in his early years, however deep his sense of social responsibility. He had first to discover responsibility to himself.

He had also to discover love, if that doesn't sound simple-minded. In his first phase love songs are rare, though the occasional exceptions, like "Corrina, Corrina" are beautiful. In his second period, especially in *Blonde on Blonde,* love songs occur, but tend to be disturbingly hallucinatory. *John Wesley Harding,* however, ends with "I'll Be Your Baby Tonight," a simple song of heterosexual love: which is a two-way relationship between individuals. The point, if obvious, is important: for Dylan is no longer concerned with himself in opposition to the external world, nor with the mazes of his dream or nightmare; he's concerned with himself in relationship to another human being. Superficially, the music seems corny, ragtimely, almost cosy, whilst the quietly comic words forestall emotional indulgence. Yet the time, lyrically extended in the silence of the night, is so beautiful that in total effect the song, far from being comfortable, almost stills the breath. The music tells us that it's *true* that there's "no need to be afraid": that all the bleeding and dying and all minatory Thin Men are banished from this silent room and warm bed. The tune's climax, rising from C to F and then leaping up an octave, marvellously liberates; while at the same time the "squeezed" notes, edging upwards, make us aware that we can't take love's joy without also accepting its pain. The harmonica postlude emphasizes this: the whining country instrument indeed carries us "out of this world" to the room of love, which is haven and heaven; yet there's a hint of lacrimae rerum in its wailing. The song leaves us warm and at peace—yet also vulnerable; we live through the experience of love in a way it would hardly be extravagant to call magical. So the song, though it seems homelier, is really no less mysterious than Dylan's other great lyrical songs, "Mr. Tambourine Man" and "Sad Eyed Lady."

This song could have been written only by a young man; none the less its balance of stresses—between tenderness and irony, joy and pain—is remarkably mature. Perhaps Dylan has never equalled it since, though it's the springboard from which most of his later songs derive. The disc *Nashville Skyline* effects a rebirth of country and western music, in which eroticism and heterosexual lovingness are experienced, not commercially manipulated. A rock-bottom reality song like "Lay Lady Lay" is complemented by the happy boogie rhythm of "Peggy Day," nostalgically barrelhouse in style yet ironically self-aware, with a deflatory black-and-white-minstrel-show coda that doesn't deprive Peggy of her seductiveness or Dylan of his solicitude.

It's interesting that for this disc Dylan seems to have acquired a new voice: deeper, rounder, more "musical" in the conventional sense; and it's still more interesting that his reborn country love-music should have been issued in Nashville, home of the vast pop music industry. The love and acceptance, being genuine, hit back at a world's corruption. In this sense Dylan didn't cease to be radical when he abandoned protest.

For this reason I don't agree with those who think Dylan's latest songs are a betrayal, any more than I agree with those who thought his acceptance of electronic gadgetry a traitorous act. I had qualms over the curious double album *Self Portrait* on which, for the first time in years, Dylan sings other people's songs as well as his own; but I suspect Dylan means to leave us uneasy, wondering if the bathos is genuinely a part of the self he celebrates. The latest disc, anyway, carries on direct from *John Wesley Harding* and *Nashville Skyline*. The lovesongs on *New Morning*—such as "The Man in Me," or "If Not For You" —are passionate yet terse: while the country songs—such as "Time Passes Slowly" or "Went To See the Gypsy"—function both poetically and musically at a level deeper than the conventional country recipe, since they relate the country experience to the city man's alienation from Nature. Most remarkable is the song "If Dogs Run Free," which returns to a theme never far below the surface of Dylan's art—that of freedom and responsibility. If dogs run free, the song asks, why shouldn't we, doing our own thing, regardless. Dylan's voice flatly speaks, as in his early days, rather than sings, and the words' irony is his sense of responsibility. Yet the music, with its ecstatic piano arabesques riddled with painfully blue false relations, haloed by the loonily scatting voice of a girl, counteracts the words, since its richly jazzy freedom sounds like an act of affirmation.

So the balance between freedom and responsibility is no less delicate than the interaction of security and vulnerability in "I'll Be Your Baby Tonight"; and this disc once more justifies its title: the morning it welcomes *is* new—everlasting and unfallen, as Thoreau put it.

And the newness brings us to Dylan's originality: which lies not so much in the idiom and conventions he uses as in *how* he uses them. His materials are traditional; he transmutes them by an act of creative imagination, so that the only legitimate comment on his "originality" is analysis of what happens in the songs, from bar to bar, to the interrelationship between words and music. Moreover, with a pop-folk singer it isn't merely the words and the notes: techniques of vocal production, oddities, even apparent inadequacies, of instrumental skill are part of the effect; so that comprehensive analysis could be achieved only by way of talk, possibly at a piano, certainly with the aid of the recorded sounds. None the less, the inevitably brief hints offered in these pages do at least, backed by the recordings, demonstrate the manner in which Dylan, unlike most pop artists, has grown up and offers potential for future development. His significance lies in the fact that he cannot be categorized. At bottom he's a traditional folk artist, a white drifter and outsider; yet he's seen this experience as directly relevant in an urban metropolis and in so doing has called upon industrial techniques and even "commercial" values. In this respect there are parallels between Dylan and the two pop composers of indubitable genius from an earlier generation, Gershwin and Ellington. Gershwin as Jewish Outsider, Ellington as Negro Outsider, "incarnated" values that denied Tin Pan Alley; yet they made it possible for their public to accept a range of experience which it didn't know it could apprehend, let alone believe in. Dylan began as the Adolescent Outsider, with Nashville substituting for Tin Pan Alley. He has an advantage over his predecessors in that he has a public that identifies with him and is (even intellectually) aware of what he stands for. It remains to be seen, however, whether Dylan's young public can grow older with him, or whether the superficially articulate militants will carry the day in maintaining that Dylan has been a Judas in moving from callow denunciation of other people's values to a recognition of mutual responsibility. Dylan resembles his own equivocally titled Judas Priest in that the Enemy is no longer THEM, over there. The Outsider is now inside too: which is why Dylan's late love songs are so different from the pop songs of the twenties and thirties which—apart from the occasional exception such as Gershwin's—were normally escapist, whether through hedonism or nostalgia.

In sheerly musical inventiveness Dylan cannot compete with Gershwin or Ellington; in the conventional sense he cannot sing and is an indifferent guitarist and pianist; his verse, as such, is slipshod and technically incompetent. Yet he uses his gifts with intuitive genius and in so doing reveals—as do the great folk or blues singers—that what appears to be technical incompetence is no such thing. His ability to develop is thus inseparable from his "loneness"; and in this he may be contrasted with the only pop artists of his own generation who, in imaginative potency, can hold a candle to him. The Beatles were also intuitive artists, but conditioned by their corporate identity, which made it possible for them to express the "tribal consciousness" of the young. The more they sought to reconcile this tribal consciousness with a sensitive awareness of individual awareness of individual experience, the more they gravitated towards "art," towards collaboration with George Martin, and towards the recording studio: out of which flowered *Sgt. Pepper,* the consummation of and, I suspect, a pretty permanent monument to the pop explosion of the sixties. Yet it would seem that *Pepper,* as an artefact, could be achieved once only. The Beatles' "togetherness" couldn't last beyond it, and the twilight of the gods has overtaken them as the Lennon-McCartney composing duo has disintegrated—Paul into charm, John into self-indulgent disgruntlement. Dylan, being alone, not necessarily reliant on other artists or on machines, alone has the capacity to GO ON, as a real folk artist or jazzman can, but as an however talented artist of the pop industry cannot. The Beatles have disbanded, Gershwin died young, Irving Berlin, Crosby and Sinatra remained permanently adolescent, Cole Porter survived by becoming exclusively deflatory. Can Dylan preserve his folk-like integrity from youth through the middle years and even into a venerable old age? If so, he'll be a phenomenon, as well as a great song-maker. I wish I could be alive in the year 2000, if only to know the answer.

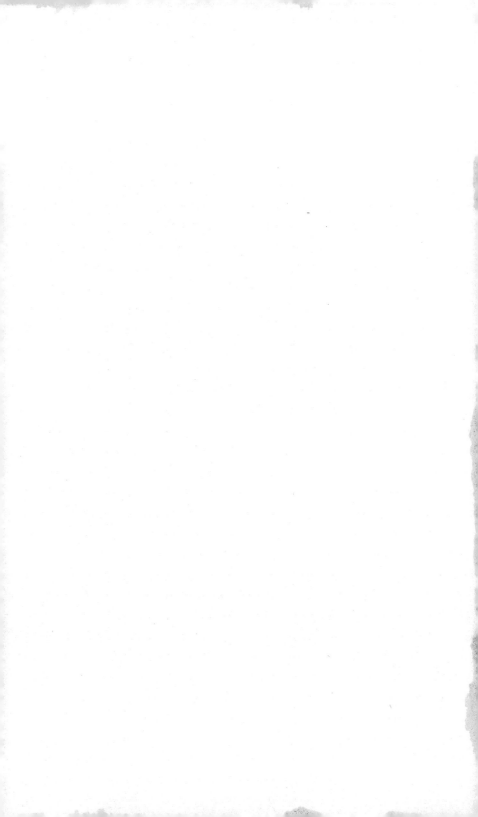

Printed in the United States
32872LVS00003B/95

9 780306 804168